# THE
# IMPACT
# OF
# PARTIES

To
Gunilla, Beatrice, Belinda and William

# THE IMPACT OF PARTIES

## Politics and Policies in Democratic Capitalist States

Edited by

# Francis G Castles

Sponsored by the European Consortium
for Political Research / ECPR

330.9
I 34

*For information address*
SAGE Publications Ltd
28 Banner Street, London EC1Y 8QE

SAGE Publications Inc
275 South Beverly Drive
Beverly Hills, California 90212

**British Library Cataloguing in Publication Data**

The Impact of parties: politics and policies
   in democratic capitalist states.
   1. Capitalism—Political aspects 2. Economic
history—1945
   I. Castles, Francis G.
   330.9     HB501     81-85190

   ISBN 0-8039-9787-6

# Contents

# Acknowledgements

**This volume presents** the initial findings of the research group on Party Differences and Public Policy, which was formed in 1978 at the European Consortium for Political Research conference in Grenoble. The membership of the research group has fluctuated over the three-year gestation period of the book and, in addition to those who have contributed to this volume, has included Sten Borg (University of Leeds), Olof Petersson (University of Uppsala), Heikki Paloheimo (University of Turku) and Chris Rootes (University of Kent).

The research group as a whole would like to acknowledge the intellectual encouragement it has received from the European Consortium, and the invaluable financial help from the ECPR Research Committee which made possible the series of discussions on which this volume is based. In particular, we would wish to record our sincerest thanks to Professors Jean Blondel and Rudolf Wildenmann of the Research Board, without whose efforts we could never have succeeded in making the project a reality.

The Universities of Amsterdam, Konstanz and Tübingen and the Open University also gave generous support to the authors of this volume, and the latter made available the resources to perform the arduous editorial activity inherent in an international collaborative endeavour of this kind. Our gratitude is also due to the German Research Foundation (DFG), which provided funding for the research assistance necessary for the collection and computation of much of the cross-national data.

The individual contributors take full personal responsibility for the chapters that appear under their names, but would simultaneously wish to acknowledge the extent to which their views have evolved and been modified by joint collaboration in the research group. Those contributors for whom English is not their mother tongue would wish to thank the editor, without whose tireless effort this book could never have been presented to an English-speaking audience.

Finally, the manuscript could never have been prepared without the magnificent secretarial assistance of Enid Sherward, Michelle Kent, Yvonne Honeywell and Doreen Beacham of the Open University. To the last of these, the editor gives his special thanks for work well beyond the call of duty.

# 1

# Introduction:
# Politics and Public Policy

Francis G. Castles
Open University

**The academic study of politics** is rapidly acquiring a renewed
relevance. In place of a preoccupation with the structure and
mechanics of government, more and more studies are concen-
trating on the impact of politics. That inevitably means greater
relevance, in so far as that impact is a function of the way in which
the policies of governments impinge on the lives and fortunes of individual men and women. Today, political scientists have become
as interested, as professional politicians and voters have always
been, in questions like whether it makes a difference for whom we
vote or how we participate in public affairs. From such a perspective, politics ceases to be merely the analysis and description of the
ways in which human communities choose among alternative
courses of action, but focuses as much on the substance of the
choices made and the reasons why they are chosen. The new approach — which has illustrious antecedents in political theory from
Aristotle to Marx — rejects the orthodoxy of an 'end of ideology',
and replaces it with an investigation into the ways in which different political ideas, expressed through parties, factions and
groups, interact with social and economic structures to produce the
diversity of public outcomes that characterize modern states.

The new approach to politics and public policy is inherently comparative and necessarily interdisciplinary. It is inherently comparative because the focus on diversity means a shift away from the
earlier Marxist and functionalist belief that, for good or ill, all industrialized capitalist states are moving along the same trajectory
of change. To locate the causes of diversity in public policy out-

comes, we must examine and compare the social, economic and political structures of such states. The new approach is necessarily interdisciplinary because, to the degree that it accepts the constraints of pre-established disciplinary boundaries, it degenerates into a futile debate about the primacy of political, social or economic explanation. The body of research comprising comparative public policy studies has too often started out with the objective of demonstrating the rival claims of politics or economics and has, in consequence, failed to analyse the reciprocal interaction of diverse, political, economic and social factors in the determination of public policy.

This volume takes its point of departure from what is clearly a political phenomenon, in so far as it attempts to isolate the role of political parties in shaping policy outputs and outcomes and to specify under what circumstances party politics does matter. However, an assessment of that role necessarily involves an attempt to get away from the more one-sided disciplinary interpretations of the genesis of policy outcomes and to replace them with an analysis of how political and socioeconomic factors together shape the consequences of policy-making. Thus, the basic research question in each of the following contributions is: to what extent, and under what circumstances, is the political composition of governments and the role of political parties in the political system an important variable which accounts for observable differences in policy outputs and policy outcomes in democratic capitalist states?

The five substantial essays that comprise the volume each examine the impact of political parties on a major component of the policy output of contemporary capitalist democracies.The three essays that make up Part I focus on the factors determining diverse patterns of public expenditure and different macroeconomic policy mixes. What we are trying to understand here is why governments have such varied priorities; why some favour enormous expenditure on welfare while others try desperately to limit the fiscal burden on the state; why some deploy enormous resources for maintaining military defence while others try to minimize such expenditure; why some struggle against the odds to maintain full employment while others are willing to deflate at the first breath of adverse economic conditions. The remaining essays, which make up Part II, examine how the policies of governments combine with other factors to affect the livelihood, the incomes, of citizens. The issues raised here involve both the inter- and intra-class distribution of economic rewards stemming from policy choices and are clearly relevant to the perennial political question of the degree to which purposive political action can ameliorate the structures of inequality in capitalist societies. The central focus on political parties is not because of any a priori assumption on the part of the authors that parties are the most important determinant of outcomes in these policy areas, but rather because some political parties claim that their objective is to fashion public expenditure and macroeconomic policy in such a way as to alter the reward structure of contemporary society. An assessment of the validity of that claim, usually identified with the democratic Left, is a contribution both to our knowledge of the factors associated with particular policy outcomes and to our understanding of the role of ideology in the modern state.

Although the five essays examine different aspects of contemporary public policy, and although the authors of each have approached their tasks from diverse theoretical traditions, there is a strong core element of commonality of approach, focus and purpose, which it is hoped makes the volume more than just a survey of several discrete dimensions of public policy. Probably the most important single element that unites the five contributions is a belief on the part of all the authors that explanation of public policy outcomes in terms of any single paradigm is unlikely to be a fruitful way forward in comparative public policy. The time has come to counterpose the rival claims of paradigms and disciplines, not with the objective of demonstrating the superiority of any single one in a general way, but rather with the aim of pointing to the interaction of the multiplicity of factors which may be presumed to influence different policy areas at different times. For this reason, each author has attempted to survey the whole range of explanations emanating from the different disciplines and to test them empirically in such a way as to make it possible to bring out the patterned interrelationships between supposedly rival explanatory factors. Thus, the volume should be seen, as a whole, as an attempt to bring together and assess the findings of comparative public policy studies of the democratic capitalist state in such a way as to fashion a sort of synthesis of what has gone before and as a more secure platform for launching further research.

## Common problems and a common approach

As we have said, what gives a unity of perspective in this volume is the approach adopted by the authors rather than any inherent similarity of initial perspective or substantive conclusions. That unity of approach stems from a joint recognition of the promise of comparative public policy studies to shed illumination on major questions concerning the operation of the contemporary state and a simultaneous realization that the approaches adopted in much of the emerging literature were in various respects problematical. Throughout, the Research Group worked on the basis that there was no necessity that essays on diverse aspects of public policy would come to similar conclusions in respect of the determination of policy outcomes, but that there must be a genuine effort to adopt a mode of analysis that would make it possible for all researchers in the field to accept the basic thrust of the conclusions so derived. In summary, the central criticism of much existing research was that many of its conflicting conclusions were inherent in the theoretical paradigms from which research proceeded and the methodological strategies adopted to conduct that research. What we have sought to achieve is an approach that avoids these problems of tautological argument in order that diverse conclusions should no longer be seen as further fuel for the battle of paradigms, but rather as a set of cumulative findings that require reconciliation at a further stage in public policy research.

Although each contribution to the volume surveys the range of conflicting explanations and analytical problems that arise in the literature dealing with a particular policy field, the best way to give an idea of our common approach is to provide a brief overview of the problems as they pertain to the field as a whole and to point to the way in which we have attempted to tackle them. While it will become immediately apparent that these problems are closely inter-related, it is possible to describe them separately as the problem of competing paradigms, the problem of the universe of discourse, and the problem of statistical interpretation.

*Competing paradigms*

The problem here is not so much that there are diverse explanations of the derivation of public policy outcomes, but rather that these explanations are so closely bound up with competing interpretations of social and political reality that research has often been conceived more in terms of demonstrating the truth of a particular paradigm than in terms of understanding the complexity of public policy. Most particularly, the academic debate has centred around the rival claims of political and socioeonomic explanatory frameworks.

On the one hand, there is a strong school of thought that attributes observed variance in public policy outcomes to political factors. Such factors include the degree of political institutionalization (Huntington, 1968); the extent of political centralization (Wilensky, 1976); the influence of labour unions and socialist parties (Lenski, 1966); the capacity of voters to influence party programmes through representative elections (Erikson, 1976); the differential ability of political elites to respond to opportunities for 'political learning' (Heclo, 1974); and the varied potential of interest groups and political parties to articulate and aggregate interests (Almond and Coleman, 1960). In the vast majority of the arguments that posit a relationship between political factors and policy outcomes, the question of party influence and party control plays a central role. This is manifestly true of those theories that suggest that labour union and socialist preferences will be translated into higher levels of state interventionism. It is scarcely less so in other theories in what may be broadly described as the 'pluralistic politics paradigm', which have been premised on the view that the content, the distributive and redistributive features and the timing of policy outputs are dependent on the structure of the political market, the relative strength of competing political forces, the preferences of voters, perceptions and strategic considerations of the political leadership, characteristics of the political culture and the strength and cohesion of the governing and opposition parties.

Such views proceed from two assumptions. The first involves a denial that the socioeconomic structure is in some sense more fundamental as a determinant of policy outcomes than are the political arrangements of society. The second assumption is that 'parties are the central intermediate and intermediary structure between society and government' (Sartori, 1976; ix), and that, therefore, it makes an important difference to public policy how they interact and which is in power at any particular time. This perspective is clearly one that would be embraced by virtually all practising politicians, and would seem a natural starting place for public policy research conducted by the political science profession. It is also a perspective that is inherent in the ideological self-conception of the liberal democratic state. What price democracy, if it doesn't matter who you vote for or what party is in office?

On the other hand, this 'politics matters' perspective is strongly challenged by another school of thought, which argues that public policy outcomes are largely determined by socioeconomic factors and that party control and influence are more or less irrelevant. The scholars who have arrived at this conclusion have done so from very divergent intellectual premises. There are those who have proceeded from the sociological hypotheses of the convergence of advanced democratic societies and the closely related thesis of the 'end of ideology'. The convergence hypotheses, stated variously by Clark Kerr et al. (1960), J.K. Galbraith (1967) and many others, suggests that there is a logic of industrialism in which the exigencies of modern technology and an advanced economy override political factors making for diversity, and progressively shape social structures and public policies in a similar mould. The 'end of ideology' thesis can be seen as a sub-theme in the growing similarity of advanced societies in so far as it points to the lessened salience of party conflict, the growing acceptance of a consensus on the middle-ground of politics. As one commentator put it, '[I]t has become ever more difficult to distinguish the policies and goals of socialist and non-socialist parties. Dealing with common problems and appealing for majority support, both find it necessary to offer roughly similar programs' (Christenson et al., 1971: 274).

Where policies and goals can no longer be distinguished, the question of which party is in office ceases to have any practical importance. On the other hand, a basically similar conclusion is reached by those approaching the matter from a neo-Marxist position. In this perspective, policy outputs and outcomes are seen not as a consequence of a logic of industrialism as such, but as political translations of social class struggles inherent in the capitalist structure. Policy in this view is dependent on the social weight of competing and conflicting social classes or class fractions. Policy-making is viewed as a reaction of the state and political ruling class to the results of, and requisites arising from, class struggles. The directive capacity of the state and of the governing parties are in this view periodically promoted or constrained by the configuration of class conflicts (see, for example, Albers et al., 1971, and Parkin, 1971).

Irrespective of the source of the challenge to the 'politics matters' paradigm, the independent variable seen as fundamentally affecting the variance of policy outcomes is the socioeconomic structure. In the convergence/'end of ideology' case, the determining factor is technological change, which produces consensus and similarity.

Admittedly, the neo-marxist position is anything but monolithic, and varies from a stance in which the 'logic of *capitalist* industrialism' serves a similar mechanistic explanatory role as socioeconomic factors in the convergence theory to one that an hypothesized 'relative autonomy of the state' allows the influence of party some limited impact in respect of 'competing strategies and policies' (see Gough, 1979: 44). Nevertheless, neo-Marxist views necessarily stress the manner in which the mode of production predetermines in greater or lesser detail the outcomes of social conflicts. None of these views would concede more than the most marginal role to party control, and to changes in the balance of parties represented in the legislature, as factors determining the shape of public policy in the contemporary democratic state. Both the 'politics matters' perspective and its various opponents clearly have resort to empirical evidence to support their respective claims and to refute their challengers. In essence, the evidence required by the former school of thought is of dissimilarities in policy outcomes, which can be interpreted in terms of political dissimilarities between states; whereas a refutation of political influence requires evidence of both substantial similarity, which can be attributed to the underlying similarity of socioeconomic structures, and policy dissimilarities, which can be causally related to differential socieconomic structures. The problem is that it is relatively easy to provide evidence of both kinds from the experience of contemporary democratic capitalist states. The trick involved in interpreting reality exclusively from one perspective or the other would seem to be either to ignore counter-indications to trends supporting a particular viewpoint or, more frequently, to suggest that the ways in which public policy outcomes are similar or differ are essentially trivial.

Our reading of the evidence, derived from research produced within the framework of the competing paradigms, is quite different and shapes the approach we have taken in this volume. We would argue, a priori, that the accumulation of evidence from the past decade or more of comparative public policy studies has demonstrated that an understanding of the factors determining policy outcomes is far more complex than can be encompassed by any single paradigm. We seek not to ignore counter-indications, or to underplay them, but rather to interpret their existence as evidence of an interplay between political and socioeconomic factors in the determination of public policy. Furthermore, we are inclined to the view that the discovery of underlying similarity in one area of policy and dissimilarity in another may well be due to major differences in the causal factors operative in different public policy spheres. That such a conclusion has not emerged from the battle of the paradigms is largely attributable to the wish to generalize from a restricted body of evidence to the nature of the policy process as such. Our decision to focus on a wide range of the policy outputs of the contemporary democratic state was a conscious reflection of our expectation that the determination of policy outcomes was most unlikely to be a singular process, but would differ from one policy area to another. In particular, we would expect, and the studies in this volume confirm, that policy areas in which the state has direct competence (i.e. deciding expenditure priorities, modifying income distribution by taxes and transfers) are more likely to be affected by overtly political factors than policy areas in which the state has to rely on persuasion of individuals acting within an economic market environment (i.e. controlling inflation and unemployment).

The contributing authors would all acknowledge that it is neither possible nor desirable completely to stand outside the paradigms that comprise scholarly endeavour. In fact, the authors are variously proponents of many of the viewpoints summarized above. However, what each has attempted to do is to make a conscious effort to think through and test explanations deriving from the whole range of paradigms. Such an effort has been facilitated precisely because it occurred within the context of a research group in which one's conclusions had to be justified to researchers steeped in alternative paradigms of explanation. Interestingly, this process of interaction has led to quite major modifications of interpretation in the period of nearly three years involved in the gestation of this book. In all cases, the conscious attempt to understand diverse explanatory frameworks and alternative sources of evidence has resulted in less one-sided and more complex conclusions, which point up the reciprocal influence of socioeconomic, political and structural factors. It is precisely because there has been this genuine bringing together of diverse perspectives that we would argue that this volume represents a synthesis of much of the work hitherto conducted in the area of comparative public policy studies. In departing from the false dichotomies and unreal certainties of the battle of the paradigms, it also sets out a new, and infinitely more complex, agenda for future research.

## The universe of discourse

Research that explores hypotheses concerning the structural similarity or political diversity of states is inherently comparative in nature. There are, however, certain problems associated with the choice of which states it is appropriate to compare in the endeavour to uncover the factors determining policy outcomes in democratic capitalist states. There are two possible strategies that can, and have been, adopted in selecting the universe of discourse for comparison. One is to investigate the widest possible sample of states and to seek to discover the similarities between countries manifesting particular levels of policy outcome. An example of a study utilizing such a strategy would be Wilensky's investigation of the determinants of social security spending in 64 nation-states (Wilensky, 1975). The alternative strategy is to focus only on a particular category of states (i.e. capitalist democracies) and seek to discover the correlates of the differences in policy outcomes they manifest. An example of a study embodying this latter strategy would be Hibbs's analysis of differing trade-offs between inflation and unemployment in 12 advanced states (Hibbs, 1977). This choice of research strategies is, of course, that between a 'most different' and 'most similar' mode of comparison (see Przeworski and Teune, 1979: 31-9), and depends crucially on the purposes for which comparison is being utilized. The choice of a 'most different' (i.e. maximizing the universe of discourse) mode of analysis is most appropriate where we wish to account for similarities, despite the seemingly disparate contexts in which they occur. The choice of the 'most similar' strategy (i.e. limiting the comparison to a categorized universe of discourse) is appropriate where our aim is to account for differences, since such a procedure makes it easier to identify residual differences which may serve to explain the observed variance.

The problem is, of course, that the hypotheses concerning the determination of policy outcomes that stem from rival paradigms make quite opposite assumptions about whether our task is to explain similarity or diversity. Thus, one might presume that those who proceed from the view that the logic of industrialism or structure of capitalism imposes substantial similarity on the countries in which they occur would favour wider comparisons in which such similarities could emerge in contrast to countries with less developed economic systems. Conversely, one would expect the 'politics matters' perspective to be tested in the context of essentially similar nations in which remaining political differences were the primary candidate for explaining policy differences. In fact, it is precisely this dichotomy of approach that we find in the empirical studies that purport to support the rival paradigms. Thus, those studies that have argued strongly for the overwhelming impact of economic development and related socioeconomic factors on public policy outcomes have usually been based on samples (usually very large) of nations with a wide spread of economic levels. Conversely, the researches that have located the importance of party influence and control have been restricted to samples (necessarily smaller) of countries that are economically advanced. It seems by no means improbable that the statistical findings of both sets of researches are broadly correct and broadly compatible; in other words, the early stages of economic development have a marked effect on policy outcomes, but, once a threshold point has been reached, a variety of other factors are required to explain policy diversity in advanced states. Indeed, findings by Jackman that the relationship between social equality and economic development is curvilinear in character suggest precisely such a conclusion (Jackman, 1975). What cannot be correct or compatible in the two sets of researches is the overarching conclusions drawn from them concerning the relative importance of political and socioeconomic factors in policy determination. What scholars with these diverse views have often tended to do is to generalize from a wide sample to a non-randomly chosen sub-sample (an example would be the argument that socioeconomic development is the crucial determinant of policy outcomes in the advanced countries, just because it is in the wide sample including countries at very diverse economic levels) or alternatively to generalize from a small sample to countries in general (e.g., because political factors appear to be important in the advanced countries, they must constitute the major explanatory framework for understanding the nature of policy variation). Neither type of generalization appears to be logically defensible or, in reality, fruitful for understanding the relative importance of the multiplicity of factors that affect public policy outcomes.

The joint belief of the authors of this volume that many of the defects of earlier analysis stem from generalization beyond the limits dictated by the chosen universe of discourse does not, of course, obviate the difficulty that a common universe of discourse had to be elaborated for this study. For each author to adopt a widely divergent sample of countries for analysis would have clearly limited the cumulative impact of our findings, since divergences of interpretation could as readily have been attributed to sample choice as to genuine differences among policy areas. For a number of reasons, we decided to focus on a 'most similar' universe of discourse, comprising some 21 democratic capitalist states. First, just because we were not engaged in the battle of the paradigms, and consequently were not concerned to elaborate broad generalizations, it was not difficult for any of the authors to concede that, in contrast to economically underdeveloped countries, there were broad similarities between industrialized and capitalist states, which profoundly influence their public policy. Since, in essence, that is the sum of the contention of writers, like Wilensky, who have discussed public policy outcomes in the context of the widest possible universe of discourse, we need not engage in an analysis that would merely reproduce a well-known finding. Second, because our focus of interest centred around questions of party influence and control, we had to make comparisons within a universe of discourse where party differences were a meaningful variable. That is not possible in a sample containing totalitarian dictatorships, traditional oligarchies and military regimes, and seemed to be possible only where there was a genuine potential for competition between political parties expressing diverse ideological views. Third, and most important, it appeared to us that all the theoretical perspectives utilized to explain public policy diversity should hold for the universe of democratic capitalist states. The 'politics matters' perspective holds for it as a matter of course; countries characterized by strong parties (or governments dominated by) Left, Centre or Right should manifest significantly different policy configurations. The convergence and 'end of ideology' theories, although they might be expected to show up most starkly in a comparison of developed and underdeveloped countries, were actually advanced to explain changes occurring within the industrialized countries, and must, therefore, be presumed to be relevant to a universe of discourse, the levels of economic development and industrialization in which vary from Ireland and Italy at the bottom of the distribution to the United States and Sweden at the top. Neo-Marxist theories must also be presumed to be pertinent, and have been extensively utilized, in a set of countries characterized by possession of capitalist class structure, but varying in the degree of development of the mode of production and class relations. It is our view, therefore, that an analysis focusing on the diversity of policy outcomes in democratic capitalist states neither predetermines the nature of our conclusions nor rules out any of the major categories of explanation that have emerged in the comparative public policy literature.

## Statistical interpretation

The major problems of statistical interpretation that arise in the context of the essays contained in this volume are not in any sense intrinsically related to the particular subject under investigation, but are rather general problems that emerge from the use of the methods of applied social statistics in the context of a limited universe of discourse. Stated most simply, the problems arise because comparisons of more than a very few cases require the use of statistical techniques which can serve as a surrogate control for spurious explanations, but the limitation to a relatively restricted universe of discourse offers grounds for only a partial degree of confidence that such control is effective and a less than adequate basis for distinguishing the reciprocal and interactive impact of a wide range of independent variables.

These problems may, in general terms, be conceived in terms of 'the overdetermination of observed difference' which is a feature of all comparison within a restricted frame of reference, since the number of cases may be too small to establish which of a number of differences among the cases is the cause (or effect) of the observed variance (see Roberts, 1978: 294). In more specific statistical terms, the problems arise from the instability of estimation which is inherent in analysis of a limited range of cases. As Blalock points out, the correlation techniques, which are the basis of virtually all the statistical work in this and related fields of study, involve both measures of variance and covariance and 'the magnitude of the correlation coefficient depends on the range and variability in both variables' (Blalock, 1979: 401). In effect, correlation is the numerical equivalent of type construction, but, because single extreme values can greatly influence the level of measured covariance in a small sample, reported correlation coefficients between two or more variables can fluctuate wildly, dependent on the particular cases chosen for analysis. There are a number of statistical responses to these difficulties, but none are particularly applicable in the context of our study. Having once established that the sample population is normally distributed, one can rely on tests of statistical significance to establish the probability of a determinate relationship between the stipulated variables. However, in a statistical sense the population of advanced capitalist states is not a sample, but a complete enumeration of the relevant universe of discourse. It is impossible to extend the range of variability 'to counteract the effects of numerous uncontrolled variables' (Blalock, 1979: 401) because the number of cases is inherently limited to the 20 or so instances of the phenomenon under observation. It is also impossible to opt for the alternative strategy of excluding the more extreme cases on any major scale, since the population would be reduced further to a point where 'the overdetermination of observed difference' becomes an even more serious problem. These difficulties are clearly exacerbated when use is made of multiple correlation techniques, since different countries may display extreme values on different variables. Indeed, with a little ingenuity and a lot of statistical rectitude, it would be possible to conclude that all cases should be excluded from the analysis because they are extreme in one way or another.

Critics of the use of applied statistical method in the social sciences have been prone to see in these difficulties a reason for eschewing anything but the most limited comparative analysis. Our own view is that, while such problems point to the need for extreme caution in the interpretation of statistical findings, the potential contribution of the comparative method to the understanding of the processes involved in the determination of policy outcomes is sufficiently great to justify researches of this kind. On the whole, we are inclined to think that criticisms of the use of statistical methods in the public policy field are, in fact, more a consequence of the failure of previous studies to exercise caution in the conclusions they draw from statistical findings than of anything inherent in the nature of statistically based comparisons. In particular, there has been a failure to utilize a variety of strategies which might serve to minimize the risks of unwarranted and premature conclusions.

Two such strategies are of particular importance, and have shaped the general approach taken by all the contributions in this volume. One frequent, and often quite deserved, criticism of researches in the comparative public policy field is that their findings have derived from the analysis of only one or a very limited number of dependent variables. Such analyses are open to criticism, not merely on the general ground that their findings may be an artefact of the existence of instability of estimation in a limited universe of discourse, but also on the ground that the results may be biased by the particular measure of the dependent variable utilized and that the causal links postulated may be less a consequence of general processes of policy determination and rather a reflection of processes particular to a particular area or element of public policy or a given period of time. In this volume, the danger of generalizing from one policy area to another is inherently limited by the explicit attention paid to a diverse range of policy outcomes, but even within the context of individual contributions authors have attempted to survey a range of policy components, rather than letting one serve as a proxy for all. Moreover, wherever the available data permitted, the authors have utilized the same dependent variables measured at a variety of time-points during the period of the early 1960s to the mid-1970s. Not only does this allow us to measure change and to analyse the processes involved in that change; it also offers the opportunity to assess the degree to which the policy determination process is invariant over time. By focusing on a range of policy outcomes occurring at different times, each author seeks to build up a pattern of the major factors associated with a given policy area. In this endeavour, what is most significant is not the interpretation of particular correlation coefficients, which may well be the artefact of the cases studied, but rather the overall explanatory thrust of the pattern seen as a whole.

Searching for a pattern among policy outcomes is one strategy for minimizing the risk of unwarranted conclusions. The other strategy we utilize involves explicit analysis of the interrelation between the independent variables demonstrated to be associated with policy variance. Here, too, there is reason for criticism of some previous research: on the one hand because, in the context of the battle of the paradigms, some scholars have rested content to show the degree of bivariate association between a very limited number of socioeconomic or political variables and a particular policy outcome, and on the other because those who have attempted to uncover the interaction of factors in the policy determination process have tended to rely on multivariate methods, which are almost invariably too ambitious given such a limited universe of discourse. The approach that has been adopted here is to rely on simple bivariate analysis throughout, but to supplement that method by careful attention to the interrelationships between the very considerable range of independent variables utilized in each study. In effect, that has implied a search for patterned relationships between major aspects of the social, economic and political structures of contemporary democratic capitalist states. It is for this reason that much of this volume is taken up by discussion of such relationships as that between the party system and the development of international trade patterns, or between corporatist forms of social organization and the ideological goals of political parties. It is our basic contention that in structured interactions of this kind we are most likely to discover the basic determinants of the patterns of public policy manifested in modern societies.

## The agenda for future research

The agenda for future research in the comparative public policy field can best be highlighted by what we feel to be the inherent limitations of our own analysis. There are at least four major tasks that we would like to have accomplished, but which proved impossible given the restrictions imposed by data availability, time constraints and the need to present our findings at a reasonable length. In particular, we would have wished to pay greater attention to changes in policy outcomes over time; to focus on particular cases, and the contrast between cases, in order to illustrate and test particular hypotheses; to give more attention to the possible trade-offs between policies; and to give a fuller account of patterned sequences in the development of public policy in democratic capitalist states.

The authors of this volume have adopted various mixtures of a cross-sectional and longitudinal design. In Chapter 5 on wage policy, the basic instrument of analysis is a set of time-series analyses of the individual countries under study. In Chapters 2 and 3 on the welfare state and macroeconomic policy, given the general non-availability of adequate time-series data, a conscious effort has been made to avoid the pitfalls of a purely cross-sectional statistical design. Throughout the analysis, wherever possible, either the explanatory variables were measured with indicators aggregated over time or the initial conditions were explicitly taken into the analysis. These various choices of research strategy were adopted to cope with the limitations inherent in cross-sectional analysis. Whereas cross-sectional analysis can effectively uncover a variety of major factors associated with policy variance, it often remains necessary to employ a time-series design in order to understand the exact interrelation of the causal sequence involved. To provide a single example, we may discover a strong degree of association between a party of a given ideological complexion and a particular type of policy outcome by means of a cross-sectional analysis. That does not, however, imply that we are entitled to conclude that the electoral victory of such a party will lead to such an outcome, which might just as well be a consequence of that party's influence on other parties or its impact on the balance of the party system, irrespective of whether it holds office. The only way to establish whether policy is a direct concomitant of office-holding is to employ an integrated times-series-cross-sectional design. Ideally, cross-sectional analysis and time series for each of the individual countries should always be used together, but at the moment problems of data availability and assembling data for comparative study make that very difficult. Part of the agenda for research in the comparative public policy field must be to rectify this situation.

Although our general approach has never been to let statistical results speak for themselves, but rather to interpret them as far as possible in terms of our knowledge of the particularities of individual countries' development, it has not been possible to pay as much attention as we would wish to the unique context of policy-making in each of the countries that comprise our universe of discourse. What is required is some means of integrating the findings that emerge from comparative studies and political history in order to reduce the very considerable degree of unexplained variance that remains in this and every other study, utilizing the applied statistical method. Moreover, the need for the detailed analysis of individual cases is not merely a question of supplying historical context, but may also be helpful in illustrating or testing hypotheses. Thus, the argument that party difference is a crucial factor in influencing policy would possibly be best tested by examining the experience of countries in which long periods of single-party hegemony has been succeeded by a dramatic shift in party control (e.g. Australia between 1972 and 1975 or Sweden since 1976). In a similar way, we might wish to examine in great detail a number of what appear to be, in terms of the overall comparison, deviant cases; cases where statistical analysis tells us precisely how little we can explain. There is room in this area of individual case-studies for a literally endless stream of public policy research. Some is already being conducted, but the only caveat we would enter is that there is much to be said for a development in which comparative and individual studies cross-fertilize each other, since comparison seems to be an essential means of isolating the questions to which case studies can provide the answers.

The question of trade-offs between areas of policy is one that is suggested by an overall reading of the findings contained in this volume. It is a reasonable conclusion from the analysis that, while democratic capitalist states may be characterized by a range of different policy outcomes and policy mixes, there are certain structural limitations on total policy mix. To put it crudely, there are costs attached to what we want, and to have more of some things we must have less of others. This dilemma is clearly shown up in wages policy, where trade unions may have to choose between a militant policy to improve the balance between wages and profits or acceptance of a wage restraint imposed by a socialist government with the goal of procuring social reforms conducive to greater social equality. It is also apparent in the difficulties experienced by governments in attaining a macroeconomic policy mix conducive to successful political control of the economy. In order to analyse the wider pattern of trade-offs across the whole range of public policy outcomes, it would be necessary to employ a research design in which each component of policy was analysed in relation to an identical array of indepedent variables. We did not consider that practicable at this preliminary stage of research, where, despite a common approach of the kind already indicated, we wanted to leave authors free to explore the factors that appeared most pertinent to specific and diverse policy areas. Obviously, the question of the interaction between policy choices implied in the notion of trade-off must be an important subject for future research, since the real dilemma of policy-making in the contemporary state is just how it is possible to achieve a whole range of what appear to be, and may in reality be, incompatible policy objectives.

A further conclusion, which seems to be strongly suggested in certain contributions to this volume, is that there are important differences in the factors determining policy outcomes in periods of economic prosperity and economic crisis. This also is a matter that deserves more attention than was possible in the context of studies, the primary objective of which was to establish the significant factors shaping different policy areas rather than overarching constraints impinging on all aspects of policy-making at a given time or in a given economic climate. Again, the use of consecutive cross-sectional designs is probably less useful in this context than time-series analysis. Most optimistically, what we should be seeking to produce is a developmental history of public policy in the democratic capitalist state. It may well be that if and when research has advanced to the stage where such a goal is possible, we shall see the differential policy performance revealed in the following pages as a long drawn-out accretion of a series of alternative responses to the constraints imposed by the development of the modern state.

# REFERENCES

Albers, D. et al. (1971). *Klassenkampfe in Westeuropa*. Reinbek bei Hamburg: Rowohlt.

Almond, G. and Coleman J. (1960). *The Politics of Developing Areas*. Princeton: University Press.

Blalock, H. Jr (1979). *Social Statistics*. Tokyo: McGraw-Hill Kogakusha.

Christenson, R.M. et al. (1971). *Ideologies in Modern Politics*. London: Nelson.

Erikson, S. (1976). 'The Relationship between Public Opinion and State Policy: A New Look Based on some Forgotten Data', *American Journal of Political Science*.

Galbraith, J.K. (1967). *The New Industrial State*. London: Hamish Hamilton.

Gough, I. (1979). *The Political Economy of The Welfare State*. London: Macmillan.

Heclo, H. (1974). *Modern Social Politics in Britain and Sweden*. New Haven, Conn.: Yale University Press.

Hibbs, D. (1977). 'Political Parties and Macroeconomic Policy', *American Political Science Review*.

Huntington, S.P. (1968). *Political Order in Changing Societies*. New Haven, Conn.: Yale University Press.

Jackman, R.W. (1975). *Politics and Social Inequality: A Comparative Analysis*. London: John Wiley.

Kerr, C. et al. (1960). *Industrialism and Industrial Man*. Cambridge, Mass.: Harvard University Press.

Lenski, G. (1966). *Power and Privilege: A Theory of Social Stratification*. New York: McGraw-Hill.

Parkin, F. (1971). *Class Inequality and Political Order*. London: MacGibbon & Kee.

Przeworski, A. and Teune, H. (1970). *The Logic of Comparative Social Enquiry*. London: John Wiley.

Roberts, G. (1978). 'The Explanation of Politics: Comparison, Strategy and Theory', in Lewis, P.G. et al., *The Practice of Comparative Politics*. London: Longman.

Sartori, G. (1976). *Parties and Party Systems*. Cambridge: University Press.

Wilensky, H. (1975). *The Welfare State and Equality*, Berkeley: University of California Press.

Wilensky, H. (1976). 'The "New Corporatism" Centralization and the Welfare State', *Sage Professional Papers*, Series/Number 06-020.

# I

# The Priorities
# of Governments

# 2

# The Impact of Parties
# on Public Expenditure

Francis G. Castles
Open University

## Introduction

**This chapter attempts** to employ a relatively straightforward
methodology in analysing the determinants of the main components of public expenditure and, in particular, of public welfare
expenditure. This methodology does not rely on complex statistical
manipulations, but rather uses simple bivariate analysis as a means
of uncovering patterns of relationships between expenditure and a
variety of social, economic and political factors. In essence, the
argument is that, if the pattern of factors associated with a number
of a priori related policy areas is similar, or if similar factors are
associated with a particular policy area at different times, then this
gives us stronger reasons to make causal influences than if the focus
of study is a single policy variable at a particular time.

The literature concerning the determinants of public expenditure
in general and public welfare in particular is quite extensive, and
the early sections of the chapter examine the major hypotheses advanced in the field as well as surveying certain problems that arise
in analysing the relationships between politics and public policy.
Thereafter a research design is elaborated which attempts to utilize
aggregate data on the broad divisions of public expenditure in the
advanced capitalist states as a means of locating patterns among
associated social, economic and political factors. The period under
review is broadly that from the early 1960s until the mid-1970s.
Essentially, it covers the period of economic expansion and optimism that preceded the first oil crisis of the 1970s. It is by no

means apparent that the factors determining public expenditure in a given period are generally applicable for all periods, and the following chapter returns to some of the same issues for the ensuing period of economic crisis.

In respect of findings, this chapter has three major objectives. First, we wish to pay special attention to the question of whether democratic capitalist states were becoming more or less similar in their patterns of public expenditure during the 1960s and early 1970s. In other words, are we looking at a process of convergence or divergence? The question is important because so many strands of sociological analysis point to the increasing similarity of advanced societies, and the increased role of state as a revenue-gathering and expenditure-generating mechanism is a central feature of these societies. Second, we wish to locate what role, if any, party politics has in the processes that lead to greater or lesser expenditure in a variety of policy fields. Third, we are concerned to understand whether whatever linkages there are between patterns of public expenditure and patterns of politics are mediated via the choices made by individual electors or through the pre-established structures of the party system. Although our conclusions in respect of this last are the most speculative of all, they are also, perhaps, the most significant in a sense that extends beyond policy analysis. In the introduction to this volume, we have pointed out that the time has come to go beyond the simple dichotomies of the 'politics matters' debate. This is the more so, since our conclusions suggest that, while politics does indeed matter, it does so in a way that allows only limited scope for individual political choice.

## Politics and welfare: conflicting views

The debate on the relative importance of socioeconomic and political factors in the determination of public policy has concentrated very heavily on the field of public expenditure and, in particular, on public expenditure on welfare. The reasons for this are obvious enough. A distinctive feature of the contemporary state — and accepted as such by Marxist and non-Marxist scholars alike — is the assumption by government of a vast range of new responsibilities funded through the public domain. Such responsibilities generally include the maintenance of minimum levels of income, adequate standards of public health and basic education provision, and may in some instances go so far as to cover a duty to provide public housing or comprehensive accident compensation. These new functions of the state can be provided only by the extension of public revenue on a substantial scale, so that, by the late 1970s, no advanced capitalist state was collecting less than 25 percent of GDP as current revenue and several were collecting in excess of 50 percent. Clearly, this century has seen a transformation in the range and extent of public policy, and it would have been cause for surprise only if scholars had not made the central features of that transformation the main focus of their attention.

Moreover, a focus on welfare levels was a particularly appropriate area in which to raise the issue of whether politics matters. On the one hand, the proponents of democratic pluralist theory had argued that responsiveness to popular demands should lead to the state intervening to provide services to its citizens. On the other, democratic socialists have prophesied, and many labour movements have had as a central assumption, that the growth of a working-class voice in politics would result in the state taking a role in curbing the operation of the free market with the end of securing greater welfare. However much there might be disagreement between the protagonists of these views about the nature of the causal mechanism involved, both were agreed in the presumption that politics matters: that differences in democratic structures and participation or working-class control of the levers of political power would determine the extent of welfare expenditure. But both of these views seem flatly to contradict the two major themes in the sociological analysis of advanced capitalist societies. In the funtionalist scheme, the main engine of social change — and, by implication, the agency shaping the role of the contemporary state — is the process of differentiation brought about by industrialization. In the dominant economistic strand of Marxist theorizing, the processes of capital concentration determine class relationships and conflicts, of which political alignments are a mere reflection. For both theories, the extent of state activity and its nature are determined primarily by socioeconomic factors; there may be a coincidence of political alignments and the role of the state, but that is only a consequence of the fact that both are similarly shaped by such factors as the industrial or class structure.

The marked divergence of views on the determinants of state activity has been reflected in the early development of an empirical 'policy science' (Dye, 1976: 22). As we have seen in the Introduction, the basic thrust of empirical investigation was directed to the question of whether politics matters. Understandably, that concern was no less central to the empirical investigation of patterns of public expenditure. Indeed, it was here that the debate centred, both because of the salience of public expenditure in the modern state and because of its theoretical and ideological importance, as well as the fact that the outpourings of government statistical agencies made it one of the most available areas for study. The 'politics matters' paradigm may no longer be an appropriate focus for investigation of policy outcomes, since the accumulation of evidence suggests a departure from a simplistic either/or formulation of the question. Nevertheless, a survey of some of the major themes in the empirical discussion of the determinants of public expenditure in general and welfare spending in particular is essential in order to locate both the inadequacies of the earlier approach and as a preliminary to mapping new avenues for research, which is an important aim of this essay.

## Public expenditure and citizen participation

The earliest empirical studies of divergent expenditure outcomes related to the American states, and for that reason were less concerned with the partisan composition of government than with the extent of citizen participation in the political arena. Indeed, the pioneering work, V.O. Key's study of *Southern Politics*, was devoted to discovering whether the absence of a choice of partisanship affected the possibility of securing programmes of expenditure that would serve the interests of those on low incomes. His conclusion was that inter-party competition facilitates expenditure decisions favouring the 'have-nots' in society:

> All in all the striking feature of the one-party system, the absence of organised and continuing factions with a lower-bracket orientation, is but one facet of an issueless politics.... The factional system simply provides no institutionalized mechanism for the expression of lower-bracket viewpoints.... [T]he grand objective of the haves is obstruction, at least of the haves who take only a short-term view. Organisation is not always necessary to obstruct; it is essential, however for the promotion of a sustained program on behalf of the have-nots. [Key, 1949: 307-9]

This argument has generated a vast literature on the determinants of levels of public expenditure in the American states. In this literature, there has been a clear divide between those, such as Thomas Dye, who have argued that, once one has controlled for various measures of economic development (such as per capita personal income, urbanism, industrialization and educational level), the apparent connection between party competition and state expenditure disappears (Dye, 1966), and others, such as Sharkansky and Hofferbert, whose findings indicate that, particularly in respect of welfare expenditures, political factors like party competition and voter turnout have a substantial impact (Sharkansky and Hofferbert, 1969). Moreover, the literature has acquired a cross-national dimension with contrasts and comparisons between democratic and communist nations. Here, the argument of those pointing to a socioeconomic explanation is fundamentally that '(i) if the basic economic circumstances (in Marxist terminology "productive forces") are similar, and if the policy dilemmas are similar, it should not be surprising that the decisions are roughly similar' (Pryor, 1968: 310), while one variant of the 'politics matters' school suggests that in democratic systems 'we expect a greater association between environmental factors like socio-economic development and policy outcomes' (Cnudde and Neubauer, 1969: 524).

Although pioneering, the literature generated from Key's original hypothesis has two substantial defects as a basis for future study. The most fundamental has been noted by Thompkins in pointing out that, not only has the basic question posed remained unresolved, but it was likely to continue to do so while scholars largely 'ignored the direct and indirect relationships among the independent variables themselves' (Thompkins, 1975: 396). In other words, the focus on demonstrating whether or not politics matters obscured the need to examine a variety of causal sequences by which socioeconomic and political factors might interact to determine expenditure patterns. Moreover, the diversity of findings reported in the literature is perfectly compatible with the view that different policies at different times are determined in different ways. That they have not been so interpreted is, on the one hand, a consequence of the difficulty of subjecting a vast body of data to adequate analysis and, on the other, the felt need to come down on one side or another of what almost certainly is a false dichotomy between socioeconomic and political causation.

The second defect in this approach stems from the difficulty of generalizing it beyond the American states or crude distinctions between democratic and non-democratic nations. The specification of the political variables in the American context relates to such factors as turnout and party competition, which are basically concerned with the existence and extent of 'institutionalized mechanism[s] for the expression of lower-bracket viewpoints'. But in what is necessarily the most fertile area for acquiring an understanding of the determinants of public expenditure patterns — namely, those advanced capitalist nations that devote a substantial percentage of their gross domestic product to welfare and other public purposes — the extent of party competition is by no means the most obvious political source of divergent policy outcomes. In nations that, with the exception of the USA and, to a lesser extent, Canada, have major party organizations which explicitly advocate policies conceived to be in the interest of the working class, the focus must shift to whether the strength of these parties and those that oppose them is the primary determinant of patterns of expenditure by the state. Where partisanship is already firmly established and recognized as the basic factor in electoral choice, it is to partisanship we must look in examining the impact of politics on public policy.

## Ideology, partisanship and welfare

To see partisanship as a crucial dimension shaping patterns of public expenditure rests on the prior assumption that the political organizations among which the electorate chooses have diverse ideological leanings, which are translated into diverse patterns of policy implementation. The 'issueless politics' created by an absence of electoral competition disappears, to be replaced by a politics structured by the conflict of parties articulating views based on competing conceptions of social organization. But it is at this point in the argument that both the functionalists and Marxists enter their caveats. Whereas both might concede that, in the turbulence engendered by the Industrial Revolution and the entry into politics of the working class, there was a polarization of ideological intensity, postwar developments have seen a decline in ideology or repression of working-class consciousness to a point where nothing divides the parties other than the desire to take the spoils of office. Politics again becomes issueless, not because there is no party competition, but rather because that competition has become meaningless.

The classic formulation of this view is to be found in S.M. Lipset's *Political Man*, which attributes the 'end of ideology' to the process of socioeconomic change in advanced democratic states:

> Economic development, producing increased income, greater economic security, and widespread higher education, largely determines the form of the 'class struggle', by permitting those in the lower strata to develop longer time perspectives and more complex and gradualist views of politics. A belief in secular reformist gradualism can be the ideology of only a relatively well-to-do class.... .
>
> Increased wealth and education also serve democracy by increasing the lower classes' exposure to cross-pressures which reduce their commitment to given ideologies and make them less receptive to extremist ones. The operation of this process...means involving those strata in an integrated national culture as distinct from an isolated lower-class one.... . [Lipset, 1960: 61-5]

Similar arguments, diversely formulated, became the orthodoxy of the 1950s and 1960s. As early as 1955, Tingsten was deploring the loss of vitality of Swedish politics, where '[t]he actual words "socialism" or "liberalism"' are tending to become mere honorifics, useful in connection with elections and political festivities' (Tingsten, 1955: 145). By the 1960s, Kirchheimer was describing a wholesale 'waning of opposition' in which 'diminished social polarisation and diminished political polarisation are going hand in hand' (Kirchheimer, 1964: 287). In parallel with the 'end of ideology' thesis went the argument that advanced democratic states were being pushed by the twin imperatives of economic and technological change towards a convergence described variously as 'pluralistic industrialism' (Kerr, 1960), the 'new industrial state' (Galbraith, 1967) or 'post-industrial society' (Bell, 1973). All these discussions of convergence displayed a similar paradox. On the one hand, political factors are subordinate to economic and technological imperatives in shaping social structure and institutional arrangements; and, on the other, a political institution par excellence — the state — is seen as acquiring a more dominant role than hitherto, in terms of its capacity both to dispose of resources (public expenditure) and to co-ordinate the economy. The convergence and 'end of ideology' theses are closely interlinked, not merely because both postulate increasing similarity in society, state and politics, but because the decline in partisanship is simultaneously a product of socioeconomic development and a precondition for social conflicts developing in the context of post-industrial change to be worked out in an essentially similar way.

Both theses are also basically conservative in orientation, since, by implication at least, political action to reshape society in the interests of the have-nots is seen as unrealistic. Marxist analysis, whether or not of an economist variety, tends to agree with the substance of this diagnosis. To Marcuse the 'repressive tolerance' of the contemporary state has dissipated the critique of industrial society which attained concreteness 'in the consciousness of the two great classes which faced each other in society: the bourgeoisie and the proletariat' (Marcuse, 1964: 11). In its place has arisen '[a]n over-riding interest in the preservation and improvement of the institutional *status quo* [which] unites the former antagonists in the most advanced areas of contemporary society' (Marcuse, 1964: 11). Moreover, the nature of the capitalist state not merely conditions the views of the contesting classes, it also shapes the policy options available. Thus, Claus Offe, from a more overtly economistic viewpoint, suggests that 'no government can afford to expand welfare services beyond a certain limit without being pushed by inflation, unemployment or both' (Offe, 1972: 485). Socioeconomic factors are seen as paramount, and the conservative critique of the welfare state as 'creeping socialism' is partly correct, 'not because it is socialism but because it creeps' (Offe, 1972: 485).

The strong theoretical emphasis on the decline of partisanship and the primacy of socioeconomic forces making for policy convergence has offered fertile ground for cross-national empirical study of the patterns of similarity and dissimilarity displayed by national patterns of welfare policy and expenditure. Using 'social insurance program experience' (i.e. the length of time such programmes have been in existence) as his dependent variable, Cutright has shown that, for a sample of 76 nations, the best explanation of variance is economic development as measured by levels of energy consumption (Cutright, 1965). In an influential study, Wilensky examined the joint impact of GNP per capita, age of social security system and age structure of the population on the percentage of GNP devoted to social security. His conclusion, derived from an analysis of 60 nations, is that 'the primacy of economic level and its demographic and bureaucratic correlates is support for a convergence hypothesis; economic growth makes countries with contrasting cultural and political traditions more alike in their strategy for constructing the floor below which no one sinks' (Wilensky, 1975: 27). The root cause of the general level of welfare expenditure is seen as economic growth, but the mechanism that translates economic change into public policy is the transformation of the demographic structure which simultaneously creates 'a population in need and a political force for further social security development' (Wilensky, 1976: 13).

But that political force is not, in Wilensky's view, a particular political party with a specific ideological slant. Rather, his conclusions can be taken to support the 'end of ideology' thesis, since he explicitly pays attention to parties as potential carriers of diverse orientations to welfare and finds that 'two measures of ideology [the index of belief in 'planning for equality' and 'equality of opportunity'] consistently add nothing' to the explanation of social security expenditure (Wilensky, 1976: 48).[1] Similar studies, employing large samples of nations, have continued to point to similar conclusions, with a recent analysis of educational expenditures in 100 national political systems pointing to the crucial influence of such factors as levels of communication, health, industrialization, literacy, urbanization and wealth (Verner, 1979: 184).

Although frequently statistically sophisticated, these various studies, which purport to provide empirical backing for the convergence of welfare expenditures and the nugatory influence of political ideology, have in common a methodological flaw which vitiates much of the strength of their findings. Each is based on a large sample of countries at extremely diverse levels of economic and social development. As previously noted by Castles and McKinlay, the distribution of countries around any of the measures of socioeconomic development commonly used in such studies is bimodal in character (Castles and McKinlay, 1979: 184). Rather than demonstrating that as countries gradually become more industrialized or richer they also gradually extend the sphere of expenditure on welfare and associated purposes — in crude summary, the essence of the convergence thesis — all that Cutright, Wilensky and others have shown is that welfare programmes are more extensive and welfare expenditures are higher in industrialized and rich countries. Such an unsurprising finding effectively disguises the very real possibility that the relationships between socioeconomic, political and policy variables may be very different within each group of industrialized and non-industrialized countries considered separately. Moreover, that such is the case is very strongly suggested by the findings of Jackman, who, in a study of 60 countries, demonstrates the existence of a curvilinear relationship between economic growth and a number of welfare indicators (Jackman, 1975: 28-43). In other words, while variance in the welfare levels of less developed countries is substantially attributable to economic level, other factors must be sought to explain differences between the welfare levels of advanced nations.[2] As argued in the introduction to this volume, the danger of the distorting effects of a bimodal distribution is a reason for preferring to study a group of nations at a roughly comparable socioeconomic level. It is also a reason, the arguments of the 'end of ideology' and convergence theses notwithstanding, that we should not prematurely reject a possible linkage between the partisan composition of government and public expenditure patterns in advanced capitalist states.

### Party, class politics and political structure

Given both the tenor of socioeconomic determinism in the prevailing theoretical orthodoxy and the distorting effect of choosing to work with large samples of countries, it is hardly surprising that the occasional studies that have attempted to show a link between political factors and policy outcomes on the basis of cross-national analysis have been largely atheoretical and restricted to a relatively small compass. Indeed, in many cases the basic rationale seems to have been less to advance theory construction than to provide an underpinning for the claim of political science to be an explanatory discipline. This explains much of the one-sidedness of the argument in the 'politics matters' debate, since, if political factors were not relevant to the explanation of behaviour, and especially behaviour pertaining to that most political of arenas, the state, why should their study not be subsumed as a branch of political sociology or political economy, as the more fervent of the protagonists of the functionalist and Marxist frameworks had suggested? In the context of the debate, what was important was not so much what political factors explained, but rather that they explained anything at all.

All such studies adopted a similar universe of discourse: a larger or smaller sample of the advanced democratic states of Europe, North America and the old Commonwealth. This was not so much in recognition of the dangers of wider samples, but because, in making the primary focus the variance that could be explained by political factors, a choice had to be made of countries that had certain political attributes in common. Overwhelmingly the most frequently chosen attribute has been the strength of socialist parties, although some attention has also been paid to differences in the nature of class politics and to types of political system and political structure within the common liberal democratic framework. That socialist partisanship has found favour is due both to the fact that such an emphasis provided an implicit hypothesis for testing, since such parties professed different goals from other parties, and goals particularly relevant to patterns of public expenditure, and to the fact that the common attribute to be measured was readily defined in terms of such parties' adherence to those goals expressed in terms of a common rhetoric. Other groups and parties could not so readily be compared, since they possessed no similar common denominator.

A study that explicitly sets out to test the relative explanatory power of the various hypotheses current in the public policy field is Hewitt's analysis of 'The Effect of Political Democracy and Social Democracy on Equality in Industrial Societies' (Hewitt, 1977: 450-64). While being mainly concerned with the redistributive effects of taxation, some attention is also paid to social service expenditures as an element in redistribution. Based on a sample of 17 advanced democratic states, it is argued that the length of existence of a liberal democratic framework for partisan competition is an insufficient explanation of variance in equality, since controlling for GNP per capita makes the apparent relationship disappear.[3] The same is not true in the case of the party variable, and Hewitt concludes that 'socialist experience is significantly related in the predicted direction of redistribution through government budgets and to the share of national income going to the top income groups' (1977: 460). From this one might deduce that the case for the influence of socialist partisanship had been made; but, in fact, the results are heavily dependent on the socioeconomic variables used as controls. In another study, in this case centrally directed at the extent of public expenditure, Cameron also finds that 'the rate of growth in the economic affluence of a nation does not contribute to the expansion of the public economy' (Cameron, 1978: 1251). However, the degree of openness of the economy — measured as a function of the importance of imports plus exports in the economy (IMEX) — is of considerably greater explanatory significance than socialist strength, which he conceives as a variable mediating the effects of an open economy. Thus, 'the openness of the economy contributes to the expansion of the public economy by facilitating the development of the social infrastructure upon which Social Democratic and Labor party electoral support rests' (Cameron, 1978: 1257).

One of the major advantages of an analytic focus on the advanced states is the relative completeness of the data-base. Whereas a time-series of large samples of nations widely disparate in economic level is made virtually impossible by the poverty of prewar data, such studies are possible in the context of advanced states. A very considerable research endeavour is in progress at the University of Cologne on the growth and determinants of welfare state activity in Europe since the early beginnings of social insurance programmes in the late nineteenth century. The findings of this research have a very considerable bearing on the relationship of partisanship and the development of the modern welfare state. In summary, it is argued that:

> Political forces have decisively shaped social insurance development *only before World War II*. Until the turn of the century, authoritarian regimes, whose legitimacy was threatened by the political mobilisation of the working class, were most active. Between 1900 and 1915, parliamentary democracies under liberal rule took the lead in program extension. The inter-war period saw the greatest growth when socialist parties held governmental power or scored electoral success. After the Second World War, expansionist social policies appeared to be a by-product of prosperity throughout Western Europe, independent of the inner-political situation. Growth was greatest in those countries which had previously been among the European laggards of social insurance coverage. [Alber, 1979; Abstract; italics added]

Here we find a rather different interpretation. Politics did matter in the early development of the European welfare state, but the findings are compatible with an imputed subsequent decline in ideological differences and quite explicitly suggest a process of convergence in the postwar era. The nuances of this conclusion, and particularly the overall finding that the determinants of public policy may vary over time, are especially interesting, since they do suggest a willingness to depart from entrenched positions in the 'politics matters' debate. The task for subsequent analysis may well be seen as a question of mapping where and when politics matters, rather than entering into a sterile debate as to whether it matters at all.[4]

Alber's discussion of the political factors related to the development of the welfare state makes an important distinction between the mobilization of the working class and socialist governmental power. This distinction is important for a number of writers, who argue either that socialist cabinet strength and working-class organizations are separate forces conducive to both welfare reform and extension of the role of the state, or that the major victories for the working class have been won against the incumbents of state power, whether of bourgeois or social democratic complexion. A recent book embodying the first perspective is Stephens's *The Transition from Capitalism to Socialism*, in which he argues that socialist reform in the advanced democracies is possible on the basis of a mass movement of organized labour in which 'trade union and parliamentary activity are equally important' (Stephens, 1979: 88). This argument for the importance of class politics is supported by an empirical analysis which demonstrates a strong positive correlation between socialist rule and non-military public expenditure in 1970, and a similarly high correlation between the socialist vote and union membership as a percentage of the labour force (Stephens, 1979: 99-105). Although conceding that sweeping victories by working-class parties can effect some changes, Ian Gough is more pessimistic about the parliamentary role of social democracy and emphasizes instead 'the degree of class conflict and, especially the strength and form of the working class struggle' (Gough, 1979: 64). In terms of this perspective, the changes in the state apparatus implied by welfare state activity are defensive strategic reactions of a ruling class under threat. Irrespective of the assumptions from which a class politics analysis proceeds, it shares with the other approaches already discussed in this section the notion that public policy conducted by the state is not merely a reflection of socioeconomic factors, but is at least further shaped by the conscious political actions of individuals, movements or parties working through or in opposition to established political structures.

Those studies that have concentrated their attention on factors other than socialist or working class strength in the effort to demonstrate the importance of politics have adopted disparate approaches. Castles (1978) and Castles and McKinlay (1979a, 1979b) have focused on the strength of parties of the Right as determinants of welfare outcomes, including the level of transfer payments, educational spending and infant mortality rates. This approach, which focuses on the differential impact on policy of parties with diverse ideological leanings, will figure largely in this chapter. Anthony King, in an examination of the diverse welfare performance and level of state activity in Britain, Canada, France, Germany and the United States, suggests that it is the prevailing American ethos of the limited role of government that explains the vast differences between that country and the others (King, 1978). Guy Peters, testing an hypothesis he derives from the work of Lijphart, argues that the type of political system — whether the polity has a fragmented or homogeneous political culture and whether political elites adopt competitive or coalescent behaviour patterns — has an impact on policy configurations (Peters, 1978).[5] In particular, he notes that coalescent systems have significantly higher levels of welfare spending than competitive types (1978: 94).

Finally, a number of studies have taken up the question of the link between political structure, conceived in terms of the diverse levels of political centralization in federal and unitary states, and a variety of public policy variables. Interestingly, and with the exception of King's study, whose results are definitely biased by the presence of three federal states in this restricted sample, this is one area in which the conclusions all point in a similar direction: federal states are lesser providers of welfare and have a less active role in the economy than unitary states. Wilensky finds lower social security spending in the least centralized of his richer sub-sample of states (Wilensky, 1975: 52-3); Cameron argues that federalism 'dampen[s] the degree of expansion of the public economy' (Cameron, 1978: 1253) and Castles and McKinlay suggest that the federal/unitary variable is of even greater explanatory power than the measure of right-wing partisanship they utilize (Castles and McKinlay, 1979a: 179-80). In each case, the basic rationale of the finding is that political elites in centralized states can more easily overcome the resistance to new departures in state activity. Here, then, is a political factor with some promise for understanding at least part of the variance in public expenditure patterns, but it should be noted that it is one apparently very different from partisan allegiance, since the latter is seemingly subject to periodic fluctuation, while institutionalized forms of political centralization are virtually unchanging.

## Problems of analysing politics and public expenditure

It was argued previously that the political factors isolated by the democratic pluralists as important in explaining the variance of policy among the American states were likely to be less relevant in cross-national analysis. Moreover, the discussion of the studies purporting to test the socioeconomic convergence thesis pointed to the methodological problem of employing large samples of nations at disparate levels of development. These are sufficient reasons why progress in acquiring knowledge of the complex interaction of socioeconomic and political factors in the determination of policy outcomes must come from studies of nations at similar levels of economic development and with comparable political structures and partisan alignments.[6] Thus, in so far as our interest is in the development of public expenditure patterns in the modern welfare state, it is inappropriate to draw conclusions based on the experience of those nations that have not yet achieved even minimal levels of educational, health and public income maintenance provision; and, among those that have, the choice must be restricted to those with a sufficient similarity of political behaviour to make statements about the variation in such attributes meaningful. That this is the case more or less predetermines that the universe of discourse for our study of patterns of public and welfare expenditure will be the 20 or so nations that have in common a relatively advanced capitalist economy, a more or less developed welfare infrastructure, and the political institutions and alignments predicated on the existence of a liberal democratic state. However, this choice of a universe of discourse, and the nature of the political factors it suggests as possible causes of policy variation, has its own very real problems, which must be examined in some detail before it is possible to develop a viable strategy for further analysis.

## The search for patterned relationships

The most fundamental problems stem from the methodological and statistical implications of an analysis that is based on such a small number of countries. It has already been suggested that the total of democratic capitalist states that may appropriately be compared is 21, but most studies have worked with several fewer, since, even for the advanced countries, wholly comparable data are rarely fully available. Methodologically, a small universe of discourse leads to the problem of 'the overdetermination of observed difference' (Roberts, 1978: 294), which means, in effect, that the number of cases is too small to settle which of several differences among the cases may be regarded as the cause (or effect) of the observed variance. To take an extreme instance, the problem posited by King, of why the United States has a much lower degree of state activity than four other countries, is not strictly open to resolution, since any one of the multitudinous factors that differentiate the United States from these countries could be the cause of the observed difference in state activity. Bringing more cases into the comparison serves progressively as a control for spurious explanations, but, certainly, 20 or so cases at the best can only discriminate among the most obvious.

The statistical problems that arise from instability of estimation in a small population of cases have already been discussed in the Introduction. The simultaneous need to increase population size to control for spurious explanation and to minimize it to exclude extreme variability suggests that considerable caution should be exercised in interpreting statistical findings. The strength of a relationship can be tentatively indicated by significance levels; and, from an exploratory point of view, the correlation techniques from which they result are useful in generating preliminary insights into the linkage of variables, which might not be immediately apparent from inspection of a two-by-two classification of cases. While the normal function of significance testing is inappropriate in the context of a total population with no possibility of sampling error, it does make sense as a test of postulated causal relationships against what Blalock calls 'chance-processes' alternatives (Blalock, 1979). However, the preliminary and tentative nature of statistical findings based on such a small number of cases must always be remembered, and we should not be prepared to arrive at conclusions unless analogous findings emerge in other contexts. It is for this reason that we propose to focus on patterns of public expenditure and welfare in this chapter. If partisan alignment, for instance, can be shown to be related to a variety of policy variables at different times, it adds substantial strength to the imputation of a causal link of some kind. It may, therefore, be regarded as a measure of the collective strength of the argument of the 'politics matters' school that so many studies have reported moderately strong, direct or indirect, linkages between socialist partisanship and indicators of welfare and equality.[7] On the other hand, it must be considered a weakness of the majority of individual studies that they restrict themselves to a very limited selection of dependent variables.[8]

The need to locate patterns of variation is further intensified if it is our intention to examine the complex interactions of a series of economic, social and political factors. Given the scope for instability of estimation in a small population, there are very real problems in assessing the relative explanatory power of two or more independent variables. The normal procedure in step-wise multiple regression analysis is to concentrate attention on the strongest statistical relationship and to focus attention on other variables only in so far as they add to the explanation of variance. However, by definition, those that add most will be those relatively unrelated to the strongest independent variable. This means that, when there are several strong explanatory variables, which are themselves highly intercorrelated, it will be frequently a matter of pure chance which is selected as the central locus of analysis. There are certain techniques — in particular, path analysis — by which this danger can be minimized, but only by a prior theoretical specification of causal relationships, and with results only as adequate as the hypotheses from which it is derived. Often what has passed for theory has been little more than post hoc rationalization designed to produce the best fit with a single dependent variable. What seems essential in the analysis of policy outcomes is some greater attention to the patterns of interrelationship of a wide range of independent variables over a wide range of policy areas. If for instance, as we shall subsequently find, the openness of the economy and the strength of the political Right are strongly intercorrelated, we should be concerned not merely with which provides the better fit with a single set of policy-related data, but whether similar relationships hold in respect of other policy areas. Thereafter, what is required is theoretical speculation not only as to why one or other variable is most strongly related to policy (assuming that this does not fluctuate, as it frequently will), but also as to the nature of the relationship between the independent variables. Drawing attention to such problems of multicollinearity as statistical pitfalls to be avoided by the wary is not sufficient. Only in the study of patterns of intercorrelation and patterns of outcomes have we the intellectual means to iron out the fluctuations of data pertaining to our restricted universe of discourse.

It is also very important to realize the full implications of the search for patterned relationships. Obviously, we would optimally wish to explain separately variations in discrete areas of policy and variations in a single policy area over time. But the necessity to use related policy areas or the same policy at diverse time periods as controls for the inherent fluctuations of the data-base implied that this is possible only to a limited extent. If, for instance, we locate a moderately strong relationship between economic growth and educational spending for a five-year period, but do not discover any comparable relationship in the preceding or succeeding periods, we should be more entitled to dismiss the relationship as a consequence of instability of estimation than to conclude that different relationships pertained in the different periods. Similarly, if we hypothesize that socialist partisanship is related to welfare expenditures in a variety of areas, and find that this is apparently the case in only one area, it may well be premature to seek post hoc reasons why that area should differ from others. This is neither to suggest that distinguishing between the differential causes of policy outcomes at different times and in different areas is impossible, or to argue against post hoc reasoning as such. What is necessary is sufficient evidence to discern that for related policies at a particular time, or for particular policies over time, there exists a set of more or less patterned relationships. Where those relationships are un-predicted by theory — and that is the more likely the larger the range of independent variables brought into view by the analysis — there is always room for that reasoning from unanticipated results, which is often the most fruitful stimulus to new theoretical insight.

## Socioeconomic change and structured political choice

There are further problems, this time conceptual in nature, when we come to consider just what it is that the various studies that have examined the relationship between socioeconomic, political and policy variables are attempting to prove. The vehemence of the 'politics matters' debate, and the fact that it is tied in with the con-flict of sociological functionalists and Marxist structuraiists on the one side and the pretensions of a political science discipline premis-ed on the exercise of human choice on the other, suggests that the issues are fundamental, relating to the extent to which the struc-tured socioeconomic processes of contemporary societies leave room for conscious reshaping of policy and institutional ar-rangements. The possibility that both determinism and choice can, and should be, encompassed by a single theoretical framework is argued by some proponents of both functionalism (see Almond, 1973) and Marxism. Thus, for one Marxist analyst of the political economy of the welfare state, what distinguishes this latter theory

is not the view that a particular class dominates the institution of the state (though this is the normal state of affairs), but that whoever occupies these posi-tions is constrained by the imperatives of the capital accumulation process. But at the same time the separation and relatively autonomy of the state permits numerous reforms to be won, and it in no way acts as the passive tool of one class. Within these constraints there is room for manoeuvre, for competing strategies and policies. There is scope for the various organs of the state to in-itiate policies, to reverse them, to make choices and to make mistakes. [Gough, 1979: 43-4]

# TABLE 1
## Change in socioeconomic and political factors
## (18 nations)

| (a) Socioeconomic | | (b) Political | 1951-60 with 1961-70 |
|---|---|---|---|
| GNP per capita 1960 with 1973 | 0.94 | Right parliamentary seats | 0.91 |
| GNP growth rate 1950-59 with 1962-69 | 0.69 | Right cabinet seats | 0.80 |
| Imports and exports (IMEX) as% | | Social democratic parliamentary seats | 0.97 |
| GNP 1960 with 1975 | 0.95 | Social democratic cabinet seats | 0.71 |
| | | Union density (16 countries, 1960 with 1970) | 0.87 |

Sources: Data on GNP per capita and growth rates (annual rate at constant prices averaged over the period) from World Bank (1976). Data on IMEX from OECD *National Accounts* (1958-67, 1975). Data on parliamentary seats is calculated from Mackie and Rose (1974); that on cabinet seats is calculated from *Keesings Contemporary Almanac*. Data on union density is from Stephens (1979).

Such a balanced perspective, although not necessarily Marxist in tenor, is very desirable from a conceptual viewpoint, but it has not been easy to translate it into empirical practice.

The basic difficulty is in making the necessary linkages between the imputed causal mechanisms and the phenomena signifiying them. It would be assumed that the measures signifying the dynamic of the capital accumulation process (or socioeconomic processes, in functionalist terms) would change little in their relative magnitudes over time, since they tapped basic structural attributes, while the indicators relating to the political dimension (i.e. strategies, choices and manoevures) would be much more subject to fluctuation. Yet an examination of the types of variation most commonly surveyed in the literature does not reveal such a contrast. This is shown in Table 1, which reports correlation coefficients for values of a variety of socioeconomic and political factors at two time-points separated by between 10 and 20 years. As would be expected, cabinet participation, which depends on the specific balance of forces at a given time, is more variable than parliamentary representation, which depends on the relatively stable alignments in the electorate and normally unchanging constitutional rules. Moreover, there is obviously some tendency for greater fluctuation, the greater the period of time brought into view. Even so, by including another six years in the analysis, 1951-60 to 1967-76, the correlation for social democratic seats is only reduced to 0.57 and the relationship in respect of right-wing cabinet seats and parliamentary seats for both political tendencies remains almost unchanged. Moreover, as already noted, certain political factors, like the degree of political centralization, are almost wholly invariant. Over periods of several decades the same appears to be true of such factors as the competitive or coalescent behaviour of elites and the somewhat divergent measures of the political complexion of government and political system used in this volume.

That the majority of significant political factors should be relatively unchanging over long periods should come as little surprise. The institutionalized forms of political centralization and electoral choice are prescribed in constitutional arrangements that are intended to be permanent. Moreover, at a more informal level, what we know of the impact of processes of political socialization and the crystalization of party alignments with the extension of universal suffrage (see Lipset and Rokkan, 1967) suggests that here too we should expect to find relatively stable and structured features. Indeed, when contrasting socioeconomic and political factors, it is in certain of the former that one would expect the greater variability. This applies particularly to rate of change variables, such as economic growth rates, inflation rates, and demographic change rates, which may be postulated to fluctuate in response to short-term factors, despite certain long-term regularities stemming from institutional features of the economic infrastructure. It should be noted that the majority of policy studies have neglected such change variables, and have preferred to relate both levels and changes in policy to *levels* of socioeconomic and political activity.[9] Such an emphasis has been appropriate, because both the functionalists and Marxists and the adherents of a political science perspective have, in reality, been interested in the same phenomenon, that is, the manner in which the variation in the structures of contemporary societies affects the nature of public policy outcomes.

Assuming only that the protagonists in the debate are willing jointly to concede that the imperatives stemming from economic and social forces are necessarily mediated through structures of political choice, the controversy must be resolved into a search for patterned relationships between relatively enduring socioeconomic and political structures. Such a concession need not be difficult for a Marxist, like Gough, so long as the room for manoeuvre and competing strategies in class politics is seen as subject to institutionalized limitation. For the more empirical political science all that is required is a reorientation of perspective. There are some signs that such a reorientation may, in any case, be taking place simply because it yields better results. Thus, Dryzek, in a recent study of impact of politics and economics on inequality, which starts in the familiar 'politics matters' mould, moves on to employ a factor analysis, which combines together the degree of economic resource use with the extent of political development as twin dimensions of what he calls 'development' (Dryzek, 1978: 402). Moreover, the explanatory power of this factor is tested against another socio-political measure of 'class politics'. Dryzek's own conclusion, that 'the determinants of cross-national differences in social equality should not be categorized as either socioeconomic or political', is one that is likely to be just as appropriate throughout the public policy field, where, par excellence, economic and social needs are made provision for through the structures of political choice.

## The specification of variables

Finally, the analysis of the determinants of patterns of public policy involve a further category of problems concerning the specification of both independent and dependent variables. Although these will be discussed further in the context of elaborating our research design, they merit some brief consideration in relation to our general overview of the field of study. The major problems to be confronted here are the difficulty of distinguishing between types of political explanation, of operationalizing party variables, and of ensuring adequate comparability in the policy-related data.

Distinguishing among the types of political explanation that have been offered for policy variation is difficult, simply because the criteria for classification are rarely such as to make it possible to apply decisive tests between a variety of competing hypotheses. In effect, this is once more to say that 'the overdetermination of observed difference' in a small population makes it difficult to

## TABLE 2
### Intercorrelations of political variables,
### 1965-74 (18 nations)*

|  | 1 | 2 | 3 | 4 | 5 | 6 | 7 | 8 | 9 |
|---|---|---|---|---|---|---|---|---|---|
| (1) Right-wing parliamentary seats | 1.00 | 0.81 | -0.02 | -0.34 | -0.80 | -0.29 | -0.81 | -0.43 | -0.48 |
| (2) Right-wing cabinet seats |  | 1.00 | 0.02 | -0.39 | -0.65 | -0.11 | -0.70 | -0.56 | -0.36 |
| (3) Social democratic parliamentary seats |  |  | 1.00 | 0.75 | 0.48 | 0.11 | 0.14 | -0.67 | 0.64 |
| (4) Social democratic cabinet seats |  |  |  | 1.00 | 0.75 | 0.08 | 0.36 | -0.50 | 0.79 |
| (5) Complexion of government and political system (GAPS) |  |  |  |  | 1.00 | 0.25 | 0.75 | 0.11 | 0.66 |
| (6) Federal/ unitary |  |  |  |  |  | 1.00 | 0.00 | 0.04 | 0.32 |
| (7) Competitive/ coalescent |  |  |  |  |  |  | 1.00 | 0.34 | 0.47 |
| (8) Other cabinet seats |  |  |  |  |  |  |  | 1.00 | -0.04 |
| (9) Union density, 1970 (17 countries) |  |  |  |  |  |  |  |  | 1.00 |

*Variables (6) and (7) are dummy variables (federal = 0, unitary = 1; competitive = 0, coalescent = 1). The rationale for the complexion of government and political system (GAPS) variable as used in this chapter is found on p. 60 below, as is also the method of calculation (see n. 16).

come to firm conclusions, except on the basis of repeatedly observed patterns. This point can be made statistically by examining the intercorrelations of a variety of political variables for a particular period.

As demonstrated in Table 2, the problem is that every variable, apart from political centralization, is significantly related to two or more others. To take but one example, when we discover that the correlation coefficients measuring the relationships between educational expenditure in 1960 and right-wing cabinet seats and coalescent political systems are $-0.52$ and $0.47$ respectively, how do we distinguish between the explanations of rightist non-intervention and of elite compromise, when we know that the correlation between the two independent variables was $-0.81$ for the period 1951-60? In this case the answer may be relatively obvious, since there is reason to believe that the two phenomena may be reverse sides of the same coin and because they display the same close interrelation throughout a longish period (1951-76). What we seem to have here is one phenomenon conceptualized in different ways. Other instances may be much less obvious, and, given the inherent instability of estimation in our population, may not be readily resolvable by the usual statistical techniques. This being so, our conclusions are once again necessarily dependent on patterns of association either over time or in related policy areas.

That the political factors, with the exception of the federal/unitary variable, tend to demonstrate strong patterns of intercorrelation does not mean that care need not be exercised in specifying and operationalizing the independent variables for analysis. As Borg and Castles (1981) have pointed out in respect of party variables, the choice of independent variable and the manner of measuring it can have crucial causal implications. Thus, although there has been a strong emphasis on socialist parties in the literature, the dimensions of left-wing influence have been defined in diverse, and sometimes conflicting, ways. Some studies have chosen to focus on social democratic and labour parties, taking adherence to the Socialist International as the defining criterion for allegiance to common goals (see Castles, 1978; Hewitt, 1977; and Tufte, 1979); while others have included all parties of the Left (see Dryzek, 1978) or have adopted the midway stance of discussing parties of the non-Communist Left (see Jackman, 1975). But, clearly, to equate the influence of social democratic parties, which frequently hold office in liberal democratic systems, with other leftist parties, which are almost invariably excluded as 'anti-system' parties, is to make implicit or explicit judgements as to the mechanism by which socialist strength shapes public policy. Basically, it seems to involve an acceptance of the view that the extension of the welfare state is a process by which beleaguered elites allocate 'benefits to the less privileged...to damp down radical or revolutionary movements' (Parkin, 1971: 124).[10] Such a class politics hypothesis is perfectly tenable, but it is at odds with the presumption that guides the actions of the social democratic parties, that, in order to change the fabric of capitalist society, it is necessary to gain political control of the levers of economic power. To assess the strength of this latter explanation, it is necessary to relate socialist success in gaining governmental status to subsequent policy change. Obviously, there is likely to be considerable inter-correlation between the diverse variables used in the literature to operationalize socialist and working-class strength, suggesting simultaneously that imputations as to the causal mechanisms at work need to be made with some caution, that the linkages between particular independent and dependent variables should be carefully specified, and that conclusions should emerge only from a substantial survey of research findings.

Similar difficulties are encountered in respect of the way in which the impact or strength of party variables is actually measured (Borg and Castles, 1981). There are at least four commonly used measures in the literature: percentage of the total vote, percentage of seats in the legislature, number of years in office, and percentage of cabinet seats held. Again, these definitions have diverse causal implications. Percentage of the total vote measures opinion in the electorate, while parliamentary seats assesses the extent to which that opinion is reflected in the law-making arena. Number of years in office might be regarded as a measure of the degree to which a party possesses a veto on the formulation of policy, while cabinet strength taps the positive potential to shape policy in a mould consonant with party ideology. Although, as has already been indicated in Table 2, some of these measures are likely to be highly interrelated, this will not necessarily be the case. Thus, Borg and Castles have shown that during some periods (see note 25 below) there is a much stronger relationship between legislative strength and years in office for parties of the Right than for social democratic and labour parties (Borg and Castles, 1981). Quite apart from the significance of that particular finding for understanding the difficulty that radical opinion may experience in being translated into influence on policy formulation, this does, once again, suggest the care that must be taken in the specification of party variables.

Last, but by no means least, there is a range of difficulties in specifying the dependent, policy-related, variables for analysis. This is partly the familiar problem of all cross-national studies of obtaining data with optimum coverage of the relevant universe of discourse. However, it is even more fundamentally an issue of making inferences from indicators that are more or less directly related to the subject under investigation (see Castles, 1978: 58-60). Optimally, we would wish to measure a whole range of policy outcomes, in the sense of examining the impact of health policy in terms of the wellbeing of the community, the impact of education policy in terms of individuals' abilities to function adequately within their social environment, and the impact of public income maintenance programmes in terms of the level-of-living of individuals in circumstances where they are deprived from income from employment. However, data pertaining to welfare outcomes are only rarely routinely collected by statistical agencies, and then, only exceptionally, in a form that makes even the most elementary cross-national comparisons possible.[11] Because this is so, the majority of studies are restricted to cross-national analysis of the policy outputs of governments, which are routinely collected and, frequently, collated in a reasonably comparative way by internatinal governmental agencies, such as UNO, UNESCO, ILO and OECD. Such data are only indirectly related to the achievement of welfare and related purposes, since societies may be characterized by different views as to how such purposes should be realized — in particular, the choice between realization through the market or state activity. Moreover, even though it is possible to discern a shift away from private welfare schemes in advanced countries in recent years (OECD, 1976: 15), there remains a substantial diversity in the methods by which a government may attempt to achieve policy objectives (Kaim-Caudle, 1973: 50). The levels and changes in policy outputs most frequently examined — total government revenue or expenditure, transfer payments, government consumption, spending on health, education and public income maintenance programmes — should not, therefore, be taken as more than approximate indicators of government effort in welfare and related fields.[12] Nevertheless, given the very real diversity of patterns of public expenditure among the advanced capitalist states, the question of why the degree of effort should vary so considerably is of some importance. Moreover, it is a question that seems to tie in with the major partisan divide of our epoch: the diverse stance of the political parties on the positive role of the state in promoting welfare and equality.

## Research design

The basic conclusion that emerges from the preceding survey of the literature devoted to the determinants of welfare spending and its associated problems is that future research is likely to be most fruitful where we are able to bring into view the widest possible range of dependent and independent variables in the hope of being able to discern recurrent patterns of relationships either as between related policy areas or as between the same policy area at different times. With such an objective in mind, it is our intention, in the remaining sections of this chapter, to examine some of the major dimensions of public expenditure in the 1960s and 1970s, as well as the change that took place over the period, and to attempt to relate these to patterns of socioeconomic and political factors. In doing so, it will not be possible, for all the reasons already stated, to come to definitive conclusions about the causation of particular policies at particular times. Rather, it is hoped to offer sufficient basis for intelligent speculation concerning some of the major influences on patterns of public expenditure, and to provide a part of that evidence that would form the basis of an overall assessment of the relationship between party difference and public policy in general.

### The dependent variables

The availability even of output data is all too frequently of a kind that makes the search for patterned relationships extremely difficult. Thus, information concerning related policy areas may not be forthcoming for a sufficient range of cases, or the cases surveyed may differ from policy area to policy area, thereby markedly increasing the distorting impact of instability of estimation. Moreover, in so far as we would wish to analyse related policies over a given time-span, there are almost invariably difficulties in data collection. Indeed, assembling the necessary data-base is, in itself, a substantial research project. This being so, we are particularly fortunate in being able to rely on the material provided by a continuing research endeavour on public expenditure trends conducted under the auspices of the Organization for Economic Cooperation and Development (OECD). The major objectives of this research have been to examine 'the factors lying behind the past growth in public expenditure [and] the likely future development of demands for public expenditure and the costs incurred in meeting these demands' (OECD, 1978: 8). The first of these objectives is virtually identical to our own, and, indeed, it might seem almost an act of supererogation to subject to analysis data that have already been so meticulously studied with similar purposes in mind. However, as the authors of an earlier study in the same OECD series point out, the economic analysis, which it is their task to undertake, does not provide a full explanation of public expenditure trends, since 'differences in countries' institutional structures, reflecting other factors of a social, historical and political nature, play a larger role than income differences in accounting for the inter-country variations in the relative importance of the government sector in this field' (OECD, 1977: 15). It is these 'other factors', considered beyond the scope of the OECD research, that are the focus of the investigation in this chapter.

The dependent variables that feature in this analysis are either drawn or calculated from the material presented in the summary volume, *Public Expenditure Trends*, which constitutes a synthesis of OECD's work in this area during the last decade (OECD, 1978). The data relate to major categories of public expenditure and elements of welfare spending and give more or less complete coverage for 18 out of 21 advanced democratic states. The exceptions are Iceland and Luxembourg, which, at least in terms of population base, are no major loss, and Israel, which in terms of atypicality caused by massive defence expenditures might in any case distort the picture. Although it has not always been possible to assemble data for the same years, a roughly comparable time-span is covered, from the early 1960s to the mid-1970s. In our original data-set, processes of change were characterized in terms of both first-order change (i.e. as a percentage of GDP) and as ratios (i.e. level at time $n+1$ as a percentage of level at time $n$). While the former may be seen as a measure of the real transformation that occurs over a period, the latter might possibly be regarded as a better indicator of a change in public policy stance. However, on the whole there was little difference between the findings based on the two measures, and with one exception, necessitated by a lack of data, only first-order changes are presented in the following tables. On the few occasions where consideration of ratios might influence our assessment of processes of change, this is discussed in the text. All data are presented in terms of percentages of gross domestic product (GDP) in order to provide a basis for cross-national comparison.

The data relating to levels and changes in the major categories of

public expenditure are to be found in Table 3. The reasons for
focusing on each of these categories requires separate explanation.

(1) *Total public expenditure.* This may be taken as an alternative
measure to government revenue in indicating the extension of the
'public economy'. Thus, Cameron's findings concerning the joint
impact of the openness of the economy and partisan control of
government should be replicated here. Indeed, the level of public
expenditure is one of the more obvious measures of the degree to
which government has substituted public control for the operation
of market forces, which has always been a primary aim of socialist
parties.[13] Since the period surveyed was one of extremely rapid extension of public expenditure — in 12 of the 18 nations the share of
public expenditure in GDP has increased by more than a third in
the last two decades — it would be a major refutation of the efficacy of democratic socialism's capacity to effect change if it were
shown that it had not contributed to that development. Finally, it
should be noted that there is scope in this area for an explanation in
terms other than purely economic, since the OECD analysis itself
rejects all variants of the convergence thesis, and, indeed, argues
that 'the evidence points on the contrary to a growing international
dispersion in the relative size of public sectors (OECD, 1978: 13).

(2) *Public consumption expenditure.* This may be taken as an
approximate measure of the extent of the state itself, since it includes the costs of the various services provided direct to the
citizen. This expenditure is overwhelmingly devoted to the wages
and salaries of public employees. However, since there is rarely
much scope for increased productivity in the provision of public
services, their relative share in GDP is likely to increase irrespective
of further extensions in service. It is for this reason that we have
chosen to present public consumption expenditure data in terms of
constant (1970) prices. In terms of current prices, the share of
public consumption expenditure in GDP has on average increased
by around 5 percent in the last 20 years, but in constant terms expenditure has been remarkably stable. Nevertheless, as Table 3
demonstrates, there are marked differences in the levels of public
consumption expenditure in different countries and also in the extent and direction of change over the period. Moreover, a measure
of the extent of the state is particularly relevant to an inquiry into
the impact of partisan differences, since the role of the state has
been a major issue separating the parties from their earliest
development. To the degree that there is a choice concerning the
manner of service delivery, whether directly from the state or in-

# TABLE 3

## Major categories of public expenditure in the OECD area

Percentage of GDP

| | Australia | Austria | Belgium | Canada | Denmark | Finland | France | Germany | Ireland | Italy | Japan | Netherlands | NZ | Norway | Sweden | Switzerland | UK | USA |
|---|---|---|---|---|---|---|---|---|---|---|---|---|---|---|---|---|---|---|
| Total public expenditure (cu.p)*, 1967-69 average | 26.4 | 36.4 | 35.6 | 33.0 | 35.5 | 33.4 | 39.4 | 33.1 | 33.7 | 35.5 | 19.2 | 42.6 | n.a. | 37.9 | 41.3 | 25.0 | 38.5 | 31.7 |
| Total public expenditure (cu.p)*, 1974-76 average | 32.8 | 39.9 | 43.0 | 39.4 | 46.4 | 37.3 | 41.6 | 44.0 | 49.4 | 43.1 | 25.1 | 53.9 | n.a. | 46.6 | 51.7 | 33.5 | 44.5 | 35.1 |
| Elasticity of total public expenditure (cu.p)*, 1960-76 | 1.26 | 1.16 | 1.21 | 1.21 | 1.38 | 1.16 | 1.09 | 1.23 | 1.31 | 1.19 | 1.13 | 1.28 | 1.02 | 1.25 | 1.38 | n.a. | 1.21 | 1.17 |
| Change in total public expenditure (cu.p)*, 1967-76 | 6.4 | 3.5 | 7.4 | 6.4 | 10.9 | 3.9 | 2.2 | 10.9 | 15.7 | 7.6 | 5.9 | 11.3 | n.a. | 8.7 | 10.4 | 12.5 | 6.0 | 3.4 |
| Public consumption expenditure (co.p)*, 1962-64 average | 11.8 | 16.6 | 13.5 | 17.5 | 17.2 | 15.7 | 15.5 | 17.5 | 14.5 | 14.3 | 11.6 | 19.6 | n.a. | 13.9 | 19.8 | 10.8 | 18.8 | 19.9 |
| Public consumption expenditure (co.p)*, 1974-76 average | 13.6 | 14.2 | 14.2 | 18.6 | 20.5 | 16.9 | 13.1 | 17.9 | 17.6 | 13.1 | 8.6 | 15.3 | n.a. | 15.1 | 22.7 | 11.4 | 18.9 | 17.7 |
| Change in public consumption expenditure (co.p)*, 1962-76 | 1.8 | -2.4 | 0.9 | 1.1 | 3.3 | 1.2 | -2.4 | 0.4 | 3.1 | -1.2 | -0.7 | -1.7 | n.a. | 1.2 | 2.9 | 0.6 | 0.1 | -2.2 |
| Transfers and subsidies (cu.p)*, 1967-69 average | 6.4 | 14.7 | 15.1 | 8.2 | 11.8 | 10.8 | 19.2 | 13.2 | 12.6 | 17.1 | 5.2 | 18.1 | 6.8 | 16.0 | 12.3 | 8.8 | 11.3 | 7.1 |
| Transfer and subsidies (cu.p)*, 1974-76 average | 9.3 | 15.8 | 19.3 | 11.8 | 15.8 | 13.4 | 21.9 | 16.9 | 19.7 | 21.5 | 8.4 | 27.3 | 9.1 | 22.3 | 19.3 | 13.6 | 14.7 | 11.2 |
| Change in transfers and subsidies (cu.p)*, 1967-76 | 2.9 | 1.1 | 4.2 | 3.6 | 4.0 | 2.6 | 2.7 | 3.7 | 6.9 | 4.4 | 3.2 | 9.2 | 2.3 | 6.3 | 7.0 | 4.8 | 3.4 | 4.1 |
| General govt. expenditure minus total welfare (cu.p)*, early 1960s | 14.4 | 12.5 | 12.1 | 18.0 | 14.6 | n.a. | 19.3 | 17.1 | n.a. | 18.8 | 12.0 | 20.2 | n.a. | 20.5 | 19.1 | n.a. | 21.6 | 19.2 |
| General govt. expenditure minus total welfare (cu.p)*, mid-1970s | 19.2 | 17.2 | 20.0 | 22.0 | 20.6 | n.a. | 19.4 | 21.5 | n.a. | 22.3 | 14.5 | 22.1 | n.a. | 26.8 | 27.5 | n.a. | 27.7 | 18.3 |
| Change in gen. govt. expenditure minus total welfare (cu.p)*, early 1960s – mid-1970s | 4.8 | 4.7 | 7.9 | 4.0 | 6.0 | n.a. | 0.1 | 4.4 | n.a. | 3.5 | 2.5 | 1.9 | n.a. | 6.1 | 8.4 | n.a. | 6.1 | -0.9 |

*cu.p. = current prices; co.p. = constant (1970) prices.

Source: OECD (1978).

directly through transfers, subsidies or redistribution through the tax system, it might be hypothesized that socialist parties would prefer the former and bourgeois parties the latter. In other words, even if we were to assume that partisan differences did not impinge on the extent of state activity as a whole, we might expect divergence in the way in which that activity was structured.

(3) *Transfers and subsidies*. This is a measure of the resources taken from the community in revenue and redistributed to individuals and groups. More than any other category of public expenditure, this has increased in the last two decades, with the OECD average going from 7.5 percent of GDP in 1955-57 to 13.9 percent in 1974-76 (OECD, 1978: 17-18). Very substantial proportions of that part of the total devoted to household transfers is accounted for by the activities commonly associated with the welfare state — in particular, pensions, health benefits, unemployment benefits and children's allowances. Although, as we have just noted, bourgeois parties might be expected to prefer welfare delivery through this channel to direct provision of state services, it is nevertheless the case that extension of welfare transfers is at the heart of the democratic socialist strategy for promoting social equality. As such, the very marked differences in levels and rates of change presented in Table 3 are of relevance in our inquiry into the effects of the partisan composition of government.

(4) *General government expenditure minus total welfare*. In some broader sense, all that the government does — even defence — might be regarded as contributing to the public welfare. However, as we shall see below, the definition of welfare adopted by the OECD basically covers the three major programmes of the welfare state: education, public income maintenance and health. Since it is of some interest to assess whether public policy in the welfare state arena has different root causes from those that are operative for the other functions of government, we have used an indicator of general government expenditure minus total welfare. The major items included are the costs attached to the administration of government, defence spending, interest on the public debt, aid to agriculture and industry, public housing and expenditure related to the development of urban infrastructure. With the possible exceptions of defence (where the Right has often been an adherent of the strong state) and agriculture (where subsidies might be assumed to be favoured by rural-based parties), expansion of these expenditure areas might be hypothesized as involving the sort of statist activity favoured by a socialist ideology. It should be

## TABLE 4
## Public welfare expenditure in the OECD area

Percentage of GDP in current prices

| | Australia | Austria | Belgium | Canada | Denmark | Finland | France | Germany | Ireland | Italy | Japan | Netherlands | NZ | Norway | Sweden | Switzerland | UK | USA |
|---|---|---|---|---|---|---|---|---|---|---|---|---|---|---|---|---|---|---|
| Public education expenditure, 1960 | 2.4 | 2.6 | 3.8 | 3.5 | 4.0 | 4.8 | 2.1 | 2.1 | 3.0 | 3.2 | 3.0 | 2.8 | 2.8 | 4.1 | 4.0 | 2.5 | 3.7 | 3.6 |
| Public education expenditure, 1970 | 3.8 | 4.0 | 4.9 | 6.5 | 7.0 | 5.6 | 3.2 | 3.0 | 4.9 | 4.0 | 2.6 | 5.9 | 4.4 | 4.9 | 5.9 | 3.6 | 4.4 | 5.3 |
| Change in education expenditure, 1960-70 | 1.4 | 1.6 | 1.1 | 3.0 | 3.0 | 0.8 | 1.1 | 0.9 | 1.9 | 0.8 | -0.4 | 3.1 | 1.6 | 0.8 | 1.9 | 1.1 | 0.7 | 1.7 |
| Public income maintenance expenditure, 1962 | 4.7 | 14.1 | 11.7 | 5.4 | 6.5 | 6.7 | 11.8 | 11.9 | 5.3 | 7.5 | 2.1 | 8.6 | 7.6 | 5.1 | 6.0 | n.a. | 4.4 | 5.5 |
| Public income maintenance expenditure, 1972 | 4.0 | 15.3 | 14.1 | 7.3 | 9.9 | 9.9 | 12.4 | 12.4 | 6.4 | 10.4 | 2.8 | 19.1 | 6.5 | 9.8 | 9.3 | n.a. | 7.7 | 7.4 |
| Change in public income maint. exp., 1962-72 | -0.7 | 1.2 | 2.4 | 2.9 | 3.4 | 3.2 | 0.6 | 0.5 | 1.1 | 2.9 | 0.7 | 10.5 | -1.1 | 4.7 | 3.3 | n.a. | 3.3 | 1.9 |
| Public health expenditure, 1962 | 2.5 | 2.9 | 3.1 | 2.5 | 3.7 | 2.5 | 3.1 | 2.5 | 2.8 | 2.9 | 1.9 | 2.8 | 3.3 | 2.5 | 3.6 | 2.0 | 3.2 | 1.2 |
| Public health expenditure, 1974 | 5.0 | 3.7 | 4.2 | 5.1 | 6.5 | 5.5 | 5.3 | 5.2 | 5.4 | 5.2 | 3.5 | 5.1 | 4.2 | 5.3 | 6.7 | 3.5 | 4.6 | 3.0 |
| Change in health expenditure, 1962-74 | 2.5 | 0.8 | 1.1 | 2.6 | 2.8 | 3.0 | 2.2 | 2.7 | 2.6 | 2.3 | 1.6 | 2.3 | 1.1 | 2.8 | 3.1 | 1.5 | 1.4 | 1.8 |
| Total welfare expenditure, early 1960s | 9.6 | 19.6 | 18.6 | 11.4 | 14.2 | 14.0 | 17.0 | 16.5 | 11.1 | 13.6 | 7.0 | 14.2 | 13.7 | 11.7 | 13.6 | n.a. | 12.6 | 10.3 |
| Total welfare expenditure, mid-1970s | 12.8 | 23.0 | 23.2 | 18.9 | 23.4 | 21.0 | 20.9 | 20.6 | 16.7 | 19.6 | 8.9 | 29.1 | 15.1 | 20.0 | 21.9 | n.a. | 16.7 | 15.7 |
| Change in total welfare expenditure, early 1960s to mid-1970s | 3.2 | 3.4 | 4.6 | 7.5 | 9.2 | 7.0 | 3.9 | 4.1 | 5.6 | 6.0 | 1.9 | 14.9 | 1.4 | 8.3 | 8.3 | n.a. | 4.1 | 5.4 |

*Source:* OECD (1978).

noted that our conclusions in respect of this category of expenditure must be more tentative than for the others, since OECD data were not available for Ireland, Japan, New Zealand and Switzerland.

In addition to presenting data on aggregate categories of public expenditure, *Public Expenditure Trends* also provides a functional breakdown of the major components of welfare spending in the advanced democratic states. This constitutes a second element in our analysis of patterns of public expenditure, the data for which are to be found in Table 4. The same 18 countries are covered in respect of spending in three areas.

(1) *Education expenditure*. Whether this area may be legitimately seen as an aspect of welfare has been the subject of dispute. On the one hand, free public education has been seen by many socialists as an essential component in removing restrictions on equal opportunity and as a major channel of social mobility (see Crosland, 1963: 189-207). On the other hand, educational opportunity may be regarded as an essential element in producing the 'human capital' necessary to run the advanced industrial state, and as such, a prerequisite of all technological societies. Furthermore the fact that in many countries private resources are a substantial element in the finance of education and that the public resources for that purpose tend to be monopolized by the middle classes can also be taken as evidence that education is in some sense different from other aspects of the welfare state (see Wilensky, 1975: 3-7). Nevertheless, the extent of educational expenditure is of some interest, since, objections notwithstanding, the only educational opportunities available to those who typically support socialist parties lie through the activities of the state. Again we should note that, since education is almost exclusively an element of public consumption expenditure, there could well be a divergence between socialist parties attempting to restrict services to those offered by the state and others shifting the duty to the private sector via tax benefits.

(2) *Public income maintenance expenditure*. The items falling under this heading are primarily the welfare state benefits disbursed as household transfers. Under the title of 'social security', they constituted the measure of welfare used in Wilensky's study, which found benefits to be closely related to the bureaucratic and demographic correlates of economic development and wholly unrelated to ideological factors. Moreover, it was these programmes of expenditure whose coverage Alber saw as linked to socialist

partisanship in the interwar period, but now subject to a process of convergence. If we were to discover that such programmes of income maintenance were unrelated to partisan difference, this could also be a possible consequence of the desire of non-socialist parties to concentrate on indirect delivery of welfare or of the use of such benefits in the 'competitive overbidding' of modern electoral politics. None the less, all such findings and speculations jibe with the prevalent impression of socialist practice in the 1960s: that, on attaining office, such parties massively increased public spending in precisely this area.

(3) *Health expenditure*. This element in public expenditure cuts right across the categories of public consumption expenditure (the employment of health service staff) and household transfers (sickness and invalidity benefits). As in the case of expenditure on education, there is a significant private sector in medical care, with somewhat over 20 percent of expenditure being accounted for in this way. Further, there is a disparity between the cross-national distribution of total health spending and public expenditure for the same purpose, indicated by an intercorrelation between the two of only 0.46.[14] However, while this might seem to be evidence of a major divergence between public health outputs and health outcomes, such a conclusion ignores the fact that much of the disparity is a reflection of the vast level of private health provision in one country, the United States, as well as the fact that private medicine generally benefits a small and privileged section of the community (see Castles and McKinlay, 1979a: 812-3). As with education, it is only through public provision that the lower social strata can have access to extensive benefits, and for this reason health expenditure is also likely to be the subject of partisan divisions.

The measures of expenditure surveyed above constitute a basis for discerning patterned interrelations with a variety of socioeconomic and political factors. In particular, they offer an arena in which we might expect to find differences premised on ideological divisions between parties of the Left and Right. Having suggested reasons why socialist parties might advocate higher expenditure under each heading, the simple assumption would be that partisan differences would have an impact on all categories and functions. Alternatively, there could be a pattern in which expenditure most directly related to the provision of services by the state (public consumption expenditure as a whole, education and, to a lesser degree, health) would reflect partisan differences more than areas in which the state distributes revenues (transfers and public

income maintenance expenditure). Another possibility is a change
of pattern over time, with expenditures being diversely affected by
the partisan control of government in the early 1960s and
mid-1970s. Given the major economic growth experienced in this
period, such a pattern might be reasonable, since within the
democratic framework it is difficult for even the most ardent advocate of enhanced welfare to increase expenditure substantially
without additional resources. Finally, of course, there may be no
discernible relationship with partisan control. However, if that
were so in an arena so heavily infused with ideological division, it
might well suggest that the nature of partisanship in advanced
capitalist societies was of little practical consequence.

## The independent variables

The public expenditure data in Tables 3 and 4 will be analysed
primarily by means of regressing each dependent variable on to a
series of independent socioeconomic and political variables. Since
the basic objective is less the explanation of variance in particular
policy areas and more the location of patterns of association across
time and/or related policy areas, the main emphasis will be on the
recurrence of bivariate relationships, not only as between dependent and independent variables, but also between different independent variables. In the case of the independent variables, space
precludes the presentation of the raw data, since the majority of
variables had to be coded separately to match the time-periods
covered by the expenditure series. However, major issues in the
operational definition and calculation of the independent variables
are treated in the discussion below.

The socioeconomic factors that we examine are those that have
greatest currency in the literature, and the majority of them are
relevant to one or other variant of the convergence thesis. GNP per
capita at current prices is used as the measure of level of economic
development. The most clear-cut version of the covergence thesis
would suggest the presence of a linear relationship between levels of
economic development and levels of public expenditure. However,
a more sophisticated argument might postulate that 'at some level
in public goods provision, the perceived benefits that accrue to the
ruling majority in a democracy from public goods begins to
decline' (Wade, 1972: 31). This decreasing marginal utility effect
would imply a stabilization of the scope of government in the most

developed countries, and a consequent catching-up effect for those that have not reached that level. In our analysis, we test for this effect by relating changes in public expenditure to the initial level of expenditure. Strong negative correlations would indicate the presence of the catching-up phenomenon. Another variant of the convergence thesis sees the impact of economic development being mediated through the demographic structure, with affluence producing a large economically non-active sector, particularly the old, who may be regarded as the dependent group most in need of state assistance and as a political force pushing for the further extension of social security provision. In order to test the validity of this hypothesis, which is particularly relevant to the three explicitly welfare functions, we regress these expenditures on to demographic ratios expressing the relative proportions of the school-age population, the aged and the dependent population as a whole. A final factor pertinent to the convergence thesis is the rate of economic growth. Since we might, a priori, argue that economic growth provided the resources for the extension of public expenditure, we examine the association of growth rates with both levels and changes in public expenditure. It should be noted, however, that the literature on rapid economic growth is by no means unanimous about the nature of its impact, especially in the short term. Indeed, Wildavsky has gone so far as to argue that public expenditure may vary inversely with growth, since in high-growth economies higher demand for services can be met with a lower share of the national product, while in lower-growth economies similar demands must be met by a shift of national resources into the public sector (Wildavsky, 1975: 232-5).

There is one further socioeconomic variable that is systematically used throughout the analysis. This is Cameron's openness of the economy measure operationalized as the total of imports plus exports (IMEX) as a percentage of gross national product. On the basis of his finding that the openness of the economy is the strongest predictor of the extension of the public economy, Cameron advances a structural hypothesis suggesting that the high degrees of industrial concentration necessitated by a small domestic market lead in turn to strong trade union development and frequent leftist-dominated governments, both of which exercise pressures for publicly financed services (Cameron, 1978: 1256-8). This is precisely the type of structural socio-political explanation that we earlier suggested might be most fruitful in furthering understanding of the determination of public policy. However,

Cameron's findings were based on the change in a single policy variable over a 15-year period. In order to assess the applicability of his hypothesis over a wider compass, we shall examine whether it holds for the various categories of public expenditure and components of welfare spending taken separately.

There are nine political variables used in our analysis. The reasons for choosing several of them are readily apparent. Throughout our discussion, we have noted the emphasis in the literature on the impact of socialist partisanship. It is to assess the strength of that impact that we include measures of social democratic or labour parliamentary representation and cabinet participation. The choice of social democratic or labour allegiance rather than wider definitions of the Left is based on a wish to test the claim that it is the control of the levers of political power that decisively shapes the formulation of policy. Within our universe of discourse only Finland has experienced any substantial cabinet participation by a major party to the Left of the social democrats. The inclusion of both parliamentary representation and cabinet participation is intended as a means of distinguishing between the direct impact of socialist partisanship through holding the reins of government and the potential indirect influence conferred in virtue of being a substantial opposition with a veto power stemming from representation of a major section of opinion in the electorate and from the possibility of being called upon to form the next government. Moreover, we have also included a measure of union density (i.e. percentage of trade unionists within the labour force) as an indicator of the strength of class politics outside the parliamentary and government arenas. If the arguments of writers such as Gough are to be confirmed, we should expect union density to be more strongly associated with high levels of expenditure than is socialist cabinet incumbency.

Apart from testing for the impact of socialist partisanship, we have also chosen to investigate the influence of two of the more structural factors that appear in the literature. As we have already mentioned, there is a general consensus that low degrees of political centralization, as signified by the existence of federal arrangements, are associated with a tendency towards restricted public expenditure, particularly in the field of welfare. This finding is worth examining, both because it is one of the very few that seems uncontroversial and because, as Table 2 demonstrated, the federal/unitary variable is unusual in being largely unrelated to other sources of political differentiation. We have also chosen to utilize the political system variable indicating competitive and coalescent leadership styles. However, here the reason is precisely because this variable is strongly related to others, and particularly to the strength of the parliamentary and governmental Right. Political analysis of the smaller European democracies has tended to emphasize the impact of coalescent leadership in creating distinctive patterns of policy-making (see Lijphart, 1968, and Heisler, 1974), and it therefore seems desirable to counterpose this explanation to others, which, in selected contexts, seem to fit the data just as well.

What is distinctive in this analysis is a focus that widens the scope of interest in partisanship beyond the impact of socialist parties. I have argued elsewhere that there is evidence that policy outputs and outcomes are more decisively influenced by the strength of parties of the Right than by the extent of socialist partisanship (see Castles, 1978; Castles and McKinley, 1979a, 1979b; Borg and Castles, 1981). The hypothesis on which this argument rests is a structural one relating class interests to the historical structuring of party systems:

If the welfare state is seen largely in T.H. Marshall's terms as conferring 'equality of status', it is not merely in the interests of the industrial working class, but also of the vast majority of wage earners, to secure as great 'a reduction of risk and uncertainty' as possible. If it is reasonable to believe that a large portion of the middle stratum of society is willing to forgo some small immediate benefits in a Rawlsian attempt to 'maximise the minimum', there may be less need to push for welfare than is commonly assumed. The only stratum that has a clear interest in opposing welfare initiatives insofar as they involve a redistribution of wealth will be that which is extremely privileged compared with the majority of the population. In absolute numbers, such a social stratum is likely to be relatively small, *but its political influence will depend on the historical and structural forces which have shaped the party system.* My hypothesis is that, to the degree that such forces have led to the emergence of a large and united party of the Right which can act as the political instrumentality of the privileged stratum, there will be a strong impediment to welfare. It will be noticed that this is a negative hypothesis. A large party of the Right will tend to impede welfare state provision but, in its absence, the degree of such provision will depend on the choices of those whom the people select to govern them. [Castles, 1978: 75]

This hypothesis is obviously equally applicable to the field of public expenditure in general. Not only has the contemporary extension of the public economy been largely a consequence of vastly increasing outlays on welfare provision, but also the very idea of the strong state is antithetical to the laissez-faire strand in right-

wing ideology. In an attempt to test this hypothesis further we include among our independent variables measures of both
parliamentary and cabinet strength of parties of the Right.

It will be noted that the last sentence of the above quotation
leaves open the question of the impact of parties representing the
views of groups other than the working class and privileged strata.
It might be assumed that such middle or centre groups would be
under marked cross-pressures, given their diverse social composition, with the mass of white-collar workers having few resources to
finance private welfare provision and the professionals and certain
of the self-employed having greater resources and a tradition of independence. Further, such groups will be subject to the ideological
views of the strata and parties that flank them. Although it seems
probable that these conflicting pressures will be worked out in different ways in different countries, this assumption suggests that the
impact of parties of the centre is likely to be indeterminate. This
supposition will be tentatively assessed by relating patterns of
public expenditure to the strength of parties other than those of the
Right and democratic socialist persuasion. In this case, we restrict
ourselves to a measure of cabinet seats, since an hypothesis based
on assumptions about the behaviour of the middle strata cannot be
tested by data relating to the strength of anti-system parties of
Right and Left. In the case of cabinet seats, the only anomaly is the
Finnish Communist Party, which has briefly attained cabinet status
on several occasions.

The categorization of parties as 'Social democratic/labour',
'Right' and 'Other' appears in Table 5. Clearly, questions of operationalization are of considerable importance here, particularly in
respect of the distinction to be made between parties of the Right
and other parties. Since the hypothesis predicting a negative impact
on public expenditure by parties of the Right is premised on the unity of the political instrumentality acting as a carrier of privileged
strata interests, the single strongest party of the Right must be
selected. This presents substantial difficulties only in the case of
countries where the Right of the political spectrum is occupied by
both a sizeable secular party and a party of Christian democratic
persuasion. Since the latter attract cross-class support in virtue of
their confessional status, we would obviously prefer to include only
secular parties of the Right. However, this leads to the paradox of
both Germany and Italy being characterized as possessing negligible right-wing strength. This problem has been resolved on an ad
hoc basis by a distinction between countries in which a secular

**TABLE 5**
**Classification of parties in 18**
**democratic capitalist states**

|  | *Major party of the Right* | *Other governing parties* | *Social democratic/ labour party* |
|---|---|---|---|
| Australia | Liberal/Country* | — | Labour |
| Austria | People's | Freedom | Socialist |
| Belgium | Liberal | Christian Social (linguistic parties) | Socialist |
| Canada | Conservative | Liberal | New Democratic |
| Denmark | Conservative | Liberal Radical | Social Democratic |
| Finland | National Coalition | Centre Swedish People's Democratic Union | Social Democratic |
| France | Gaullist | Independent Republican Radical | Socialist |
| Germany | Christian Democratic | Free Democratic | Social Democratic |
| Ireland | Fine Gael | Fianna Fail | Labour |
| Italy | Christian Democratic | Liberals Social Democratic | Socialist |
| Japan | Liberal Democratic | — | Socialist |
| Netherlands | Liberal | Catholic People's Anti-Revolutionary Christian Historical Democrats '66 | Labour |
| New Zealand | National | — | Labour |
| Norway | Conservative | Liberal Centre Christian People's | Labour |
| Sweden | Moderate Unity | Centre Liberal | Social Democratic |
| Switzerland | Christian Democratic (formerly Conservative People's) | Radical Democrats Swiss People's | Social Democrats |
| United Kingdom | Conservative | — | Labour |
| United States | Republicans | Democrats | — |

*Votes and seats for the Liberal and Country parties are combined, since we accept Sartori's view that the parties are not a mere coalition, but a 'coalescence' (Sartori, 1976: 188).

party of the Right has consistently polled 10 percent of the vote and those in which they have not. In the former, the secular party is classified as the party of the Right, and in the latter the Christian democratic party is so classified. This has the disadvantage that it does not wholly coincide with the conclusions of studies examining the relative ideological positioning of the European Christian democratic parties (see Irving, 1979). However, the resulting classification of parties of the Right does correspond very closely to survey evidence concerning individuals' perceptions of parties' positioning on a left-right spectrum (see Inglehart and Klingemann, 1976: 225). Socialist parties are much more readily defined in terms of adherence to the Socialist International. Other parties constitute the residue after socialist and right-wing cabinet participation has been measured. Their complexion is primarily Christian, centrist or liberal, with the only substantial exception being those parties of the Right that fail to qualify on the size criterion.[15] In Table 5, only those other parties that have polled at least 5 percent of the vote are classified.

Among the goals set themselves by the authors of this volume of studies of the determination of public policy is the wish to explore the potential of a variety of variables designed to maximize the measurement of partisan impact. In a subsequent chapter, indicators will be developed on the basis of the assumption of the essential unity of ideas and stance binding the parties of the bourgeoisie. This assumption contradicts our own view that the impact of parties of the centre is likely to be indeterminate. For this reason, we have developed our own composite measure of the 'complexion of government and political system' (GAPS). The manner of calculation of these various indicators is similar save only that in the later chapter bourgeois parties in coherent and consistent alliance are grouped together, while here the only criterion for dominant governing status is the attainment by the major party of the Right or the social democratic party of 66 percent of cabinet seats over 66 percent of a stipulated period, and only these parties enter into the equation of the relative size of parties.[16] GAPS, therefore, attempts to maximize the measurement of certain factors hypothesized to have an impact on public policy — the strength of both Right and socialist partisanship and the balance between them — without making any prior assumptions as to the proclivities of other bourgeois parties. Apart from the issue of whether these factors do have a substantial policy impact, the explanatory power of GAPS will depend on the degree to which these other parties do, in fact, influence policy, and in what direction. Moreover, it should be noted that if such parties adopt diverse stances in different policy areas — e.g., macroeconomic and welfare policies — the various indicators will have a different explanatory potential in each area.

With the exception of the dummy variables measuring federal/unitary states and competitive/coalescent styles of leadership, which do not change over the entire period of our investigation, the remaining political variables have been calculated as averages for five- and ten-year periods preceding each level measurement of the dependent variables. In the case of change, the political variables have been calculated for the entirety of the period. Given the very high degree of stability of these variables measured over time reported in Table 1, there was very little difference between the results obtained using five- or ten-year averages, and only the latter are reported in our subsequent discussion of the factors associated with levels of public expenditure.

## Patterns and speculations

The bivariate relationships for the major categories of public expenditure and for the components of public welfare are reported in Tables 6 and 7. In this concluding section, we shall attempt to locate and analyse the emergent patterns of interaction among the dependent and independent variables as well as to speculate upon the nature of the structural processes of policy determination that these processes may indicate. Moreover, since the expenditure data cover, in greater or lesser detail, the entire range of governmental activity for at least a decade, we would hope that the analysis presented here would have a relevance in furthering our understanding of the contemporary functioning of the democratic capitalist state.

### Convergence or divergence?

We have already cited the OECD view that, looked at in terms of aggregate expenditure, the 1960s and early 1970s was a period of 'growing international dispersion in the relative size of public sectors'. That no simple process of convergence was taking place is also apparent from even the most cursory glance at the relationship

# TABLE 6
## Bivariate relationships for major categories of public expenditure

| | GNP per capita (current prices)[1] | Growth in GNP per capita (constant prices)[2] | Initial level of expenditure (only for change variables)[3] | Level of imports and exports (IMEX) as % of GNP[4] | % of population aged 65 or over[5] | Union density[6] | Right-wing parliamentary seats[7] | Right-wing cabinet seats[8] | Social democratic parliamentary seats[9] | Social democratic cabinet seats[10] | Other cabinet seats[11] | Complexion of government and political systems (GAPS)[12] | Federal = 0 Unitary = 1[13] | Competitive = 0 Coalescent = 1[14] |
|---|---|---|---|---|---|---|---|---|---|---|---|---|---|---|
| | | | | | | Percentage of GDP | | | | | | | | |
| Total public expenditure (cu.p)*, 1967-69 average (17)+ | 0.12 | -0.60** | — | 0.41 | 0.63** | 0.32 | -0.46* | -0.52* | 0.19 | 0.43* | 0.15 | 0.55** | 0.39 | 0.30 |
| Total public expenditure (cu.p),° 1974-76 average (17)+ | -0.08 | -0.38 | — | 0.71** | 0.53* | 0.38 | -0.55** | -0.65** | 0.23 | 0.42* | 0.27 | 0.57** | 0.43* | 0.29 |
| Elasticity of total public expenditure (cu.p),° 1960-76 (17)+ | 0.00 | -0.17 | n.a. | 0.48* | 0.33 | 0.61** | -0.63** | -0.61** | 0.14 | 0.52* | 0.12 | 0.53* | 0.08 | 0.44* |
| Change in total public expenditure (cu.p),° 1967-76 (17)+ | -0.18 | -0.20 | 0.04 | 0.58** | 0.05 | 0.16 | -0.47* | -0.39 | 0.09 | 0.21 | 0.20 | 0.35 | 0.13 | 0.15 |
| Public consumption expenditure (co.p),° 1962-64 average (17)+ | 0.45* | -0.14 | — | 0.10 | 0.25 | 0.05 | 0.03 | -0.10 | -0.09 | 0.12 | 0.05 | 0.18 | 0.03 | 0.10 |
| Public consumption expenditure (co.p),° 1974-76 average (17)+ | 0.21 | -0.61** | — | 0.15 | 0.29 | 0.44* | -0.41 | -0.59** | 0.20 | 0.54* | 0.09 | 0.41 | 0.06 | 0.22 |
| Change in public consumption expenditure (co.p),° 1962-76 (17)+ | -0.01 | -0.25 | -0.13 | 0.33 | 0.07 | 0.53* | -0.46* | -0.48* | 0.29 | 0.42* | 0.06 | 0.39 | 0.19 | 0.25 |
| Transfers and subsidies (cu.p),° 1967-69 average (18)+ | -0.26 | -0.17 | — | 0.49* | 0.66* | 0.04 | -0.40* | -0.34 | 0.04 | 0.29 | 0.21 | 0.24 | 0.38 | 0.23 |
| Transfers and subsidies (cu.p),° 1974-76 average (18)+ | -0.08 | 0.04 | — | 0.68** | 0.56** | 0.10 | -0.47* | -0.47* | -0.05 | 0.11 | 0.38 | 0.48* | 0.43* | 0.28 |
| Change in transfers and subsidies (cu.p),° 1967-76 (18)+ | 0.06 | -0.08 | 0.35 | 0.55** | 0.08 | 0.18 | -0.60** | -0.37 | -0.14 | 0.05 | 0.33 | 0.27 | 0.32 | 0.27 |
| General govt. expenditure minus total welfare (cu.p),° early 1960s (14)+ | 0.36 | -0.52* | — | 0.10 | 0.17 | -0.28 | -0.10 | -0.11 | -0.15 | 0.09 | 0.05 | 0.21 | 0.20 | -0.12 |
| General govt. expenditure minus total welfare (cu.p),° mid-1970s (14)+ | 0.05 | -0.60* | — | 0.41 | 0.44 | 0.46* | -0.50* | -0.58* | 0.42 | 0.61** | -0.03 | 0.53* | 0.35 | 0.26 |
| Change in gen. govt. expenditure minus total welfare (cu.p),° early 1960s—mid-1970s (14)+ | -0.17 | -0.19 | -0.20 | 0.42 | 0.46* | 0.84** | -0.47* | -0.37 | 0.75*** | 0.77** | -0.39 | 0.67*** | 0.24 | 0.51* |

° cu.p. = current prices; co.p. = constant (1970) prices.
+ figures in parenthesis indicate number of cases — significance levels vary accordingly.

## TABLE 7
### Bivariate relationships for public welfare expenditure

| | GNP per capita[1] (current prices) | Growth in GNP per capita[2] (constant prices) | Initial level of expenditure[3] (only for change variables) | Level of imports and exports (IMEX) as % of GNP[4] | % of population aged 65 or over[5] | Union density[6] | Right-wing parliamentary seats[7] | Right-wing cabinet seats[8] | Social democratic parliamentary seats[9] | Social democratic cabinet seats[10] | Other cabinet seats[11] | Complexion of government and political systems (GAPS)[12] | Federal = 0, Unitary = 1[13] | Competitive = 0, Coalescent = 1[14] |
|---|---|---|---|---|---|---|---|---|---|---|---|---|---|---|
| | | | | Percentage of GDP in current prices | | | | | | | | | | |
| Public education expenditure, 1960 (18)° | 0.15 | -0.34 | — | 0.17 | — | 0.25 | -0.41* | -0.52* | 0.14 | 0.47* | 0.16 | 0.40 | 0.42* | 0.47** |
| Public education expenditure, 1970 (18)° | 0.37 | -0.42* | — | 0.35 | — | 0.36 | -0.66** | -0.69** | -0.08 | 0.32 | 0.43* | 0.59** | 0.18 | 0.59** |
| Change in public education expenditure, 1960-70 (18)° | 0.35 | -0.53* | 0.04 | 0.40 | — | 0.14 | -0.33 | -0.40 | -0.14 | 0.05 | 0.35 | 0.19 | -0.16 | 0.41* |
| Public income maintenance expenditure, 1962 (17)° | -0.10 | 0.35 | — | 0.13 | 0.54* | -0.17 | -0.18 | -0.19 | 0.14 | 0.11 | 0.15 | 0.26 | -0.19 | 0.20 |
| Public income maintenance expenditure, 1972 (17)° | 0.14 | -0.19 | — | 0.58** | 0.57** | 0.02 | -0.43* | -0.39 | 0.11 | 0.22 | 0.22 | 0.51* | 0.07 | 0.51* |
| Change in public income maint. exp., 1962-72 (17)° | -0.07 | -0.06 | -0.04 | 0.64** | 0.03 | 0.07 | -0.73** | -0.50* | -0.03 | 0.20 | 0.37 | 0.75** | 0.32 | 0.58** |
| Public health expenditure, 1962 (18)° | -0.28 | -0.17 | — | 0.39 | 0.50* | 0.48* | -0.32 | -0.37 | 0.49* | 0.45* | -0.07 | 0.38 | 0.54** | 0.20 |
| Public health expenditure, 1974 (18)° | -0.02 | -0.26 | — | 0.32 | 0.22 | 0.45* | -0.44* | -0.55* | 0.22 | 0.45* | 0.13 | 0.38 | 0.42* | 0.24 |
| Change in public health expenditure, 1962-74 (18)° | 0.06 | -0.11 | 0.10 | 0.13 | -0.13 | -0.01 | -0.39 | -0.45* | -0.12 | 0.18 | 0.28 | 0.37 | 0.14 | 0.14 |
| Total welfare expenditure, early 1960s (17)° | -0.10 | 0.21 | — | 0.26 | 0.68** | -0.02 | -0.34 | -0.36 | 0.30 | 0.27 | 0.20 | 0.50* | -0.01 | 0.36 |
| Total welfare expenditure, mid-1970s (17)° | 0.22 | -0.27 | — | 0.69** | 0.55* | 0.19 | -0.69** | -0.64** | 0.10 | 0.34 | 0.34 | 0.77** | 0.15 | 0.68** |
| Change in total welfare expenditure, early 1960s to mid-1970s (17)° | 0.05 | -0.16 | 0.04 | 0.64** | 0.03 | 0.09 | -0.81** | -0.66** | -0.10 | 0.23 | 0.47* | 0.65** | 0.22 | 0.62** |

° figures in parenthesis indicates number of cases — significance levels vary accordingly.

# Notes on Tables 6 and 7

*Numbers of cases and significance levels*

With very minor exceptions, the data for the independent variables are complete in respect of all 18 cases. However, data for the dependent variables are on occasions restricted as a consequence of reliance on a single source — OECD's *Public Expenditure Trends*. In most instances, the number of cases is either 17 (with either New Zealand or Switzerland missing) or 18. In the case of 'General government expenditure minus total welfare' the number of cases is restricted to 14 (excluding Finland, Ireland, New Zealand and Switzerland).

In the text of the tables significance levels are indicated as follows:

* = significant at 0.05 level

** = significant at 0.01 level

Because the number of cases varies from expenditure component to expenditure component, similar correlation coefficients will not always indicate similar levels of significance. It should further be noted that, with the exception of the correlations reported in respect of 'Complexion of government and political systems', all statistics involve the use of Pearson's correlations. Since 'Complexion of government and political system' (GAPS) is a rank ordering of types of political systems, Spearman's rho was used in that instance.

*Footnotes to tables*

1. GNP per capita at market prices for four dates (1960, 1967, 1970 and 1963). Source: World Bank (1976). Reported correlations are based on the nearest data point.

2. Growth in GNP per capita at constant (1970) prices. The data are averages of annual growth rate — either for the 10 years preceding a measurement of the level of expenditure or for the entire period involving the measurement of change. Source: Madsen (1978).

3. Initial level of expenditure. These data are used only in respect of change variables and are to be found in Tables 3 and 4 above; they are derived from *Public Expenditure Trends*.

4. Level of imports plus exports (IMEX) as a percentage of GNP for three dates (1960, 1970 and 1975). Source: OECD *National Accounts* (1958-67 and 1975). Nearest data point.

5. Percentage of the population aged 65 or over for two dates (1960 and 1970). Source: World Bank (1976). Nearest data point. (Note that figures were also computed for youthful population (below 14 years of age) and dependent population (aged + youthful). They are not reported in the tables, since they yielded no significant results whatsoever.

6. Union density measured as union membership as a percentage of the labour force for two dates (1960 and 1970). Source: Stephens (1979: 115). Nearest data point. Ireland and Japan excluded.

7. Right-wing parliamentary seats. Annual percentages averaged for either the 10 years preceding a measurement of level of expenditure or for the entire period involving measurement of change. Source: Mackie and Rose (1974).

8. Right-wing cabinet seats — method of calculation as in n. 7. Source: *Keesings Contemporary Almanac*.

9. Social democratic parliamentary seats — source and method of calculation as in n. 7.

10. Social democratic cabinet seats — method of calculation as in n. 7; source as in n. 8.

11. Other cabinet seats — method of calculation as in n. 7; source as in n. 8.

12. 'Complexion of government and political system (GAPS)'. Calculated as in end footnote 16. Source: Mackie and Rose (1974).

13. Federal v. unitary. This is a dummy variable with Australia, Austria, Canada, Germany, Switzerland and United States scored 0 and all other countries scored 1.

14. Competitive v. coalescent. This is a dummy variable with Australia, France, Germany, Ireland, Italy, Japan, New Zealand, the United Kingdom and the USA scored 0 and all other countries scored 1. Source: Peters (1978): n. 8, p. 92.

between level of GNP per capita and expenditure levels and changes. Only one relationship is statistically significant, and even that is not quite what it appears on the surface. The finding concerning public consumption expenditure and level of GNP in the early 1960s would appear to be an artefact of the strong positive impact of economic level on defence expenditure. Although the available OECD data make it impossible to test for the effect of defence spending at the precise date reported in Table 6, calculations for a time only five years later show that controlling for this factor renders the relationship between per capita income and public consumption expenditure quite negligible.[17] It is arguable that our chosen measure of change in first-order terms is not sensitive to the magnitude of the efforts made by lower-income countries to emulate the levels of expenditure of the richer initial high-spenders. Such an effort would certainly be presumed in those variants of the convergence thesis, that conceive of diffusion of innovation as an important mechanism in the cross-national spread of government expenditure programmes (see Gordon, 1969). In order to test for this possibility, all the change variables were also calculated as ratios, which tap the dimension of magnitude of effort in so far as small first-order changes are magnified if they occur in the context of a low level of expenditure. However, this procedure yields only one further significant relationship: in this case, between level of GNP per capita and the change ratio for health expenditure (0.41*). But this is interesting precisely because it contradicts the convergence argument. The positive correlation suggests that during this period it was the richest countries that were making the greatest efforts to expand their health facilities. This finding, taken in conjunction with a strong negative association between the change ratio for health expenditure and the initial level of expenditure ($-0.62**$), suggests, by implication, that the catching-up effort that seems to have characterized this aspect of public expenditure in the 1960s was, at least in part, an effort by the richer countries to redress their previously inadequate level of provision.

The period under review was one of very marked economic growth for all the nations that compose our universe of discourse. Between 1960 and 1973 even in the United Kingdom, the laggard in this respect, GNP per capita increased by 225 percent (35 percent in constant prices), while in Japan, quite outstandingly the leader, it increased by an enormous 846 percent (319 percent in constant prices). If a convergence process was at work, we should expect to find some signs that changes in expenditure over the period would be positively related to rates of economic growth, and we might similarly expect levels of expenditure to be positively associated with the growth of the national resource base in the previous decade. At first sight, the evidence seems to suggest that, on the contrary, educational expenditure was increasing least where economic growth was highest and that total public expenditure and non-welfare expenditure in the 1960s and public consumption expenditure and non-welfare expenditure in the early 1970s was least where prior economic growth was greatest. This could be read as support for Wildavsky's alternative hypothesis that public expenditure will tend to vary inversely with economic growth. In reality, the support is only partial. The Japanese case seems to illustrate that very high growth economies can meet increased demands for services with a more or less constant share of the national product. However, once the Japanese case is discounted, there remain no significant relationships between growth rates and public expenditure for the remainder of our universe of discourse.[18] This leaves unproven the further argument of Wildavsky that in low-growth economies similar demands have to be met by a shift of resources into the public sector. Indeed, it seems probable that this hypothesis could be tested only by a comparison with a period in which economic growth was much lower than that experienced in the 1960s. For the decade under review all that can reasonably be concluded is that, with the exception of Japan, differences in the rates of economic growth experienced by the advanced states appear to have had no appreciable direct impact on patterns of public expenditure (but see below, Chapter 3).

The authors of the OECD report on *Public Expenditure Trends* suggest that the evidence shows 'no obvious tendency for those countries which started from a relatively low level of public welfare services to increase their share of public expenditure in an effort to catch up' (OECD, 1978: 13). The findings in Tables 6 and 7 in respect of the relationship between first-order change and initial levels of expenditure fully support that conclusion. However, if the effort to catch up is not seen solely in terms of matching the level of expenditure of the big spenders, but is rather conceptualized as the magnitude of the current effort compared with that of the past (i.e. as the change ratio), there would appear to have been some effort to catch up in respect of both health expenditure and transfer payments. Moreover, it would seem that there is a connection between these two exceptions to the rule that the 1960s witnessed no attempts to catch up, since the change ratios for health expenditure

and transfer payments are positively associated (0.45*). Interestingly, neither the change ratio for public income maintenance expenditure nor that for educational spending is similarly associated with
the change ratio for transfer payments. Indeed, a picture is beginning to emerge, which will be confirmed subsequently, that the health
sector differs quite markedly from other welfare areas. Unlike
them, the effort to expand health provision has been, at least in
part, a consequence of the richer countries attempting to catch up,
and in that effort there seems to have been a substantial reliance on
transfer payments rather than on the provision of direct service
through the extension of public consumption expenditure. We shall
return to the question of the singularity of the health sector in the
context of our subsequent discussion of the impact of party difference on expenditure patterns.

On the whole, the evidence provided by changing patterns of
public expenditure in the 1960s and early 1970s appears to offer little positive support to the idea of convergent trends developing
directly from the operation of economic forces. However, given the
very significant levels of association between demographic and expenditure variables reported in both Table 6 and Table 7, it is worth
paying some attention to Wilensky's argument that demographic
development mediates the impact of economic development. A
variety of demographic variables — levels and changes in the
youthful, dependent and aged populations — were included in our
data-set, although the only significant results relate to the level of
those aged 65 and over. In line with Wilensky's own findings, based
on analysis of levels of social security provision, there is a strong
bivariate relationship between age structure and levels of public income maintenance expenditure. In addition, there are equally
strong relationships with total welfare and total expenditure, of
which public income maintenance expenditure programmes have,
in recent decades, taken a progressively larger and larger share. The
same applies, not surprisingly, to transfer payments, which constitute the major delivery system for social security payments.
Finally, there is evidence that in the earlier period age structure was
linked to the level of health expenditure and that recent change in
non-welfare expenditure may have been marginally associated with
the same factor. Only in the areas of educational spending and
public consumption expenditure are demographic factors of any
kind of no obvious relevance. Although the absence of a link between the size of the youthful population and the level and change in
educational provision may seem surprising, it is a finding that coin-

**TABLE 8**
**Correlations between welfare components,**
**1960s and 1970s**

|  | (a) 1960s | | | | (b) 1970s | | | |
|---|---|---|---|---|---|---|---|---|
|  | 1 | 2 | 3 | 4 | 1 | 2 | 3 | 4 |
| (1) Education | 1.00 | -0.40 | 0.13 | -0.15 | 1.00 | 0.17 | 0.48* | 0.50* |
| (2) Income maintenance |  | 1.00 | 0.29 | 0.94** |  | 1.00 | 0.13 | 0.92** |
| (3) Health |  |  | 1.00 | 0.51* |  |  | 1.00 | 0.42* |
| (4) Total welfare |  |  |  | 1.00 |  |  |  | 1.00 |

cides with the OECD view of trends in education during the 1960s (OECD, 1978: 27).

Since pensions for the old constitute such a substantial element in public income maintenance expenditure, and that in turn is so large a part of welfare spending, the findings reported might well be regarded as a single syndrome associated with the number of aged in population. Clearly, this syndrome requires explanation, but Wilensky's hypothesis does not seem particularly persuasive, since for our sample of 18 countries there is no evidence of any association between economic level and the percentage of the aged (1970 = 0.11).[19] Further, we should note two points that cast serious doubt on Wilensky's argument that the old constitute 'a political force for further social security development'. First, there is absolutely no support in the data for the view that the massive increases in public income maintenance expenditure, health spending or total public expenditure during the period under review were associated with either the level or the change in the aged population. Indeed, in the case of health the relationship that did exist in the early 1960s has ceased to be significant by 1974. This hardly squares with the view that the old are an independent and active political force in the contemporary democratic state, making an impact on welfare provision irrespective of the party currently in office. Second, even though both health spending and public income maintenance expenditure are associated with the presence of an older population structure, it is apparent that in other respects there is little similarity in the relationship between these welfare components from country to country. This is illustrated in Table 8, which reports the correlations between the various programmes in both the early 1960s and mid-1970s. On the one hand, these figures demonstrate the point made above that public income maintenance is such a major component of total welfare that the close association of both with age structure is, in effect, part of a single syndrome. On the other hand, neither in the 1960s nor in the 1970s was there a relationship between the levels of health and public income maintenance provision. This being so, it seems somewhat inappropriate to seek in the demographic structure a common direct explanation of this diversity of performance. This is not to imply that the age structure is irrelevant in either case, but rather involves the supposition, which will be investigated below, that age may have diverse effects when mediated through diverse political structures.

The analysis presented in this section suggests that there is little evidence in the field of public expenditure developments in the 1960s that is compatible with the existence of an economically determined process of convergence in the advanced democratic states. The OECD conclusion that 'dispersion in the relative size of public sectors' was the dominant trend can be readily affirmed by examination of the raw data presented in Tables 3 and 4, with the grossest contrast in most cases being between the consistent low spending of Japan and the vastly expanded public expenditure of the Netherlands. Patterns of aggregate expenditure as between nations became less similar, but with the corollary, clearly illustrated in Table 8 above, that expenditure patterns for welfare programmes within nations were becoming more similar. Thus, for instance, there is a clear trend for educational spending to come more into line with other welfare components during the decade. While in the early 1960s high levels of educational expenditure seem to have been virtually an alternative to income maintenance programmes, by the early 1970s it would appear that in a number of countries they were becoming complementary. While our earlier conclusion was that differences between countries in respect of rates of economic growth had, with the exception of Japan, very little impact on expenditure levels, it may be that the general expectation of an expanding resource base serves to explain the increasing similarity as between the extent of programmes within a given country. A limited resource base prior to the 1960s meant that even countries in which the demand for public welfare expansion was great were faced with a limited capacity to respond, and had to be content with a trade-off between different types of welfare programme. In the decade following 1960, the general optimism engendered by the prospect of high and continued economic growth permitted those countries in which the demand for public expenditure was high to expand simultaneously on several fronts. Such an analysis can help us to understand the exceptional expenditure in the Netherlands, where the general optimism of the 1960s was compounded by the special circumstances of the windfall discovery of North Sea Gas. On the other hand, it needs to be emphasized that there is nothing in this analysis that explains why the demand for public expenditure was so markedly greater in some countries than in others.

While convergence does not appear to be a feature of expenditure development in the 1960s, it would be misleading not to mention that certain features of welfare systems in the advanced countries were becoming more similar during the period. There is a tendency, remarked in much of the OECD literature, for the expansion of the public economy in the 1960s to be associated with a catching-up process in terms of coverage of welfare programmes and the emergence of greater similarities in respect of welfare delivery systems. The undoubted move towards universal coverage offers support for Alber's view that the postwar extension of social security programmes followed a different pattern from previously. The most significant change in welfare delivery systems is a blurring of the distinction 'between those countries that had relied on the social insurance principle and which have extended the scope of public aid or social assistance, and those that had relied on more or less flat-rate universal benefits, and which have seen moves towards the supplementation of these by earnings-related contributions and benefits' (OECD, 1976: 15). The implications of this distinction and its subsequent attenuation will play an important role in our later discussion.

## Party difference and public expenditure

While differences in levels of economic development, rates of economic growth and initial levels of expenditure appear to have had little effect on public expenditure patterns, the same was not true of variance in the age structures of advanced states. However, even age structure was unconnected with certain categories of expenditure, and had virtually no impact on the very substantial expenditure changes that occurred in the 1960s. This somewhat negative picture that emerges from an appraisal of the most commonly adduced socioeconomic hypotheses is not duplicated in respect of the party variables featuring in our analysis. Both the parliamentary and governmental strength of the major party of the Right are strongly associated with one or more aspect of each category of public expenditure and each component of welfare, as well as having a significant relationship with the major dimensions of change during the period. The individual impact of socialist and other parties is clearly less, but social democratic incumbency also manifests a relationship with several elements of public expenditure. Moreover, in respect of both right-wing and social democratic incumbency the direction of the relationships is exactly as predicted: the Right spends less, the social democrats are more generous. The patterns of association between parties and public expenditure offer us fertile grounds for speculation as to the nature of the role that political actions play in democratic capitalist states, and this will be discussed in the concluding sections of this chapter. Here, however, our focus will be on the patterns of public expenditure themselves and the way in which they are affected by party differences.

The first point to notice is a very clear pattern of change over the period as a whole. At the beginning of the period, right-wing or social democratic cabinet incumbency is associated only with educational and health spending, and even then the degree of 'explained' variance is not very impressive. Our first reported finding for total public expenditure is also significant in respect of both right-wing and social democrats, but that is for the later 1960s. By that time, although not separately reported in Table 6, public consumption expenditure was associated with right-wing incumbency ($-0.51^*$), but not with social democratic cabinet seats (0.35). In the early 1970s, with the single exception of public income maintenance expenditure, every category of public expenditure and every component of public welfare reflected the impact of right-wing incumbency. Even that exception is only partial, since both first-order and ratio change in public income maintenance expenditure manifested the strong negative impact of right-wing governments. This overall process of change can be characterized as the very opposite of convergence, since it involved a pronounced tendency for the countries that were already the leaders in one field of expenditure to move ahead in other areas as well.

In the context of a summary presentation of this kind, it is impossible to make specific mention of the performance of each nation in respect to level and change in each category of public expenditure and component of public welfare. What we have attempted to do in Figure 1, by presenting the scattergrams for educational and total welfare regressed against right-wing cabinet seats, is to demonstrate the two basic patterns manifested by the data. Pattern (a) is, as we have already noted, the least common, in so far as partisan control government is already associated with expenditure by the early 1970s. Pattern (b) represents the more normal situation, in which change was more or less strongly associated with right-wing incumbency in such a way that by the early 1970s there was a clear relationship between the level of expenditure and partisan control. A number of important points emerge from an examination of these scattergrams, which are generally applicable in respect to all our expenditure data. First, it must be emphasized that change is not solely a function of the expansion or contradiction of expenditure levels, but is also a consequence of alterations in the partisan composition of government. Thus, for instance, the change in the USA's position relative to the regression line as between (a) 0.1 and (a) 0.2 is not a result of a change in that country's educational provision vis-à-vis other countries, but is solely a consequence of the fact that administrations in the 1950s were largely Republican (i.e. right-wing) and for much of the 1960s were Democratic (i.e. non-right-wing). Second, it should be noted that the degree of change in the relative positioning of countries in respect of each expenditure variable is only moderate. Thus, the correlation between educational expenditure in 1960 and 1970 is 0.67**, and between total welfare in the early 1960s and in the early 1970s is 0.72**. This implies that the approximately 50 percent of the variance in 1970s expenditure levels can be 'explained' by the state of public expenditure in the 1960s. Third, and most important, the degree of change in the party variables is, as already illustrated in Table 1, typically much less than that for the expenditure variables. This implies that the expenditure change associated with right-wing partisan control in the 1960s was more a consequence of right-wing parties being reluctant to expand provision than, as might alternatively be argued, of a tendency for countries with a low public expenditure propensity to be conducive to right-wing government.

Fourth, and unsurprisingly, given the level of the correlation coefficients reported in Tables 6 and 7, there are frequently major exceptions (outliers) to the trends that dominate the picture. The case of the Netherlands is consistently an outlier in respect to change in total public expenditure, transfers, public income maintenance and, as illustrated in Figure 1, total welfare expen-

# FIGURE 1
## Two patterns of public expenditure

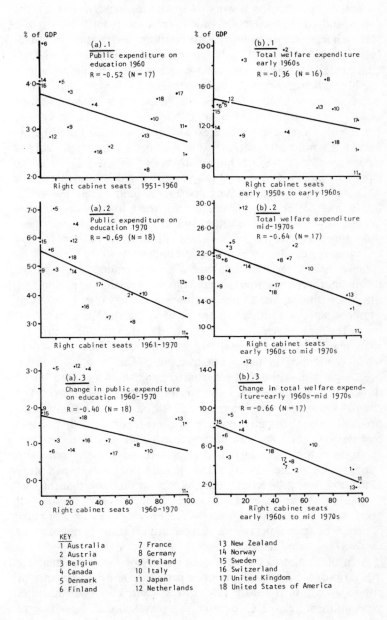

KEY
| | | |
|---|---|---|
| 1 Australia | 7 France | 13 New Zealand |
| 2 Austria | 8 Germany | 14 Norway |
| 3 Belgium | 9 Ireland | 15 Sweden |
| 4 Canada | 10 Italy | 16 Switzerland |
| 5 Denmark | 11 Japan | 17 United Kingdom |
| 6 Finland | 12 Netherlands | 18 United States of America |

diture. In all these instances, the growth of expenditure was very substantially more than would have been expected, even given the predominantly non-right-wing character of government in the 1960s. Indeed, if the Netherlands is removed from the otherwise clearly linear picture in (b) 0.3, the resulting correlation improves from − 0.66** to − 0.81**. We have already pointed to special circumstances relating to optimism concerning economic growth in the Netherlands, which may serve to explain these exceptions. It is, however, of some note that the Netherlands is also a major outlier in respect to the change in public consumption expenditure. Here, rather than expenditure expanding more than would be expected, it is markedly reduced against the general trend, possibly as a consequence of the fact that an absence of a right-wing influence was not matched by any substantial socialist presence. The Netherlands case should be an important reminder that, despite the importance of the general tendency for there to be an association between right-wing incumbency and lower levels of public spending, this phenomenon by no means constitutes a full explanation of expenditure patterns in the period under review.

Nevertheless, the fact that such a general tendency is apparent throughout our data would seem compatible with the notion that the propensity of democratic capitalist states to expand the extent of public activity is, in part, determined by the ideological structuring of the party system. Irrespective of the strength of this propensity, new departures in public expenditure can come about only when economic resources are available. This was, of course, precisely the situation that confronted policy-makers in the 1960s, the era of apparently unlimited and rapid economic growth. The countries that appear to have capitalized on the opportunity were precisely those that had governments of centre or social democratic complexion. The Right saw economic growth in quite other terms, as an opportunity for increased returns to private enterprise and initiative. Given the very considerable inertia of public expenditure in the downwards direction, it seems most improbable that the vast gaps in expenditure levels established by the early 1970s will decrease appreciably in the near future, although in an era of more limited economic expectations there is little reason to suppose that they will increase further.[20]

A further point to notice is the diversity of factors influencing the various categories of public expenditure and components of public welfare in the early 1960s. Most conspicuously, education expenditure is related to right-wing strength, health spending to social democratic strength and class politics, and public income maintenance seems unaffected by political considerations. These differences seem explicable at least partly in terms of ideological and cultural preferences for particular forms of state activity. In the early 1960s, our data show no association between partisanship and public consumption expenditure. However, the reported relationships are probably somewhat distorted by the inclusion of defence expenditure, and certainly by 1967-69 there is a strong relationship, with right-wing cabinet seats and a moderate one with social democratic imcumbency (see note 17). On the other hand, although right-wing parliamentary seats are marginally associated with transfer payments in the 1967-69 period, a significant relationship with right-wing incumbency appears only in the mid-1970s. Thus, we might tentatively suggest that, while parties of diverse ideological complexion had not wholly dissimilar attitudes to the use of transfer payments for much of the period, they were more divided about public consumption expenditure, which through the employment of public service workers directly enhances the scope of the state. But it is precisely education and, only to a somewhat lesser extent, health that were financed through direct services provided by state employees in schools, universities and hospitals. In other words, the earliest areas of welfare state development to manifest partisan differences in respect of expenditure levels were those in which financing presented substantial ideological difficulties for parties of a non-socialist complexion.

In contrast, public income maintenance programmes are necessarily financed largely through transfer payments. Here there need be no inherent ideological antipathy for non-socialist parties, so long as such programmes were based on the insurance principle of benefits in proportion to contribution, and it was this principle that prevailed throughout much of mainland Europe (in particular, Belgium, France, Germany, Austria, Italy and the Netherlands). This explains a further paradox in that coverage of social security programmes was clearly related to socialist strength in the interwar years (see Alber, 1979), and yet expenditure levels in the 1950s were, if anything, lower in countries where socialism was dominant. Admittedly, there were already signs of a catching-up process in respect of coverage, but the dominant contrast was of universal, minimum flat-rate benefits in Scandinavia and those countries influenced by the British example and of more restricted access to insurance-linked benefits in mainland Europe. The former countries were characteristically those with a strong socialist parliamentary presence, while the latter, in the early 1960s, were dominated by parties of the Right and Centre. The next decade saw a partial convergence of social security programmes, with mainland Europe extending coverage and other countries adopting earnings-related schemes. The overall consequence was that by the end of the period most nations had universal coverage, but that partisan differences now showed up in expenditure levels, with the complexion of government and political system accounting for about a quarter of the inter-nation variance.

Further, we might surmise that ideological preferences may affect the manner in which citizen needs or demands are translated into public policy. The age structure of the population is, as we have already noted, positively associated with public income maintenance programmes throughout the period and with the level of health expenditure in the early 1960s. In the former area, we have seen that policy-makers made different choices as to coverage and level of benefit, at least partly on ideological grounds. The singularities of the health area have already been mentioned in the previous section, but they are compounded by the fact that it is the only component of welfare where there is a clear association with measures of socialist strength and working-class influence prior to the emergence of a significant relationship with the Right. Health is, therefore, the only area in which one can unequivocally argue that social democracy and/or the trade unions gave the lead. It seems probable that this finding is a reflection of the fact that socialist and working-class organizations had fewer scruples about catering for public needs by the direct provision of state services through the mechanism of public consumption expenditure. It is also noteworthy that, although first-order changes in health expenditure indicate no success on the part of laggards in catching up with the initial leaders, consideration of the change ratio suggests that a real effort was made. A number of the non-socialist countries that made the most conspicuous effort in this direction did so by devising health delivery systems in which the doctor remained in private employment and received remuneration through the less ideologically objectionable mechanism of transfer payments to patients.[21] Thus, despite the singularities of the health area, and despite the undoubted impact of demographic factors in the early period, party difference remains important, both because it appears as a factor explaining some countries' early leadership in this field, and because countries dominated by parties of a non-socialist kind tended, for ideological reasons, to prefer transfer payments as a means of attempting to catch up.

Finally, the findings concerning general government expenditure minus total welfare should be mentioned as a further illustration of the impact of party difference. While the very high correlation coefficients reported for socialist strength and class politics may well be an artefact of the smaller number of cases, what is particularly interesting is that first-order change was so much more strongly associated with these measures than with indicators of right-wing strength. Nowhere else is such a pattern apparent, and it seems arguable that the finding reflects the diverse priorities of the parties during the period. The social democratic priority was expenditure that enhanced the reach of the state: growth in public investment, development of the urban infrastructure, expansion of public housing and increased direct state employment. The extension of welfare expenditure was only a subsidiary objective, and was significantly related to socialist strength only in the health area. For the Right, one may surmise that the priority was keeping expenditure as low as possible, although, given the danger of reducing non-welfare expenditure to a level where the viability of the state as an agent of private interests could be called into question, the more stringent control seems to have been exercised in respect of welfare expenditure. The expenditure stance of other, primarily centre, parties was characteristically ambiguous. While in the forefront in respect to the expansion of total welfare, their influence was noticeably, if not significantly, in a statistical sense, directed against the expansion of the non-welfare functions of the state. The structural conditions underlying this ambiguity of the centre is among the topics that will be explored further in the next section.

## Open economies and closed political systems

Our discussion hitherto has attempted to locate the separate impact of socioeconomic and partisan differences on public expenditure patterns within the democratic capitalist states. However, as that discussion proceeded, it became apparent that such factors were linked with partisan difference mediating the effects of economic expectations and citizen needs stemming from the age structure of the population. Thus, our analysis of public expenditure trends confirms the view that the dichotomy between political and socioeconomic explanation in this field obscures more than it reveals. At this point, it is relevant to pay some explicit attention to an hypothesis that is premised on the integral relationship between economic structure and political action.

Cameron's argument, that we can understand the expansion of the public economy in the 1960s and early 1970s only in the context of socialist and trade union pressures for greater public expenditure, which are themselves conditioned by the relative openness or closure of the economy, implies just such an integral relationship. The novel element in this thesis is the role of the open economy as a primary factor simultaneously fashioning the strength of the labour movement as a whole and creating a need for an interventionist stance by the government. On the one hand, a strong export economy tends to lead to concentration of ownership with a concomitment push towards density of unionization and extension of the scope of collective bargaining. This is a major factor in strengthening the industrial wing of the labour movement, which, in virtue of intensifying the salience of class politics, is a positive stimulus to socialist political allegiance and parliamentary strength. On the other hand, dependence on overseas markets limits a government's capacity to manage aggregate demand and control unemployment, and generally serves as an impediment to effective control over the economy. It is Cameron's contention that the extension of the role of the state through increased public expenditure is a mechanism by which governments can seek to reassert control. Obviously, where there is a powerful labour movement, with an ideological preference for diminishing the role of the market and enhancing employment opportunities and welfare expenditure, the incentive to expand the public economy is built into the system.

The population of democratic capitalist states that is under review here is an appropriate one to replicate Cameron's findings, since the only difference in cases is our inclusion of New Zealand and exclusion of Spain (because of its very recent attainment of democratic status). Cameron's measure of the extent of the public economy is total government revenue, but using our very similar measure of total public expenditure gives analogous results.[22] In respect of the change in expenditure from 1960 to 1976, both the level of imports plus exports as a percentage of GNP (IMEX) and measures of social democratic cabinet seats and union density yield significant degrees of association. Moreover, our data confirm that the same factors were significantly related to levels of total public expenditure in the periods 1967-69 and 1974-76. On the face of it, these findings constitute further validation for Cameron's hypothesis. However, if we seek a pattern in respect of

## TABLE 9
### Interrelations between the openness of the economy and political variables, early 1960s and mid-1970s

| | Right-wing parliamentary seats | Right-wing cabinet seats | Social democratic parliamentary seats | Social democratic cabinet seats | Other cabinet seats | GAPS | Federal/ unitary | Competitive/ coalescent | Union density (1960) |
|---|---|---|---|---|---|---|---|---|---|
| (a) 1960s (political variables for 1958-62) IMEX 1960 | -0.63** | -0.68** | 0.41* | 0.37 | 0.39 | 0.70** | 0.36 | 0.59** | 0.39 |
| (b) 1970s (political variables for 1970-74) IMEX 1975 | -0.72** | -0.66** | 0.22 | 0.25 | 0.50 | 0.62** | 0.42* | 0.60** | (1970) 0.60** |

the separate categories of expenditure and components of welfare spending, the nature of the relationships involved becomes somewhat more complex. While the level of IMEX is closely associated with levels of transfers and subsidies, public income maintenance expenditure and total welfare spending, the degree of openness of the economy seems to have no explanatory power in respect of public consumption expenditure, health, education and non-welfare expenditure. This is decidedly peculiar, since the variables with which IMEX is associated are precisely those that are least related to measures of socialist partisanship and class politics. Cameron argues quite explicitly that the strength of the socialist milieu will lead to 'an unusually large increase in publicly funded income supplements' (Cameron 1978: 1258), but it is in this area that socialist and working-class strength is the weakest predictor of performance. In fact, in respect of all but the aggregate data, which, naturally, reflect the forces at work in all areas of public expenditure, it would appear that the openness of the economy and the strength of the socialist milieu are mutually exclusive, rather than complementary, explanations.

Before dismissing Cameron's conclusions as the consequence of an accidental conjuncture in a single set of data, it is worth examining the general relationship between openness of the economy and the full range of political variables. This is done in Table 9, which reports correlations for periods roughly coincident with the beginning and end of our period of investigation. The table offers clear enough evidence that the level of IMEX is closely associated with a number of political factors, but that socialist partisanship is only marginally among them. This being so, it seems appropriate to speculate on how we may reconceptualize the links between the openness of the economy and the political sphere.

There would appear to be a number of possible relationships between right-wing partisanship, the most highly intercorrelated of the political variables, and the international aspects of the economy. It might be possible that parties of the Right have ideological preferences for development through 'balanced growth', while socialist and other parties favour development through industrialization for export markets. However, it should be noted that this does not square readily with laissez-faire beliefs in free trade, and seems incompatible with an historical development in which the now advanced nations had settled their trade postures largely prior to the extension of the suffrage, and the consequent emergence of party cleavages. More reasonably, one might argue for an alternative scenario, in which parties of the Right mediated the impact of the structure of international trade.[23] However, mediation may be the wrong concept here. It implies either that a political instrumentality shapes public policy in a way consonant with economic structure, or, as in Cameron's hypothesis that socialist governments attempt to offset the potentially deleterious effect of an open economy on full employment, that it serves as a sort of negative feedback mechanism. The chapter on macroeconomic policy demonstrates that, if governments of a particular partisan complexion do attempt to carry out this countervailing function, they achieve remarkably little. Moreover, there is no apparent relationship between integration into the world economy and the successful management of fluctuations in employment (see p. 136 below). The fact that, throughout our data on public expenditure, it is apparent that parties with a right-wing political stance seem remarkably adept at achieving outputs consonant with their ideological beliefs might well suggest that the trade structure has no particular implications for the extent of public expenditure, and that partisan strength was the crucial determinant.

Probably the most persuasive surmise as to the interrelationship between the openness of the economy and contemporary party systems is that both have common roots in the conjunction of economic, class and electoral circumstances in the late nineteenth and early twentieth centuries. Certainly, it is clear that, although either or both of these factors seems strongly associated with public policy outputs, neither is particularly of recent provenance. While the crystallization of party systems was completed in the 1920s with the extension of the suffrage to the lower classes, contemporary party cleavages still reflect the impact of earlier dimensions of conflict and compromise (see Rokkan, 1970: 112-40). Most particularly, they reflect divisions in ruling-class interests as a consequence of conflicts between church and state and between rural and urban interests. The former type of conflict is perpetuated in the existence of religious parties and the latter in competing parties of Right and Centre. But the appearance of conflicting rural and urban interests was itself intimately related to the economic structure and trading opportunities of particular nations.

In oversimplified schematic terms, there would appear to have been three alternative economic configurations for development in the late nineteenth century. Small nations with no substantial agricultural surplus could only rely on industrialization for export markets. This pattern, which typified the smaller European countries, made for inevitable conflicts between pre-industrial landed elites and new urban classes dependent on manufacturer, as well as potential conflicts with a peasantry opposed to the landed elite in class terms and the urban milieu on cultural grounds. Larger nations, which attempted to industrialize through a strategy of balanced growth, were, in contrast, able to a greater or lesser degree to encourage 'a gradual merger of urban and rural interests' (Rokkan, 1970: 120). Although this development occurred in different ways in countries like Britain and Germany, it led to a similar coalescence of dominant class interests of a kind that might, under appropriate circumstances, lead to mobilization behind a single political instrumentality.[24] A final path towards development lay in industrialization through reliance on the export of primary products. The countries of the New World that adopted this course — Australia, New Zealand, Canada and, to a certain extent, the United States — also avoided ultimately fissiparous conflicts among the ruling class, with the landed interest acting as the guarantor for a fledgling industry shielded from outside competition by protective tariffs. Thus the countries that industrialized through balanced growth and balanced trade and those of the New World, which industrialized through an asymetric pattern of trade, were simultaneously the countries that minimized the potential for lasting cleavages in the party system prior to the emergence of lower-class political opposition.

If this extremely simplified picture is reasonably accurate, it suggests that both the strength of the political Right and the relative openness of the economy have their roots in the structural conditions, and that partisan differences in the policy field would be expected to be a consequence not only of the development of working-class organizations and socialist ideology, but also of the existence of non-socialist centre parties with an ideological independence conditioned by the manner in which the crystallization of the party system has enshrined earlier cleavages among the bourgeoisie. In the relatively closed economies in which such cleavages were minimized, there occurred another type of closure: the ideological closure brought about by the dominance of a political party espousing right-wing views. The centre or other partties of the more open economies could gradually become more responsive to the emergent interests of the growing class of white-collar and petit bourgeois voters in greater educational opportunity, better health facilities and enhanced income maintenance programmes. They could take the distinctive, if ambiguous, stance, described in the last section, of maintaining great caution in enhancing the non-welfare functions of the state, while simultaneously being in the forefront of the effort to protect the individual from undeserved misfortune. Within the closed economy, the newly emergent social strata of the advanced industrial society had only the choice between socialist and right-wing parties, and to the extent to which anti-statist attitudes swayed them towards the latter, their fortunes were bound up with parties whose ideological rationale and origins lay in the protection of privilege and the status quo. That such a closure in the direction of greater equality and welfare persists to this day, we need only recall the response of the Right to the opportunities afforded by the economic growth of the 1960s to create the infrastructure of a fairer society.

## Partisanship, party structure and political structure

Of the nine political variables included in our analysis, two are outstandingly better predictors of the level and change in public expenditure than the others: our two measures of the strength of the major party of the Right. To a somewhat more moderate extent, three more variables — social democratic cabinet seats, the composite measure of the complexion of government and political system (GAPS) and the nature of elite behaviour — are also clearly associated with expenditure patterns. As shown in Table 2 above, the correlation between right-wing parliamentary representation and cabinet participation is very high, and its pattern of fluctuation of approximately 0.80 and 0.90 for the entire period under review suggests no reasons for a separate analysis or to demur from the common-sense view that parliamentary representation is directly transformed into cabinet strength with immediate implications for policy formulation. As might be surmised from the fact that social democratic cabinet participation is much more closely associated with public expenditure variation than is social democratic parliamentary representation, the strength of the relationship between these two measures of socialist strength is markedly less than occurs at the other end of the political spectrum. Indeed, it is sometimes the case that the intercorrelation is as low as 0.65 and is actually exceeded by a negative correlation between right-wing and social democratic cabinet participation.[25] This result is consistent with the earlier finding of Borg and Castles that 'social

Democratic/Labour office-holding may be partially regarded as an artifact of the presence of strong Right' (see Borg and Castles, 1981). Although it would probably be misconceived to generalize this finding to all periods, the fact that it is persuasive in some is itself a measure of the inadequacy of an explanation of policy variation which rests primarily on the impact of socialist partisanship.

In general, the high degree of intercorrelation between variables measuring similar dimensions of partisan strength is not conducive to making fine distinctions concerning the causal influences which may be operative. For instance, class politics as measured by union density is closely associated with both social democratic cabinet participation and parliamentary representation. Which relationship is the stronger varies from time to time during the period, but both fluctuate between around 0.70 and 0.80. Union density is a better predictor of policy variation than parliamentary representation, but is substantially inferior to cabinet participation. On this basis, and given that union density is associated with public expenditure only when social democratic cabinet participation is also a significant predictor, it is quite impossible to determine whether class politics has an effect independent of cabinet incumbency. The case is rather similar in respect of our composite variable of complexion of government and political system, which was designed to tap the joint impact of cabinet dominance and the balance of partisan opinion in the electorate. Although this variable is among the better predictors, there is only one instance where it locates a relationship that is not identified by the simple partisan variables. This exception is, however, quite interesting, since it suggests the impact of partisanship on total welfare in the early 1960s, a finding obviously in line with social democratic and right-wing influence on both education and health expenditure in that period. Otherwise, although strongly intercorrelated with measures of both right-wing and social democratic strength (see Table 2), the composite measure picks up nothing that is not at least equally well located by the simple partisan measures. In these terms, the composite indicator of complexion of government and political system must be regarded as somewhat less promising than might have been hoped.

The results reported in Tables 6 and 7 do not demonstrate any very substantial association between 'other' cabinet seats and expenditure levels and trends. At most, one might suggest a tendency for these parties to be associated with higher levels of educational expenditure by the end of the 1960s and to be a marginal factor in increased total welfare during the period as a whole. Looked at in terms of the wider aggregates of expenditure, the overall impression is largely consistent with our initial hypothesis that the impact of parties of the centre is likely to be indeterminate. However, as we have already noted, a closer focus suggests nuances to this conclusion. If one were to characterize the position of 'other' parties vis-à-vis the social democrats and the Right, it would appear that they were closer to the former in the strictly welfare area, occupied a more or less intermediate position in respect of the extent of the public economy and public consumption expenditure, and took a somewhat anti-statist stance in respect of the non-welfare elements of public expenditure. Such a profile is wholly consonant with the ideological stance of liberal, centre and religious parties, whose constituents would seem to have as much to gain from the welfare state as the skilled working class, which forms the backbone of social democratic support, but who retain a bourgeois distrust of the overmighty state. Moreover, it should be noted that the policy configuration of 'other' parties conforms with the assumption built into GAPS. That measure was devised on the assumption that 'other' parties would have a neutral policy stance, and the fact that the measure was a relatively successful predictor of expenditure variation tends to point to the correctness of that view.

The analysis so far would appear to lend support to the view that partisan control of government is among the factors influencing levels and changes in public expenditure, with strong parties of the Right acting as an impediment to expansion and social democratic and other parties, jointly or separately, serving as a stimulus. This conclusion is, of course, based on a simple bivariate analysis in which the best measure of partisan control typically 'explains' between 20 and 50 percent of the variance in expenditure. Multivariate analysis, although fraught with difficulties in a population so subject to instability of estimation, does not fundamentally alter that conclusion.[26] One or other of the indicators of right-wing strength (including GAPS) is generally a major predictor of policy variation and, having controlled for its impact, neither measures of socialist strength nor those of 'other' cabinet participation add a great deal to the degree of 'explained' variance.

However, before finally concluding that the partisan configuration is a major determinant of patterns of public expenditure, we need to examine the relationships between the dependent variables and our measure of elite behaviour (competitive/coalescent) and political structure (federal/unitary). Coalescent leadership is premised on the capacity of elites to work together and is, not surprisingly, strongly associated with the absence of major cabinet participation by the Right. Indeed, the only two cases in our population which do not conform with this generalization are Austria, where coalescent behaviour emerged precisely out of former violent enmity of Right and Left, and Ireland, where a dominant party of the centre competes simultaneously against Right and Left.[27] These two cases are substantially the explanation for the marginal divergence between the results reported for the strength of the Right and the leadership variable. At the beginning of the period Ireland was relatively backward economically, with low levels of public expenditure, transfer payments and public consumption expenditure, whereas Austria was the reverse in all respects bar economic development. What appears to have occurred during the 1960s and early 1970s was a catching-up process in which, despite similar patterns of economic growth, Ireland managed to achieve similar levels of public expenditure performance by the end of the period.

The diverse profiles of these two countries are not unambiguously attributable to the nature of elite leadership. The initial level of expenditure in Austria is probably more easily explained by the traditional social insurance pattern it had in common with a number of other mainland European nations from an early date, together with the very considerable strength of socialist cabinet participation. In contrast, Ireland had inherited the less financially onerous flat-rate coverage system from the British and, in addition, had no significant socialist political presence. But neither had it a dominant party of the Right which could serve as an impediment to expansion of the public economy under the propitious circumstances of increasing national prosperity in the 1960s. In Austria, the People's Party was becoming stronger throughout the 1960s, and it was only with the advent of a social democratic government in 1970 that public expenditure and welfare spending started to accelerate once again. This picture is complex, involving diverse configurations of welfare delivery systems, economic growth and political change. Rightly, it should be more complex, since it seems likely that Austria's much older demographic structure also contributed to higher levels of initial expenditure. Such a multiplex picture is to be expected once we descend from statistical generalization to the particularities of individual cases. There would, however, appear to be nothing here to make us prefer elite behaviour as an alternative general explanation to the structure of partisanship.

The pattern of relationships displayed by federal states varies quite strongly from that associated with our other political or, for that matter, socioeconomic measures. This is, of course, what might have been expected, given the absence of significant intercorrelations reported in Table 2. Over the range of factors examined in this chapter no obvious pattern emerges at all: some of the countries have relatively low GNP per capita (Australia, Austria); some high rates of economic growth (Austria, Germany and Switzerland); some have open economies (Austria and Switzerland); some have strong socialist parliamentary representation (Australia, Austria and Germany); and some have strong 'other' party cabinet participation (Canada, Switzerland, and the USA). Four of the countries have had extensive right-wing cabinet participation, but one of those that has not (Switzerland) has infinitely the worst all-round public expenditure performance. Indeed, were it not for the case of Switzerland, it seems probable that we could subsume the impact of federalism as an artefact of right-wing strength, adding as a rider that decentralized political structures may be particularly favourable to parties seeking to defend the status quo.[28] It could be argued that there is little to choose between two of the parties which together have a permanent majority in Switzerland's Federal Council in terms of rightist ideology (i.e. Christian Democrats and Radical Democrats); but, while that rescues the thesis of rightist influence on policy outputs, it is at the cost of creating a major exception to our hypothesis that such influence is excercised only 'where historical and structural forces have led to the emergence of a large and united party of the Right' (Castles, 1978: 75). Given the small number of cases characterized by federal status, and the exceptionally poor policy performance of Switzerland, it is impossible to reach any firm conclusions as to the determinate impact of decentralized political structure. While the Swiss policy formulation process might be affected by the multiple access points provided for opponents of state expenditure by the canton structure, it could equally well be influenced by any one or combination of the historical socioeconomic or political factors that make Switzerland distinctive. Certainly, on the political front, it is notable that Switzerland has, in addition to a federal structure, two other unique features which might well be regarded as impediments to change. One is the permanent coalition within the Federal Council, which effectively makes all decisions subject to minority veto, and the other is the prevalence of decisive referenda, which provide a much used channel for opposing government initiatives.

Overall, the impact of neither elite behaviour nor political structure seems sufficient to disturb the conclusion that emerges from the analysis of patterns of public expenditure that partisan control of government is a major determinant of policy outputs. However, it is important to be clear as to the implications of this finding. What it does seem to imply is that the ideological preferences for greater or less state activity or greater or less welfare have a direct impact on the policies that parties pursue. What it does not imply is that changes in electoral opinion are readily translatable into changed policies. Party ideology is structured by persistent cleavages, which have their origins in the alignments of classes and interests at the time of the extension of the suffrage. Despite periodic fluctuations in ruling parties and landslide electoral victories, all measures of partisan strength demonstrate remarkable stability over time (see Table 1). Indeed, since the Second World War there appear to have been only two appreciable changes in the political complexion of government and political system. Moreover, these changes, which allowed social democracy to become the dominant party of government in both Austria and Germany, seem at least as much attributable to changes in the class structure consequent upon military defeat as to the immediate effects of a reformist strategy pursued by this party. Thus, to accept that the partisan control of government is an influential aspect in policy formulation is not necessarily to argue for an historical and non-structural viewpoint. Politics clearly matter in the sense that party political structures institutionalize class and interest cleavages and make them continuingly policy-relevant. But the nature of such cleavages can and does change, and a much longer time perspective than is inherent in a study of little more than a decade would suggest that these changes must eventually be reflected in new institutional structures, new ideologies and new policies.

# NOTES

1. There are very real statistical problems with Wilensky's treatment of the effects of ideology. He argues that, even discounting the influence of socioeconomic factors, there remain substantial differences between the welfare levels of the rich countries in his sample. He goes on to suggest that one popular explanation of this difference is ideology, and proceeds to test the idea by correlating factors derived from a content analysis of party programmes with welfare performance. The problem is that the sample of 22 countries utilized for this testing procedure is not the same group of countries to which the popular explanation could reasonably be supposed to apply. As he points out in a discreet footnote, the sample includes Bulgaria, Greece (pre-junta), India, Nicaragua, Paraguay, Portugal, Tunisia, Turkey and Uruguay (see Wilensky, 1975: 43). None of these could be considered markedly relevant to understanding the causes of variance in the welfare performance of the richer countries!

2. This is, incidentally, borne out by an anlysis of the data Wilensky himself presents. Although he does not calculate the correlation coefficient for the relationship between GNP per capita and social security expenditure as a percentage of GNP in his sub-sample of rich countries (Wilensky, 1975: 30-1), the data he provides make it possible to do this. The result is a very small negative correlation, suggesting that, when we have controlled for economic level, the entire variance in welfare level remains to be explained.

3. The measure of political democracy utilized is the number of years for which states have simultaneously been characterized by universal adult male suffrage, the secret ballot and responsible government (see Hewitt, 1977: 457).

4. It should be noted that Alber mentions a point that is of considerable relevance to our subsequent inquiry: that his basic dependent variable, social insurance coverage, 'taps only one aspect of social policy expansion' (Alber, 1979: 12). Indeed, he mentions that for his sample of European nations there is a negative correlation between coverage and expenditure for 1970, which leaves it entirely open as to whether partisan control of government may be a significant explanation of the latter.

5. As operationalized by Peters, competitive elite behaviour corresponds to the adversary style of the traditional parliamentary system, while coalescent elites 'approximate a "grand coalition" style of politics, with each major grouping involved in making decisions' (Peters, 1978, 73). Peter's categorization of states according to this typology is to be found in the footnotes to Tables 6 and 7.

6. It is not surprising that the pioneering work on public policy outcomes was conducted by those interested in variation among the American states. Comparisons amongst sub-state units have the advantage of automatically controlling for a vast number of historical and cultural factors as well as establishing basic parameters of socioeconomic and political variation. Other useful work has been done on the West German states (see Schmidt, 1980) and Swiss local communities (Frey and Pommerehne, 1978).

7. The interest of those examining the impact of socialist partisanship on issues of redistribution and inequality is related to the expressed goals of those parties, just as is the issue of welfare provision. While the literature review in the previous sections has focused on discussions of welfare, and of public expenditure in general, it

should be noted that many of the works cited also deal with questions of redistribution. In particular, this is true of Jackman (1975), Hewitt (1977) and Peters (1978). The literature that concentrates its attention on equality will be examined in Chapter 6. In general, it is fair to say that this literature displays very similar emphases and problems to those encountered in the discussion of welfare.

8. This comment should be taken in context. Studies vary very considerably in the range of policy areas they encompass. Thus, at one extreme, Sharkansky reports correlations between three measures of economic status and 42 policy variables for the American states (Sharkansky, 1969: 192-4), while at the other Cameron discusses only one, the increase in percent of GDP represented by all governments' revenues, 1960-75 (Cameron, 1978). Moreover, considering difficulties in data collection and analysis and the normal restrictions of article-length presentation, a self-denying ordinance on the number of variables utilized is quite understandable.

9. The only major exception is the attention sometimes paid to the relationship between economic growth rates and policy outcomes. Interestingly, the reported relationships between economic growth and change in public revenue (Cameron, 1978: 1251) and equality (Jackman, 1975: 43-9) are inverse, which, if true over longer periods, would have implications very difficult indeed to square with the convergence thesis.

More typically of the literature, Cameron's finding in respect to the positive link between openness of the economy and the growth in the public economy is based on the relationship between the level of IMEX in 1960 and the change in the size of the public economy over the subsequent 15 years. Given the nature of the factors mediating between the openness of the economy and its public extension — industrial concentration, union strength and leftist-dominated government — the choice of a change variable would hardly have been defensible, since changes in these factors are hardly very likely in the short term. Indeed, it should be noted that our own data for change in IMEX and change in public expenditure over the same period give a correlation of − 0.31. This should in no way be taken as a refutation of Cameron's finding, which shows up just as strongly when the level of IMEX is related to either level of or change in public expenditure. What it does demonstrate is the substantial difference there may be between structural and shorter-term explanations.

10. This hypothesis has been advanced in some contexts in which confusion with the potential governmental role of socialist parties does not seem problematical. This is true of Alber's already cited view that prior to 1900 authoritarian regimes conceded welfare advances when threatened by the political mobilization of the working class, since at that time, no socialist parties had achieved governmental status. It is also applicable to the analysis of welfare in the United States, where mass radicalism has not been mobilized through the socialist movement at all (see Piven and Cloward, 1972). However, the genuine problem of distinguishing between the impact of socialist governmental status and extra-parliamentary working-class strength is clearly demonstrated by the 0.79 correlation between socialist cabinet seats and union density in Table 2.

11. The only routinely collected data available would appear to be unemployment statistics (see Chapter 3), infant mortality statistics (discussed in Castles and McKinlay, 1979a) and data relating to income inequality (see Chapter 6). However, even in respect of this last, there are very major difficulties involved in making the categories of analysis comparable over more than a very few nations (see Sawyer, 1976). Educational enrolment ratios are sometimes taken as a measure of educa-

tional outcome, but, in reality, they refer far more to the quantity of education provided than to its quality. The basic difficulty is that data pertaining to policy outcomes are generally of the qualitative kind that can be obtained only by sample surveys. To my knowedge, the most ambitious attempt to acquire cross-national data on the more qualitative aspects of level-of-living has been that of the Research Group for Comparative Sociology of the University of Helsinki, which is, however, restricted to the Scandinavian countries.

12. It should be noted that the terminology here is somewhat at variance from that used by Wilensky, who uses the term 'outputs' to describe per capita expenditures on welfare, rather than the percentage of GNP devoted to such purposes, which is the measure of output utilized in this chapter (see Wilensky, 1975: 17).

13. Note, however, that total public expenditure excludes one element which often features centrally in socialist analysis of public control of the economy, i.e. the expenditure of those government-owned enterprises or public corporations which primarily sell the goods and services they produce in the market.

14. Calculated from data in *Public Expenditure on Health* (OECD, 1977: 10).

15. It should be noted that we have broken our own operational rules by classifying the Swiss Christian Democratic People's Party as the party of the Right instead of the Radical Democrats, which currently obtain around 20 percent of the vote. The reason for this is the Christian Party (under another name) was the traditional conservative party of Switzerland. In fact, since both parliamentary representation and cabinet participation of these two parties are now virtually identical, this classification makes no difference whatsoever to our results.

16. The rank ordering is obtained by scoring the two underlying dimensions as follows:

| *Dominant governing party* | *Relative size of party* |
|---|---|
| 1 = dominance of right wing in government (whenever the share of cabinet seats aggregated over period = 66% + and if the party is in office for 66% + of the period) | 1 = when the right-wing party is stronger than the social democratic by at least 5% of the popular vote |
| 2 = neither Right nor social democrats dominant | 2 = when the right wing and social democrats are separated by not more than 5% of the vote |
| 3 = dominance of social democrats in government (similar criterion) | 3 = social democrats stronger than right wing (similar criterion) |

The two scores are totalled and one is deducted, since there are only five possible combinations.

17. The data available in *Public Expenditure Trends* allows certainty only for the 1967-69 period. Public consumption expenditure at current prices and GNP per capita show a positive correlation of 0.62**, while the comparable figure at constant (1970) prices is 0.59**. When defence expenditure at current prices is deducted from current public consumption expenditure, the correlation is reduced to 0.18. Incidentally, this procedure also increases the negative association of right-wing cabinet seats and public consumption expenditure (1967-69) at current prices from −051* to −0.61**. Similarly, the relationship between public consumption expenditure and social democratic cabinet seats increases from 0.35 to 0.47*.

18. The Japanese case illustrates very clearly two points discussed earlier in this

chapter. First, there is the question of the distinction between effort or output and outcomes. In the period 1960-76 total public expenditure as a percentage of GDP at constant prices rose by only 13 percent in Japan. During the same period real expenditure per capita increased roughly fourfold. Second, the extraordinarily high Japanese growth rate illustrates the problem of the instability of estimation in a small population. In respect of this variable, Japan is clearly an outlier. To give one example, by removing Japan from the sample, the reported relationship between growth rate and total public expenditure in 1967-69 declines from $-0.60$ to $0.005$. Moreover, Japan is extreme in a number of other respects: it has a very low proportion of those above pensionable age; among the least open economies, among the strongest parties of the Right; and consistently has the lowest rank order score for GAPS. It should be noted however, that, while removing Japan from our population for these measures does quite frequently (although by no means invariably) decrease the level of association reported in Tables 6 and 7, it only rarely decreases them below the level of statistical significance.

19. Wilensky again makes the error of assuming that a relationship that shows up strongly in a diverse population, in this case with a bimodal distribution of demographic structures, will automatically be present in any subset of that population.

20. Although Peacock and Wiseman's hypothesis of a ratchet effect in the growth of public expenditure, the motive force of which is wartime expansion of spending levels, seems to have been falsified by the peacetime advance in the 1960s and early 1970s, their discussion of the problems of reducing levels of expenditure remains pertinent (Peacock and Wiseman, 1967). Above and beyond purely economic and institutional factors, it should be noted that, in so far as a country's ideological structuring tends to be extremely stable, at least one of the factors conducive to high achieved levels of public expenditure remains relatively constant.

21. Cf. 'Some other countries have been unwilling to contemplate the increase in the role of the public sector thought to be consistent with a universal health scheme and have instead directed public expenditure towards assisting particular groups for whom proper access to health is most difficult; notably Medicare for the old and disabled and Medicaid for the poor in the United States, and the AWBZ for long illnesses in the Netherlands' (OECD, 1977: 45).

22. It should be noted that Cameron's data give a substantially higher result for IMEX than for socialist government control. It would appear that this divergence between our findings and his are a consequence of his measurement of change in terms of the number of percentage points by which the public economy increased as a function of GDP, whereas our measurement of change in this particular instance is expressed as a ratio relating the degree of change to the initial level of public expenditure.

23. Throughout this section it should be clear that imputations of the causal impact of parties of the Right are only the reverse side of demonstrating the impact of socialist plus other partisanship. In some ways, the causal sequences are made clearer by emphasizing the latter, since the Right can achieve its objects in a negative way, i.e. by taking no action. On the other hand, the impact of socialist and other partisanship is by no means identical, and deserves separate treatment.

24. Such an instrumentality did not necessarily have to take the form of a political party. The capacity of the modernizing elites which guided the fortunes of Wilhelmine Germany and post-Meiji Restoration Japan to create a coalescence of

rural and urban interests served an identical function and arose in a similar economic context.

25. This finding and the conclusion which derives from it may have applicability only during certain periods. In our data set this pattern of interrelationships is found only for the 1950s and early 1950s, but not thereafter. This was an era in which the Right was particularly strong in a substantial number of advanced democratic states, and stronger correlations between social democratic parliamentary representation and cabinet participation begin to emerge at just the time when democratic socialism was enjoying its greatest electoral upsurge since the prewar period.

26. The problem with step-wise multiple regression techniques when we are seeking to establish patterns across a broad range of dependent variables is that small differences in the degree of fit lead to substantial changes in the causal ordering of the independent variables from one area to another. However, when the same set of independent variables maintain roughly similar magnitudes of bivariate association in related policy areas or over time, it seems more appropriate to deduce that the same configuration of factors is involved.

27. Interestingly, the strength of the centre in Ireland appears to have led to a coalescence between Right and Left of sufficient strength to permit the formation of coalition cabinets in 1973 and 1981.

28. It should be noted that, for a substantial number of the dependent variables, data for Switzerland were missing. It seems reasonable to suppose that, had this not been the case, there would have been far more statistically significant relationships reported for the political structure variable. On the other hand, all those which were reported did include Switzerland. Of these, only the relationship between political structure and health spending in 1962 remains significant with the deletion of the Swiss case.

# REFERENCES

Alber, J. (1979). 'The Growth of Social Insurance in Western Europe: Has Social Democracy made a Difference?', International Political Science Association (Moscow).

Almond, G. (ed.) (1973). *Crisis, Choice and Change*. Boston: Little, Brown.

Bell, D. (1973). *The Coming of Post-Industrial Society*. New York: Basic Books.

Blalock, H. Jr (1979). *Social Statistics*. Tokyo: McGraw-Hill Kogakusha.

Borg, S. and Castles, F.G. (1981). 'The Influence of the Political Right on Public Income Maintenance Expenditure and Equality', *Political Studies*.

Cameron, D. (1978). 'The Expansion of the Public Economy: A Comparative Analysis', *American Political Science Review*.

Castles, F.G. (1978). *The Social Democratic Image of Society*. London: Routledge & Kegan Paul.

Castles, F.G. and McKinlay, R. (1979a). 'Does Politics Matter: An Analysis of the

Public Welfare Commitment in Advanced Democratic States', *European Journal of Political Research*.

Castles, F.G. and McKinlay, R. (1979b). 'Public Welfare Provision, Scandinavia, and the Sheer Futility of the Sociological Approach to Politics', *British Journal of Political Science*.

Cnudde, C. and Neubauer, D. (1969). 'New Trends in Democratic Theory', in Cnudde and Neubauer (eds) (1969), *Empirical Democratic Theory*. Chicago: Markham.

Crosland, A. (1963). *The Future of Socialism*. London: Jonathan Cape.

Cutright, P. (1965). 'Political Structure, Economic Development and National Social Security Programs', *American Journal of Sociology*.

Dryzek, J. (1978). 'Politics, Economics and Inequality: A Cross-National Analysis', *European Journal of Political Research*.

Dye, T. (1966). *Politics, Economics and the Public: Policy Outcomes in the American States*. Chicago: Rand McNally.

Dye, T. (1976). *Policy Analysis*. University of Alabama Press.

Frey, B. and Pommerehne, W. (1978). 'Towards a More Theoretical Foundation for Empirical Policy Analysis', *Comparative Political Studies*.

Galbraith, J. (1967). *The New Industrial State*. London: Hamish Hamilton.

Gordon, T.J. (1969). *A Study of Potential Change in Employee Benefits: National and International Patterns*, Vol 2. Middleton, Conn.: Institute for the Future.

Gough, I. (1979). *The Political Economy of the Welfare State*. London: Macmillan.

Heisler, M.O. (ed.) (1974). *Politics in Europe*. New York: David McKay Company.

Hewitt, C. (1977). 'The Effect of Political Democracy and Social Democracy on Equality in Industrial Societies: A Cross-National Comparison', *American Sociological Review*.

Inglehart, R. and Klingemann, H. (1976). 'Party Identification, Ideological Preferences and the Left-Right Dimension among Western Mass Publics', in Budge, Crew and Farlie (eds), *Party Identification and Beyond*. New York: John Wiley.

Irving, R. (1979). 'Christian Democracy in Post-War Europe: Conservatism Writ-Large or Distinctive Political Phenomenon?', *West European Politics*.

Jackman, R. (1975) *Politics and Social Equality: A Comparative Analysis*. New York: John Wiley.

Kaim-Caudle, P. (1973). *Comparative Social Policy and Social Security*. Oxford: Martin Robertson.

Kerr, C. (1960). *Industrialism and Industrial Man*. Cambridge, Mass.: Harvard University Press.

Key, V.O. (1949). *Southern Politics*. New York: Alfred A. Knopf.

King, A. (1978). 'Ideas, Institutions and the Policies of Governments: A Comparative Analysis', reprinted in P. Lewis, D. Potter and F.G. Castles (eds), *The Practice of Comparative Politics*, 2nd ed. London: Longman.

Kirchheimer, O. (1964). 'The Waning of Opposition', in Macridis and Brown (eds), *Comparative Politics*, Homewood, Ill.: Dorsey Press.

Lijphart, A. (1968). 'Typologies of Democratic Systems', *Comparative Political Studies*, vol. I.

Lipset, S.M. (1960). *Political Man*. London: Heinemann.

Lipset, S.M. and Rokkan, S. (1967). *Party Systems and Voter Alignments*. New York: Doubleday.

Mackie, T. and Rose R. (1974). *The International Almanac of Electoral History*. London: Macmillan.

Madsen, H.J. (1978). 'Poetics'. University of Aarhus, mimeo.

Marcuse, H. (1964). *One Dimensional Man*. London: Routledge & Kegan Paul.

OECD (various years). *National Accounts 1958-67*. Paris: OECD.

OECD (1975). *National Accounts 1975*. Paris: OECD.

OECD (1976). *Public Expenditure on Income Maintenance Programmes*. Paris: OECD.

OECD (1977). *Public Expenditure on Health*. Paris. OECD.

OECD (1978). *Public Expenditure Trends*. Paris: OECD.

Offe, C. (1972). 'Advanced Capitalism and the Welfare State', *Politics and Society*.

Parkin, F. (1971). *Class Inequality and Political Order*. London: MacGibbon & Kee.

Peacock, A. and Wiseman, J. (1967). *The Growth of Public Expenditure in the United Kingdom*, 2nd ed. London: Allen & Unwin.

Peters, G. (1978). 'Types of Democratic Systems and Types of Public Policy', reprinted in P. Lewis, D. Potter and F.G. Castles (eds), *The Practice of Comparative Politics*, 2nd ed. London: Longman.

Piven, F. and Cloward R. (1972). *Regulating the Poor*. London: Tavistock.

Pryor, F. (1968). *Public Expenditures in Communist and Capitalistic Nations*. Homewood, Ill.: Richard D. Irvin.

Roberts, G. (1978). 'The Explanation of Politics: Comparison, Strategy and Theory', printed in P. Lewis, D. Potter and F.G. Castles (eds), *The Practice of Comparative Politics*, 2nd ed. London: Longman.

Rokkan, S. (1970). *Citizens, Elections, Parties*. Oslo: Universitetsforlaget.

Sartori, G. (1976). *Parties and Party Systems*. Cambridge: University Press.

Sawyer, M. (1976). 'Income Distribution in OECD Countries', in *OECD Economic Outlook*. Paris: OECD.

Sharkansky, I. (ed.) (1969). *Policy Analysis in Political Science*. Chicago: Markham.

Sharkansky, I. and Hofferbert, R. (1969). 'Dimensions of State Politics, Economics and Public Policy', *APSR*.

Schmidt, M. (1980). *CDU and SPD an der Regierung*. Frankfurt: Campus.

Stephens, J.D. (1979). *The Transition from Capitalism to Socialism*. London: Macmillan.

Thompkins, G. (1975). 'A Causal Model of State Welfare Expenditure', *The Journal of Politics*.

Tingsten, H. (1955). 'Stability and Vitality in Swedish Democracy', *The Political Quarterly*.

Tufte, E. (1979). 'Political Parties, Social Class and Economic Policy', *Government and Opposition*.

Verner, J. (1979). 'Socioeconomic Environment, Political System and Educational Policy Outcomes', *Comparative Politics*.

Wade, L. (1972). *The Elements of Public Policy*. Columbus, Ohio: Merrill.

Wildavsky, A. (1975). *Budgeting: A Comparative Theory of Budgetary Processes*. Boston: Little, Brown.

Wilensky, H. (1975). *The Welfare State and Equality*. Berkeley: University of California Press.

Wilensky, H. (1976). 'The "New Corporatism", Centralization and the Welfare State', *Sage Professional Papers*, Series/Number 06-020.

World Bank, (1976). *World Tables 1976*. Baltimore: Johns Hopkins University Press.

# 3

# The Role of the Parties in Shaping Macroeconomic Policy

Manfred G. Schmidt
University of Konstanz

## Introduction

**This chapter focuses** on the determinants of macroeconomic policy in the advanced capitalist states. The policy areas examined overlap to some extent with those surveyed in Chapter 2, mainly because the extent of the tax state, which is one of our central concerns, is both a factor conditioning the nature of economic policy as such and the immediate revenue source for public expenditure of whatever kind. However, there are three major differences in the emphasis of the two chapters. First, while Chapter 2 was concerned with aspects of expenditure, we focus on the major elements of macroeconomic policy: the revenue base, the rate of unemployment and of inflation. Second, while Chapter 2 was restricted in its analysis to the expansionary period of the 1960s and early 1970s, we shall examine policy in the subsequent period of economic constraint heralded by the oil crisis of 1973. Third, whereas Chapter 2 proceeded from an overtly non-theoretical stance, our analysis is grounded in an approach that contextualizes policy in the macrosocietal structures of advanced capitalism.

In summary terms, we may characterize capitalist democracies by three macrosocietal structures which they have in common:

1. a mode of production characterized by wage-dependent labour, by private profit-maximizing behaviour and by structurally given economic instabilities;

2. a political system that is characterized by competing political

parties, pluralistic structures of decision-making and a democratic electoral system;

3. a state that, on the one hand, is largely dependent on resources extracted from the private sector of the economy and which, on the other hand, indulges in substantial interference with the private economy and with the institutional and substantive arrangements of civil society.

Although these macro-societal structures are common to all capitalist democracies, the degree of political control of the economy, the scope, the timing and the outcome of economic policy vary enormously from country to country.

A combination of capitalist economic structure and democratic political arrangements seems compatible with widely divergent policy stances. There are at one extreme the countries in which state intervention flavours all major aspects of policy: there is active intervention in the market economy, a tax system that extracts more than half the national income, and redistributive mechanisms, ranging from industrial subsidies to public income maintenance programmes, that reallocate a substantial proportion of national income for welfare state purposes. The Scandinavian countries, and more recently the Netherlands, may be taken as the exemplars of such a policy stance. In other countries, state intervention is far less pronounced and the various aspects of welfare state provision is much more muted. Japan, Switzerland and the United States are consistent examples at this other extreme. Moreover, capitalism and democracy coexist in nations whose macroeconomic profile is of high inflation and low unemployment and also in nations where the authorities have made vast efforts to control inflation, even if this was seen as involving the risk of high and increasing rates of unemployment.

Further, the response to economic crisis has not been uniform across the capitalist democracies. All advanced states were hit by the economic constraints of the mid-1970s, but there was a wide range of variation in both political initiatives and macroeconomic outcomes. In some countries, the United Kingdom being a prominent example, there was a dramatic increase in both the rate of unemployment and the rate of inflation. In others the authorities managed to hold unemployment down, usually, although not always, with the consequence of an increase in consumer prices. Austria is an example of a country that succeeded in both, whereas the cost of low unemployment in Norway and Sweden was a constant battle with rising prices.

The central research questions that will be addressed in this chapter are all related to the variation in macroeconomic policy manifested by democratic capitalist states. Fundamentally, we wish to examine the reasons why economic policy varies as much as it does; why, for instance, countries with similar macrosocietal structures have such a diversity of approaches to problems such as unemployment and inflation. Moreover, we hope to gain additional purchase on some of the issues first raised in the earlier context of the discussion of public expenditure by focusing on the range of variation in the size and rate of expansion of the tax state. In approaching these issues of macroeconomic policy, the basic thrust of our investigation will be, as throughout this volume, the extent to which variation in policy outcomes can be accounted for by differential economic and socioeconomic structures and developments, and the degree to which explanations must be sought in diverse political structures and in conscious and deliberate political choice.

Debate concerning these questions is by no means new. Political scientists and practising politicians have been long concerned with the causes and consequences of state intervention into the institutions and processes of the capitalist economy. One perennial issue has been whether the major determinant of economic policy has been conscious political choice or the structured socioeconomic imperatives inherent in the capitalist mode of production. Another has been the extent to which the apparent growth in state intervention has enabled governments to exercise successful control over the economy.[1] Prevailing schools of thought on these matters cannot readily be divorced from political tendencies. Thus, according to one school, which has primarily been espoused by radical socialists whose intellectual framework derives from Marxist and neo-Marxist thought, the dynamics of capitalism was the essential law of motion that shaped the policies pursued by governments in contemporary states. Effectively, this view suggests that the relative autonomy of the private sector of the economy vis-à-vis the state either prevents or undermines efforts to control the economy or to soften the practice of capitalism via labour market policies and redistributional welfare policies. On this basis, it was concluded that the rise of state intervention and the evolution of the welfare state had at best only marginally affected the sphere of distribution, but had certainly made no major change in the basic characteristics of the capitalist mode of production.

According to another school of thought, which is politically closely linked to social democratic and reform-oriented bourgeois tendencies, and which intellectually owes much to the work of liberal social scientists and economists, the reward structure, the laws of motion and the imbalances of a capitalist market economy are basically amenable to political control. They can be changed, provided that governments, and especially labour movements, are willing and politically strong enough to overcome the resistance of entrenched business interests. In this view, the evolution of the welfare state, and the introduction of economic planning, demand management and labour market policies, are seen as the in- struments for realizing the reform potential of the state. The development of the Swedish welfare state is generally taken to be the epitome of the successful realization of that potential. In a re- cent comparative analysis of the impact of organized labour on public policy, which relies heavily on the Swedish example, John D. Stephens goes so far as to claim that the 'socialization of income and control rights', brought about by social democratic govern- ments backed up by a strong labour movement, opened the parliamentary road to the 'transition to socialism' (Stephens, 1979). The underlying assumption inherent in this school of thought is remarkably similar to that which is the shared basis for the political science fraternity: that differential political structures and processes have a differential impact on the course, the content and the impact of public policies.

## Competing explanations of macroeconomic policy

Political science assumptions have, quite naturally, featured pro- minently in the emerging field of public policy analysis, and several of the most recent and influential contributions in this area have argued explicitly that the partisan composition of government is among the more important factors accounting for differences in economic policy and macroeconomic outcomes in the Western democracies. These studies have interpreted the available empirical evidence as being compatible with the view that social democratic parties and their allies are both more willing and more able to con- trol economic imbalances in a way that favours the core class base among the organized working-class movement. On the basis of a comparative analysis of rates of unemployment and inflation in a number of Western democracies in the 1960s, Douglas Hibbs has attempted to demonstrate that the policies of social democratic governments have been markedly divergent from those of a non-socialist complexion (Hibbs, 1977). According to Hibbs, social democratic governments put a far higher priority on full employment, despite the concomitant risk of higher inflation, whereas bourgeois administrations were, on the whole, much more reluctant to take positive measures against unemployment, since their primary objective was the containment of prices. The general conclusion of this study is 'that the macroeconomic policies pursued by left- and right-wing governments are broadly in accordance with the objective economic interests and subjective preferences of their class-defined core political constituencies' (Hibbs, 1977: 1468).

Other studies come to broadly similar conclusions. For instance, Andrew Cowart's study of monetary and fiscal policies in the major European nations in the 1970s yielded results that vary from those of Hibbs only very marginally.

> Governments of the left appear to have taken more dramatic action in response to domestic economic change — whether for the purposes of maximizing employment or minimizing inflation...The responses of governments of the right are simply more muted in most cases. [Cowart, 1978: 311]

Focusing on a wider range of economic policies, Tufte, in a major appraisal of the field, again emphasizes the vital importance of ideology and partisan control of government.

> [J]ust as the electoral calendar helps to set the timing of policy, so the ideology of the political leaders shapes the substance of economic policy. [Tufte, 1978: 71]

> The single most important determinant of variations in macroeconomic performance from one industrialized democracy to another is the location on the left-right spectrum of the governing political party. Party platforms and political ideology set priorities and help decide policies. The consequence is that the governing party is very much responsible for major macroeconomic outcomes — unemployment rates, inflation rates, income equalization, and the size and rate of expansion of the government budget. [Tufte, 1978: 104]

Finally, Cameron's analysis of the expansion of the public economy in 18 capitalist nations from 1960 to 1975, which presents a somewhat more complex picture of the determinants of public policy, nevertheless must be counted as a study that supports the partisan control hypothesis. Despite the fact that the relative openness the economy is presented as the major determinant of the expansion of the tax state, the party control variable is the crucial mediating factor, providing a push towards greater generosity of welfare provision where the labour movement is strong. To Cameron, a strong social democratic party is sufficient, although not a necessary, condition for an expansive tax state (Cameron, 1978).

Furthermore, it is quite easy to find instances of dramatic change in the partisan composition of government in individual countries which seem to lend force to the 'party control does matter' hypothesis. For example, the advent of a long period of social democratic rule in Germany in the 1960s may be regarded as an important factor in the social, cultural and political modernization of West German society, as well as the initiating force for a range of economic policies, including a greater emphasis on planning, demand management and incomes policy (see Nahamowitz, 1978). Similarly, the change from a labour government to a coalition of bourgeois parties in Israel in 1977, and the Conservative Party take-over in Britain in May 1979, both heralded a dramatic reversal of previous economic policy. The new administrations in each case adopted a monetarist stance with a strong emphasis on public expenditure cuts.

The 'party control does matter' hypothesis, whether supported by cross-national empirical analysis or one-off observations of particular countries, tends to rest on a particular model of the relationship between civil society and the political system. The cleavage structures in civil society are, in this view, reproduced in the political system with policy-relevant consequences. Policy is seen as the outcome of the competing demands and interests of the various parties' class constituencies, together with the relative ability of each party to gain and hold governmental office. This line of reasoning rests on a number of macro-societal assumptions, which are by no means held by all analysts of capitalist society. First, it assumes that governments, in their policy-making activities, have extensive room for manoeuvre in respect of the inherent constraints imposed by the economic structure. Second, it assumes that social democratic parties are, in fact, willing to utilize the state apparatus to its fullest extent. Third, it assumes that the reward structure and laws of motion of the capitalist mode of production are, both in the short and long term, amenable to successful political intervention. It should be readily apparent that these assumptions, which permeate the 'party control does matter' view, are closely interlinked and readily compatible with the moderate social democratic political stance.

The empirical evidence on which these conclusions are based is, however, far from conclusive, and the theoretical arguments and assumptions that imply a very highly developed relative autonomy of the state are not as convincing as they seem at first sight. All studies of capitalist democracies are necessarily limited in respect of the availability of cases, with the consequence, already remarked in the introductory chapter, that the findings are liable to be distorted by the inherent instability of estimation in a small sample. Such would, for instance, appear to be the case in respect of Hibbs's study of the determinants of rates of unemployment and inflation, which was based on an analysis of only 12 countries. Separate re-analyses by Payne and Schmidt, using differently composed samples of nations and a number of additional variables, led to substantial changes in parameter estimates. Indeed, the conclusions from these latter studies suggest that the relationship between the dominant power in government and macroeconomic outcomes is either the reverse of that reported by Hibbs or, at least, very considerably weaker than predicted by his model (see Payne, 1979; and Schmidt 1979: 112-15). The basic reason for this divergence of findings is that Hibbs's study excluded most of the 'deviant cases'; for example, nations with bourgeois-dominated governments and low rates of unemployment (Japan, New Zealand and Switzerland) and nations with social democratic governments and lowish rates of inflation (Austria, Switzerland and Luxembourg).

Exactly the same problem is apparent in the arbitrary selection of individual cases of dramatic change in policy consequent on a change in the partisan composition of government. Such cases do exist, but they are not necessarily representative of all cases of change in partisan control. In contrast to the dramatic change that occurred in Israel and the United Kingdom, we may counterpose the change from social democratic to bourgeois coalition government in Sweden in 1976. Although the social democrats had been in office continuously for 40 years, the consensus of commentators is that the political transformation had virtually no impact on the style and content of economic policy-making. Indeed, the new bourgeois coalition continued to expand the public sector and extend active labour market policies at a pace similar to, or even faster than, their predecessors. The West German experience from the mid-1970s points in the same direction. Whatever impetus there had been in the initial politics of domestic reform had by now run out of steam, and the Social Democratic Party was seen by a number of commentators as merely a modernized version of Christian Democratic politics (see Narr, 1977).

Given the inconclusive nature of the evidence in this field, it would be inappropriate to consider the 'party control does matter' hypothesis as the only suitable candidate for empirical study in the context of the analysis of the determinants of the observed variation in macroeconomic outcomes in the capitalist democracies. The evidence that has been accumulated in the field of public economic policies is at least partially compatible with two other hypotheses. One is a fundamentally socioeconomic hypothesis, according to which socioeconomic imperatives and constraints are primarily responsible for shaping the actions of governments, irrespective of their political complexion. The other is a class politics hypothesis, according to which policy outputs and outcomes are primarily predetermined and fashioned by the political constellations of social forces in extra-parliamentary arenas.

The type of socioeconomic hypothesis examined here is not, at least in its theoretical assumptions, of the mechanistic kind that enters into the convergence thesis already surveyed in the earlier chapter on public expenditure. Rather, like the class politics hypothesis, it tends to be advanced in studies that focus either on the unstable dynamics and the economic disequilibrium in capitalist economies, and on the restrictive conditions that are thus given for independent state action, or on the dynamics of political conflicts between social classes and their impact on the state.[2] In modern Marxist theories of the state, for example, it is argued on the one hand, that the state is largely excluded from the economic market and from the process of production and, on the other, that, as a tax-dependent state, it is simultaneously dependent on the continuous economic transactions of labour and capital and forced to comply with the twin imperatives of supporting the process of accumulation and procuring adequate legitimation. According to this view, the problems of capital — such as business cycles, centralization, waste of resources and environmental pollution — combined with the need for legitimation have created the agenda for the modern state's activities, largely irrespective of which political tendency is in power.

Authors who write in terms of a class politics paradigm argue, in addition, that conflicts between social classes, the growth and strength of the labour movement and of business power, and the strategies of social demand anticipation on the part of governments have determined public policies within the scope of the autonomy available in a capitalist structure.[3] In this view, it is not party control that matters, but rather the balance of competing forces in the society as a whole. In terms of this perspective, the evolution of the welfare state may be seen as a consequence of class conflicts, social demands of the working population and the growth and monopolization of the process of capital accumulation. Furthermore, radical contributions to the theory of political business cycles have been grounded in a class politics paradigm. Following Kalecki's political theory of full employment (Kalecki, 1943; 322-31), Boddy and Crotty have, for example, argued that the major goal of macroeconomic policy is not to eliminate cyclic fluctuation, but to guide it in the way that is most compatible with the interests of the capitalist class, taking into account the constraint provided by the relative strength of the labour movement (Boddy and Crotty, 1975: 1-19).

It is readily apparent that the major schools of thought concerning the nature of macroeconomic policy-making in capitalist democracies are reflected in the competing hypotheses surveyed in this section. Political science assumptions and, on occasions, social democratic preconceptions tend to be built into those cross-national and single-nation studies, which have concluded that party control does matter, and, in particular, that social democratic governments behave in a markedly different fashion from bourgeois governments of Right and Centre. Marxist and neo-Marxist assumptions are equally apparent in the socioeconomic hypothesis that the state's relative autonomy is severely constrained by the need to reconcile the processes of accumulation and legitimation, and that such limitations effectively mean that policy is a concomitant of ineluctible economic structures and processes. The class politics hypothesis is in a sense a hybrid of the two schools of thought. In theoretical substance, it proceeds from Marxist assumptions concerning the laws of motion of the capitalist mode of production; but, in simultaneously pointing to the role played by the structures, strategies and outcomes of the class struggle engendered by that mode of production, it concedes that politics may be relevant to the shaping of macroeconomic policy. Thus, the debates in this field are debates not merely about questions of fact, but also about the assumptions concerning the macro-societal structures of capitalist societies held by the respective protagonists. The two major issues involved concern the relative autonomy of state and economy (which divides political scientists and social democrats from Marxists and neo-Marxists) and the nature of the political levers that move the state to action within its sphere of autonomy (which divides the protagonists of partisan control from those of class politics). Public policy studies have often failed to make explicit the assumptions from which they proceed or to contrast findings based on rival hypotheses. In our subsequent analysis of the deteminants of the expansion of the tax state, rates of unemployment and inflation, it is our intention to examine which of the hypotheses provides the best understanding of the macroeconomic policy of the contemporary capitalist state.

## Basic features of the research design

In view of the contradictory hypotheses and inconclusive evidence, it is necessary to devise a rigorous test procedure in order that conclusions concerning the determinants of macroeconomic policy can be more firmly grounded than hitherto. The research design appropriate for such a test procedure must, at a minimum, fulfil certain stipulated criteria (see, Schmidt, 1979: 102-22). Given the relatively small number of cases and the dangers of instability of estimation, it is necessary to select a sample that minimizes the danger of biased findings of the kind that are apparent in Hibbs's study of unemployment and inflation. It is also necessary to devise a set of reliable and valid indicators of the political complexion of governments, the structure of the economy and the structures of extra-parliamentary power distribution. Because it is our intention to test certain hypotheses emerging from an explicitly Marxist framework of thought, these indicators will not necessarily be the same as those developed in the context of the earlier discussion of public expenditure. In addition, it is necessary to provide a full specification of the various explanatory models, given the restrictions imposed by the low number of cases, and to specify a period of investigation, the changing circumstances of which allow for a powerful test of the specific hypotheses under investigation. Finally, the choice of dependent variables must be such as to tap policy areas and policy contents which are closely related to both the structural imbalances of capitalist economies and to the types of state intervention that are typically used to attempt to control the economy.

In light of these criteria, we have developed a research strategy that has the following characteristics.

1. The focus is on all 21 countries which are both capitalist in

economic structure and have been characterized by democratic political procedures since 1950.[4]

2. The political composition of governments is measured by various indicators of the duration and strength of 'bourgeois' (liberal, conservative and centre parties) and 'left-wing' parties (social democrat and communist) in government. Indicators of the relative size of both tendencies and indicators of the relative cohesiveness of the bourgeois and the left-wing tendency were separately constructed in order to account for both the overall power distribution within civil society and the political room for maneouvre for the incumbent tendency.[5] It is most important for the reader to note that, since our theoretical concern is with the relative strength of bourgeois and working-class-oriented political formations, the nature of these indicators depart radically from those used in the chapter on public expenditure: that chapter was developed in terms of the party control paradigm, and the measures of political strength utilized there are almost exclusively concerned with the individual impact of particular parties seeking office.

3. In an attempt to assess the nature of structures of extra-parliamentary political action, we have used a variety of indicators. These include union strength, levels of industrial conflict and the development of corporatist structures.[6]

4. In order to minimize the danger of mis-specification of models, a conscious effort has been made to include, in addition to the major political and socioeconomic factors, all those variables for which plausible hypotheses have been suggested in the existing literature and for the measurement of which secondary data were available (for details, see the next three sections). Given the low number of cases, a full specification of models could only be approximated by a set of bivariate analyses and a set of multivariate analyses with not more than two independent variables.

5. Apart from the analysis of the expansion of the tax state, which covers the entire period from the 1950s to the 1970s, the period under review is from 1974 to 1978. This period of economic recession throughout the Western World is ideal for testing the reactions of capitalist democracies under conditions of sustained economic instability and crisis.

6. Three dependent variables feature in our analysis. All of them are related to important dimensions of macroeconomic policy outputs and outcomes. The literature on reform policy-making and state intervention suggests that a comparatively large and powerful tax state is a necessary, although not a sufficient, condition for

reform policies in favour of the lower classes and for the successful control of the economy. The size and rate of the expansion of the tax state was measured by relating total revenues of general government (including social security contributions) to gross domestic product.[7] Furthermore, the literature on capitalist economies suggests that there is a structurally given tendency of inflationary pressure and of cyclical and structural unemployment, both of which require counteractionary measures by the government. Rates of unemployment and rates of inflation can thus be viewed as two of the major outcome measures by which we can evaluate whether the state has successfully managed to control the economy. In order to cope with problems of limited cross-national comparability of inflation and unemployment rates, recoded versions of the figures published by the OECD and the ILO were employed.[8]

Finally, before turning to the substantive analysis of these elements of macroeconomic policy, it should be re-emphasized that our concerns are different both theoretically and substantively from those of the earlier chapter on public expenditure. Whereas that chapter's theoretical objective was to assess the relative explanatory power of the convergence thesis and the 'party control does matter' hypothesis, ours is to juxtapose the latter hypothesis against a number of approaches that emerge from a Marxist or neo-Marxist framework. Moreover, while the substantive interest of the earlier chapter was on how governments expend their resources, our concern is with the way in which they obtain revenue and their general capacity to control the economy. It is worth mentioning that the impact of taxation, unemployment and inflation affects the welfare of the individual citizen at least as much as patterns of public expenditure.

### The expansion of the tax state in the capitalist democracies after World War II

In the period following World War II, the role of government in most of the developed capitalist democracies increased dramatically.[9] The public economy, defined in terms of the extractive capacity of the state, was in most cases enormously expanded.[10] A major growth in public consumption and in government transfers for the provision of social services and income supplements were the most important components in this expansion of the role of government.

# TABLE 1
## The size and the rates of expansion of the tax state

| | Size | | | Rates of expansion | | | Dominant tendency in government** | | |
|---|---|---|---|---|---|---|---|---|---|
| | Tax state* 1950 | Tax state* 1960 | Tax state* 1975 | Tax state* 1950-60 | Tax state* 1960-75 | Tax state* 1973-77 | 1950-60 | 1960-75 | 1974-77 |
| Australia | 20.5[2] | 25.5 | 31.6 | 5.0 | 6.1 | -2.8 | 1 | 2 | 3 |
| Austria | 28.0 | 31.0 | 39.1 | 3.0 | 8.1 | 5.0 | 3 | 3 | 5 |
| Belgium | 24.0[1] | 27.5 | 40.6 | 3.5 | 13.1 | 5.4 | 2 | 2 | 2 |
| Canada | 24.7 | 26.0 | 37.1 | 1.3 | 11.1 | 0.2 | 1 | 1 | 1 |
| Denmark | 21.8 | 27.5 | 45.3 | 5.7 | 17.8 | 2.0 | 3 | 3 | 4 |
| Finland | 30.4 | 31.6 | 39.8 | 1.2 | 8.2 | 5.0 | 3 | 2 | 1 |
| France | 32.8 | 34.0 | 40.5 | 1.2 | 6.5 | 3.6 | 2 | 1 | 3 |
| FRG | 31.5 | 35.4 | 41.0 | 3.9 | 5.6 | 2.3 | 1 | 3 | 4 |
| Iceland | 27.6[2] | 27.8[5] | 26.6 | 9.4[6] | -1.2[7] | 1.3 | 1 | 1 | 3 |
| Ireland | 23.4 | 24.5 | 36.8 | 1.1 | 12.3 | 0.7 | 2 | 2 | 3 |
| Israel | 14.4 | 28.7 | 38.9[4] | 14.3 | 10.2 | n.a. | 4 | 4 | 2 |
| Italy | 21.0[2] | 29.8 | 35.2 | 8.8 | 5.4 | 3.6 | 1 | 2 | 2 |
| Japan | 21.7[3] | 20.2 | 23.6 | -1.5 | 3.4 | 1.3 | 1 | 1 | 1 |
| Luxembg. | 32.5[3] | 32.5 | 50.6 | 0.0 | 18.1 | 13.7 | 3 | 1 | 3 |
| NZ | 27.0[1] | 28.4 | 31.4 | 1.4 | 3.0 | 7.9 | 3 | 2 | 3 |
| Netherl. | 32.8 | 33.1 | 52.6 | 0.3 | 19.5 | 4.8 | 2 | 2 | 3 |
| Norway | 29.7[2] | 34.5 | 49.7 | 4.8 | 15.2 | 1.6 | 5 | 3 | 5 |
| Sweden | 25.9 | 34.9 | 52.6 | 9.0 | 17.7 | 12.3 | 4 | 5 | 4 |
| Switzerl. | 25.1 | 25.1 | 32.1 | 0.0 | 7.0 | 5.5 | 2 | 2 | 2 |
| UK | 32.6 | 29.3 | 41.1 | -3.3 | 11.8 | 3.6 | 2 | 3 | 4 |
| USA | 23.9 | 28.2 | 30.6 | 4.3 | 2.4 | 0.8 | 1 | 1 | 1 |

*Tax state: Revenues from tax and social security contribution of general government as percentage of GDP (Source: OECD National Accounts Statistics, various volumes and United Nations: National Accounts Statistics, various volumes).

**Dominant tendency in government (for details of measurement see end note 5):
1 = Bourgeois hegemony
2 = Bourgeois dominance
3 = Balance
4 = Social democratic dominance
5 = Social democratic hegemony

1. 1953. 2. 1951. 3. 1952. 4. 1974. 5. 1961. 6. 1951-60. 7. 1961-75.

However, the general process of welfare state development took place on the basis of quite different initial conditions, and at a rate that varied substantially from country to country. In some countries, such as France, the Netherlands and Britain, development occurred within the context of a public economy, which was already of a considerable size by the early 1950s. The share of the tax state as a percentage of GDP has increased particularly fast in Sweden, the Netherlands, Norway, Ireland, Denmark, Belgium and Canada, whereas the rate of change in Japan, the United States and Switzerland has been rather modest. Both the absolute size and rates of change of the tax state for various periods are indicated in Table 1.

Why the size and rate of change of the public economy varies to such an extent has been a topic of some controversy.[11] Economists have tended to argue that the size and rate of expansion of the tax state varies positively — in a linear or nonlinear way — with levels of economic wealth, rates of economic growth, population increase and degrees of urbanization and technological innovation, and inversely with the size of the agricultural sector of the economy. According to this view, the expansionary impetus stemmed from the reaction of the authorities to the pressures of rapid economic growth and technological change, to the revolution of rising expectations, which were fuelled by the experience of postwar prosperity, and to the social problems generated by rapidly changing social structures and institutions.

In addition, Marxist writers have suggested that the increase in state revenues and expenditures is a function of inherent strains consequent on the development of capitalism and, in particular, of the class conflicts accompanying the process. To a large degree, the expansion of the tax state is seen as a mechanism by which the capitalist state formulates and implements policies designed to secure the long-term reproduction of capitalist social relations.[12] However, in contrast to the economists' view, Marxists have tended to put a greater emphasis on the limits for the growth of the tax state. While there is a growing need for measures of state intervention, there is at the same time an impediment to the fundamental expansion of the extractive capacities of the state. State activities must neither violate profit-maximizing strategies nor undermine incentives to work: otherwise unintended consequences, such as partial investment strikes, increasing capital export and reduction of work discipline, are likely to lead to economic decline, increasing unemployment and reduced volume of revenue.

The Marxist analysis is valuable in diagnosing the common structural problems of the nations under study, but its focus on the general nature of such problems provides lesser explanatory power in respect of the variation in the size and rates of expansion of the public economy in the capitalist democracies. Nor are the general modes of economic explanation fully compatible with the actual manifestation of variation in these states. For instance, the economists' views cannot readily make sense of the experience of countries, such as the United States, Japan and Switzerland, where the tax state grew, if at all, very slowly, and where the transformation in the social fabric was very rapid and the rate of economic growth comparatively high. Ad hoc explanations for these exceptional cases have been advanced, but only at the cost of making the general economic hypothesis more tenuous. In the Swiss case, it has been suggested that both political culture and unique institutional structures act as barriers to reform policies and increasing state intervention (Schätti, 1978). In the Japanese case, Wildavsky has argued that economic growth rates have been so high that, even with a constant share of GDP devoted to the tax state, sufficiently large growth dividends were available to finance increasing state activities (see Wildavsky, 1975: 232-35 and note 18 of Chapter 2 above).

A more general criticism of some of the conventional economic explanations of the expansion of the public economy has been voiced in the recent OECD survey of public expenditure trends:

> It no longer seems plausible to assume that in peacetime the public sector grows at a rather slow and steady pace, being forced up during wars to higher levels from which it does not subsequently fall back.... . Nor are there any marked signs of a typical 'time-profile' of the demand for public expenditure, with particularly strong demands emerging at some point in the process of industrialisation and then tapering off as higher income levels are reached.... . There is no marked tendency for rapid increases in total public expenditure/GDP ratio to be associated with [either] low per capita real income [or] high population growth rates. [OECD, 1978: 13]

According to this OECD study, the data-base of which is extensively re-analysed in the previous chapter on public expenditure, the major factors contributing to the extension of the tax state were increases in public consumption expenditure, a rising share of government transfers to households, a major expansion in programme coverage and the impact of demographic structure. The OECD study does not, however, offer a convincing explanation of

why the various components of expenditure developed as they did,
and why the authorities acted, or did not act, in the way they did.

The prevailing economic and socioeconomic explanations of the
growth of the tax state have, to an increasing extent, been challenged in recent years by the work of a number of sociologists and
political scientists. Anthony King, for example, has argued that the
comparatively small public sector in the USA was nothing but a
reflection of the dominant values and preferences inherent in
American public opinion: 'The state plays a more limited role in
America than elsewhere because Americans, more than other people, want it to play a limited role' (King, 1973: 418). Clearly, such
an hypothesis is compatible with the previously mentioned ad hoc
argument used to demonstrate why Switzerland has experienced
such modest public sector growth in the postwar period. Recent
contributions from studies on politico-economic linkages also lend
further support for a sociological and political explanation. Bruno
S. Frey and others have been able to show that governments pursued expansive policies whenever their popularity deficit came close
to a threshold that was critical for their re-election prospects.[13] In
addition, they noted that the degree of expansion varies with the
political complexion of governments, with social democratic
governments being more willing, on the whole, than bourgeois
governments to intervene actively in the economic market. Finally,
in seeking to outline the major hypotheses in this field, it is again
necessary to mention Cameron's seminal study, which has already
been discussed in some detail in the previous essay on public expenditure and in the introduction to this chapter. Cameron's argument
is important because it adds an international economic aspect to the
explanation of the expansion of the public economy.   By
demonstrating that the relative openness of the economy serves to
shape the social infrastructure on which partisan support rests, his
hypothesis departs from the simple antitheses of the 'politics matters' debate and sets the influence of the governmental and extra-
parliamentary forces of the Left in the context of the functioning of
the international economy of capitalism (see Cameron, 1978).

In what follows, we shall re-analyse those hypotheses that
emerge from the literature on the determinants of the tax state and
that can be tested in the context of a research design utilizing cross-
national, secondary, data. In particular, we shall focus on the 'party control does matter' hypothesis, the international, the politico-
economic, the economic, the institutional and the class conflict
explanations.[14] In order to avoid the pitfalls commonly associated

with cross-sectional analysis, especially the ecological fallacy, our study will combine comparative analysis of the size and rate of expansion of the tax state with a set of time-series analyses of the individual countries constituting our sample. Three different time periods are used: (1) the period from 1950 to 1960, i.e. the period of postwar reconstruction; (2) the period from 1960 to 1975, i.e. the period under investigation in the essay on public expenditure, and that which features in Cameron's investigation; and (3) the period from 1974 to 1977, i.e. the period of the economic crisis of the mid-1970s. Analysis beyond 1977 is impossible within the ambit of his study owing to the absence of reliable and comparable data.

## Correlates of the size of the tax state in 1975

Although there is a seeming duplication of the previous analysis of public expenditure patterns by starting from the size of the tax state in 1975, we focus on a substantially greater number of independent variables, particularly in respect of the nature of extra-parliamentary forces and the structure of the economy. It is our contention that the results of such a broad focus on the determinants of the tax state, when taken in conjunction with findings derived from the analysis of other major aspects of macroeconomic policy, must seriously modify the conclusion of the previous essay 'that partisan control of government is a major determinant of policy outputs' (see p. 88 above).

If our explanation of the size of the tax state in the capitalist democracies in 1975 were to be based exclusively on a cross-sectional analysis, the basic conclusion would be that, with the exception of the economic hypotheses, most of the arguments contained in the literature received some measure of support. As demonstrated in Table 2, the findings derived from cross-sectional analysis are statistically compatible with the 'party control does matter' hypothesis, with the class politics explanation, resting on the balance of extra-parliamentary forces, and with the explanation premised on the impact of the relative openness of the economy. Thus, the size of the tax state in 1975 is the larger:

— the more social democratic parties participated in government, whether alone or in coalition;
— the more the power distribution between labour and capital is skewed toward organized labour;

— the more the power distribution in civil society comes close to a
balance of strength of the left-wing and bourgeois milieux;
— the more the national economies are integrated into, and dependent on, the world market.
This broad conclusion of compatibility with a range of hypotheses
remains even utilizing a multivariate design and controlling for differential initial conditions, socioeconomic and political constellations.

In a sense, these results, derived from cross-sectional analysis,
pose more questions than they answer. First, there is the issue of
the indecisiveness of the conclusion. Only the economic and social
structure and the institutionalized centralization of the state seem
ruled out as explanations of the size of the tax state. Second, it is
more than a little difficult to credit that none of the aspects of
economic and social structure investigated had any connection with
the dimensions of the public economy. Explanations of this order
must be considered to constitute the basic orthodoxy of the field,
and to reject them outright on the basis of a single finding could be
regarded as more than premature. Just as in the previous analysis
of public expenditure, what we require to establish our conclusions
more firmly is an examination of the patterns manifested by the
data. Here, however, the appropriate focus is on patterns over
time, and for that reason our analysis of the expansion of the tax
state in the period up to 1975 employs a pooled, cross-national and
longitudinal research design.

### The expansion of the tax state in the 1950s (the period of reconstruction)

Our reservations concerning the findings of the cross-sectional
analysis of the size of the tax state in 1975 are supported by an
analysis of the expansion of the tax state in the postwar period of
economic reconstruction.[15] As Table 3 shows, the complex relationships between international economic dependence, class politics,
structures of the party system and political composition of governments are substantively different in the 1950s from what might
have been expected on the basis of the earlier findings. The expansion of the tax state in the 1950s is characterized primarily by a pattern that may aptly be called 'the politics of convergence'. The
'late-comers', i.e. nations with a comparatively small tax state in
the early 1950s, tended to have the highest rates of expansion (for

## TABLE 2
## Correlates of the size of the tax state (1975)

| Hypothesis | Indicator | Result[3] |
|---|---|---|
| 'Party control does matter' | Dominant tendency in government, 1960-75 | $r_s = 0.41$ |
| | Social democratic prime minister (% of months, 1960-75) | $r = 0.46$ |
| | 'Left-wing parties' in government (percentage of months, 1960-75) | $r = 0.30$ |
| 'Structure of party system and structure of the political tendencies' | 'Left-wing seats' (average share, 1960-75) | $r = 0.34$ |
| | Relative dominant party, 1960-75 | $r_s = 0.45$ |
| | Cohesion of the bourgeois tendency, 1960-75 (1 = weak, 0 = strong) | $r = 0.37$ |
| | Cohesion of left-wing tendency, 1960-75 (1 = strong, 0 = weak) | $r = 0.12$ |
| 'Extra-parliamentary distribution of power' | Left-wing vote (average share, 1960-75) | $r = 0.44$ |
| | Social democratic vote (average share, 1960-75) | $r = 0.38$ |
| | Corporatism | $r_s = 0.11$ |
| | Strikes—long-run change in involvement (1 = decrease, 2 = stable, 3 = increase)[1] | $r_s = -0.35$ |
| | Union density[1] | $r_s = 0.38$ |
| | Importance of union confederation in collective bargaining[1] | $r_s = 0.48$ |
| 'Institutions' | Federalism ( = 1)/centralism( = 0) | $r = -0.30$ |
| 'Integration in the world market' | Imports and exports (%GNP, 1975) | $r = 0.57$ |
| 'Economic and social structure' | Economic growth rates (average increase per capita at constant prices, 1960-75)[2] | $r = -0.21$ |
| | Inflation (consumer price index average, 1960-75) | $r = -0.35$ |
| | Size of agricultural sector, 1975 | $r = -0.31$ |
| | Size of wage and salary dependent labour force, 1975 | $r = 0.32$ |
| | Population, 1975 | $r = -0.37$ |
| 'Initial size of tax state' | Tax state, 1960 | $r = 0.75$ |

$(N = 21)$

1. N = 18.
2. N = 20
3. $r_s$ = Spearman's rank-order correlation coefficient; $r$ = Pearson's product moment correlation coefficient. For intercorrelations between independent variables, see Appendix 1.

*Source:* Korpi and Shalev, 1979.

## TABLE 3
### Macrosocietal determinants of the growth of the tax state (bivariate relationships)

| Hypothesis | Independent variables | 1950-60 | 1960-75 | 1974-77 |
|---|---|---|---|---|
| 'Party control does matter' | Dominant tendency in government[1] | 0.18 | 0.29 | 0.26 |
| | 'Left-wing-party' prime minister | 0.49 | 0.42 | 0.07 |
| | Left-wing parties in office | 0.31 | 0.26 | 0.31 |
| 'Structure of party systems and political tendencies' | Left-wing seats | 0.24 | 0.34 | 0.41 |
| | Dominant party in party system[1] | 0.21 | 0.51 | 0.42 |
| | Cohesion of bourgeois tendency (1 = weak, 0 = strong) | -0.21 | 0.40 | -0.29 |
| | Cohesion of left-wing tendency (1 = strong, 0 = weak) | -0.21 | 0.34 | 0.26 |
| 'Extra-parliamentary distribution of power' | Left-wing vote | 0.25 | 0.30 | 0.41 |
| | Corporatism (1 = weak, 2 = medium, 3 = strong)[1] | | 0.13 | 0.37 |
| | Strike | | -0.52[2] | -0.37[3] [8] |
| | Union density[1] | | 0.36[2] | 0.29[4] |
| | Importance of trade unions confederation in collective bargaining[1] | | 0.43 | 0.37 |
| 'Institutions' | Federalism (= 1)/Centralism (= 0) | -0.09 | -0.32 | -0.35 |
| 'Openness of the economy' | Import and export as % GDP at t-1 | -0.35 | 0.53 | 0.54[5] |
| | Import and export as % of GDP, change between t and t-1 | 0.52 | 0.17 | |
| 'Economics and social structure' | Economic growth rates (per capita, constant prices) | 0.41[6] | -0.11[6] | -0.72 |
| | Size of agricultural sector at t-1 | 0.19[6] | -0.32 | -0.19[5] |

**TABLE 3 (continued)**

| | | | |
|---|---|---|---|
| Change in size of agricultural sector between t and t-1 | -0.08[6] | 0.30 | |
| Size of wage and salary dependent labour force at t | -0.17 | 0.14 | 0.46[5] |
| Change of size in wage and salary-dependent labour force between t and t-1 | -0.63 | -0.07 | |
| Rate of inflation | 0.14 | -0.34 | -0.22 |
| 'Tax state in previous period' Tax state at t-1 | -0.67 | 0.36 | 0.29 |
| Number of cases | 21 | 21 | 20[7] |

*Notes to Table 3*

1. The coefficients are Spearman's rank-order correlation coefficient. All other coefficients are Pearsonian product—moment correlation coefficients. Since our sample is identical with the population we did not report significance levels. Those who really go in for significance tests will remember that with 21 cases the critical value of the coefficients at the 0.1 level is some ±0.3 and some ±0.37 at the 0.05 level.

2. Data taken from Korpi and Shalev (1979). The indicators cover the total postwar period.
3. For the measurement of the strike indicator see end note 6.
4. Pearson's r. The data on union density are for the mid-1970s.
5. 1975 data for import/export.
6. Number of cases: 20.
7. Data for Israel were not available.
8. N=18.

For intercorrelations between independent variables see Appendices 1, 2 and 3.

example, Israel, Australia and Italy), whereas the governments that already presided over an extensive tax state at that time were, apart from Sweden, much more hesitant to increase the tax and social security burden $(r = -0.67)$. One can plausibly argue that the expansion of the tax state in the late-comer nations was a reaction of the governments to gaps in the provisions of public goods and services, which tended to become both politically and economically more dangerous with developing imbalances within the capitalist structure. Such imbalances include increasing competition from abroad, a factor obviously enhanced by the degree of integration into the world market, and the growing problem of reconciling the accumulation and legitimation requirements of states simultaneously attempting to realize democratic goals within a structure imposed by the imperatives of capitalist production.

It was, however, under specific economic and domestic political conditions that those requirements and imperatives were actually translated into policy. To a degree, and with complex relationships, which vary, the expansion tended to be more pronounced the more that external dependence increased $(r = 0.52)$, thereby necessitating rapid assertion of control over the domestic repercussions of enhanced integration into the world market. Similarly, we find a positive association with economic growth rates $(r = 0.41)$, presumably because the expansion of the economic resource base allowed for a greater growth in the public economy without strong opposition. On the political side, there is a relation between expansion of the tax state and left-wing control of the major offices of state $(r = 0.49)$; and, in at least some countries, it appears that a larger public sector was a more feasible objective where organizational and ideological splits within the bourgeois political tendency allowed governments a greater room for manoeuvre.

Looking at the individual countries demonstrates the mixed picture in respect of the impact of partisan control of government. While the general tendency is for there to be a greater expansion in the extractive capacity of the state where the political composition of government is skewed to the Left, three out of five of the leaders in this process — Australia, Iceland and Italy — were characterized by 'bourgeois hegemony' (see Table 1). Of the three nations in which social democracy was either hegemonistic (Norway) or dominant (Israel and Sweden) in the 1950s, the latter two were also among the leaders and Norway came seventh, just after Denmark, which itself had a long tradition of social democratic government. On this basis, there is some support for the view that partisan control does really matter, but it is by no means as conclusive as has been suggested in some parts of the literature. Moreover, it seems clear that, at best, social democratic political ascendency is a sufficient rather than a necessary condition for the expansion of the tax state.

A similar conclusion is appropriate in respect of Cameron's explanation in terms of the impact of integration into the world economy. Although it is the case that governments tended to expand their extractive capacity in order to control the domestic consequences of a rapid increase in external dependence, some nations deviated from this trend. Thus, it seems necessary to specify more fully the economic and political structures and processes that intervene in the complex interrelationship between international dependence, the political complexion of governments and policy inputs. In the 1950s differential economic growth rates and the need to make up for lost time seem to be the most important intervening variables. This conclusion does not preclude the real possibility of idiosyncratic factors also playing a major role in conditioning the extractive capacity of the state. Certainly, it would seem that the zero growth of the tax state in Switzerland in the 1950s must be put down to a combination of the political culture and institutional barriers to reform. Nevertheless, the conclusion may be regarded as a valid indicator of the overall trend in the 21 countries under investigation.

## The expansion of the tax state between 1960 and 1975

In the 1960s and early 1970s most governments expanded the extractive capacity of the state very considerably. The rates of expansion of the tax state exceeded by far those typical of the postwar period of reconstruction. A large proportion of the resources extracted from the economy was, during this period, shifted into welfare state programmes, educational and health expenditure. Many of the reasons for these developments are discussed in great detail in the earlier contribution on patterns of public expenditure, and here we shall only outline the broad characteristics of the upsurge in the extent of the tax state that are necessary to understand the nature of the postwar development as a whole.

The findings reported in Table 3 concerning the expansion of the public economy from 1960 to 1975 again offer support for both the 'party control does matter' hypothesis and an explanation in terms of international economic dependency. The major differences in comparison with the 1950s are that structures of class conflict gain more importance as determinants of tax state expansion, that convergent tendencies disappear, and that economic growth rates no longer appear to be systematically related to the development of the public economy. Of these changes, the most dramatic is the cessation of the catching-up phenomenon, and the appearance of evidence that it was nations that possessed a major extractive capacity in the early 1960s that most rapidly expanded the extent of the public economy in the subsequent period ($r = 0.36$).

Thus, while the political composition of government and the relative openness of the economy continue to be conducive to the expansion of the tax state, there emerge in the 1960s a new set of intervening factors, which are important predictors of variation among the capitalist democracies. These factors include the degree of cohesiveness of the bourgeois tendency, the power distribution between the Left and the bourgeois milieux, and the relative strength of organized labour. The role played by the structuring and size of the bourgeois tendency is of particular interest, because, clearly, some of the influences involved are the same as those previously identified in the negative impact of parties of the Right on patterns of public expenditure. However, our conceptualization of the situation differs from that advanced in the earlier essay. We see the influence of the bourgeois tendency not exclusively in terms of their control of the levers of governmental power, but rather in terms of varying constellations of class forces opposing or being open to pressure to foster the expansion of the tax state. Indeed, the fact that bourgeois governmental control is only one of a number of factors involved is actually suggested by the findings presented in the earlier chapter, in so far as there are more strong relationships reported for right-wing parliamentary seats than for right-wing cabinet seats. This is, at least, indicative that it is the overall strength of rightist tendencies that is the decisive factor (see pp. 62-63 above).

What is evident is that, whether governmental power was held by bourgeois or leftist parties, organizational and ideological splits within the bourgeois tendency created fewer impediments to the expansion of the public economy than where a large and politically united bourgeois tendency disposed of strong veto power within the political system ($r = 0.40$). Thus, a government made up of social democratic and left-wing parties, committed to reform policies, comprehensive labour market intervention and macroeconomic demand management, which was confronted with an organizationally and ideologically split bourgeois opposition (e.g. Sweden until 1976; Norway and Denmark) had much more room for manoeuvre than the Social Democratic-Free Democratic coalition in West Germany from 1969 onwards. Even under bourgeois rule the lack of cohesion of the bourgeois tendency facilitated the expansion of the tax state, in particular in those cases where a left-wing party was the single major party and in which the labour movement was strong. One can distinguish between three major constellations in this respect: first, a case where one of the parties in a bourgeois coalition government — usually the strongest one — has close links to the trade unions and comparatively strong working-class support, and is thus more sensitive to demands for enhanced state intervention (e.g. Belgium and the Netherlands); second, the case of those bourgeois coalitions in which consensus-building and the practice of mutual overbidding results in an expansion of state expenditures, thereby requiring an increased extractive capacity of the state (e.g. Denmark and Norway under bourgeois coalitions in the late 1960s); third, the case of bourgeois governments faced with a power distribution between the left-wing and bourgeois milieux which approximates to a situation of balance and in which the single largest party is left-wing in complexion. It is under these conditions that even conservative parties are, more often than not, under strong indirect pressure to adopt some of the demands aggregated by the opposition parties.

At least in some countries, of which Denmark, the Netherlands and West Germany might be the best examples, the impact of the cleavage between leftist and bourgeois milieux was further reinforced by the combined influence of two factors. On the one hand, these countries experienced a 'resurgence of class conflict' in the 1960s and early 1970s, which had the effect that, over a period of time, the burden that labour imposed on capital was shifted over to the state. Moreover, this reappearance of class conflict also tended to disrupt formerly stable modes of conflict resolution with the breakup of the Dutch system of 'pillarization' being the most dramatic example. On the other hand, the growing importance of so-called 'post-materialistic' values in many Western nations also created an impetus for government intervention, particularly in respect of expanding educational provision. Where intensified class struggle was conjoined with new values and faced by weakened decision-making structures, the pressures for a strong upsurge in the extent of the tax state were irresistible.

Finally, it should be mentioned that, in terms of the sources of revenue accruing to the state, the expansion of the public economy was primarily financed by the absolute extension of indirect taxes and by the absolute and relative extension of the direct taxes and social security contributions (OECD, 1978). The increasing importance of indirect taxation was particularly dramatic under social democratic rule, which is surprising in so far as one might have expected governments of this complexion to have favoured the more potentially redistributive mechanism of direct taxes. Indeed, there is an implication here that the growth of the tax state did not necessarily have any major redistributive impact. This view is supported in so far as the OECD tax progression indicator does not vary systematically with indicators of the political composition of governments (OECD, 1978: 57).

*The development of the tax state*
*in the crisis of the 1970s*

It is frequently argued that the vast expansion of the 1960s and the early 1970s was strongly facilitated by the favourable economic conditions in this period. Rates of economic growth were, generally speaking, high, and rates of unemployment and inflation were relatively low. Governments were, therefore, in a position in which they could expand the extractive capacities of the state without causing dangerous political opposition from those who ultimately had to pay the bill. The question that must now be examined is what happened to the tax state in the crisis of the 1970s, when, for the most part, growth rates declined and rates of unemployment and inflation went up.

The governments of the advanced democratic states adopted very diverse strategies to cope with the new situation. Some of them continued to expand the tax state at the same rate as before or even at a faster pace (e.g. Austria, Luxembourg and Sweden). Some of them slowed down the rate of expansion (e.g. Norway and Denmark), and some of them more or less halted growth of the tax state (e.g. the USA and Canada). Only in Australia did the size of the tax state actually manifest a significant decline. Apart from the nations in the first group, the governments seem to have paid tribute to the conventional notion that too rapid an expansion of the public sector can provoke reaction by social groups aiming to restore their accustomed share of income and output, and that such a competition for scarce resources can be a major source of inflationary pressure and aggravate the risk that future growth prospects will be diminished by conflict over resources allocation.

When we come to examine the impact of political and socioeconomic factors on tax state development during this period, we are confronted with the problem that our measurement of the dependent variable tends to inflate the figures whenever the economy is depressed. This is because it relates total revenues to GDP, and because, in periods of economic crisis, unemployment insurance, the social wage and early retirement schemes expand the costs of social security both in absolute terms and relative to GDP. Thus, it is hardly surprising that, overall, nations with low levels of economic growth tended to expand the tax state strongly and that nations with a more resilient economy manifested the opposite tendency. Thus, it was low-growth nations, such as Sweden, New Zealand, Luxembourg and Switzerland, that report the strongest expansion of the public economy in this period, whereas Norway, whose high economic growth was largely predicated on oil wealth, only increased the share of the tax state as a percentage of GDP by some 1.6 percentage points (see Table 1). The general strength of this tendency is indicated by the fact that some 50 percent of the total variance in the expansion of the tax state during this period is statistically 'explained' by economic growth rates alone.

However, an examination of the residuals suggests additional insights into the policy processes that characterized the crisis period. As Table 4 demonstrates, once we have accounted for that proportion of the variance that is explained by economic growth, there remain important political factors at work. Relative to what one would expect on the basis of bivariate regression estimates, the expansion of the tax state was markedly overproportionate under social democratic rule (e.g. in Austria and Sweden until 1976) and in countries where the dominant tendency in government was balanced (e.g. Luxembourg). In contrast, in certain countries where the bourgeois tendency was either hegemonic or dominant the expansion of the public economy was much lower than might have been expected on the basis of economic growth rates alone (e.g. Australia, Canada, Iceland and Switzerland).

The inverse relationship observed between the average rate of economic growth and the expansion of the tax state seems at first sight to be compatible with the conventional view of many conservative economists, that economic growth tends to be stronger to the

**TABLE 4**
**The expansion of the tax state between 1973 and 1977**
**(regression with economic growth rates)**

| Country | Actual rate of expansion (Y) | predicted rate of expansion (Y')[1] | Residuals (Y-Y') |
|---|---|---|---|
| Australia | − 2.8 | 3.6 | -6.4 |
| Austria | 5.0 | 1.2 | 3.8 |
| Belgium | 5.4 | 3.6 | 1.8 |
| Canada | 0.2 | 2.9 | -2.7 |
| Denmark | 2.0 | 2.6 | -0.6 |
| Finland | 5.0 | 5.6 | -0.6 |
| France | 3.6 | 2.1 | 1.5 |
| FRG | 2.3 | 2.1 | 0.2 |
| Iceland | 1.3 | 3.4 | -2.1 |
| Israel | — | — | — |
| Italy | 3.6 | 4.9 | -1.3 |
| Japan | 1.3 | 0.6 | 0.7 |
| Luxembourg | 13.7 | 9.8 | 4.9 |
| New Zealand | 7.9 | 8.5 | -0.6 |
| Netherlands | 4.8 | 3.9 | 0.9 |
| Norway | 1.6 | -1.1 | 2.7 |
| Sweden | 12.3 | 7.0 | 5.3 |
| Switzerland | 5.5 | 8.6 | -3.1 |
| UK | 3.6 | 4.1 | -0.5 |
| USA | 0.8 | 2.1 | -1.3 |

1. The linear prediction equation was $Y' = 5.95 - 1.69 (X)$, $r = -0.72$
where $Y'$ is the predicted rate of expansion and $X$ is the average annual rate of economic growth per capita at constant prices.

extent that the state refrains from excessive intervention in the private economy. Time-series analyses for the individual countries do not, however, support this view, either for the 1960s or 1970s.[16] Moreover, the conservative view would imply a moderate to strong inverse relationship between the size of the tax state before the crisis set in and the rate of economic growth in the subsequent years. Our analysis suggests, however, that such a relationship does not exist (the correlation between the size of the tax state in 1973 and the average rate of economic growth per capita in real terms between 1973 and 1977 is $r = 0.29$ with 20 cases). Indeed, it is apparent that consciously adopted policies of state intervention may foster high economic growth. The altogether favourable economic performance of Austria is, for instance, largely a consequence of compensatory demand management combined with incomes policy, a hard currency policy approach and a wide variety of selective labour market measures.[17] The Norwegian case points in much the same direction. During the mid-1970s Norway was able to combine a very high growth rate with one of the largest public economies among the capitalist democracies. While Norway's good fortune in possessing adequate domestic energy resources facilitated this development, it is quite clear that the government's demand management, labour market and industrial policies contributed to the outcome.[18]

As a final point concerning the impact of economic factors during the crisis, it should be noted that our findings also reaffirm the importance of the relative openness of the economy in promoting the growth of the public economy ($r = 0.54$). Since in this period the openness of the economy was not strongly correlated with economic growth rates ($r = 0.35$), we may safely conclude that both of these factors have an independent impact on the development of the tax state. However, an economic explanation in these terms remains incomplete in so far as it fails to specify the linkages through which the pressures and imperatives inherent in economic circumstances are fed into the policy formulation process and ultimately translated into policy outputs. To understand these linkages, we must focus our attention on a number of political factors.

The picture in respect of the impact of the political composition of governments is far from straightforward. We have already noted that some social democratic governments expanded the public sector far more than would have been predicted on the basis of their economic growth rates. However, in general terms the 'party control does matter' hypothesis is not systematically supported, and there is no clear dividing line between the policies pursued by governments of different political complexion. The differential performance of governments with strong social democratic parties helps to illustrate this point. In the period 1973-77 Austria and Norway were ruled exclusively by their respective social democratic parties, while in Denmark, Germany, Sweden and the United Kingdom the social democrats were the dominant parties of government. However, as we have already seen, it was only in Austria and Sweden that there was a substantial concomitant increase in the size of the tax state, a performance largely reflecting those countries' reliance on active demand management and labour market policies. In contrast, the expansion of the tax state was much more muted in Norway, Denmark and West Germany. The performance of the United Kingdom falls roughly between these two groups.

There would seem to be evidence for the view that the low degree of expansion of the tax state in certain social democratic countries was a consequence of government reaction to the threat imposed by tax protest movements: the Progress Party in Denmark, which suddenly in 1973 became the second largest party; the Anders Lange Party in Norway; and the fear on the part of the Social Democratic-Free Democratic coalition in Germany that they might lose decisive parts of their electoral base to a new tax protest party, which Herman Fredersdorf, a former member of the SPD, planned to organize.[19] Tax protest movements made the governments in these countries extremely sensitive concerning tax policy issues, since further distributive or redistributive policies on the part of the social democrats risked their potential demise at the hands of a coalition of conservative elements plus disaffected former supporters.

Moreover, the muted expansion of the tax state in these countries has to be seen in perspective. In all of them, the size of the tax state was comparatively great throughout the period under review, and the same pattern holds true as far as government expenditure is concerned. Public spending on income maintenance, education, public health and general welfare, measured as a percentage of GDP in 1974, was, and is, very high in these countries, as it is also in other countries that have experienced long periods of social democratic rule.[20] In other words, it might be argued that Denmark, Norway and Germany could afford a pause in the expansion of the public economy, since they had adequate funds and levers at their disposal to cope with the social and political repercussions of the economic crisis while simultaneously pursuing structural policies and applying demand management.

While the expansion of the tax state in the mid-1970s is largely independent of which party is in power, the extra-parliamentary distribution of power is an important explanatory factor. The increase in the size of the public economy was the stronger:
— the higher the left-wing vote and, thus, the greater the power distribution between the left milieu and the bourgeois milieu was balanced ($r = 0.41$);
— the greater the strength of trade union organization ($r = 0.37$);

— the more the power of the labour movement was institutionalized in corporatist arrangements ($r_S = 0.37$);
— the lower the strike volume ($r = -0.37$);
— the higher the share of wage- and salary-dependent labour as a
percentage of the civilian labour force ($r = 0.46$).

The fact that the influence of the various indicators of extra-
parliamentary distribution of power is so consistent suggests that
here we are tapping an independent explanatory factor of some importance, and this conclusion is reinforced by the absence of any
strong interrelationship with the economic factors already identified as causes of the expansion of the tax state during the
economic crisis.

In summary, the results of our analysis suggest that, in the
mid-1970s the development of the tax state was determined largely
by a syndrome of economic circumstances, of which economic
growth and integration into the world economy were the most important, conditioned by the impact of the extra-parliamentary
power distribution on the course of governmental policy. As will
become apparent subsequently, such a finding is broadly compatible with the trends apparent in the determination of other aspects
of macroeconomic policy in the 1970s. The extra-parliamentary
power distribution between the leftist and bourgeois tendencies, the
organizational strength of the labour movement and its strength
within corporatist institutions shape the general course of governmental policies, quite frequently almost wholly regardless of which
party is in office.

## The determinants of the tax state

Our analysis has shown that the causal mechanisms that shape the
size and the rates of expansion of the tax state vary over time. One
would, however, be justified in concluding that the evidence derived from the entire period points to a complex relationship, in which
a constellation of socioeconomic and political factors combine to
produce a large and expansive tax state. Those factors include:
— an economy relatively open to world trade;
— a power distribution between the left and the bourgeois milieux
which comes close to a balance;
— a strong and united labour movement, whose strength is, addi-
tionally, institutionalized in corporate modes of conflict resolution;

— an ideologically and organizationally divided bourgeois tendency;

— a very strong government made up of social democratic parties and left-wing allies.

The consequences of a highly developed tax state in terms of equality and welfare have been much debated in the literature on the development of the welfare state, and some conclusions concerning the relative generosity of the capitalist democracies in terms of public income maintenance expenditure, health and educational spending were reported in the chapter on patterns of public expenditure. However, our primary concern in the remaining sections of this chapter will be with the question of the extent to which the differential size of the tax state has had an impact on the successful political control of pending system problems in capitalist societies. Did all those governments that dispose of a large tax state, and thus control many levers for steering the economy, really employ their resources in such a way as to bring the basic and structurally given instabilities of a private economy under control? In particular, did they succeed in controlling the inflationary pressures and unemployment problems that characterize contemporary capitalism? Finally, were there systematic differences in respect of these aspects of macroeconomic policy under social democratic and bourgeois rule? It is to these issues that we now turn.

## Macro-societal determinants of rates of unemployment (1974-1978)

After a long postwar period of economic prosperity, many capitalist economies have been plagued by poor economic growth, high inflation and substantial unemployment since the early 1970s. These economic conditions are generally acknowledged to be the root cause of a variety of major political and social problems experienced in the contemporary capitalist democracies. Low growth and high unemployment reduce the state's revenue and increase the demand for social and economic intervention by the state. Thus is created a fiscal crisis of the state. In addition, low growth simultaneously reduces the potential for wage increases for the dependent labour force and tends to squeeze the margin available to profit. Together, these factors tend to undermine the strong industrial consensus brought about by postwar prosperity in many of the industrial societies of the West. High rates of inflation change the distribution of real income and wealth both within and between classes. It tends to worsen the position of low-income groups and of groups with small to medium wealth, and it also tends to affect negatively those taxpayers who contribute disproportionately to the financing of the expansion of the public sector. High unemployment reduces not only the overall standard of living, but also the quality of life and the degree of social integration of those who are laid off. Looked at from the point of view of the working-class movement, high rates of unemployment also have the effect of undermining the economic power of organized and unorganized labour.

During the economic crisis there has been a general consensus on the part of employers, trade unions and the state that high levels of economic growth should be a primary objective of economic policy. However, serious conflict has emerged concerning the relative priority of low inflation and low unemployment. The trade unions and the Left in general have been typically far more willing to tolerate higher rates of inflation if unemployment could be minimized. In contrast, the employers and the bourgeois tendency as a whole saw the foremost objective as containing the price explosion, even if this involved serious dangers on the employment front.

Although all the capitalist democracies were confronted with economic crisis from 1974 onwards, the political response of the authorities, trade unions and employers differed considerably. So too did the macroeconomic outcomes of the policies adopted. International comparisons reveal a wide range of variation in labour market policies and labour market outcomes, such as the rate of unemployment and the change in the labour force participation ratio. Thus, Austria, Sweden, Norway, Japan, Switzerland, Iceland and Luxembourg continuously reported low unemployment figures, whereas the USA, Britain, West Germany, France, Italy and many other countries have found it much more difficult to control unemployment in the 1970s. In this section we focus on the determinants of the rate of unemployment in the capitalist democracies since the onset of the recession in 1973/74, and in the next we examine the variation in inflation rates for the same period.

*Hypotheses*

Comparative research on the determinants of rates of unemployment across the full range of capitalist democracies has, hitherto, been a somewhat undeveloped area of study.[21] Analysis has generally been restricted to one-country studies or, at best, has taken in a relatively small sample of countries. The overall findings of research on the determinants of unemployment have, moreover, been somewhat contradictory. Generally speaking, one can distinguish between two competing explanatory models, one socioeconomic and the other political in character. According to the socioeconomic model, rates of unemployment are primarily dependent on economic, demographic and labour supply variables. According to the political model, political business cycles, preferences of governing parties and the structures of extra-parliamentary political arenas are the major determinants of rates of unemployment. A more detailed literature review reveals that the following eight hypotheses seem to be particularly important (see Schmidt, 1979: 91-99).

1. *Economic hypotheses.* Economic hypotheses state that the level and the expansion of the rate of unemployment vary strongly with indicators of the state of economic development. Marx's law of accumulation, for example, predicts a strong direct relationship between the size of the industrial reserve army and the level of economic development. Keynesian and radical political economists and econometricians have further suggested that the rate of unemployment varies positively with the level of technological development and inversely with levels of aggregate demand, business cycles, the rate of profit and the rate of inflation (see Nowotny, 1974; and Hunt and Sherman, 1978).

2. *Labour supply hypotheses* (see, for example, Havemann, 1978). Labour market studies in the 1960s and 1970s supplement the economic explanations of the incidence of unemployment with a stress on the importance of the availability of labour and the structure of the labour market. For example, it was argued that the expansion and the level of unemployment vary directly with the level, the composition and the expansion of the labour force and of the population between 15 and 64 years of age, and, further, with the degree to which labour markets are segmented. One could complete this list with what might be called the 'foreign labour force' hypothesis. It is well known that all nations with a relatively large foreign labour force established restrictive immigration controls in the early 1970s and have thereafter tended to treat migrant workers as an easy target for exporting unemployment (Krane, 1979). One might, therefore, hypothesize that countries with a substantial

foreign labour force in the early 1970s would, by the mid-1970s, be characterized by comparatively low domestic rates of unemployment owing to the export of their industrial reserve army.

3. *The world market integration hypothesis.* In our earlier discussion of the expansion of the tax state, we confirmed the importance of the relative openness of the economy as a factor influencing that aspect of macroeconomic policy. Although it was not the major focus of the original study by Cameron, he premises his whole argument concerning the expansion of the public economy on the macroeconomic problems of control imposed by involuntary exposure to world economic trends. Clearly, these problems are likely to be particularly acute in the field of employment policy.[22] On the basis of Cameron's study, and an awareness that integration into the world economy has political as well as purely economic aspects, it might be argued that the rate of unemployment is directly related to the degree to which nations are economically and politically integrated in the world market and its political superstructure (i.e., EEC, NATO, etc). On this supposition, one would expect that the government's capacity and willingness successfully to steer the labour market is the more restricted the more the national economies are dependent on the world market and the more the relative autonomy of the state is limited by integration into the political organization of the world market.

4. *The constant structure hypothesis.* It is frequently suggested that much policy-making can be understood in terms of incrementalism. A parallel pattern may be discerned in respect of economic systems. The structure, dynamics and the outcomes of an economy at time $t$ is strongly dependent on the structure, dynamics and outcomes at time $t - 1$. One might thus argue that the differential rates of unemployment in the 1970s would be strongly associated with differential rates of unemployment in the preceding period.

A major drawback of the prevailing socioeconomic explanations of rates of unemployment is that they do not fully specify the linkages that relate economic and socioeconomic characteristics to policies and macroeconomic policy outcomes. Recent contributions from sociologists and political scientists suggest that there are genuinely political structures and processes that act as the intervening variables which ultimately determine labour market policies and outcomes.

5. *The politicized labour markets hypothesis.* Since the outset of the labour market crisis in the mid-1970s, it has been frequently argued that the most restrictive barrier to full employment policy

was neither insufficient aggregate demand nor excess labour supply, but rather what may be described as the 'politicization' of
labour markets. Politicization of labour markets may be taken to
denote a phenomenon whereby the welfare policies of the state and
the egalitarian wage policies of the trade unions have restructured
and segmented labour markets to such an extent that market forces
are no longer operative, and with the unintended outcome that
unemployment increases, or at least remains constant, even in the
absence of economic recession. Comprehensive unemployment insurance schemes, minimum wage laws and employment protection
safeguards for particular segments of the labour force have been
identified as the major culprits in this process.[23] Thus, it might be
hypothesized that the rate of unemployment is the higher, the more
the practice of capitalism is softened by welfare state intervention,
and, conversely, that unemployment is least where the welfare state
is least developed.

6. *The 'party control does matter' hypothesis.* According to
many political scientists, policies are largely a function of politics.
As we have previously noted, Douglas Hibbs has argued that social
democratic governments tend to pursue policies that are keyed to
full employment irrespective of the consequences for prices, while
right-wing and centrist governments reverse these priorities (Hibbs,
1977). The general conclusion of this study is that the differential
macroeconomic policies pursued under social democratic and
bourgeois rule are broadly in accordance with the differential objective economic interests and subjective preferences of their
respective class constituencies.

7. *The party milieu hypothesis.* Research by Schmidt and Payne
has challenged the validity of Hibbs's findings, since his result is
not replicated where the sample of nations has a changed or extended composition (Schmidt, 1979: 102-13; Payne, 1979). It is,
however, interesting to note that the strength of the socialist milieu
(as measured by the left-wing vote) manifests a consistent inverse
relationship with the rate of unemployment. Here again there is a
suggestion that what is important in terms of policy determination
is the extra-parliamentary distribution of power, with a strong
socialist milieu acting as a real barrier against an unequal distribution of the costs of the economic crisis at the expense of wage-
dependent labour, irrespective of the party in office. However, as
became clear in the context of the development of the tax state, the
impact of the party milieu is also crucially conditioned by the
ideological and organizational cohesion of the bourgeois tendency.

Thus, we might also expect to find a relationship between the rate of unemployment and bourgeois cohesion, as well as with the overall power distribution between the rival tendencies as indicated by our measure of party dominance.

8. *'Corporatism does matter' hypotheses*. The extent of corporatist organization taps a further dimension of the extra-parliamentary distribution of power within the capitalist democracies. The debate on corporatist modes of policy formation and the regulation of class conflict suggest two contradictory hypotheses concerning the nature of macroeconomic policy outcomes.[24] According to one school of thought, corporatism indicates both a powerful trade union movement and a strong social integration of the labour movement into the policy network (Stephens, 1979: 123). In this view, stable corporatism presupposes successful political exchange. Trade unions tend to be more moderate in their wage policies if employers pursue moderate price policies and if the state is willing to offer compensation in other areas. Two classes of compensation are regarded as particularly important: first, policies that offer trade unions the organizational means to recruit new members and exercise effective control of rank-and-file demands; and, second, policies, such as active labour market measures, that favour the social base from which the trade unions draw their strength. On the basis of this argument, one might suggest the hypothesis that, the stronger the corporatist mode of regulating class conflict, the lower will be the rate of unemployment. However, an hypothesis premised on an equal exchange between wage moderation and employment policy may be contradicted where the corporatist arrangement is seen as involving a situation of unequal political exchange. Thus, recent studies by Leo Panitch and Harmut Wiesenthal have suggested that corporatism is quite often biased against the interests of labour as far as short-term tangible outcomes and indulgence-deprivation ratios are concerned (see Panitch, 1977; Wiesenthal, 1979). According to this school of thought, corporatism implies a strong social control over the labour movement, and such arrangements are a measure of the weakness, rather than the strength, of labour. Thus, an hypothesis deriving from the assumption of unequal political exchange would suggest that strong corporatist arrangements are likely to be found in conjunction with high rates of unemployment and, simultaneously, with high degrees of industrial consensus.

*Results of the empirical analysis*

In what follows, we shall examine the various socioeconomic and political explanations of the differential rates of unemployment in 21 capitalist countries between 1974 and 1978; 1974 is the first year of the world-wide economic recession and 1978 is the last year for which reliable data were available. The dependent data are the average rates of unemployment — expressed as a percentage of the civilian labour force — during the period under investigation.[25] The original data were taken from OECD and ILO publications. The dependent variable is trichotomized in terms of high, medium and low rates of unemployment. 'High unemployment' is defined as a rate of unemployment that exceeds the 5 percent mark. 'Medium' rates of unemployment are larger than 2 percent and equal to or smaller than 5 percent. 'Low' rates of unemployment are equal to or smaller than 2 percent.

Although rank ordering results in a loss of information as compared with the originally reported data, it is in fact both a useful and an appropriate device. First, it goes much of the way towards solving the problem of the universally accepted limited comparability of unemployment statistics. We cannot safely treat the OECD and ILO figures as interval scale variables; but we can safely say that Ireland's rate of unemployment is higher than that of Germany, and the rate of Germany is higher than that in either Austria or Sweden. Second, the cut-off point at 2 percent (low versus medium) is not as arbitrarily chosen as might appear. The 'normal' frictional rate of unemployment in developed capitalist economies is generally taken to have its upper limit at the 2 percent mark. In addition, a low rate of unemployment is one of the most fundamental prerequisites for creating the potentiality of reform policy, whereas medium and high rates of unemployment are in the long term detrimental to the maintenance and expansion of welfare capitalism.[26]

In addition to the independent variables discussed in previous sections, certain other indicators were utilized. Demographic aspects of labour supply were measured by the change in the population of working age (15 to 64) as a percentage of the total population between 1974 and 1976 (data for 1978 were not yet available). In addition, labour force participation ratios were used, but data were available for only nine countries.[27] A high welfare/low welfare dichotomy was employed to test the politicization of labour markets hypothesis. Integration into the world

## TABLE 5
### Rates of unemployment and political and economic determinants, 1974-1978

| | Ave. rate of unemployment, 1974-78 | Ave. rate of unemployment, 1960-73 | Corporatism, (1974-78) | Left-wing vote, 1974-78 | Dominant tendency in government, 1974-78 | Ave. annual rate of economic growth p.c. (real terms) 1974-78 | Ave. annual rate of inflation (consumer prices) 1974-78 |
|---|---|---|---|---|---|---|---|
| Australia | High | Low | Medium | 45.0 | Balance | 1.66 | 12.8 |
| Austria | Low | Medium | Strong | 51.5 | Soc. dem. hegemony | 2.86 | 6.9 |
| Belgium | High | Medium | Medium | 29.6 | Bourgeois dominance | 2.10 | 9.2 |
| Canada | High | High | Weak | 16.6 | Bourgeois hegemony | 2.24 | 9.2 |
| Denmark | High | Medium | Medium | 41.2 | Soc. dem. dominance | 1.38 | 11.0 |
| Finland | Medium | Medium | Medium | 43.3 | Balance | 1.34 | 13.8 |
| France | Medium | Low | Weak | 42.5 | Bourgeois hegemony | 2.54 | 10.7 |
| FRG | Medium | Low | Medium | 44.5 | Soc. dem. dominance | 2.24 | 4.8 |
| Iceland | Low | Low | Medium | 32.6 | Bourgeois dominance | 2.28 | 39.8 |
| Ireland | High | High | Weak | 14.1 | Bourgeois dominance | 2.82 | 15.3 |
| Israel | Medium | Medium | Medium | 37.8 | Balance | 2.90 | 35.0[1] |
| Italy | Medium | Medium | Weak | 41.9 | Bourgeois dominance | 1.58 | 17.0 |
| Japan | Low | Low | Strong | 38.4 | Bourgeois hegemony | 2.32 | 11.3 |
| Luxembourg | Low | Low | Medium | 48.3 | Balance | 0.70 | 7.9 |
| New Zealand | Low | Low | Medium | 42.8 | Balance | -0.92 | 13.8 |
| Netherlands | Medium | Low | Medium | 36.8 | Bourgeois dominance | 1.78 | 7.8 |
| Norway | Low | Low | Strong | 47.5 | Soc. dem. hegemony | 4.12 | 9.5 |
| Sweden | Low | Low | Strong | 48.2 | Balance | -0.10 | 10.3 |
| Switzerland | Low | Low | Strong | 26.4 | Bourgeois dominance | -0.44 | 4.1 |
| UK | Medium | Medium | Weak | 40.0 | Soc. dem. dominance | 1.10 | 16.1 |
| USA | High | Medium | Weak | 0.0 | Bourgeois hegemony | 1.80 | 8.0 |

1. 1973-77

## TABLE 6

### Hypothesized relationships and results of the empirical analysis — determinants of average rates of unemployment, 1974-78

| Research hypothesis | Empirical indicator | Hypothesized relationship | Actual relationship[1] | Conclusion |
|---|---|---|---|---|
| 'Constant structure' | Average rate of unemployment, 1960-73 | Positive | 0.63 | Confirmed |
| 'Economic hypotheses' | GDP per capita, 1978 (US$) | Positive | -0.17[4] | Not confirmed |
| | % wage labour, 1975 | Positive | -0.44 | Not confirmed |
| | Economic growth, 1974-78: GDP per capita, real terms (average annual change) | Inverse | 0.25 | Not confirmed |
| | Average annual rate of inflation, 1974-78 (consumer prices) | Inverse | 0.09 | Not confirmed |
| 'Demographic and labour supply — hypotheses' | Population between 15 and 64 as % total population, 1974-76 (first difference) | Positive | -0.39 | Not confirmed |
| | Foreign labour-importing countries (= 1; else = 0) | Inverse | 0.13[2] | Not confirmed |
| 'World market integration hypothesis' | 1 = strong political and economic integration: 0 = else | Positive | 0.29[2] | Not confirmed |
| 'Politicized labour markets' | 1 = strong welfare state; 0 = else | Positive | 0.10[2] | Not confirmed |
| 'Party control does matter' | Dominant tendency in government, 1974-78 | Inverse | -0.25 | Not confirmed |
| | Left-wing parties in government, 1974-78 | Inverse | -0.32 | Weakly confirmed |

**TABLE 6 (continued)**

| 'Structure of the party system' | Cohesion of bourgeois tendency (1 = weak; 0 = strong) | Inverse | 0.16[2] | Not confirmed |
|---|---|---|---|---|
| | Dominant party | Inverse | -0.33 | Weakly confirmed |
| 'Extra-parliamentary distribution of power', | Left-wing vote, 1974-78 | Inverse | -0.48 | Confirmed |
| 'Corporatism' | Corporatism | Inverse[3] | -0.67 | Confirmed |

*Notes:*

1. Spearman's rho if not otherwise indicated, $N = 21$.
2. lambda$_a$.
3. Inverse relationship hypothesized for the 'equal exchange hypothesis'.
4. $N = 20$.

market and its political superstructure was also measured as a
dichotomous variable (high/low — based on imports/exports as a
percentage of GNP and on membership in strongly integrated
economic and military alliances). The constant structure hypothesis
was made testable by predicting a direct relationship between
average rates of unemployment from 1960 to 1973 and from 1974
to 1978.

Excerpts from the data base are presented in Table 5. Table 6
summarizes the hypothesized relationships and the overall results
of the empirical analysis.

## The impact of economic and socioeconomic structures and processes

The relationship between the rate of unemployment in the earlier
period from 1960 to 1973 and in the later period of economic crisis
is of medium strength ($r_S = 0.63$). A cross-tabulation makes it possible to think in terms of nations with constant and changing performance. While the majority of nations with low unemployment in
the earlier period came close to full employment in the mid-1970s as
well, the labour market performance of West Germany, France,
Australia, Belgium, Denmark, the USA and the Netherlands
deteriorated with varying degrees of seriousness. In these latter nations, and in those that maintained constant profiles of medium
and high unemployment, the economic crisis of the 1970s had a
direct and fairly strong impact on the labour market, whereas
labour market problems in the low-unemployment countries seem
to have been more muted or even totally absent. It is this differential responsiveness of the labour markets of the capitalist
democracies that requires explanation.

Such an explanation is not to be found in either the economic or
the labour supply hypothesis, as the results in Table 6 reveal. There
is no systematic evidence in support of the assumption that the rate
of unemployment is directly dependent on rates of economic
growth or inflation, and these findings are further confirmed by
time-series analysis for the individual countries in the 1960s and
1970s.[28] Moreover, the negligible relationship in the data between
inflation and unemployment clearly contradicts the conventional
wisdom of an inverse inflation-unemployment mix. The trade-off
characteristic of these two aspects of macroeconomic policy is an
important aspect of Hibbs's argument, and the absence of em-

# TABLE 7
## Responsiveness of labour markets to economic growth — results of time-series analyses, 1970-78

| Country | $r^2$ | Linear regression estimates | Durbin-Watson statistics | Type of responsiveness |
|---------|-------|------------------------------|---------------------------|------------------------|
| | (1) | (2) | (3) | (4) |
| Australia | 0.59 | $Y = 1.72—0.512 (X)$ | 2.82 | Strong |
| Austria | 0.01 | $Y = -0.02—0.014 (X)$ | 2.0 | Low |
| Belgium | 0.42 | $Y = 1.54—0.24 (X)$ | 1.16 | Strong |
| Canada | 0.67 | $Y = 1.24—0.256 (X)$ | 1.44 | Strong |
| Denmark | 0.48 | $Y = 1.4 —0.356 (X)$ | 1.05 | Strong |
| Finland | 0.65 | $Y = 1.4 —0.269 (X)$ | 1.26 | Strong |
| France | 0.17 | $Y = -0.88—0.124 (X)$ | 1.67 | Medium |
| FRG | 0.79 | $Y = 1.2 —0.304 (X)$ | 1.4 | Strong |
| Iceland[1] | 0.48 | $Y = 0.1 —0.079 (X)$ | 1.52 | Low |
| Ireland | 0.58 | $Y = 2.5 —0.680 (X)$ | 2.65 | Strong |
| Israel[2] | 0.48 | $Y = 0.41—0.08 (X)$ | 2.36 | Low |
| Italy[3] | 0.07 | $Y = 0.68—0.109 (X)$ | 1.9 | Medium |
| Japan | 0.14 | $Y = 0.2 —0.018 (X)$ | 2.6 | Low |
| Luxembourg[1] | | | | Low |
| New Zealand | 0.08 | $Y = 0.08—0.102 (X)$ | 2.2 | Low |
| Netherlands | 0.30 | $Y = 0.9 —0.188 (X)$ | 1.06 | Medium |
| Norway | 0.02 | $Y = -0.6 +0.039 (X)$ | 2.14 | Low |
| Sweden | 0.48 | $Y = 0.14—0.113 (X)$ | 1.71 | Medium |
| Switzerland[1] | 0.59 | $Y = 0.1 —0.032 (X)$ | 2.5 | Low |
| UK | 0.23 | $Y = 0.76—0.138 (X)$ | 1.59 | Medium |
| USA | 0.74 | $Y = 1.09—0.383 (X)$ | 2.5 | Strong |

*Notes:*
1. Very low range of variation.
2. 1970-75.
3. Figures should be interpreted with care because the measurement of the official rate of unemployment changed in this period.

Column (1): $r^2$ indicates the amount of variation explained.

Column (2): Regression estimates for intercept and slope. The slope indicates, for example in the case of Australia, that a 1% downward (upward) change in the rate of economic growth would cause an upward (downward) shift in the rate of unemployment of 0.512 percentage points.

Column (3): Indicates the extent of autocorrelation. Broadly speaking, values that deviate strongly from the 2.0 mark indicate autocorrelation.

Column (4): A 'low' responsiveness indicates that intervening variables interrupt the quasi-automatic link between economic growth and rates of unemployment that is observable in the 'strong responsiveness' countries.

**TABLE 7 (continued)**

---

Dependent variable: Annual change in rate of unemployment $(U_t - U_{t-1})$.
Independent variable: annual economic growth rates (per capita, real terms).

*Sources:* Unemployment data from OECD and ILO publications. Data on economic growth rates from OECD; *National Accounts of OECD Countries, 1960-1977,* vol. I (OECD; 1979a) and *OECD Economic Outlook,* July 1979 (OECD; 1979b).

---

pirical confirmation casts doubt on his hypothesis, even before we come to examine the impact of the party composition of government on unemployment rates. At least, the simple variant of the labour supply hypothesis seems inapplicable, since, in contradiction to expectation, unemployment tends to be lower where the working-age population constitutes a greater proportion of the total population. Similarly, there is no evidence that countries with a substantial proportion of migrant workers were better able to avoid the labour market consequences of the economic crisis.

These findings do not necessarily imply that the impact of the economic factors is unimportant. The essential point is that the labour market responded immediately and directly only in certain countries, and that in others a number of intervening variables interrupted the normal relationship between economic recession and labour market crisis. The time-series findings for individual countries reported in Table 7 bring out three types of responsiveness: countries with a strong primacy of the economy; nations with medium responsiveness; and states in which low responsiveness appears to be a consequence of the relative importance of political control of the economy. It can be plausibly argued that intervening political mechanisms account for these different patterns of responsiveness.

### The impact of political structures on the rate of unemployment

Contrary to what many labour market analysts believe, and contrary to Hibbs's 'party control does matter' hypothesis, highly politicized labour markets did not result in high rates of unemployment; nor is there much support for the view that countries under social democratic rule pursued policies that were consistently different from those with bourgeois governments. Contrary to expectation, certain of the countries with politicized labour markets seem to have been able to use the levers provided by an extensive public economy to combat labour market difficulties. The dominant tendency in government seems to be important for differential labour market outcomes only beyond a certain threshold. The strongest support that might be offered in our findings for Hibbs's hypothesis is that hegemonic social democratic government (Austria, Norway and Sweden until 1976) is a sufficient, but not a necessary, condition for low rates of unemployment. Moreover, as we shall see, even that support may be more reasonably interpreted as an artefact of the coincidence of the dominant tendency in government and the extra-parliamentary balance of power in these countries.

It is aspects of this latter dimension of politics in the capitalist democracies that our empirical analysis demonstrates to be of substantial importance in determining rates of unemployment. A strong socialist milieu, whether measured in terms of the average left-wing vote or the presence of a strong and dominant party of the left within the political system, exerts a strong pressure on government to practise active labour market policies ($r_S = -0.48$ and $r_S = -0.33$). In addition, the influence of the socialist milieu appears greatest where the Left is united and ideologically cohesive and the bourgeois tendency is lacking in cohesion. In general, the political impact of the left-wing milieu and of organized labour seem to be the more pronounced to the degree that it is institutionalized in strong and united parties, in strong and united trade unions and in corporatist modes of regulating the conduct of the class struggle.

Of these aspects of the extra-parliamentary distribution of power, it is corporatism that is the single best predictor of differential rates of unemployment ($r_S = -0.67$). Corporatism, as we have operationalized the concept, relates to a syndrome in which trade unions and employers practise a social partnership ideology, in which strike volume is low, and in which the government refrains from imposed wage policies (see note 6). All the countries with low rates of unemployment during the crisis of the 1970s were characterized by either strong or medium degrees of corporatist conflict resolution. A strong corporatism is a sufficient, but not a necessary, condition for low rates of unemployment (i.e., Iceland, Luxembourg and New Zealand combine low unemployment and a

medium degree of corporatism). The opposite holds true for countries in which class conflict is regulated in either an authoritarian or
competitive manner: a weak corporatism is a sufficient, but not a
necessary, condition for high rates of unemployment (i.e.,
Australia, Belgium and Denmark combine high unemployment and
a medium degree of corporatism). States characterized by corporatist arrangements of medium strength manifest the most
diverse pattern. Some of the countries in this group — Finland,
Germany, Israel and the Netherlands — were faced with medium
rates of unemployment, but the remainder were as likely to be
characterized by high as by low rates.

Although the majority of the capitalist democracies conform to
the pattern predicted by the corporatist hypothesis predicated on
equal political exchange, there are important exceptions. These latter are the countries in which a medium degree of institutionalization of class conflict has not been matched by favourable outcomes
in terms of low rates of unemployment. However, it may be that, in
the countries where corporatist arrangements have not produced
full employment, alternative compensations to the labour movement have been available, in particular more generous welfare state
policies. Such an hypothesis would appear to be compatible with
the data, in so far as the countries with a medium degree of corporatism and with high or medium unemployment are generally
characterized by expansive welfare states, which are geared to
softening the practice of economic rationalization and modernization by reactive monetary compensations.

The overall importance of aspects of the extra-parliamentary
distribution of power are clearly established, but difficulties of interpretation remain, particularly where it is necessary to untangle a
series of political factors, both extra-parliamentary and governmental, which might be presumed to have an impact on levels of
unemployment. On the one hand, we encounter circumstances
where the internal dialectic of factors that might individually be
propitious for labour market outcomes together operate in a
somewhat different fashion. Thus, the very moderate protest of
West German trade unions against an unsatisfactory labour market
outcome in the context of established modes of conflict resolution
can be partly explained in terms of trade unions' fear that action on
their part would endanger the tenure of a social democratic government. On the other hand, it is difficult to distinguish which factors
are decisive in a given context. Thus, the only three nations in
which social democratic government was hegemonic (Austria, Nor-

## TABLE 8
### Intercorrelations (Spearman's $r_s$)

|  |  | V01 | V02 | V03 | V04 | V05 | V06 |
|---|---|---|---|---|---|---|---|
| Rate of unemployment, 1974-78 | (V01) | 1.0 |  |  |  |  |  |
| Rate of unemployment, 1960-73 | (V02) | 0.63 | 1.0 |  |  |  |  |
| Corporatism | (V03) | -0.67 | -0.53 | 1.0 |  |  |  |
| Left-wing vote, 1974-78 | (V04) | -0.48 | -0.45 | 0.44 | 1.0 |  |  |
| Dominant party in party system, 1974-78 | (V05) | -0.33 | -0.18 | 0.45 | 0.75 | 1.0 |  |
| Dominant tendency in government, 1974-78 | (V06) | -0.25 | -0.08 | 0.40 | 0.69 | 0.75 | 1.0 |
|  | $N = 21$ |  |  |  |  |  |  |

way and Sweden until 1976) were simultaneously the only three countries in which strong corporatism was conjoined with a strong left-wing milieu. Which set of factors was responsible for low unemployment in these countries, or whether they all are, is a matter that can ultimately be settled only by detailed one-country studies; although, given the overall direction of our findings, the balance of probability must rest with the crucial impact of the extra-parliamentary distribution of power (see Table 8).

### Why and how does corporatism matter?

Generally speaking, rates of unemployment in the 1970s were primarily dependent on the degree of corporatism, on the distribution of power between the Left and the bourgeois milieux, and on the structure of the labour market in the previous period. Although, as Table 8 demonstrates, these variables are to some extent interrelated, it is possible to specify the causal mechanisms involved with somewhat greater precision. The structure of the labour market between 1960 and 1973 is a background condition for subsequent development. In countries with full employment in the 1960s, the structure of the economy and the expectations and values guiding policy-makers were generally much more favourable to a continuation of full employment policy, despite the problems imposed by economic crisis. Governments in countries that had experienced comparatively high unemployment in the 1960s were economically and politically more inclined to let unemployment figures go up as the recession took hold. However, the effect of the historical experience of unemployment in the capitalist democracies is mediated by two intervening political variables — established corporatist arrangements and a balanced distribution of power between Left and a bourgeois milieu — which seem, in most instances, to guarantee low rates of unemployment, even in periods of economic crisis.

Why and how do corporatism and the distribution of power between the Left and the bourgeois milieu influence the rate of unemployment? One can very broadly distinguish between five mechanisms.

1. The presence of a strong corporatist mode of conflict resolution and the presence of a strong left-wing milieu increase the salience of unemployment as a political issue. Both political factors tend to put indirect pressure on the policy choices of whatever party is in office, and restrict the government's capacity to shift the burden of the economic crisis, in its entirety, to labour.

2. Corporatist arrangements tend to increase the capacity for societal guidance. Thus, within the corporatist context, incomes policy is designed to achieve, and frequently does achieve, favourable conditions for both capital accumulation, with 'reasonable' if not necessarily maximum levels of profits, and more or less full employment.

3. Corporatist arrangements tend to be associated with the practice of hoarding labour and overmanning on the part of industrial firms.

4. Corporatism and a strong left-wing milieu tend to be conducive to active labour market policies, often in conjunction with comprehensive counter-cyclical demand management on the part of the government.

5. A further mechanism that facilitates successful control of the labour market is the range of external economic policies and immigration controls, which are typically utilized, where corporatism and left-wing milieu are strong, to shelter the domestic economy and the domestic labour force.

In general terms, corporatist arrangements tend to be based on a high degree of industrial consensus and moderate wage demands, the latter assuming a particular importance in periods of economic crisis. The behaviour of organized labour in corporatist states is characterized by middle-class-oriented deferred gratification patterns, in which low industrial militancy and moderate wage demands are consciously adopted in order to keep the economy on an even keel. However, the politics of deferred gratification by no means invariably favours the labour movement, as medium to high rates of unemployment in Germany, the Netherlands and Belgium clearly indicate.

Whether corporatism involves a process of equal or unequal exchange depends crucially on the attitudes of industrial managements and their willingness to offer real concessions. Such a willingness may be a function of either the development of a bourgeois ethos, in which the values of acquisitive competition are somewhat muted, or the demonstrated compatibility of the interests of labour and capital under specified conditions. The strong continuing influence of paternalistic elements in Japanese capitalism is an illustration of the fact that the value system of the bourgeoisie is not everywhere identical. The limited role of a laissez-faire ideology in the process of modernization in a number of European countries — in particular, Sweden, Norway and Austria — has been similarly conducive to a model of corporatism which stresses the reciprocal advantages to be gained from cooperation (see Castles, 1978: 140-2). On the other hand, under certain circumstances the management of private firms may learn that, given a high degree of integration into the world market, co-operative policies towards labour may be compatible with, or even favourable to, profitable economic expansion and international competitiveness. Such circumstances are most likely to occur in small nations with comparatively strong consociational structures, a higher density of communication among elites and less economic heterogeneity, all of which factors combine to foster integration and lessen problems of governability.

It is important to emphasize, however, that the type of concessions that industrial managements in some countries are willing to offer are not, by themselves, enough to ensure high levels of employment. A structural barrier is inherent in the requirement, which characterizes ail capitalist enterprise, that there is an adequate return on capital investment. This imperative drastically reduces the economy's capacity to hoard or absorb surplus labour. Thus, in order to maintain low rates of unemployment, it is quite essential that private labour market measures are backed up by comprehensive public labour market policies. Certainly, the evidence suggests that the authorities in all the capitalist democracies were aware of the necessity of active labour market intervention if the unemployment consequences of the economic crisis were to be contained.[29] There was no country where the government took the risk of adopting a purely laissez-faire approach in its crisis management. Although rates of unemployment rose in the 1970s to a level unparallelled in the two preceding decades, the style of government activity was very different from the deflationary approach of the 1930s. Whatever their political composition, the governments of the capitalist democracies in the 1970s made conscious efforts to reduce unemployment. Nevertheless, the most dramatic and successful measures were adopted in the countries where corporatism and/or the left-wing milieu was strongest. What appears to have happened is that, in those countries where equal exchange had hitherto been the principle of co-operation between the social partners in the labour market, the government now stepped in to right the temporary imbalances created by the economic crisis.

Even among those countries that took the most activist labour market stance, there was considerable variation in the exact nature of the policies adopted. The most comprehensive and overtly interventionist schemes were adopted in five countries (Austria, Luxembourg, New Zealand, Norway and Sweden), all of which experienced social democratic rule for some or all of the crisis period. This should not, however, be taken to imply that partisan control was necessarily the decisive factor, since in the period from 1960 to 1978 all but Austria had continuous low rates of unemployment, despite changes in government. What it probably does suggest is that comprehensive measures to combat unemployment are more likely to be adopted where the left-wing milieu is strong and has a potential lien on power. In all these countries, the labour hoarding practices of firms integrated into a corporatist structure were supported and supplemented by global countercyclical and selective demand management, including expansion of state expenditures, wage subsidies and assistance to depressed industries and areas. In addition, public sector employment was expanded, measures were taken to adjust labour supply (i.e. early retirement schemes, retraining programmes and, in Austria and Luxemburg, reduction of working hours), and efforts were made to improve job allocation procedures. Perhaps most dramatic of all, Sweden, which for half the period had a bourgeois government, maintained between 3 and 4 percent of the active labour force in a variety of retraining and job creation schemes throughout much of the economic crisis.

Some of these countries also made the attempt to shelter the domestic labour market by protectionist measures and by restrictive controls in respect of migrant workers.

In addition to these five countries, there were others (e.g. Japan and Switzerland) with strong bourgeois governmental and extraparliamentary tendencies, which also pursued determined policies to control unemployment. While they also took measures to protect the domestic labour supply, their activism in the labour market was of a somewhat different kind. This variation seems as much attributable to the prevailing mode of corporatist organization in each country, as to differential party political strength. Whereas the five countries already described fall into the category of 'liberal corporatism', Japan's paternalist capitalism involves a 'private corporatism' and Switzerland's segmented structure a 'societal corporatism', both of which minimize the interventionist role of the state. The Japanese authorities were, therefore, willing to go along with the most advanced European practice in respect of selective aid to industry and individuals, but drew the line at expanding public sector employment and job creation schemes in the private economy. The Swiss solution to labour market problems deviated still further from the model of the 'liberal corporatist' states. Effectively, unemployment was controlled by exporting surplus foreign workers. Restrictive demand management, monetarist policies, the almost complete absence of labour market intervention and very strict immigration controls substantially lowered the level of employment almost wholly at the expense of migrant workers. Immigration restrictions were by far the most important instrument of control, and the labour market impact of a marginal reduction in working hours and a limited degree of labour hoarding were of much lesser importance.[30] In summary, both Japan and Switzerland behaved as might have been predicted in terms of our overall analysis: because corporatist arrangements were strong, both manifested a strong urge to control unemployment; but because both were also characterized by an anti-statist corporate tradition, they made an effort to avoid the interventionist policies favoured in those countries with a stronger leftist influence.

## Inflationary pressure in the crisis
## of the 1970s

We have seen that nations characterized by strong corporatist structures and a balanced power distribution between the bourgeois and left-wing tendencies were, on the whole, able to exercise a degree of control over labour market imbalances. They quite frequently managed to hold the rate of unemployment down, despite unfavourable economic and demographic circumstances. This successful political control in the labour market is not necessarily replicable in other realms of macroeconomic policy. In some of the countries with high levels of employment, low economic growth and declining international competitiveness posed severe problems. This applies to Iceland, Luxembourg, New Zealand, Sweden and, to a much lesser extent, Austria. Moreover, the case of Sweden suggests that the highly developed active labour market policy used to tackle the employment problem could generate unintended second-order consequences: on the one hand, a growing segmentation of the labour market, with the labour market opportunities for new entrants being markedly less favourable than for established workers, and, on the other hand, a major reduction in labour mobility (Johannesson and Schmid, 1979: 55).

It is a common observation that advanced capitalist societies are plagued not only by chronic labour market problems, but also by endemic inflationary pressures.[31] It has been argued, for example, that inflationary pressure in developed industrial states is a consequence of the degree of monopolization within the economy and the commitment on the part of governments to provide full employment or, at least, to hold unemployment at a level much lower than would exist in a non-regulated market economy. Under such circumstances, trade unions dispose of much greater bargaining power than would otherwise be the case, and are often in a position to force employers to adjust by increasing price levels rather than by reducing wages or shedding labour. The consequence is an inflationary spiral, fueled by never-abating wage demands.

Strong inflationary pressure tends to undermine both economic and political stability. High rates of inflation tend to lead to drastic changes in the distribution of real income and wealth. Given the rigidities of the tax system, high inflation means a higher level of tax revenue, with the consequence of a further twist in the wage-price spiral and enhanced problems for industries competing in the world market. Together, these forces threaten governments with severe legitimacy deficits, which may well provide a strong incentive for putting price and wages control as the foremost priority on the political agenda. Table 5 above demonstrates the divergence of government performance in respect to the twin problems of labour market and inflation control. Among the low-unemployment countries, it was only Austria and Switzerland that were relatively successful in keeping prices under control. While inflation remained moderate in Luxembourg, it was at around the 10 percent level in Norway and Sweden, and higher still in Japan, New Zealand and Iceland. Among the nations with medium to high rates of unemployment, only the Federal Republic of Germany succeeded in keeping inflation below the 5 percent mark, while most of the others reported rates in excess of 10 percent.

In this section we intend to address the question of why inflation rates vary so widely and whether, and to what extent, the socioeconomic and political variables, already shown to be important factors in the determination of macroeconomic policy outputs, are also relevant here. Our dependent variable is the rate of inflation for the period 1974-78 as measured by rises in the consumer price index. The data are derived from OECD publications. Since there is a real problem of international comparability in this data set, as in all others used in this project, it was thought sensible to recode the data into broad categories. Thus, figures between 0 and below 5 percent were classified as rank 1, figures between 5 and below 10 percent were classified as rank 2, those of 10 percent and above were classified as rank 3, etc.

Following discussions of the so-called 'revised Phillips Curve', one might expect an inverse relationship between the rate of unemployment and the rate of inflation. Phillips had discovered a nonlinear inverse relationship between the rate of unemployment and the rate of change of money wage rates in Great Britain between 1861 and 1957 (Phillips, 1958). Subsequently, a revised Phillips Curve, predicting an inverse relationship between the rate of inflation and the rate of unemployment, became, for a time, almost an economic orthodoxy. Obviously, in this view, price stability and full employment were fundamentally incompatible.[32] However, certain lacunae in the evidence used to support the hypothesis motivated a strong counter-reaction. Stobbe, for example, argued that it was more reasonable to presume no direct relationship between the variables, since both depended on so many other important factors not specified in this simple bivariate model. Moreover, he pointed to historical counter-examples, such as West

Germany in the 1960s, where full employment and low inflation had gone hand in hand (see Stobbe, 1975: 404). In his Nobel lecture, Milton Friedman suggested the possibility of an inverted Phillips Curve in some of the Western nations, and he argued that 'at least in some countries, of which Britain, Canada and Italy might be the best examples, rising inflation and rising unemployment might have been mutually reinforcing, rather than separate effects of separate causes' (Friedman, 1977: 463). According to this view, the basic reason is that high inflation and an increasing variation in the actual and anticipated rate of inflation will lead to an inefficient allocation of resources, and hence, in all likelihood, to high unemployment. Seen in this way, it is the institutional and political arrangements that accompany high inflation, and in particular the increasing government intervention in a progressively more volatile price system, that are likely to prove most antithetical to the most productive use of employed resources (Friedman, 1977: 464-8). Although the details would vary from country to country, the general result would be the same: 'reduction in the capacity of the price system to guide economic activity; distortions in relative prices because of the introduction of greater friction, as it were, in all markets; and, very likely, a higher recorded rate of unemployment' (Friedman, 1977: 467-8).

However, the empirical analysis of 21 capitalist democracies, presented in Table 9, offers very little support for either the revised Phillips Curve hypothesis or the Friedman counter-hypothesis. A cross-sectional analysis suggests the absence of any inverse relationship of the kind predicted by the Phillips Curve, and a complementary time-series analysis of the countries for the period 1970-77 points to the probability that the rather marginal positive relationship is an artefact of a phenomenon present in only a few countries.[33] Both countries with low and high inflation have reported both high and low rates of unemployment, and there would appear to be no systematic trade-off between price levels and employment. This finding is important not merely because it confounds economic thinking, but also because it contradicts both of the major lines of argument that have guided policy-makers in the crisis of the 1970s. The Austrian case illustrates beautifully how misguided the conventional approaches may be. Austria went through the recession in the 1970s with low unemployment, comparatively high economic growth and low to medium rates of inflation. Thus, two seemingly incompatible economic targets were more or less reconciled by a mixture of policy choices. An active

## TABLE 9

### Determinants of rates of inflation (average, 1974-78) and change (average, 1974-78 minus average 1960-73)

| Hypothesis | Indicator | Expected relationship | Actual ave. size* 1974-78 | Relationship change* 1960-73 to 1974-78 | Conclusion |
|---|---|---|---|---|---|
| 'Phillips curve' | Rate of unemployment (average, 1974-78) | Inverse | $r_s = 0.06$ | $r_s = 0.27$ | Not Confirmed |
| 'Inflation—unemployment—null—hypothesis' | | None | $r_s = 0.06$ | $r_s = 0.27$ | Confirmed |
| 'Revised Phillips curve' | | Direct | $r_s = 0.06$ | $r_s = 0.27$ | Not confirmed |
| 'Party control does matter' | Left-wing parties in government (% months, 1974-78) | Direct | $r_s = -0.34$ | $r_s = -0.38$ | Weakly confirmed |
| | Dominant tendency in government (1974-78) | Direct | $r_s = -0.04$ | $r_s = -0.08$ | Not confirmed |
| 'Structure of party system and of political tendencies' | Social democratic prime minister (% months, 1974-78) | Direct | $r_s = -0.25$ | $r_s = -0.29$ | Not confirmed |
| | Dominant party (1974-78) | Direct | $r_s = -0.08$ | $r_s = -0.19$ | |
| | Cohesion of bourgeois tendency (1 = weak, 0 = strong) | Direct | $l_u = 0.13$ | $l_u = 0.42$ | Not confirmed |
| | Cohesion of left-wing tendency (1 = strong, 0 = weak) | Direct | $l_u = 0.13$ | $l_u = 0.13$ | |
| 'Extra-parliamentary power distribution' | Left-wing vote (1974-78) | Direct | $r_s = -0.09$ | $r_s = -0.13$ | Not confirmed |
| 'Corporatism does matter' | Corporatism | Inverse | $r_s = -0.32$ | $r_s = -0.45$ | Weakly confirmed |
| 'Industrial conflict' | Strike volume (1974-77) | Direct | $r_s = 0.58$ | $r_s = 0.56$ | Confirmed |
| 'Economic wealth' | GDP per capita (1978)** | Inverse | $r_s = -0.60$ | $r_s = -0.52$ | Confirmed |
| 'Political control of the economy' | Tax state (1976) | Inverse | $r_s = -0.10$ | $r_s = -0.27$ | Not confirmed |
| 'Historically constant structure' | Rate of inflation (average, 1960-73) | Direct | $r_s = 0.55$ | $r_s = 0.87$ | Confirmed |

$(N = 21)$

*$r_s$ = Spearman's rank-order correlation coefficient rho; $l_u$ = $\lambda_u$     **$N = 20$

labour market policy geared to maintain full employment, a hard currency policy and concerted tripartite action, leading to a decline in real wages, seem to have been responsible for an outcome that eluded policy-makers elsewhere.

## The impact of political factors on the rate of inflation

In a number of the more recent contributions to the theory of inflation, it has been convincingly argued that a satisfactory analysis must combine economic with sociological and political variables. Gunter Steinmann, for example, concluded his review of the literature by suggesting that: 'In the economic theory of inflation the exclusive focus of investigation is on how monetary growth, excess demand or cost-push lead to an increase in the level of prices, but not on why monetary growth, excess demand or cost-push come about' (Steinmann, 1979: 183).[34] Although we still do not dispose of empirically validated socioeconomic and political explanations of inflationary pressures, some recent studies in industrial sociology and political science yield at least some guidelines for the development of a more adequate theoretical framework.

We have already had occasion to mention the analysis of Douglas Hibbs, who, premising his argument on the revised Phillips Curve hypothesis, suggests that social democratic governments will tend to prefer a low unemployment/high inflation mix, while parties of the bourgeois tendency will display a reversed preference (see Hibbs, 1977). Our re-analysis of Hibbs's hypothesis, with data from the 1970s rather than the 1960s, does point to the importance of party control as a determinant of inflation, but in a rather different way from that posited in the hypothesis. On the one hand, it is not the strength of left-wing parties controlling the executive that makes the difference, but rather their mere presence in government. On the other hand, and far more important, the presence of left-wing parties in government — whether in coalition or alone — actually improves the prospects for successful control of prices. Thus, while we have already shown that a strong left milieu is conducive to low unemployment, it now appears that a left-wing presence in government is a factor promoting low rates of inflation. Phillips and Hibbs notwithstanding, there is little sign of a trade-off in macroeconomic policy outcomes.

It has already been noted that Austria, Germany and Sweden

reported rates of inflation with a range from 4 to 10 percent. However, judged by the average rate of inflation in the 21 capitalist democracies, and judged in particular by the extremely high rates in a number of bourgeois-dominated countries (e.g., Australia and Italy from 1976 onwards), this performance is not as bad as it seems at first sight. Thus, the analysis shows that, relatively speaking, at least some of the social democratic governments were more 'successful' than their bourgeois counterparts in controlling the upward gallop of the wage-price spiral, although a glance at the absolute figures makes it plain that inflationary pressure was greater in these countries in the 1970s than in the previous decade. The case of West Germany, with the second lowest rate of inflation in the sample, achieved under the auspices of a Social Democratic-Free Democratic (i.e., liberal bourgeois) coalition government, is of particular interest. The policy mix favoured by the West German authorities, and in particular by the Deutsche Bundesbank, clearly reflects the endeavour to avoid anything that might remind the public at large of the two hyperinflationary situations experienced by Germany, the first in the early 1920s and the second in the immediate aftermath of the Second World War. Simultaneously, it was apparent that all necessary steps would be taken to ensure that the competitive edge of the West German export industry would not be dulled.

The fact that governments in which parties of the Left participated were, on the whole, more successful in holding down inflationary pressures can plausibly be explained by the structure and political form of conflict resolution and, in particular, by the willingness of trade unions to hold down wage demands so long as a party of their own political complexion was in office. Those authors who argue that the rate of inflation is closely related to the level and dynamics of industrial conflict are broadly correct (see Steinmann, 1979: 127-65), although they frequently fail to specify the necessary and sufficient conditions. To put it briefly: the probability of a low inflation rate is high where the dominant mode of conflict resolution is corporatist in character, where industrial conflict is largely absent, and where the economy is wealthy and has a dominant role in the world market. If any one or more of these conditions is unfulfilled, there will be a strong probability of highish inflation. The empirical relationship between the level of the rate of inflation in the mid-1970s and corporatism is $r_S = -0.32$; with the level of industrial conflict it is $r_S = 0.58$ and with economic wealth, $r_S = -0.60$. In the case of the change of the inflation rate compared with the previous period (1960-73), the relationships are $r_S = -0.45$ for corporatism, $r_S = 0.56$ for industrial conflict and $r_S = -0.52$ for economic wealth. Together, these findings are compatible with an explanation that builds on a complex relationship between conflicts between labour and capital, forms of extra-parliamentary political arenas and power differentials in the world market.

High inflationary pressure generally leads to endeavours to regulate wages and prices, but, with the exception of those countries with strong corporatist arrangements, these efforts to create wage restraint via incomes policy provoke reaction. They are seen by wage-dependent labour and the trade union movement as a threat to living standards, and frequently culminate in high strike volumes and wage settlements which more or less compensate for the initial loss in purchasing power. This process is often accompanied by price policies on the part of firms, which contribute to a further twist in the wage-price spiral. Illustrative of this mutually reinforcing process, which is typical of the relatively less wealthy nations, is the fate of incomes policy in Britain under both Tory and Labour administrations. Similar problems over incomes policy packages have occurred in Iceland, and the conflicts over the 'scala mobile' in Italy, by which there is an automatic adjustment to wages in certain firms according to the rate of inflation, have much the same character.

In nations with strong corporatist arrangements, there is a mechanism at work that interrupts this sequence. The reasons for this are several. On the one hand, such an arrangement tends to lead to moderation in wage demands, and this is facilitated by a trade union structure in which the leadership has the capacity to control rank-and-file demands in the short to medium term, not least because governments hold out the promise of full employment as a compensation for wage sacrifice. On the other hand, there is also a tendency for less aggressive pricing policy by enterprises, either because of their competitiveness and/or because of the fact that, in corporatist nations, entrepreneurs tend to have a wider range of downward flexibility in their profit expectations. These latter points emphasize that the interruption of the wage-price spiral in corporatist nations is strongly facilitated in wealthy economies which are dominant in the world market. This provides room for manoeuvre to enact wage and price restraint and makes it possible for the rich nations to shift at least some of the impact of inflationary pressures on to the poorer nations.

**TABLE 10**
**Intercorrelations between major explanatory**
**variables (Spearman's $r_s$)**

|  |  | *V001*[1] | *V002* | *V003* | *V004* | *V005*[2] |
|---|---|---|---|---|---|---|
| GDP per capita, 1978[1] | (V001) | 1.0 |  |  |  |  |
| Rate of inflation, 1960-73 | (V002) | -0.17 | 1.0 |  |  |  |
| Left-wing parties in government, 1974-78 (% months) | (V003) | -0.34 | -0.17 | 1.0 |  |  |
| Corporatism | (V004) | 0.52 | -0.17 | 0.44 | 1.0 |  |
| Strike volume, 1973-77[2] | (V005) | -0.63<br>N = 21 | 0.09 | -0.60 | -0.70 | 1.0 |

1. N = 20
2. N = 18

The average rate of inflation in the mid-1970s was not, of course, independent of the rate of inflation in the preceding period from 1960 to 1973, since, clearly, some of the factors adduced above are not peculiar to periods of crisis. In economies with relatively high rates of inflation in the 1960s the probability of an above-average rate in the 1970s was high. Whether the level of inflationary pressure in the previous period contributed to rapid inflation in the 1970s or whether there was some move towards partial control depended on the impact of the particular conjuncture of economic and political factors outlined above.[35] In Table 10 we present the intercorrelations between these major explanatory factors.

To summarize, inflationary pressure plagues all the capitalist democracies. Governments in all of them had to cope with the obviously inbuilt inflationary structure of advanced capitalism. While none has really managed to hold inflation down to the low levels of the 1960s, there has, nevertheless, been a wide range of variation in the success of attempts to exert political control in this situation. The variation in the rate of inflation, in respect of both level and change over time, is best accounted for by a nation's economic wealth and position in the world market, whereas the degree of control seems attributable to a range of societal and political factors including the presence of corporatist arrangements, the level of industrial conflict and the presence of left-wing parties in government. Here, as so often in this volume, it would appear to be an issue not so much of whether economic or political factors matter, but rather of how they interact in determining complex patterns of policy outcomes.

## Patterns of partial political control
## in advanced capitalist economies

What conclusions can be drawn from our study of macroeconomic outcomes? To what extent were governments in the capitalist democracies capable of exercising successful control of the economy? To what extent, and under what circumstances, did the political composition of governments, the distribution of power in extra-parliamentary arenas and the nature of socioeconomic structures account for observable differences in economic policy outputs and macroeconomic policy outcomes in these 21 nations?

Our analysis suggests that, in some nations, governments expanded the tax state beyond a level held by many conservatives to be deterimental to, and in the long-run incompatible with, a market economy. In some nations governments also managed to control either unemployment problems or inflationary pressures. But there is not a single case among the capitalist democracies in the 1970s in which the government really succeeded in simultaneously organizing a potent tax state and controlling both inflation and unemployment. What seems to emerge from our analysis is a pattern of selective and partial political control of the economy. With respect to some macroeconomic instabilities, the policies pursued by governments did have the result of holding the 'laws of motion' of the advanced capitalist economy in abeyance, and this degree of control was particularly pronounced in respect of labour market policy. However, the evidence is simply not compatible with the view that social democratic governments can exercise a comprehensive or successful 'political control of the economy' as a whole. Nor is it possible to conclude, as does Stephens, that such interventions by the state have, intentionally or otherwise, created the basis for the 'transition to socialism' (Stephens, 1979). Quite the contrary: the performance of most capitalist nations in the 1970s suggests that the dynamics of the economy and its structurally given instabilities

## TABLE 11
### Patterns of political control of the economy

| Country | Rate of unemployment, 1974-78 | Rate of inflation, 1974-78 | Size of tax state/welfare state, 1977 | Degree of successful political control of the economy |
|---|---|---|---|---|
| Australia | High | High | Low | Very low |
| Austria | Low | Medium | Medium | Moderately strong |
| Belgium | High | Medium | Medium | Moderately low |
| Canada | High | Medium | Low | Very low |
| Denmark | High | High | High | Moderately low |
| Finland | High | High | Medium | Very low |
| France | Medium | High | Medium | Very low |
| FRG | Medium | Low | Medium | Moderately strong |
| Iceland | Low | High | Low | Moderately low |
| Ireland | High | High | Low | Very low |
| Israel | Medium | High | Medium | Moderately low |
| Italy | Medium | High | Medium | Moderately low |
| Japan | Low | High | Low | Moderately low |
| Luxembourg | Low | Medium | High | Moderately strong |
| New Zealand | Low | High | Low | Moderately low |
| Netherlands | Medium | Medium | High | Moderately strong |
| Norway | Low | High | High | Moderately strong |
| Sweden | Low | High | High | Moderately strong |
| Switzerland | Low | Low | Low | Moderately strong |
| UK | Medium | High | Medium | Moderately low |
| USA | High | Medium | Low | Very low |

tended, more often than not, to undermine or prevent efforts to exercise political control of the economy.

Assuming that the three elements of macroeconomic policy we have studied are of roughly the same importance, we can provide an approximate indicator of the degree of partial political control achieved in each country. In effect, the patterns of political control of the economy, which emerge from Table 11, offer a summary overview of the phenomena discussed throughout this chapter. Seven nations — Austria, West Germany, Luxembourg, the Netherlands, Norway, Sweden and Switzerland — manifest moderately strong political control, whereas the degree of control in the rest is either moderately low or very low.

If we cross-classify the advanced capitalist democracies by the

**FIGURE 1**
**Active and passive welfare state capitalisms and**
**active and passive market economies**

1974 – 78
Rate of unemployment

| | Low (<2.0) | | High (>2.0) | |
|---|---|---|---|---|
| **Large** | Austria Luxembg Norway Sweden | Active welfare capita- lism | Passive welfare capita- lism | Belgium Denmark Finland France FRG Netherlands UK |
| **Small** | | Active market economies | Passive market economies | Australia Canada Ireland Italy USA |
| | Iceland Japan Switzerland New Zealand | | | |

Public sector 1977

size of the tax state and the rate of unemployment in the mid-1970s, we can distinguish between four different groups of capitalist societies (see Figure 1). The majority of the nations with an extensive public economy are characterized by a variety of passive welfare state policies, which reactively compensate for the risks inherent in the capitalist order, but which either abstain from or fail in the effort of actively and preventatively steering market mechanisms. Only in four of the high tax state nations were measures initiated that succeeded in controlling the instabilities of the economy in such a way as to secure the goal of more or less full employment. These nations may be characterized in terms of 'active welfare capitalism'. The majority of nations with a strong market economy and a limited public economy are characterized by passivity in respect of intervention in the labour market. It is, however, of substantial interest that four of the nations with small

**FIGURE 2**
**Modes of regulating the economy and class conflict**

| | Low rates of unemployment (1974-78, $U < 2.0$) | High rates of unemployment (1974-78, $U > 2.0$) |
|---|---|---|
| **Social democratic dominance or hegemony (1974-78)** | Austria<br>Norway<br><br>Tendency towards corporatist mode of regulation and developed welfare state<br><br>Sweden<br>Luxembourg | Denmark<br>Germany<br>UK<br><br>Tendency towards liberal mode of regulation and developed welfare state<br><br>Finland<br>Israel<br>Netherlands |
| **Bourgeois dominance or hegemony (1974-78)** | New Zealand<br><br>Tendency towards corporatist and paternalist mode of regulation and weak welfare state<br><br>Japan<br>Iceland<br>Switzerland | Australia<br>Ireland<br><br>Tendency towards authoritarian and competitive mode of regula-tion or weak welfare state<br><br>Belgium<br>Canada<br>France<br>Italy<br>USA |

*Balance* (marked at the left-hand middle of the figure)

tax states do employ mechanisms to control employment fluctua-tions in a manner functionally equivalent to that of active welfare capitalism.

Thus, if our focus is on the overall political control of the economy, there is no clear-cut dividing line between bourgeois and left-wing governments. It is only if an additional set of conditions is fulfilled that party control really matters in a systematic way. For example, a hegemonic social democratic government, supported by a strongly organized and political united trade union movement and confronted by an organizationally and ideologically divided bourgeois tendency, adopts policies that differ substantially from those of a bourgeois hegemonic government. However, in nations falling between these two extremes, much of the variation in macroeconomic outcomes is accounted for by the distribution of power between the left and bourgeois milieux, the relative strength of organized labour and the degree to which it is institutionalized into corporatist arrangements. While the overall political control of bourgeois and social democratic governments is not decisively different, there is a real difference between them in the extent to which they passively and reactively soften the practice of capitalism by means of a variety of welfare state measures. Governments under social democratic rule generally dispose of a wider variety of more comprehensive and generous welfare state provisions than their bourgeois counterparts.

Given the absence of a systematic relationship between welfare state performance and the successful political control of labour market instabilities, it is interesting to pay some further attention to the strategies employed to cope with the labour market crisis. In broad terms, what seems to emerge from a cross-tabulation (see Figure 2) of party control and labour market outcomes is that, whereas success in securing full employment is largely a function of the existence of corporatist arrangements for regulating class conflict and steering the economy, the methods used in the attempt to alleviate labour market problems tend to be determined by the availability of, and the inclination to use, the levers provided by an extensive tax state. A part of this conclusion has already been demonstrated in the previous discussion of the range of mechanisms used by the nations successful in controlling unemployment (see above pp. 140-47). While all the countries in this category share the characteristic of medium to high degrees of corporatism, Austria and Norway, with strong social democratic governments throughout the period, and Sweden, Luxembourg and New Zealand, with balanced governments, used active labour market policies to protect employment, whereas Japan and Switzerland, with bourgeois governments, minimized intervention in their successful efforts to achieve the same goal. It is not unreasonable to attribute the absence of a statist strategy in these latter countries to a combination of the particular form of corporatism (paternalist and societal, respectively), the reluctance of bourgeois governments to use the state apparatus, and the weakness of the existing tax state as a basis for labour market activism.

All the countries that failed to maintain full employment had low or, at best, medium levels of corporatism, but they differ in the extent of the development of the welfare state. The combination of weak institutions of conflict resolution and economic management together with an extensive welfare state creates a situation in which there is simultaneously considerable room for manoeuvre by private capital and a range of programmes designed to cope in a reactive and passive way with the social and political problems this involves. In the absence of an extensive public economy, and thus relying largely on selective measures, the states with relatively weak economic steering mechanisms are extremely vulnerable to instablities generated by the capitalist order and to the protest associated with it. The available evidence on the incidence of industrial conflict supports this supposition, with those countries manifesting a tendency towards authoritarian or competitive modes of conflict resolution and weak welfare state provision having a markedly worse strike record than the majority of other nations (see Hibbs, 1978; Korpi and Shalev, 1979).

It needs to be stressed that the labels attached to the cells in our cross-tabulation in Figure 2 are ideal types. What we are pointing to, in reality, is the tendencies suggested by our statistical analysis, rather than determinate explanations. For instance, there is nothing in our analysis that can explain why Australia and New Zealand had different labour market outcomes in the mid-1970s, since each displayed balanced government, a medium degree of corporatism and low welfare. On the other hand, the tendencies displayed are important and give us some insight into the range of political solutions and strategies available to decision-makers confronted by the instabilities created by the macro-societal structure of capitalism. The nature of the problem in terms of the maintenance of the capitalist order is not so much unemployment as the crisis of legitimation it brings in its wake. Such a crisis can be avoided in two ways: by direct control of the economic mechanism through corporatist arrangements, or by an indirect process of buying off discontent through the mechanism of programmes designed to cushion the effect of economic instabilities. The direct route can be used by bourgeois and social democratic governments, although their respective preferences for state intervention may influence the tools they use for active control through corporatist channels. The indirect route is particularly, although not exclusively, a social democratic ploy, since it has generally been social democratic governments that have presided over the development of the extensive welfare state apparatus necessary for the purpose. Indeed, with the exception of the more activist parties in Austria, Norway and Sweden, one might conclude that social democracy had taken Voltaire's advice to heart and, realizing the impossibility of defeating capitalism and the problems of controlling it, had decided to build the best life possible behind the garden fence of the welfare state.

## The hypotheses revisited

In the introduction to this chapter, we outlined some of the competing explanations that feature in the literature on public policy in the advanced capitalist states. To conclude our presentation, we shall summarize briefly what our analysis contributes to our understanding of the validity of these explanations.

1. One general position in the literature is that increasing state intervention has created the basis for successful political control of the economy. This has been opposed by Marxist writers who have taken the position that the policies adopted in capitalist democracies were unable to cope with the structurally given instabilities of the capitalist order. Our analysis does not confirm either of these extreme positions. Rather, the evidence seems to point to what may be described as a 'partial political control' hypothesis. The imbalances of capitalist economies are amenable to varying strategies of more or less successful political control in certain areas; in particular, to interventions to expand the size of the tax state and to limit labour market fluctuations. However, the success of intervention in one area does not usually spill over into all the other aspects of macroeconomic policy. Indeed, there seems to an empirically identifiable tendency for there to be a trade-off by which success in one area necessarily limits successful control elsewhere. Because the autonomy of the capitalist economy remains considerable in all these nations, governments must necessarily order their priorities in the field of macroeconomic policy.

2. Another position, frequently adduced in the literature, is that party control will be the decisive factor in determining such priorities. The evidence for this 'party control does matter' hypothesis is somewhat mixed. In respect of the size of the tax state and the relative generosity of the range of welfare state programmes, the analysis presented in this chapter and in that on public expenditure patterns suggests that control of the reins of power is im-

portant. However, in respect of the other major aspects of macroeconomic policy — the control of unemployment and inflation — there is no clear-cut dividing line between the policies adopted by social democratic and bourgeois governments. This is not to say that the party composition of government is irrelevant for economic policy and policy outcomes: rather, our analysis repeatedly demonstrated that party control was of importance if certain other conditions were met, as in the pronounced tendency for a combination of strong corporatist arrangements and strong social democratic government to lead to active labour market policies. In such an instance, we note simultaneously the total failure of the 'party control' hypothesis to explain the level of unemployment and the fact that it is of some relevance in understanding the strategies adopted to cope with labour market fluctuation. Once again, we would stress the simplistic nature of much of the discussion in the public policy field. The real issue is not whether party control matters, but rather to what extent, and in particular in what circumstances, it matters.

3. On the whole, those explanations resting on the primacy of economic factors are not confirmed. For instance, the common view that the level and growth of economic resources directly determine the nature and extent of public policy outcomes is, by and large, incompatible with the evidence presented. But, once again, this is not to say that economic factors, like the level of resources or the degree of integration into the world market, are irrelevant. Thus, we noted that the growth of the tax state in the 1960s was markedly facilitated by the high general levels of economic growth experienced in the period. The crucial point that emerges is that, in many capitalist nations, the links between the economy and public policy are, to varying extents and in a variety of complex ways, mediated by intervening societal and political factors.

4. Perhaps the most interesting and important finding is the degree to which those mediating factors are of the kind suggested by the class politics paradigm. The view that extra-parliamentary politics is an important determinant of economic policy is strongly supported by our analysis of the rates of inflation and unemployment and the development of the tax state in the crisis of the 1970s. The structures and outcomes of extra-parliamentary political arenas, the development of corporatist structures and the power distribution between left-wing and bourgeois milieux seem to be vital factors in determining the success or failure of macro-

economic policy, more or less irrespective of the party in office.

The essays in this volume have been premised on the belief that recent contributions to the study of public policy have taken too narrow an approach, in respect of both their focus on a false dichotomy between politics and economics and the limited range of dependent and independent variables examined. Starting from such a premise, we would not wish to advocate a new orthodoxy by suggesting that only extra-parliamentary factors matter, or even that they invariably matter most. What we would wish to point out is that this analysis of macroeconomic policy suggests that such factors are of a degree of importance much greater than hitherto assumed in the public policy literature. Certainly, it would be valuable if the extra-parliamentary politics of capitalist democracies featured more prominently in future public policy research.

## NOTES

1. See for example Poulantzas (1969), Miliband (1969), Müller and Neusüß (1970), Offe (1972, 1975), Habermas (1973), Esping-Anderson et al. (1975), Ronge (1977), Tufte (1978), Castles (1978), Stephens (1979).

2. See Ronge and Schmieg (1973), Offe (1972, 1975).

3. Esping-Andersen et al. (1975), Gough (1979).

4. The following nations were included: Australia, Austria, Belgium, Canada, Denmark, Finland, France, Federal Republic of Germany, Iceland, Ireland, Israel, Italy, Japan, Luxembourg, Netherlands, New Zealand, Norway, Sweden, Switzerland, United Kingdom, United States.

5. The political composition of governments was measured by three indicators: (1) the percentage of months for which the 'left-wing-parties' or the 'bourgeois parties' were in government in a given period (this indicator measures the mere presence of the respective political tendencies in government); (2) the number of months in a given period in which the post of a prime minister (or functional equivalent) was held by left-wing parties or bourgeois parties (this indicator measures which tendency had the major role in government); (3) the left-wing parties' share of cabinet seats in a given period: the original values were converted into a rank order scale of the dominant tendency in government in order to take account of the fact that such a comparatively low level of measurement is generally more compatible with the theoretical language and the theoretical knowledge of political scientists than interval scales or cardinal scales. The scale runs from '1' to '5': '1' means 'bourgeois

hegemony government' (share of cabinet seats equals 100 percent); '2' means 'bourgeois dominance government' (the share ranges from greater than 66.6 percent to less than 100 percent); '3' means 'balance government' (the bourgeois parties' share and the left-wing parties' share is larger than one-third and equal to or less than two-thirds of the total of cabinet seats); '4' means 'social democratic-dominance government'; '5' means 'social democratic hegemony government' (the share of cabinet seats on the part of the social democratic and other left-wing allies is equal to 100 percent).

The relative size of the bourgeois and the left-wing tendency is measured by the average left-wing vote in a given period, including the last national election that precedes this period.

The cohesiveness of the bourgeois tendency was dichotomized. '1' means 'weak cohesiveness', i.e., if more than one bourgeois party scores at least 10 percent of the vote in the majority of the elections within a given period. '0' means 'cohesiveness' (any other case which does not meet the criteria stipulated under '1').

The cohesiveness of the left-wing party spectrum was scored '1' ('strong cohesiveness') whenever non-social democratic left-wing parties score less than 10 percent of the vote in the majority of the elections within a given period, and '0' for any other case which does not meet the criteria stipulated under '1'. It should be pointed out that by this decision/rule France and Italy score '0' even if the PCI is, for example, the dominant party among the left-wing parties.

In order to account for the political complexion of the centre of gravity within the party system, an indicator of the dominant party was used. It takes on three values, which are rank-ordered on a left-right scale: '1' means a bourgeois party is dominant, i.e., it is stronger than the major left-wing party by at least 5 percent of the popular vote in the majority of elections; '2' means 'balance 'or' no dominant party', i.e., the criteria stipulated for rank 1 and rank 3 are not met; '3' means that a left-wing party is dominant (classified in analogy to rank '1').

The latter four indicators were used in order to account for structures of the party system and for the distribution of power between the major political milieux (in the case of the left-wing vote indicator) which are both of crucial importance for the differential room to manoeuvre on the part of the governing political tendency. The data were taken from Mackie and Rose (1974), Spuler, Allen and Saunders (1977) and *Keesing's Archiv der Gegenwart*. Since in most of the nations under study the size of the social democratic parties by far exceeds those of other 'left-wing parties', the 'left-wing' measures employed correlate very highly with the measures of social democratic strength.

6. 'Union density' was the measured share of the dependent labour force organized by trade unions, both for the total postwar period (source: Korpi and Shalev, 1979) and for 1974 or the following year. Indicators for the 'levels of industrial conflict' were for the total postwar period, taken from Korpi and Shalev (1979) and for the period between 1974 and 1977 from ILO publications (yearly average of working days lost per total civilian employment). 'Corporatism' is a theoretical concept which relates to a particular mode of policy formation and a particular mode of regulating class conflicts in advanced democratic nations from a 'competitive' (regulation largely without the state) and an 'authoritarian' mode ('concerted action' between the state and capital under exclusion of the trade unions).

The corporatism indicator was rank-ordered. 'Strong corporatism' is the label for all those countries in which the trade union leadership and the employers' associations are committed to a social partnership ideology; in which the state, the trade unions and the employers' associations co-operate in some economic policy areas; in which the strike volume between 1974 and 1978 is very low (ratio of working days lost to total civilian employment lower than 0.1 for the average of the years from 1974 to 1978); and in which no authoritarian incomes policy was enacted by the state. Switzerland and Japan deviate from the typical West European liberal corporatism. Switzerland displays characteristics of a societal corporatism with comparatively low involvement of the state. Japan is a case of a paternalistic capitalism and a 'private corporatism'. Both arrangements are broadly functionally equivalent to the typical liberal corporatism. 'Weak corporatism' relates to countries where employers and trade unions are not co-operative (indicated by frequent lock-outs, high strike involvement, strong socialist and communist wings in the labour movement, weak industrial democracy), and where incomes policies were usually enacted from above. 'Medium corporatism' is a residual category.

The classification of the countries was based on Lehmbruch (1977), Schmitter and Lehmbruch (1979), von Beyme (1977), Kendall (1977), IDE-International Research Group (1981).

7. The data were taken from various OECD National Accounts Statistics and, for those countries which were not included in OECD publications, from the United Nations National Accounts statistics. It should be pointed out that, owing to changes in data collection and definition, the data for the period from 1950 to 1960 are not strictly comparable with the data from the beginning of the 1960s onwards, which have been standardized by the OECD. Though our measure of the tax state is very closely related to the extractive capacity of the state, its major disadvantage is that it excludes revenues from non-tax and non-social security contributions as well as borrowing, tax aids and tax credits. Unfortunately, no consistent, reliable and cross-nationally comparable figures for these items were available.

8. Problems of international comparability are for example thoroughly discussed in Vannereau (1975), Koller and König (1977), OECD (1979a). The method we employed to increase the comparability is that of an ex-post reduction in the level of measurement. For details, see the sections on the rate of unemployment and the rate of inflation. In addition, we tested the reliability of our unemployment measures and the validity of our explanation with a sample of all those nine nations for which the US Department of Labor publishes internationally comparable rates of unemployment (Moy, 1979). The retest reliability was extremely high, and our explanations of why the rates of unemployment vary as much as they do is strongly confirmed. The rate of inflation was measured by the index of consumer prices. This index was chosen because it is the inflation indicator that is most visible to the mass public and thus is politically of much more importance than other inflation indicators. The data were generally taken from OECD publications and, in case of missing data, from ILO and UN publications.

9. OECD (1972, 1978); Nutter (1978); Gough (1979).

10. A definition in these terms derives from the literature on the tax state; see Goldscheid (1917); Schumpeter (1918); and Hickel (1976).

11. For an inventory of hypotheses, see Musgrave and Musgrave (1973) and Wittmann (1978).

12. See Groth (1978); Foley (1978); Gough (1979).

13. Frey (1978); Schneider (1978); Frey and Schneider (1979).

14. For intercorrelations between the explanatory variables see appendixes 1, 2, and 3.

15. Change is measured by first differences (for example, size of the tax state in 1975 minus size of the tax state in 1960).

16. Time series analyses for the 21 nations, with the rates of expansion of the tax state as the dependent variable (measured by first differences on a yearly base) and the rate of economic growth (measured by the annual rate of change of the per capita GDP at constant prices) for the period between 1960 and 1969 and for the period between 1970 and 1977, show that a strong negative relationship between these two variables is the exception and not the rule: Denmark ($r^2 = 0.46$, $b = -0.614$, Durbin Watson: 2.4); New Zealand ($r^2 = 0.30$, $b = -0.234$, DW: 2.3); and the USA ($r^2 = 0.62$, $b = 0.24$, DW: 2.0) were the deviant cases in the 1960s, and Luxembourg ($r^2 = 0.76$, $b = -0.358$, DW: 2.3); New Zealand ($r^2 = 0.45$, $b = -0.421$, DW: 1.84); and Sweden ($r^2 = 0.4127$, $b = -0.477$, DW: 1.82) were those in the 1970s. In all other nations the relationship between economic growth and the expansion of the tax state was either insignificant or positive, and thus the reverse of what the conservative hypothesis would predict.

17. See the OECD *Economic Surveys* on Austria from 1974 onwards.

18. See the OECD *Economic Surveys* on Norway from 1974 onwards.

19. See Murphy, Rubart, Müller and Raschke (1979).

20. See OECD (1978); Sivard (1978); Castles and McKinlay (1979); Stephens (1979).

21. To my knowledge, the major exceptions are the studies by Myers and Chandler (1962a); Hibbs (1977, 1979); Payne (1979) and the collection of internationally comparable unemployment data in Moy (1979); Sorrentino (1971, 1972).

22. See, for example, the analysis of the labour market in the OECD *Economic Surveys*.

23. See Feldstein (1973); Soltwedel and Spinanger (1976; 293); Havemann (1978).

24. See Schmitter (1974); Lehmbruch (1977); Schmitter and Lehmbruch (1979); Lehmbruch and Schmitter (1980).

25. Rates of unemployment do not tell the whole story about the underutilization of the labour force. Semi-official estimates in West Germany suggest, for example, that, even by conservative estimates, the overall degree of unemployment is probably twice as large as the official figures indicate. A similar point for the USA has been made by Hunt and Sherman (1978: 326-30). Unfortunately, additional and cross-nationally comparable labour market and unemployment indicators were available for only nine countries (see for example Moy, 1979).

26. See for example the fate of the politics of domestic reforms in West Germany under the SPD-FDP-governments from 1969 onwards (Schmidt, 1978).

27. The data were taken from various ILO *Yearbooks of Labour Statistics*, from OECD figures on demographic trends, and from Moy (1979).

28. Time-series regressions between the rate of unemployment as the dependent variable and the rate of inflation as the independent variable for each of the 21 nations in the period between 1950 and 1977 on a yearly base consistently show that the relationship between both variables is either close to zero or, in some cases, significantly positive. Our analysis with yearly data thus shows that, if a relationship exists at all, it is in a direction that contradicts the revised Phillips Curve Model: inflation rates tend to be the higher, the higher the rates of unemployment are. This result is very strongly supported by two separate time-series regressions for each of the 21 nations in the periods 1960-69 and 1970-77. In these runs, the strongly autocorrelated rate of unemployment variable was replaced by a measure of the change in the rate of unemployment in comparison with the previous year (measured

by first differences). In those cases in which the regression coefficient had a negative sign, the relationships were totally insignificant.

29. The following paragraph is based on a large number of studies on the respective nations. The major sources were the annually published one-country studies in the OECD *Economic Surveys* series and the following contributions: Sorrentino (1970, 1971, 1972, 1976); Sorrentino and Moy (1974); Moy (1979); Moy and Sorrentino (1975, 1977); Schmid (1975); Walterskirchen (1977); Inoue (1978); Tuchfeldt (1978); Ernst (1978); Chaloupek (1979); Guldimann (1979); Johannesson and Schmid (1979).

30. Judged by the internationally comparable series of labour market indicators on nine industrial nations (Moy, 1979), Sweden seems to be the only country among the low-unemployment nations where even the labour force participation ratio (labour force as a percentage of the population in working age) and the employment population ratio went up. The evidence on the Japanese case is somewhat contradictory. While the total level of employment increases from 1973 to 1978, other labour market indicators, such as the employment-population ratio and indexes of total employee hours in private non-agricultural establishments, indicate a substantive decrease (Ernst, 1978; Moy, 1979: 12-13). This suggests that Japan and, as we have pointed out above, Switzerland are the deviant cases among the nations with low rates of unemployment, as the under-utilization of the labour potential seems to be lower than in the rest of the low-unemployment countries. Further research on cross-nationally comparable labour market and underemployment indicators is obviously very much needed in order to solve this problem and related ones.

31. Bergmann, Jacobi and Müller-Jentsch (1975: 47-62); Müller, Rödel, Sabel, Stille and Vogt (1978: 53-113); Solow (1975: 58).

32. For an overview see Nowotny (1974); Ramser and Angehrn (1977).

33. See n. 28 above. Time-series regressions with the annual change in the rate of unemployment (dependent variable) and the rate of inflation in the period from 1970 to 1978 indicate that positive relationships existed in not more than six countries. In Germany, Iceland, Israel, the Netherlands, United Kingdom and in the United States the rate of inflation tended to be higher the more the rate of unemployment increased. The accompanying table summarizes the results.

| Country | $r^2$ | regression coefficient | Durbin-Watson statistics |
|---|---|---|---|
| Germany | 0.38 | 0.331 | 1.86 |
| Iceland | 0.39 | 0.177 | 3.3 |
| Israel (1970-75) | 0.81 | 0.029 | 3.0 |
| Netherlands | 0.71 | 0.279 | 2.2 |
| United Kingdom | 0.31 | 0.078 | 1.62 |
| USA | 0.16 | 0.218 | 1.51 |

34. Translation by the author. For other recent reviews of the literature see, for example, in addition to Steinmann (1979), Solow (1975) and Cobham (1978).

35. It should be pointed out that our data suggest only weak support for an international explanation of inflation rates. The relationship between the inflation rate

and the average annual volume increase of exports between 1973 and 1978 is $r_S = 0.29$ and the correlation between the inflation rate and the average annual volume increase in imports between 1973 and 1978 is $r_S = -0.33$ (the data were taken from OECD *Economic Surveys* — Basic Statistics: International Comparisons).

# REFERENCES

Armingeon, K. (1979). 'Vergleichende Aggregatdatenalayse des Zusammenhangs zwischen gewerkschaftlicher Tarifpolitik und Parteikontrolle der Regierung'. Tübingen: Institut für Politikwissenschaft, *Magisterarbeit*, mimeo.

Armingeon, K. (1980). 'La politique des syndicats du DGB face à la crise (1974-1979)', in K. Armingeon (ed.), *Les Syndicats européennes face à la crise*. Grenoble: PUG.

Bergmann, J., Jacobi, O. and Müller-Jentsch, W. (1975). *Gewerkschaften in der Bundesrepublik*. Frankfurt and Köln: EVA.

von Beyme, K. (1977). *Gewerkschaften und Arbeitsbeziehungen in kapitalistischen Ländern*. München: Piper.

Boddy, R. and Crotty, J. (1975). 'Class Conflict and Macro-Policy: The Political Business Cycle', *Review of Radical Political Economics*, 7: 1-19.

Borg, S. and Castles, F.G. (1981). 'The Influence of the Political Right on Public Income Maintenance Expenditure and Equality', *Political Studies*.

Cameron, D.R. (1978). 'The Expansion of the Public Economy', *APSR*, 72: 1243-61.

Castles, F.G. (1978). *The Social Democratic Image of Society*. London: Routledge & Kegan Paul.

Castles, F.G. and McKinlay, R.D. (1979). 'Does Politics Matter? An Analysis of the Public Welfare Commitment in Advanced Democratic States', *EJPR*, 7: 169-86.

Causer, G. (1978). 'Private Capital and the State in Western Europe', pp. 28-54 in *Contemporary Europe. Social Structure and Cultural Patterns*. London: Routledge & Kegan.

Chaloupek, G. (1979). 'Vollbeschäftigung im Alleingang?-Gewerkschaftspolitik in Österreich seit der Rezession 1975', *WSI-Mitteilungen*, 32(4): 227-34.

Cobham, D. (1978). 'The Politics of Economics of Inflation', *Lloyds Bank Review* no. 128: 19-32.

Cowart, A.T. (1978). 'The Economic Policies of European Governments', *BJPS*, 8: 238-311 and 425-39.

Ernst, A. (1978). 'Arbeitslosigkeit und Unterbeschäftigung in Japan. Eine Übersicht zum Stand der empirischen Forschung', *Mitteilungen aus der Arbeitsmarkt- und Berufsforschung*, No. 1.

Esping-Anderson, G., Friedland, R. and Wright, E.O. (1975). 'Modes of the Class Struggle and the Capitalist State', *Kapitalistate*, no. 4-5; 186-220.

Feldstein, M. (1973). 'The Economics of the New Unemployment', *The Public Interest*, no. 30-3; 3-42.

Foley, D.K. (1978). 'State Expenditure from a Marxist Perspective', *Journal of Public Economics*, 9: 221-38.

Frey, B.S. (1978). 'Politico-Economic Models and Cycles', *Journal of Public Economics*, 9: 203-20.

Frey, B.S. and Schneider, F. (1978). 'An Empirical Study of Politico-Economic Interaction in the US', *Review of Economics and Statistics*, 60: 174-83.

Frey, B.S. (1979). 'Ein politisch-ökonomisches Modell. Theorie und Anwendung für die Bundesrepublik Deutschland', pp. 406-17 in W. Pommerehne and B.S. Frey (eds), *Ökonomische Theorie der Politik*. Berlin/Heidelberg/New York: Springer.

Friedman, M. (1977). 'Inflation and Unemployment' (Nobel Lecture), *Journal of Political Economy*, 85: 451-72.

Goldscheid, R. (1917). 'Staatssozialismus oder Staatskapitalismus', pp. 40-252 in Hickel (1976).

Gough, I. (1979). *The Political Economy of the Welfare State*. London: Macmillan.

Groth, K.-M. (1978). *Die Krise der Staatsfinanzen*. Frankfurt: Suhrkamp.

Guldimann, T. (1979). *Staatlich organisierter Arbeitsmarkt und die Anpassung der Arbeitslosen — Der Fall Schweden*. Frankfurt and New York: Campus.

Habermas, J. (1973). *Legitimationsprobleme im Spätkapitalismus*. Frankfurt: Suhrkamp.

Havemann, R.H. (1978). 'Unemployment in Western Europe and the United States: A Problem of Demand, Structure, or Measurement?' *American Economic Review—Papers and Proceedings*, 63: 43-50.

Hibbs, D.A. (1977). 'Political Parties and Macroeconomic Policy', *APSR*, 71: 1467-87.

Hibbs, D.A. (1978). 'On the Political Economy of Long-Run Trends in Strike Activity', *BJPS*, 8: 153-175.

Hibbs, D.A. (1979). 'Rejoinder', *APSR*, 73: 185-190.

Hickel, R. (ed.) (1976). *Die Finanzkrise des Steuerstaates. Beiträge zur Politischen Ökonomie der Staatsfinanzen*. Frankfurt: Suhrkamp.

Hunt, E.K. and Sherman, H.J. (1978). *Economics. An Introduction to Traditional and Radical Views*. New York: Harper & Row.

IDE-International Research Group (1981). *Industrial Relations in Europe*. London: Oxford University Press.

Inoue, K. (1979). 'Structural Change and Labour Market Policies in Japan', *International Labour Review*, CXVIII(2): 223-35.

Johannesson, J. and Schmid, G. (1979). *Die Entwicklung der Arbeitsmarktpolitik in Schweden und der Bundesrepublik Deutschland: Konkurrierende oder konvergierende Modelle zur Bekämpfung der Arbeitslosigkeit?* Berlin: Internationales Institut für Management und Verwaltung.

Kalecki, M. (1943). 'Political Aspects of Full Employment', *Political Quarterly*, 14: 322-31.

*Keesing's Archiv der Gegenwart*. (1945). Bonn, Wien, Zürich.

Kendall, W. (1977). *Gewerkschaften in Europa*. Hamburg: Hoffmann und Campe.

King, A. (1973). 'Ideas, Institutions and the Policies of Governments: A Comparative Analysis', *British Journal of Political Science*, 3: 291-313 and 409-23.

Koller, M. and König, I. (1977). *Internationaler Vergleich der Arbeitslosenquoten*. Nuremberg: Bundesanstalt für Arbeit.

Korpi, W. and Shalev, M. (1979). 'Strikes, Industrial Relations and Class Conflict in Capitalist Societies', *British Journal of Sociology*, 30; 164-87.

Krane, R.E. (ed.) (1979). *International Labour Migration*. New York, London, Sydney, Toronto: Praeger.

Laidler, D.E.N. (1976). 'Inflation-Alternative Explanations and Policies: Tests on Data Drawn from six Countries', pp. 251-306 in K. Brunner and A.H. Meltzer (eds), *Institutions, Policies and Economic Performance*. Amsterdam/New York: North Holland.

Lehmbruch, G. (1977). 'Liberal Corporatism and Party Government', *CPS*, 10: 91-126.

Lehmbruch, G. (1979). 'Wandlungen der Interessenpolitik im liberalen Korporatismus', pp. 50-71 in U. von Alemann and R.G. Heinze (eds), *Verbände und Staat*. Opladen: Westdeutscher Verlag.

Lehmbruch, G. and Schmitter, P. (eds) (1982). *Consequences of Corporatist Policy-Making*. Beverly Hills/London: Sage.

Mackie, T.T. and Rose, R. (eds) (1974). *The International Almanac of Electoral History*. London: Macmillan.

Miliband, R. (1969). *The State in Capitalist Society*. London: Weidenfeld & Nicolson.

Moy, J. (1979). 'Recent Labor Market Trends in Nine Industrial Nations', *Monthly Labor Review*, 101(5): 8-16.

Moy, J. and Sorrentino, C. (1975). 'Unemployment in Nine Industrial Nations', *Monthly Labor Review*, 98(6): 9-18.

Moy, J. and Sorrentino, C. (1977). 'An Analysis of Unemployment in Nine Industrial Countries', *Monthly Labor Review*, 100(4): 12-24.

Müller,W., Neusüß, C. (1970). 'Die Sozialstaatsillusion und der Widerspruch von Lohnarbeit und Kapital', *Sozialistische Politik*, no. 6/7.

Müller, G., Rödel, U. Sabel, Stille, F. and Vogt, W. (1978). *Ökonomische Krisentendenzen im gegenwärtigen Kapitalismus*. Frankfurt/New York: Campus.

Murphy, D., Rubart, F., Müller, F. and Raschke, J. (1979). *Protest. Grüne, Bunte und Steuerrebellen*. Reinbek bei Hamburg: Rowohlt.

Musgrave, R.A. and Musgrave, P.B. (1973). *Public Finance in Theory and Practice*. Tokyo: McGraw Hill.

Myers, R.J. and Chandler, J.H. (1962a). 'International Comparisons of Unemployment' *Monthly Labor Review*, 85(6): S.857-64.

Myers, R.J. and Chandler, J.H. (1962b). 'Toward Explaining International Unemployment Rates', *Monthly Labor Review*, 85(8): S.969-74.

Nahamowitz, P. (1978). *Gesetzgebung in den kritischen Systemjahren 1967-69*. Frankfurt/New York: Campus.

Narr, W.-D. (ed.) (1977). *Auf dem Weg zum Einparteienstaat?* Opladen: Westdeutscher Verlag.

Nowotny, E. (ed.) (1974). *Löhne, Preise, Beschäftigung*. Frankfurt: Fischer-Athenäum.

Nutter, G.W. (1978). *Growth of the Government in the West*. Washington, D.C.: American Enterprise Institute for Public Policy Research.

OECD (various dates). *Economic Surveys*. Paris: OECD.

OECD (1972). *Expenditure Trends in OECD Countries 1960-1980*. Paris: OECD.

OECD (1976a). *Public Expenditure on Income Maintenance Programmes*, Paris: OECD.

OECD (1976b). *Public Expenditure on Education*. OECD: Paris.

OECD (1977). *Public Expenditure on Health*. Paris: OECD.

OECD (1978). *Public Expenditure Trends*. Paris: OECD.

OECD (1979a). *National Accounts of OECD Countries, 1960-1977*, 2 vols. Paris: OECD.

OECD (1979b). *Measuring Employment and Unemployment*. Paris: OECD.

Offe, C. (1972). *Strukturprobleme des kapitalistischen Staates*. Frankfurt: Suhrkamp.

Offe, C. (1975). *Berufsbildungsreform. Eine Fallstudie über Reformpolitik*. Frankfurt: Suhrkamp.

Panitch, L. (1977). 'The Development of Corporatism in Liberal Democracies', *Comparative Political Studies*, 10: S.91-126.

Paterson, W.E. and Thomas, A.K. (eds.) (1977). *Social Democratic Parties in Western Europe*. London: Croom Helm.

Payne, J. (1979). 'Inflation, Unemployment and Left-Wing Political Parties: A Reanalysis', *APSR*, 73: 181-5.

Phillips, A.W. (1958). 'The Relation Between Unemployment and the Rate of Change of Money Wage Rates in the United Kingdom, 1861-1957', *Economica*, 34.

Poulantzas, N. (1969). *Pouvoir politique et classes sociales*. Paris: Maspero.

Ramser, H.J. and Angehrn, B. (eds) (1977). *Beschäftigung und Inflation*. Stuttgart/New York: Fischer Verlag.

Raschke, J. (1977). *Organisierter Konflikt in westeuropäischen Parteien*. Opladen: Westdeutscher Verlag.

Raschke, J. (ed.) (1978). *Die politischen Parteien in Westeuropa*. Reinbek bei Hamburg: Rowohlt.

Ronge, V. (1977). *Forschungspolitik als Strukturpolitik*. Munich: Piper.

Ronge, V. (1979). *Bankpolitik im Spätkapitalismus*. Frankfurt: Suhrkamp.

Ronge, V. and Schmieg, G. (1973). *Restriktionen politischer Plannung*. Frankfurt: Fischer-Athenäum.

Schätti, E. (1978). *Die Wirtschaftsordnung der Schweiz. Entwicklungstendenzen seit 1939*. Zürich: Juris Druck & Verlag.

Schmid, G. (1975). *Steuerungssysteme des Arbeitsmarktes. Vergleich von Frankreich, Großbritannien, Schweden, DDR und Sowjetunion mit der Bundesrepublik Deutschland*. Göttingen: Schwartz.

Schmidt, M.G. (1978). 'The Politics of Domestic Reform in the Federal Republic of Germany', *Politics & Society*, 8: 165-200.

Schmidt, M.G. (1979). *Determinanten der staatlichen Politik in industriell-kapitalistischen Demokratien. Ein Uberblick über den Stand der vergleichenden Policy-Forschung*, Universität Konstanz-Fachbereich Politische Wissenschaft/Verwaltungswissenschaft Diskussionsbeiträge no. 11/1979. Konstanz: University Press.

Schmidt, M.G. (1980). *CDU und SPD an der Regierung. Ein Vergleich ihrer Politik in den Ländern*. Frankfurt/New York: Campus.

Schmitter, P.C. (1974). 'Still the Century of Corporatism?', *Review of Politics*, 36: 85-131.

Schmitter, P.C. and Lehmbruch, G. (eds) (1979). *Trends towards Corporatist Intermediation*. Beverly Hills/London: Sage.

Schneider, F. (1978). *Politisch-ökonomische Modelle*. Meisenheim am Glan: Anton Hain.

Schumpeter, J.A. (1978). 'Die Krise des Steuerstaates', pp. 329-79 in Hickel (1976).

Sivard, R.L. (1978). *World Military and Social Expenditures, 1978*. Leesburg: WMSE Publications.

Smith, G. (1976). *Politics in Western Europe*. London: HEB.

Solow, R.M. (1975). 'The Intelligent Citizen's Guide to Inflation', *The Public Interest*, no. 34-8: 30-66.

Soltwedel, R. and Spinanger, D. (1976). *Beschäftigungsprobleme in Industriestaaten, Beiträge zur Arbeitsmarkt- und Berufsforschung BeitrAB, 10*. Nuremberg: Institut für Arbeitsmarkt- und Berufsforschung der Bundesanstalt für Arbeit.

Sorrentino, C. (1970). 'Unemployment in the United States and Seven Foreign Countries', *Monthly Labor Review*, 93(9): 12-23.

Sorrentino, C. (1971). 'Comparing Employment Shifts in 10 Industrialized Countries', *Monthly Labor Review*, 94(10): 3-11.

Sorrentino, C. 'Unemployment in Nine Industrial Countries', *Monthly Labor Review*, 95(6): 29-33.

Sorrentino, C. (1976). 'Unemployment Compensation in Eight Industrial Countries', *Monthly Labor Review*, 99(7): 18-24.

Sorrentino, C. and J. Moy (1974). 'Unemployment in the United States and Nine Industrial Countries', *Monthly Labor Review*, 97(1): 47-52.

Spuler, B., Allen, C.G. and Saunders, N. (1977): *Rulers and Governments of the World*, vol. 3; *1930-1975*. London/New York: Bowker.

Steinmann, G. (1979). *Inflationstheorie*. Paderborn/München/Wien: Schöningh.

Stephens, J.D. (1979). *The Transition from Capitalism to Socialism*. London: Macmillan.

Stobbe, A. (1975). *Gesamtwirtschaftliche Theorie*. Berlin/Heidelberg/New York: Springer.

Tuchfeldt, E. (1978). 'Die schweizerische Arbeitsmarktentwicklung: ein Sonderfall?', pp. 165-200 in O. Issing (ed.), *Aktuelle Probleme der Arbeitslosigkeit*. Berlin: Duncker & Humboldt.

Tufte, E.R. (1978). *Political Control of the Economy*. Princeton: University Press.

Vannereau, C. (1975). 'Comparability of Consumer Price Indices in OECD Countries', *OECD Economic Outlook-Occasional Series*. Paris: OECD, July: 35-56.

Walterskirchen, E. (1977). 'Arbeitsmarktpolitik in Österreich', *WSI-Mitteilungen*, 30: 293-301.

Wiesenthal, H. (1979). 'Die Konzertierte Aktion im Gesundheitswesen'. Bielefeld-Soziologische Fakultät, mimeo.

Wildavsky, A. (1975). *Budgeting. A Comparative Theory of Bureaucracy*. Boston: Little, Brown.

Wittmann, W. (1978). *Öffentliche Finanzen*. Reinbek bei Hamburg: Rowohlt.

# APPENDIX 1

## Correlations between explanatory variables size of the tax state 1975 and growth of the tax state, 1960–75

| | V001 | V002[1] | V003[1] | V004 | V005 | V006[1] | V007 | V008 | V009 | V010 | V011[2] | V012[1,2] | V013 | V014[1] | V015 | V016 | V017 | V018 | V019 | V020 | V021 | V022 | V023 | V024 | V025 | V026 | V027 | V028 |
|---|---|---|---|---|---|---|---|---|---|---|---|---|---|---|---|---|---|---|---|---|---|---|---|---|---|---|---|---|
| V001: Growth of the tax state, 1960–75 | 1.0 | 0.2? | 0.42 | 0.26 | 0.34 | 0.51 | 0.40 | 0.34 | 0.30 | 0.35 | 0.13 | -0.52 | 0.36 | 0.43 | -0.32 | 0.53 | 0.17 | 0.60 | -0.34 | -0.07 | -0.32 | 0.29 | -0.28 | 0.14 | -0.07 | 0.15 | 0.36 | 0.89 |
| V002:[1] Dominant tendency in government, 1960–75 | | 1.0 | 0.77 | 0.79 | 0.52 | 0.54 | -0.19 | 0.12 | 0.63 | 0.64 | 0.40 | -0.57 | 0.80 | 0.65 | -0.18 | 0.33 | 0.13 | 0.41 | 0.22 | 0.03 | 0.07 | 0.12 | -0.05 | 0.22 | -0.10 | 0.28 | 0.40 | 0.41 |
| V003:[1] Left-wing party/prime minister, 1960–75 | | | 1.0 | 0.73 | 0.48 | 0.82 | -0.10 | 0.41 | 0.62 | 0.70 | 0.49 | -0.42 | 0.47 | 0.47 | -0.17 | -0.10 | 0.23 | -0.03 | 0.08 | 0.23 | -0.18 | 0.11 | -0.24 | 0.27 | -0.09 | 0.32 | 0.33 | 0.46 |
| V004: Left-wing parties in office, 1960–75 | | | | 1.0 | 0.27 | 0.60 | 0.09 | 0.19 | 0.46 | 0.45 | 0.49 | -0.47 | 0.57 | 0.63 | -0.15 | 0.19 | 0.12 | -0.23 | 0.06 | 0.09 | -0.03 | -0.06 | -0.13 | 0.28 | 0.12 | 0.13 | 0.23 | 0.30 |
| V005: Left-wing seats, 1960–75 | | | | | 1.0 | 0.59 | -0.25 | 0.37 | 0.60 | 0.60 | 0.23 | -0.21 | 0.46 | 0.31 | -0.02 | 0.04 | 0.12 | 0.08 | 0.09 | 0.09 | -0.20 | 0.07 | -0.28 | 0.18 | -0.10 | 0.40 | 0.20 | 0.54 |
| V006:[1] Dominant party in party system, 1960–75 | | | | | | 1.0 | 0.03 | 0.32 | 0.77 | 0.72 | 0.49 | -0.18 | 0.54 | 0.56 | -0.18 | 0.26 | 0.12 | 0.32 | 0.09 | -0.26 | 0.04 | 0.07 | -0.23 | 0.18 | 0.04 | 0.22 | 0.18 | 0.45 |
| V007: Cohesion of bourgeois tendency, 1960–75 (0 = weak, 1 = strong) | | | | | | | 1.0 | -0.28 | -0.37 | -0.46 | -0.05 | -0.28 | -0.11 | 0.19 | 0.45 | -0.23 | -0.08 | 0.40 | -0.01 | -0.26 | 0.04 | 0.05 | 0.02 | 0.08 | 0.04 | 0.16 | 0.18 | 0.37 |
| V008: Cohesion of Left-wing tendency, 1960–75 (1 = strong, 0 = weak) | | | | | | | | 1.0 | 0.16 | 0.61 | 0.39 | -0.49 | 0.09 | 0.09 | 0.17 | -0.12 | 0.17 | -0.07 | -0.22 | 0.14 | -0.36 | 0.44 | -0.20 | 0.30 | -0.49 | -0.01 | -0.24 | 0.12 |
| V009: Left-wing vote, 1960–75 | | | | | | | | | 1.0 | 0.82 | 0.45 | -0.07 | 0.69 | 0.54 | -0.36 | 0.17 | 0.08 | 0.20 | 0.04 | 0.21 | 0.01 | -0.12 | -0.11 | 0.05 | 0.20 | 0.26 | 0.46 | 0.44 |
| V010: Social democratic vote, 1960–75 | | | | | | | | | | 1.0 | 0.54 | -0.33 | 0.59 | 0.48 | -0.07 | 0.10 | 0.11 | 0.14 | -0.14 | 0.12 | 0.20 | 0.23 | 0.11 | 0.33 | -0.15 | 0.36 | 0.26 | 0.40 |
| V011:[2] Corporatism (1 = weak, 2 = medium, 3 = strong) | | | | | | | | | | | 1.0 | -0.43 | 0.33 | 0.63 | 0.04 | 0.29 | -0.31 | -0.05 | -0.07 | 0.23 | 0.20 | -0.23 | 0.11 | -0.41 | 0.12 | -0.38 | -0.16 | -0.54 |
| V012:[1,2] Strike volume | | | | | | | | | | | | 1.0 | -0.32 | -0.68 | 0.10 | -0.54 | -0.01 | -0.52 | 0.17 | 0.14 | 0.30 | -0.20 | 0.37 | 0.00 | 0.25 | 0.28 | 0.30 | 0.38 |
| V013: Union density | | | | | | | | | | | | | 1.0 | 0.73 | -0.28 | 0.44 | -0.19 | 0.10 | 0.17 | 0.06 | 0.10 | -0.23 | -0.14 | 0.18 | 0.18 | 0.28 | 0.30 | 0.48 |
| V014:[1] Importance of trade unions in collective bargaining | | | | | | | | | | | | | | 1.0 | -0.08 | 0.56 | -0.19 | 0.63 | -0.07 | 0.20 | 0.09 | -0.26 | -0.12 | 0.04 | 0.22 | 0.28 | 0.45 | 0.48 |
| V015: Federalism/centralism (Fed. = 1, Centr. = 0) | | | | | | | | | | | | | | | 1.0 | -0.34 | -0.01 | 0.20 | -0.42 | -0.30 | -0.37 | 0.39 | -0.27 | 0.27 | -0.34 | 0.09 | -0.14 | -0.30 |
| V016: Size of agricultural sector, 1960 | | | | | | | | | | | | | | | | 1.0 | -0.29 | 0.11 | 0.06 | 0.26 | 0.08 | -0.11 | 0.03 | 0.09 | 0.11 | 0.23 | 0.26 | 0.25 |
| V017: Import and export as % of GDP, 1960 | | | | | | | | | | | | | | | | | 1.0 | 0.23 | -0.07 | 0.44 | -0.08 | 0.16 | 0.04 | -0.37 | 0.25 | 0.14 | 0.04 | 0.20 |
| V018: Import and Export as % of GDP, (change) | | | | | | | | | | | | | | | | | | 1.0 | 0.04 | -0.14 | 0.06 | -0.07 | 0.05 | -0.02 | 0.19 | 0.14 | 0.28 | 0.03 |
| V019: Rate of inflation, 1960–75 | | | | | | | | | | | | | | | | | | | 1.0 | 0.37 | 0.55 | -0.46 | 0.19 | -0.20 | -0.67 | -0.48 | -0.23 | -0.31 |
| V020: Rate in economic growth (per capita, constant prices) (1960–75) | | | | | | | | | | | | | | | | | | | | 1.0 | 0.37 | | | | 0.59 | 0.30 | -0.23 | 0.20 |
| V021: Size of agricultural sector, 1960 | | | | | | | | | | | | | | | | | | | | | 1.0 | -0.92 | 0.89 | -0.69 | 0.72 | 0.80 | -0.16 | 0.25 |
| V022: Change in size of agricultural sector, 1975–1960 | | | | | | | | | | | | | | | | | | | | | | 1.0 | -0.64 | 0.64 | -0.69 | | 0.08 | |
| V023: Size of agricultural sector, 1975 | | | | | | | | | | | | | | | | | | | | | | | 1.0 | -0.60 | -0.76 | | -0.23 | 0.03 |
| V024: Size of wage and salary-dependent labour force, 1960 | | | | | | | | | | | | | | | | | | | | | | | | 1.0 | | | | 0.03 |
| V025: Change in size of wage and salary-dependent labour force, 1975–1960 | | | | | | | | | | | | | | | | | | | | | | | | | 1.0 | 1.0 | 0.15 | |
| V026: Size of wage and salary dependent labour force, 1975 | | | | | | | | | | | | | | | | | | | | | | | | | | 1.0 | | 0.32 |
| V027: Size of tax state, 1960 | | | | | | | | | | | | | | | | | | | | | | | | | | | 1.0 | 0.75 |
| V028: Size of tax state, 1975 | | | | | | | | | | | | | | | | | | | | | | | | | | | | 1.0 |

1. Spearman's rho; in all other cases, Pearson's r.
2. N = 18, otherwise N = 21.

## APPENDIX 2

### Correlations between explanatory variables (growth of the tax state, 1950-60)

| | | V001[1] | V002 | V003 | V004 | V005[1] | V006 | V007 | V008 | V009 | V010 | V011 | V012 | V013 | V014[2] | V015 | V016[2] | V017 | V018 | V019 | V020 | V021 | V022 |
|---|---|---|---|---|---|---|---|---|---|---|---|---|---|---|---|---|---|---|---|---|---|---|---|
| V001[1] | Dominant tendency in government, 1950-60 | 1.0 | 0.68 | 0.94 | 0.68 | 0.68 | 0.14 | 0.29 | 0.63 | 0.61 | -0.44 | 0.37 | 0.19 | 0.36 | 0.07 | 0.08 | 0.16 | 0.15 | -0.08 | -0.04 | -0.08 | 0.18 | 0.18 |
| V002 | Left-wing party prime minister, 1950-60 | | 1.0 | 0.73 | 0.58 | 0.57 | 0.12 | 0.28 | 0.49 | 0.56 | -0.47 | 0.07 | 0.16 | 0.13 | 0.02 | -0.19 | 0.20 | 0.30 | -0.29 | -0.12 | -0.06 | -0.11 | 0.49 |
| V003 | Left-wing parties in office, 1950-60 | | | 1.0 | 0.57 | 0.67 | 0.19 | 0.24 | 0.54 | 0.53 | -0.35 | 0.29 | 0.32 | 0.39 | 0.10 | -0.06 | 0.04 | 0.09 | -0.12 | -0.25 | -0.20 | 0.11 | 0.31 |
| V004 | Left-wing seats, 1950-60 | | | | 1.0 | 0.80 | -0.34 | 0.25 | 0.98 | 0.85 | -0.46 | 0.15 | 0.09 | 0.38 | 0.21 | -0.06 | 0.14 | 0.21 | -0.17 | -0.32 | -0.37 | 0.13 | 0.24 |
| V005[1] | Dominant party in party system, 1950-60 | | | | | 1.0 | -0.13 | 0.33 | 0.81 | 0.78 | -0.16 | 0.19 | -0.06 | 0.46 | -0.09 | -0.20 | 0.33 | 0.36 | -0.15 | 0.12 | 0.13 | 0.12 | 0.21 |
| V006 | Cohesion of bourgeois tendency, 1950-60 | | | | | | 1.0 | -0.16 | -0.38 | -0.42 | -0.22 | 0.32 | 0.06 | -0.22 | -0.32 | 0.19 | -0.21 | -0.12 | 0.18 | 0.15 | 0.20 | 0.13 | -0.21 |
| V007 | Cohesion of left-wing tendency, 1950-60 | | | | | | | 1.0 | 0.18 | 0.61 | 0.11 | 0.35 | -0.33 | -0.25 | -0.05 | -0.41 | 0.22 | 0.30 | 0.28 | -0.14 | -0.14 | 0.05 | -0.21 |
| V008 | Left-wing vote, 1950-60 | | | | | | | | 1.0 | 0.81 | -0.43 | 0.17 | 0.08 | 0.47 | 0.02 | -0.01 | 0.10 | 0.19 | -0.20 | -0.29 | -0.35 | 0.11 | 0.25 |
| V009 | Social democratic vote, 1950-60 | | | | | | | | | 1.0 | -0.16 | 0.25 | -0.13 | 0.31 | 0.02 | -0.40 | 0.41 | 0.42 | -0.07 | -0.07 | -0.12 | 0.10 | 0.14 |
| V010 | Federalism/centralism (1/0) | | | | | | | | | | 1.0 | -0.31 | -0.03 | -0.09 | 0.00 | -0.33 | 0.03 | 0.06 | 0.35 | 0.35 | 0.48 | -0.04 | -0.09 |
| V011 | Import and export as % of GDP, 1950 | | | | | | | | | | | 1.0 | -0.31 | -0.00 | -0.62 | -0.10 | 0.10 | 0.12 | 0.35 | 0.16 | -0.00 | 0.10 | -0.35 |
| V012 | Change in import and export as % GDP (1960-1950) | | | | | | | | | | | | 1.0 | -0.00 | 0.68 | 0.44 | 0.10 | 0.08 | 0.24 | -0.31 | -0.23 | 0.10 | 0.52 |
| V013 | Rate of inflation, 1950-60 | | | | | | | | | | | | | 1.0 | -0.17 | 0.19 | 0.24 | 0.14 | -0.33 | -0.12 | -0.15 | 0.08 | 0.14 |
| V014[2] | Economic growth rates, 1950-60 | | | | | | | | | | | | | | 1.0 | 0.54 | -0.70 | -0.38 | 0.02 | -0.51 | -0.46 | -0.32 | 0.41 |
| V015 | Size of agricultural sector, 1950 | | | | | | | | | | | | | | | 1.0 | -0.69 | -0.67 | -0.06 | -0.55 | -0.60 | -0.26 | 0.19 |
| V016[2] | Change in size of agricultural sector (1960-1950) | | | | | | | | | | | | | | | | 1.0 | 0.77 | -0.42 | 0.39 | 0.30 | 0.04 | -0.08 |
| V017 | Size of wage and salary-dependent labour force (1950) | | | | | | | | | | | | | | | | | 1.0 | -0.44 | 0.53 | 0.51 | -0.03 | -0.17 |
| V018 | Change in size of wage and salary-dependent labour force (1960-1950) | | | | | | | | | | | | | | | | | | 1.0 | -0.08 | 0.08 | 0.56 | -0.63 |
| V019 | GDP per capita, 1950 | | | | | | | | | | | | | | | | | | | 1.0 | 0.90 | -0.05 | 0.01 |
| V020 | GDP per capita, 1960 | | | | | | | | | | | | | | | | | | | | 1.0 | 0.10 | 0.01 |
| V021 | Size of the tax state, 1950 | | | | | | | | | | | | | | | | | | | | | 1.0 | -0.67 |
| V022 | Growth of the tax state, 1950-1960 | | | | | | | | | | | | | | | | | | | | | | 1.0 |

1. Spearman's rho; in all other cases, Pearson's r.
2. N = 20; otherwise, N = 21.

## APPENDIX 3

### Correlations between explanatory variables (growth of the tax state, 1973–77)

| | | V001[1] | V002 | V003 | V004 | V005[1] | V006 | V007 | V008 | V009[1] | V010[2] | V011[1] | V012[2] | V013 | V014 | V015 | V016 | V017 | V018 | V019 | V020 |
|---|---|---|---|---|---|---|---|---|---|---|---|---|---|---|---|---|---|---|---|---|---|
| V001:[1] | Dominant tendency in government, 1974–77 | 1.0 | 0.86 | 0.80 | 0.83 | 0.83 | −0.22 | −0.12 | 0.60 | 0.42 | −0.47 | 0.27 | 0.47 | −0.05 | 0.37 | 0.03 | −0.08 | 0.21 | −0.14 | 0.61 | 0.26 |
| V002: | 'Left-wing party' prime minister, 1974–77 | | 1.0 | 0.74 | 0.69 | 0.76 | −0.14 | −0.08 | 0.54 | 0.47 | −0.55 | 0.37 | 0.48 | 0.06 | 0.01 | 0.17 | −0.24 | 0.35 | −0.27 | 0.58 | 0.07 |
| V003: | Left-wing parties in office, 1974–77 | | | 1.0 | 0.53 | 0.69 | −0.14 | −0.09 | 0.41 | 0.42 | −0.48 | 0.27 | 0.47 | 0.01 | 0.42 | −0.19 | 0.01 | 0.17 | −0.34 | 0.52 | 0.31 |
| V004: | Left-wing seats, 1974–77 | | | | 1.0 | 0.86 | −0.39 | −0.33 | 0.95 | 0.42 | −0.34 | 0.53 | 0.37 | −0.32 | 0.16 | −0.16 | −0.06 | 0.29 | −0.06 | 0.37 | 0.41 |
| V005:[1] | Dominant party in party system, 1974–77 | | | | | 1.0 | −0.12 | −0.11 | 0.65 | 0.51 | −0.39 | 0.48 | 0.54 | −0.05 | 0.25 | −0.19 | 0.05 | 0.26 | 0.15 | 0.56 | 0.42 |
| V006: | Cohesion of bourgeois tendency, 1974–77 | | | | | | 1.0 | 0.14 | −0.40 | −0.19 | 0.00 | −0.15 | −0.04 | 0.00 | −0.06 | 0.14 | −0.11 | 0.19 | −0.07 | 0.23 | −0.30 |
| V007: | Cohesion of left-wing tendency, 1974–77 | | | | | | | 1.0 | 0.12 | 0.23 | −0.20 | −0.39 | 0.29 | 0.02 | 0.44 | −0.25 | −0.27 | 0.29 | −0.30 | 0.31 | 0.26 |
| V008: | Left-wing vote, 1974–77 | | | | | | | | 1.0 | 0.42 | −0.66 | 0.53 | 0.46 | 0.04 | 0.13 | −0.04 | −0.07 | 0.20 | −0.22 | 0.33 | 0.41 |
| V009:[1] | Corporatism | | | | | | | | | 1.0 | −0.70 | 0.34 | 0.66 | 0.04 | 0.23 | 0.04 | 0.09 | 0.17 | −0.37 | 0.14 | 0.37 |
| V010:[2] | Strike volume, 1974–77 | | | | | | | | | | 1.0 | −0.24 | −0.67 | 0.05 | −0.28 | −0.10 | 0.21 | −0.26 | 0.56 | −0.32 | −0.37 |
| V011:[1] | Union density | | | | | | | | | | | 1.0 | 0.71 | −0.25 | 0.55 | −0.16 | −0.10 | 0.35 | 0.17 | 0.32 | 0.29 |
| V012:[2] | Importance of trade unions' confederation in collective bargaining | | | | | | | | | | | | 1.0 | −0.04 | 0.62 | −0.09 | −0.10 | 0.32 | −0.34 | 0.52 | 0.37 |
| V013: | Federalism/centralism | | | | | | | | | | | | | 1.0 | −0.41 | 0.12 | −0.29 | 0.08 | −0.42 | −0.21 | −0.35 |
| V014: | Import and export as % of GDP, 1975 | | | | | | | | | | | | | | 1.0 | −0.35 | 0.04 | 0.14 | 0.05 | 0.39 | 0.54 |
| V015: | Economic growth rates (per capita, constant prices), 1974–77 | | | | | | | | | | | | | | | 1.0 | 0.12 | −0.40 | 0.02 | 0.15 | −0.72 |
| V016: | Size of agricultural sector, 1975 | | | | | | | | | | | | | | | | 1.0 | −0.63 | 0.44 | −0.24 | −0.19 |
| V017: | Size of wage and salary-dependent labour force, 1975 | | | | | | | | | | | | | | | | | 1.0 | 0.00 | 0.21 | 0.46 |
| V018: | Rate of inflation, 1974–77 | | | | | | | | | | | | | | | | | | 1.0 | −0.39 | −0.22 |
| V019: | Size of the tax state, 1973 | | | | | | | | | | | | | | | | | | | 1.0 | 0.29 |
| V020: | Growth of the tax state (1977–1973) | | | | | | | | | | | | | | | | | | | | 1.0 |

1. Spearman's rho; in all other cases, Pearson's r.
2. N = 18; else: N = 20 (Israel excluded).

# 4

# Securing the Safety
# of the Nation-State
Hans Keman
University of Amsterdam

## Introduction

**This chapter**, like those that preceded it, is devoted to an exploration of the determinants of the priorities that governments in
democratic capitalist states assign to particular aspects of public
policy. But, whereas questions concerning overall patterns of
public expenditure (in particular, welfare expenditure) and the
nature of macroeconomic policy have received extensive coverage
in the comparative public policy literature of the last decade, issues
concerning the security of the state have received scant attention.[1]
While this omission is understandable with regard to the various
aspects of internal security — law, justice and policing — since the
available data are notoriously unreliable, it is more surprising with
regard to the external security function of the state. Here the data
are much more reliable and accessible, and the issues involved in
defence policy are generally regarded as being of the utmost importance. Like all matters pertaining to security, such issues involve
the core rationale of the state in so far as they bear directly on the
state's claim to 'the monopoly of the legitimate use of physical
force within a given territory' (Weber, 1968: 78). Whether looked
at in the philosophical terms of theorists such as Hobbes, or in the

*Author's Note. Apart from* the support of the ECPR, the preparation of this
chapter has been made possible by the Subfaculty of Political and Social Sciences of
the University of Amsterdam. I also wish to thank Dietmar Braun, Francis G.
Castles, Cees van der Eijk, Gerd Junne, Manfred Schmidt and Frans van Veen for
their support and useful comments on previous versions of this chapter.

more practical manner of the sovereign and his advisors, the traditional role of statecraft has been to ensure the integrity of the nation from foreign foes and the peace of the realm from those who
would disturb it. It is only in comparatively recent times, and with
the rise of the welfare state in particular, that the security functions
of the state, whether measured in terms of public expenditure, per-
sonnel or salience to policy-makers, have taken second place to
other aspects of public policy.

Moreover, while questions of security have receded somewhat in
terms of the priority they are accorded by democratic capitalist
governments, a substantial part of most nations' resources have
been devoted to defence during the postwar period.[2] This is shown
in Table 1, which presents figures for military expenditure expressed as a percentage of gross domestic product at the mid-point of
each postwar decade. In 1955 the mean expenditure in 18 capitalist
democracies was 4.1 percent of GDP; and, although the general
trend over the subsequent two decades was one of almost universal
decline, military expenditure still consumed 2.8 percent of national
resources in the mid-1970s.

Obviously, there is a major difference between the order of
magnitude of defence expenditure and that of welfare state expenditure, a difference that was increasing throughout the period. This
may be indicated by a comparison of military expenditure with
transfer payments to households, taken as a crude indicator of an
important dimension of welfare state development in the capitalist
democracies. Between 1955 and 1975 the mean level of transfer
payments increased from 7.3 to 13.8 percent of GDP (see OECD,
1978: 14-15). While the vast increase in the extent of the public
economy and the welfare state generally (see Wilensky, 1975, 1976;
Cameron, 1978; Schmidt, 1979) justifies the attention that comparative public policy studies have paid to these areas, external
security policy is not of negligible interest only. In the earlier
period half the countries were devoting in excess of 20 percent of
the central government budget to military expenditure, and even in
1975 eight countries were spending more than 10 percent (SIPRI,
1975, 1978).

Moreover, patterns of military expenditure are of interest
precisely because they manifest tendencies apparently quite different from those typical of the better researched areas of public
policy. Not only has military expenditure (as a percentage of GDP)
declined while welfare expenditure has expanded greatly, but the
dynamic of these tendencies also appears to be quite different.

## TABLE 1
### Levels of expenditure on external security as a percentage of GDP in 18 capitalist democracies in 1955, 1965 and 1975, and change over the entire period

| Name of country | External security in: | | | Change, 1955 – 75 |
|---|---|---|---|---|
| | 1955 | 1965 | 1975 | |
| | % | % | % | % |
| Australia | 3.6 | 3.4 | 2.8 | – 0.8 |
| Austria | 0.2 | 1.3 | 1.2 | 1.0 |
| Belgium | 3.8 | 3.2 | 3.1 | – 0.7 |
| Canada | 6.6 | 3.2 | 1.9 | – 4.7 |
| Denmark | 3.2 | 2.8 | 2.6 | – 0.6 |
| Finland | 1.6 | 1.7 | 1.5 | – 0.1 |
| France | 6.4 | 5.2 | 3.9 | – 2.5 |
| Germany | 4.1 | 4.3 | 3.6 | – 0.5 |
| Ireland | 1.6 | 1.4 | 1.7 | 0.1 |
| Italy | 3.7 | 3.3 | 2.8 | – 0.9 |
| Japan | 1.8 | 1.0 | 0.9 | – 0.9 |
| Netherlands | 5.7 | 3.9 | 3.5 | – 2.2 |
| New Zealand | 2.5 | 2.1 | 1.7 | – 0.8 |
| Norway | 3.9 | 3.7 | 3.2 | – 0.7 |
| Sweden | 4.8 | 4.0 | 3.4 | – 1.4 |
| Switzerland | 2.8 | 2.7 | 2.0 | – 0.8 |
| United Kingdom | 8.2 | 5.9 | 5.0 | – 3.2 |
| United States | 10.0 | 7.5 | 6.0 | – 4.0 |
| Mean | 4.1 | 3.4 | 2.8 | – 1.3 |

*Source:* SIPRI Yearbooks, 1975 and 1978.

## TABLE 2
### Intercorrelations of military expenditure, 1955, 1965 and 1975*

| | 1965 | 1975 |
|---|---|---|
| 1955 | 0.93 | 0.88 |
| 1965 | — | 0.98 |

*No. of cases = 18; all Pearson product – moment correlations.

Thus, while Chapter 2 substantially confirms the OECD conclusion that this period was one of a 'growing international dispersion in the relative size of public sectors' (OECD, 1978: 13), the data provided in Table 1 above indicate a high degree of stability in the relative external security output of the capitalist democracies over time. Thus, as indicated in Table 2, the intercorrelation between military expenditure in 1955 and 1975 is as high as 0.88. Furthermore, what change there is during the two decades is seemingly convergent in character with a correlation between the level of external security spending in 1955 and subsequent expenditure change being of the order of $-0.90$. Overall, it would appear that there are strong forces promoting similarity among capitalist democracies. However, it should be added that this tendency towards similarity hardly affects the differences between the countries of this study. Apart from Canada, there is no change in terms of rank order throughout the period.[3] Since one of the paramount objectives of the Research Group on Party Differences and Public Policy was to examine the diversity of factors determining the nature of public policy outcomes in different policy areas, the prima facie evidence of widely divergent trends in respect to military and welfare expenditure levels and changes suggests the value of research in the external security area as a means of extending the range of our knowledge of the factors involved in the public policy process.

A rather similar conclusion emerges if we stop to reflect on the nature of the independent variables that might be considered as major candidates for the explanation of external security levels and changes. On the other hand, we would expect to encounter some of the same factors relevant in other fields of public expenditure, e.g., the role of the domestic economy in producing the resources required to fund the military effort, and the role of ideology in shaping party differences on the importance of the external security objective. However, even in these respects we might well expect similar factors to operate rather differently in the context of external security policy. It might be that the need for external security provision is more finite than the demand for welfare, which would suggest that, once resources to achieve an 'optimum' level of military preparedness had been reached, there would be a decline in the percentage of GDP devoted to such purposes.[4] Regarding welfare expenditure and the extent of the public economy as a whole, it has been assumed that parties of the Left will demonstrate a preference for increased spending. However, given the traditional antipathy of the Left to the security functions of the capitalist state, we might expect to find the expenditure preferences of Left and Right reversed in the external security field. Alternatively, we might surmise that defence is regarded as a fundamental concern by all governments and that party differences are, therefore, much less pronounced in this area.

On the other hand, there is clearly a variety of factors which may be operative in shaping external security policy but which are not encountered in the domestic sphere, or only to a much lesser extent. External security is crucially affected by the perceived threat of events in the international sphere, as well as by the structure of the international arena. Thus, for example, the general decline in military expenditure in the period under observation is partially a consequence of the waning of Cold War tension since the 1950s, while much of the difference in expenditure between countries may be attributable to differential participation in the alliances that structure the response to the Cold War. Furthermore, a nation's military stance will be shaped by a variety of factors that are of marginal importance compared with other aspects of public policy. Some of these are geopolitical, in the sense that they pertain to influences such as distance from the contemporary centre of international conflict or a nation's size and population, all of which may be expected to have a direct effect on the perception of threat and the appropriate response to it.[5] Others may involve the direct imposition of a particular policy stance by the international community, as in the case of the demilitarized status of certain of the defeated members of the Axis Powers. Thus, irrespective of our final conclusions concerning the determination of government priorities in the external security field, we evidently cannot tackle this question without bringing into the analysis a whole range of factors largely ignored by previous contributions to comparative public policy studies.

There is one final reason why the lack of attention to external security policy is surprising, and that is the fact that the level of expenditure on defence may have direct or indirect consequences for the pursuit of other public policy priorities. Such a possibility emerges from a number of studies of fiscal processes in individual democratic capitalist states, which suggest that military expenditure in wartime or in other periods of tension may have a displacement effect in increasing the floor of acceptable levels of public expenditure with a subsequent shift of resources to other policy areas when tension declines (see Peacock and Wiseman, 1961; Musgrave, 1969; and Wildavsky, 1975). In other words, although external security policy may be less intrinsically connected with domestic politics than other areas of public expenditure, there may well be trade-off mechanisms at work, which affect domestic political concerns such as the level of welfare provision. Such a possibility is quite explicit in the traditional adage of statecraft concerning the need to provide 'guns before butter', and might well suggest a complex interaction between international politics, domestic economic constraints and policy outcomes in several areas.[6] The possibility of such an interaction between external security and various aspects of domestic policy means that the issue of what factors shape military expenditure is interesting not merely as an instance of another and different policy area, but also because it may potentially contribute to a further understanding of topics that are explored elsewhere in this volume.

## Research design

This chapter will attempt to provide answers to three basic questions: (1) What were the major determinants of levels of military expenditure in 1955, 1965 and 1975? (2) What were the causes of changing levels of expenditure during the period 1955-75? (3) Did the development of external security policy have any consequences for public policy in other areas? As in previous chapters, we shall be seeking to discover a patterned relationship between public policy outcomes and a set of independent variables.

Although we shall necessarily employ a range of independent variables somewhat different from those considered in other chapters, the nature of research design utilized is basically similar to that found elsewhere in the volume. The focus is on much the same time period, with the mid-decade time points being taken as representative of certain stages in the development of external security policy in the contemporary democratic capitalist state. The year 1955 marks a time of considerable Cold War tension and of an early stage in the European disengagement from direct forms of colonial rule. By 1965 the Cold War was fading away and decolonization was almost completed, to be replaced by a neo-colonialism, which rested more on economic than on military competition (see Barraclough, 1979; Krippendorf, 1975). Looked at from the vantage point of the early 1980s, 1975 appears as a time of changing geopolitical realities. Tension within Europe was at its nadir, but new economic realities threatened to alter relationships with the Third World, with potentially serious consequences for external security policy. In general terms, the whole period is one in which one would expect economic priorities to have a greater salience for policy-makers than military ones. The almost universal decline in military expenditure reflects these changing priorities. However, as we shall find in discussing the interaction of military and domestic policy, the balance of priorities appears to change afresh, and this could have major policy and political implications for the 1980s.

The universe of discourse chosen for analysis is essentially the same as elsewhere in this volume. Of the democratic capitalist nations, only Iceland (on grounds of having no military apparatus of its own), Luxembourg (on grounds of its small population) and Israel (on grounds of virtually permanent war status) were excluded. The one major cross-national analysis of military expenditure levels (Hill, 1978) employs a sample of as many as 109 cases. It might be argued that such a research strategy was more appropriate in the case of external security expenditure than in regard to welfare-related expenditures; since, in contrast to this latter area, the average military expenditure-GNP ratio in the democratic capitalist nations differs very little from the wider sample for which there are available data. Thus, in 1965 average military expenditure in our 18-nation sample was 3.4 percent of GDP and for all 109 nations it was 3.2 percent (see Hill, 1978: 45). However, there remain strong reasons for preferring the smaller sample. Similar averages in the two groups of countries conceal a very different range of variability. The range of spending levels in the wider sample varies from 0.1 (Panama) to 21.2 percent (South Vietnam), with an associated standard deviation of 2.9, whereas the countries in Table 1 are much more homogeneous, ranging from 1.0 (Japan) to 7.5 percent (USA), with a standard deviation of 1.7. This being so, the general argument of this volume still holds that the use of extremely diverse samples may serve to obscure the patterned similarities that pertain in countries of a particular type. Such a view is, in fact, strongly supported by findings of Hill's wider study, which not only obtained a higher degree of explained variation when the sample was stratified by nation type, but also revealed 'that the pattern of determinative forces was somewhat different for nations of relatively more or less wealth' (Hill, 1978: 53). Our own universe of discourse is also partly defined in terms of level of economic development, but has the further element of homogeneity in that it is characterized by the existence of parliamentary democratic procedures through which the electorate could potentially influence external security policy.

Finally, the mode of statistical analysis used in locating patterns of military expenditure variation is that which is common to the entire research project. Thus, our interpretation rests primarily on simple bivariate analysis as a means of uncovering consistent patterns of association in the data. Although we have similar reservations as those expressed in Chapter 2 concerning the use of multivariate techniques where sample size is small and the seemingly significant explanatory variables are interrelated, we will at certain points employ a strictly limited multivariate design. This decision is quite pragmatic, and stems from the very low degree of collinearity that happens to characterize the most important explanatory variables in our analysis.

### Possible causes of external security policy

The dependent data in this analysis are the levels of military expenditure and change in expenditure reported in Table 1. What we hope to achieve is the location of a pattern of causation that explains a large degree of the variation manifested by the data. The available literature suggests that the possible causes of military expenditure may be conveniently grouped under four headings: (1) Domestic politics; (2) Domestic policies; (3) Socioeconomic structures; and (4) Geopolitical factors.

### Domestic politics

It is possible to advance a range of diverse hypotheses concerning the effect of party preferences on the level of military expenditure. The traditional rationale for the attachment of established elites to the idea of a strong state was the need to provide external security against the possible adventurism of other nations. In their early stages, the emergent socialist movements of Western Europe were opposed to the waste of men and productive capacity entailed in what were widely seen as 'capitalist' wars. These traditional stereotypes of the Right as the party of security and the Left as the party of anti-militarism persist in most countries to the present day (see Budge and Farlie, 1977) and might lead us to expect a difference in the expenditure preferences. On the other hand, it has frequently been suggested that the general decline of ideological intensity that has typified the postwar era, combined with the perceived need to defend the advanced welfare state of mature capitalism against the aggressive designs of rival socio-political systems, has united Right and Left on just those issues relating to the preservation of the integrity of the state. This would suggest that, in contrast to the persisting stereotypes, parties would not differ with regard to actual external security outcomes, and it might even be surmised that continuing doubts about the soundness of the left-wing position on defence might push such parties in to an even more expansive stance in order to legitimate themselves with the middle ground of the electorate (see Miliband, 1969; Dankbaar and Keman, 1979).

In order to arrive at some conclusion concerning these rival views of the relationship between party preference and military expenditure, we utilize a variety of measures of party strength used in the previous chapters. They include left-wing and right-wing parliamentary seats (operationalized exactly as in Chapter 2) employed as measures of the potential for a particular ideological stance to influence external security policy. In addition, we use the composite indicator of political complexion of government and parliament (GAPS), developed in Chapter 2 of this volume, as an overall measure of the balance of party political tendencies in each nation. It is meant to denote the extent to which the Left on the one hand, and the Right on the other, exert political control regarding public expenditure.

*Domestic policies*

Both the traditional 'guns or butter' equation and the notion of an 'inspection process' of policy priorities (see Peacock and Wiseman, 1961) by electorate and political leaders regarding the distribution of public expenditure imply that there is a 'trade-off' process between military and non-military expenditure, especially in a period of economic crisis or international tension. In order to investigate this process we include non-military expenditure (expressed in percentage of GDP) as an independent variable.[7] Since other contributions to this volume have already demonstrated a strong link between total public expenditure levels and domestic politics, the trade-off argument in its simple form might lead us to expect a pattern of causation in which party preferences, levels of domestic public expenditure and military expenditure were closely linked. However, theoretical reasons might lead us to expect trade-off

processes to be rather more complex than implied by 'guns or butter', while, despite an interaction between party politics and both
aspects of public policy, the strength of the relationships may not be
adequately demonstrated by a bivariate analysis. The problem is
that the logic of the trade-off argument is the more compelling as
the situation approximates a zero-sum game. This is likely to occur
where those forces shaping government spending priorities have a
strong ideological preference for limited government expenditure,
or where the size of the public economy is sufficiently extensive to
create serious difficulties of economic stability. The former condition is most likely to occur where a right-wing government feels it
necessary to make small concessions to a vastly increased citizen demand for welfare by making disproportionately large reductions in
military expenditure. The latter condition may arise when a government — almost certainly of non-right-wing persuasion — has so increased public expenditure that the dangers of a major decrease in
defence expenditure appear less daunting than the economic
disruption that may follow from further expansion. In other
words, the governments that decrease military expenditure most are
likely to be those that hold most firmly to the fundamental objectives of both Left and Right. Between these extremes, parties willing to countenance or embrace moderate increases in public expenditure will be able to combine a comparatively modest decline in
military expenditure with greater or lesser increases in other areas
of public expenditure. This 'modified' trade-off thesis will be
discussed in the last section of this chapter.

*Socioeconomic structures*
From the earliest political economists to the most recent international relations theory, there has been a strong emphasis on the
resource relatedness of external security effort. David Ricardo
pointed to the special character of military consumption in an-
nihilating 'a capital which will never yield any further revenue'
(Ricardo, 1951: 161). Essentially, external security expenditure is
waste or 'non-reproductive' consumption, which can be funded only if there is an economic surplus above and beyond what is required for the reproduction of the society. Whether this argument
is put in the terms of early political economy, neo-Marxist analysis
(see Baran and Sweezy, 1966; Kidron, 1970; and Smith, 1977) or international relations theory (see Knorr, 1970; Russett, 1970), it
amounts to an assertion that the economic strength of a nation is a

direct cause, or at least a background condition, of anything more than a minimum external security effort. The causal argument implies that there is some threshold of economic strength below which nations will have to adopt an extremely defensive military posture, combining low levels of expenditure with either neutral status or reliance on richer allies. Only nations with appreciable economic resources will be able to abandon a defensive posture and utilize their surplus resources to fund an aggressive role in international affairs. Moreover, in such a view the richer nations will be compelled to adopt such a role in so far as other economically strong nations will be likely to interpret a lack of military preparedness as a sign of weakness. The argument that economic strength is a background condition for an appreciable military effort implies a rather similar threshold assumption, although in this case the threshold is one beyond which a substantial level of external security expenditure is a possibility rather than a necessity. In this view, the choice between an aggressive or defensive posture will be a function of a range of factors, some of which may be non-economic in character. Both arguments are compatible with an observed decline in levels of military expenditure, since the level of threat in the international arena may decrease, thereby making it possible for all nations to achieve a similar level of preparedness with less outlay, or the economic resources of all countries may increase, thereby permitting a similar level of tolerance to threat with a lower percentage of national resources.

In our subsequent analysis, we shall employ four separate variables as measures of the socioeconomic resource base of a nation. 'Total gross domestic product' is used as an indicator of the overall resource base of a nation. In strict terms, this indicates only the overall size of the economic surplus available for military consumption, and not the level of per capita resource; for, as is well-known, total GDP is composed of the elements of total population and 'GDP per capita'.[8] The latter element indicates the relative prosperity of a nation and to some extent its productivity. A (neo-) Marxist argument, premised on the 'non-reproductive' role of military expenditure — and especially its consumption — as an integral part of the domestic economy of capitalism, would suggest that, the greater the level of economic prosperity expressed in terms of GDP per capita, 'the more military expenditure is needed to maintain demand' (Smith, 1977: 66). In theory, such a phenomenon would be quite compatible with the absence of a threshold effect for the total economic strength of a nation, since we might expect to find small prosperous nations devoting a higher percentage of GDP to military expenditure than larger, less prosperous, ones. In reality, the presence of a number of large prosperous countries in our universe of discourse suggests that these effects will be to some extent confounded, but it is our hope that an analysis of the separate effects of total GDP and GDP per capita will allow us to disentangle the diverse influences of both economic strength and economic prosperity.

Finally, we shall examine the possible impact of 'Change in total GDP' and 'Change in GDP per capita' (both at constant prices) on military expenditure. As we already have noted, an overall decline in military expenditure levels remains compatible with the presence of a threshold effect. However, a negative association between per capita income change and military expenditure change would not be readily compatible with the Marxist surplus absorption thesis; for, according to this view, increased economic prosperity implies an increased surplus, which ought to be channelled into 'non-reproductive' military consumption. This is a point to which we shall return in the light of our subsequent empirical analysis.

### Geopolitical factors

Much of the recent debate concerning the determinants of military posture has centred around questions of the arms race (see Richardson, 1960; Smoker, 1964), alliance structures (see Singer and Small, 1972; Wallace, 1971) and the impact of both on a nation's position within a relatively unchanging geopolitical arena. Whereas, for wide samples of nations, such factors may involve a high degree of generalization across regional subsets, for our universe of discourse the issues may be particularized in terms of the degree of involvement of different democratic capitalist states in the Cold War. The argument that membership of alliances is conducive to higher military expenditure will be tested by the use of two dummy variables: on the one hand, alliance membership as such and, on the other, NATO membership, the latter serving as an indicator of central involvement in Cold War activity.

It should, however, be noted that neither alliance indicator fully encapsulates what we might reasonably surmise about the nature of the relationship between position in the international arena and military posture. Alliance membership distinguishes between countries that choose to band together for mutual protection and those that opt for individual neutrality, but does not distinguish between nations in terms of their position in geopolitical space. NATO membership distinguishes between countries with a particular stance towards the defence of Europe, but does not necessarily imply a positive commitment to deploy military forces at the centre of Cold War tension. Both indicators also fail to take account of the fact that some nations do not choose their military stance at all, but have it imposed upon them by the international community, as in the case of Austria, Finland and Japan. For these reasons, we have devised a rank-order scale of military stance, which attempts to take into account activity within the European theatre and the voluntary or involuntary nature of a nation's status within the international community. Another noteworthy aspect that is not captured in the alliance indicators is the existence of the so-called 'super-powers' (i.e. the Soviet Union and the USA and, perhaps to some extent of late, China). These nations are to be considered as a 'class in themselves' (Knorr, 1970: 51), for they are always and everywhere involved in Cold War structures and inherent international tension, be it in Europe or elsewhere. Consequently their military stance is fundamentally distinct from other countries, and therefore the USA is differently scored on the scale of military stance, which is as follows:

0 = imposed neutral or demilitarized status (Austria, Finland, Japan)

1 = either voluntary neutral or allied with no troops in Europe (Australia, Ireland, New Zealand, Sweden, Switzerland)

2 = allied and with troops in Europe (Belgium, Canada, Denmark, France, Germany, Italy, Netherlands, Norway, United Kingdom)

3 = super-power with troops in Europe (USA)

Not surprisingly, given the constant structure implied by the nature of the geopolitical thesis, all three variables employed here are invariant during the relatively short period of two decades.

*The interrelation of possible causes*

The variables grouped under each separate heading above are often quite closely interrelated. Obviously, the parliamentary strength of Right and Left is not wholly independent from GAPS. As we already noted, economic strength and prosperity are inherently linked, and activity in the international arena — especially in Europe — is related to NATO membership. These various degrees

## TABLE 3
### Correlation – matrix of the independent variables in 1975 and change, 1955 – 1975*

| | (01) | (02) | (03) | (04) | (05) | (06) | (07) | (08) | (09) | (10) | (11) | (12) |
|---|---|---|---|---|---|---|---|---|---|---|---|---|
| **Domestic politics** | | | | | | | | | | | | |
| (1) Soc. dem. seats | — | -0.11 | 0.76 | 0.13 | 0.03 | -0.40 | -0.16 | -0.15 | -0.14 | 0.03 | -0.23 | -0.13 |
| (2) Right-wing seats | | — | -0.63 | -0.62 | -0.61 | 0.50 | 0.01 | -0.19 | -0.26 | 0.16 | -0.08 | -0.10 |
| (3) GAPS (x) | | | — | 0.47 | 0.50 | -0.58 | -0.14 | 0.01 | 0.26 | -0.08 | -0.11 | -0.03 |
| **Domestic policies** | | | | | | | | | | | | |
| (4) Non-mil. expenditure | | | | — | 0.79 | -0.34 | -0.19 | -0.07 | 0.07 | 0.04 | 0.33 | 0.39 |
| (5) Change in non-mil. exp. | | | | | — | -0.09 | -0.08 | 0.27 | 0.37 | -0.02 | 0.28 | 0.37 |
| **Socioeconomic structures** | | | | | | | | | | | | |
| (6) GDP Total | | | | | | — | 0.24 | 0.44 | 0.44 | 0.33 | 0.47 | 0.42 |
| (7) Change in GDP total | | | | | | | — | -0.16 | 0.21 | -0.46 | -0.22 | -0.33 |
| (8) GDP per capita | | | | | | | | — | 0.90 | 0.23 | 0.29 | 0.23 |
| (9) Change in GDP pC | | | | | | | | | — | 0.01 | 0.26 | 0.10 |
| **Geopolitical factors** | | | | | | | | | | | | |
| (10) Alliance membership | | | | | | | | | | — | 0.79 | 0.79 |
| (11) NATO membership | | | | | | | | | | | — | 0.85 |
| (12) Military stance (x) | | | | | | | | | | | | — |

*The data of variables (1) – (3) are originated in the same way as in Chapter 2 above; variables (4) – (9) are taken from OECD (1977, 1978) and, if necessary, from national statistics; variables (10) and (11) are based on Banks (1975).
All results in this table are Pearson product – moment correlations except the variables marked with an (x) i.e. nos. (3) and (12), which are Spearman rank-order correlations; no. of cases = 18. All political variables are measured over the period between 1956-75 (nos. (1) – (3)) as averages, whereas the other change-variables are computed as first differences over the whole period.

of interrelationship can be judged by the correlation matrix, which appears in Table 3. Looking at the several associations under the separate headings, it will be noticed, with regard to 'domestic politics', that party differences are related to 'domestic policies'. The Right seems to possess so-called 'veto power' regarding non-military expenditure, whereas GAPS shows a positive relationship with 'domestic policies'. Both outcomes signify the importance of national political agents with regard to public policy formation, thus providing a basis for examining the 'modified' trade-off thesis.

Although many of the socioeconomic variables are comparatively highly interrelated, they never exceed the 0.60 mark, beyond which the danger of multicollinearity becomes almost unavoidable (the only exception is the interrelation between GDP per capital and change thereof). It should also be noticed that total GDP is closely related with 'domestic politics'. This seems merely a result of the fact that both the USA and Japan are among the largest populated and economically strongest countries of our universe and that both possess a very strong right-wing. In this sense both nations are to some extent deviant cases. Problems like these are almost unavoidable in an analysis with the limited number of cases employed throughout this book. At the same time, it signifies that even high bivariate relationships should be treated with care. This applies especially to the outcome of multivariate analysis, which will be examined in combination with the residuals (see Tufte, 1974). As far as the interrelations between the possible causes of external security expenditure are concerned, many of the most important dimensions do not appear highly interrelated and, to the extent that they are, not at a level incompatible with subsequent bi- and multivariate analysis. Given these results regarding the interrelation of the independent variables that figure in this chapter, we will now turn to a more detailed examination of the forces that may be operative with regard to the levels of military expenditure.

## The constant structure of external security effort

Although it is evident that the levels of military expenditure change over time, it is nevertheless the case that the differences between the various countries remain roughly the same. The only exception to this observed pattern since 1955 is Canada, which, in comparative terms, started from an extraordinarily high level, but declined more or less dramatically in the two decades since 1955. Except for this sole 'deviant' case, it cannot be stressed enough that the obvious overall similarity of the pattern of expenditure on external security in capitalist democracies is our basic point of departure in this section. Thus our main concern is to find out what factors account for this supposedly constant structure. Therefore we shall first discuss some of the properties of external security policy which all nations in this study bear in common.

The very existence of any nation-state rests on its sovereignty, which is in general acknowledged by its people and other nations. If it is not, then the supreme power of the state must be forced upon the people within the nation and be defended against enemies outside the nation-state, i.e. against other nation-states. In practice, this means that every nation must secure itself 'from the violence and invasion of other independent societies [which] can be performed only by means of military force. But the expense both of preparing this military force in time of peace, and employing it in times of war, is very different in the different states of society, in the different periods of improvement' (Smith, 1874: 541). In short, there is no political alternative to an external security policy, either in Smith's time or today. And there is still no option available to maintain a military apparatus without calling upon the national economic resources: defence is a public good and hence subject to public policy formation (see Pryor, 1968; Kennedy, 1975; and Harrison Wagner, 1975). Taking these essential properites of external security into account, the extent to which a pattern of similarity emerges among the various nations would seem to be basically a consequence of the geopolitical context and the availability of resources (finance and manpower) and finally of a domestic political consensus to devote the resources to the cause of external security. In Table 4 we give the outcome of the bivariate analysis of the independent variables in this study with regard to the levels of military expenditure. The results clearly indicate that the socioeconomic and geopolitical factors are of particular importance with regard to levels of military expenditure. Leaving aside for the moment the change-variables, all the results are around the 0.60 mark or more. It should be noticed, however, that the economic variables, unlike the geopolitical ones, tend to become less related to military expenditure at subsequent points of time.[9] It is also rather obvious that domestic politics appear to have little influence on the actual effort devoted to external security. Yet this

## TABLE 4
### Bivariate relationships of the independent variables
### with the levels of military expenditure
### (percentage of GDP)*

|  | Level of military expenditure in: | | |
|---|---|---|---|
|  | 1955 | 1965 | 1975 |
| (1) Social democratic seats | − 0.21 | − 0.17 | − 0.13 |
| (2) Right-wing seats | 0.02 | 0.13 | 0.16 |
| (3) GAPS (x) | 0.01 | 0.05 | − 0.03 |
| (4) Non-military expenditure | − 0.26 | 0.14 | 0.16 |
| (5) Change in non-military spending | — | 0.33 | 0.24 |
| (6) Total GDP | 0.80 | 0.71 | 0.59 |
| (7) Change in total GDP | — | − 0.35 | − 0.47 |
| (8) GDP per capita | 0.66 | 0.63 | 0.48 |
| (9) Change in GDP per capita | — | 0.51 | 0.32 |
| (10) Alliance membership | 0.59 | 0.58 | 0.57 |
| (11) NATO membership | 0.66 | 0.64 | 0.64 |
| (12) Military stance (x) | 0.82 | 0.80 | 0.79 |

*See explanation under Table 3; $N = 18$; all relationships in this table are computed at the same point of time as is indicated in the headings; the change variables (nos. (5), (7) and (9)) represent the periods 1955-65 and 1965-75 respectively, whereas the domestic political variables (nos. (1)-(3)) represent the respective averages between 1946-55, 1956-65 and 1966-75.

does not necessarily imply that 'politics does not matter' at all, but may signify that the complexion of parliament and government and its inherent party differences are related to matters of external security in a different manner than is the case in other fields of public policy. This observation also holds true for the relationship between non-military expenditure and military expenditure. There is, apparently, no straightforward trade-off; whether a 'modified' version can be said to occur is a question with which we will deal in the final section of this chapter. For the moment it suffices to note that the main causal effects are to be found in areas other than domestic politics and policies. However, in the following section we shall elaborate on a plausible suggestion, namely that 'politics does matter', albeit indirectly rather than directly.

## *The indirect impact of domestic politics*

It is our contention that 'domestic politics' sometimes, and under certain circumstances, may play a part with regard to the level of military expenditure. However, to a large extent the role of domestic political forces is probably a consequence of either socioeconomic or geopolitical factors and therefore indirect. Generally speaking, no political party within the existing political system denies an 'adequate' effort in the field of external security. As far as party differences are involved, these are more or less limited to discussions relating to the meaning of 'adequate' and whether or not the actual effort reflects the outcome of such a debate. So, the role of domestic politics seems to boil down to deciding on the means, but this hardly ever implies a discussion also of the end to be achieved. In most countries such a discussion is often confined to an interpretation of a nation's geopolitical position on the one hand, and to an inspection of the available resources on the other. Therefore, although we think that 'politics does matter', it seems that party control will interfere only marginally with military policy and not in any systematic (i.e. statistically significant) manner.

This indirect impact of domestic politics can be exemplified by several cases. For example, in Denmark, after the Second World War the five major parties reached a political consensus to give up neutrality and seek collective security within NATO. However, this did not mean that party differences ceased to have any influence on both foreign and defence policy (see Einhorn, 1975). The degree of Denmark's involvement in overall NATO strategies of deployment of (West) German troops and of missiles gave rise to great debate in the Folketing. At the time, the Social Democrats were dependent on the Radical Party (Det Radikale Venstre)[10] for continuing party control. The Radical party was therefore able to exert great influence on Denmark's attitude towards NATO on the one hand, and on the size of the Danish contribution to this alliance on the other. This latter aspect not only depended on geopolitical considerations, but was also induced by the country's precarious economic situation, especially in the 1950s, because of its balance of payment deficit, which only recovered in the course of the 1960s (see Einhorn, 1975: 86).

Another example is Great Britain, where the 'decline of the British Empire' and problems of economic reconstruction after the Second World War forced the government to reduce defence effort and retreat from the perspective of a 'great power'. Although this was an obvious reality throughout the 1950s and 1960s, it took a Labour government to act accordingly (see Kirby, 1972: Ch. 3). A 'European strategy' was promoted in place of the idea of an imperial military apparatus.

A third example is Canada's review of its external security policy during the 1960s. In 1963 the Liberal administration, which followed that of Diefenbaker (Progressive Conservative Party), subjected the geopolitical position in combination with the availability of national resources to a stern review (see McLin, 1967: Ch. 1), which climaxed under the leadership of Trudeau in 1970 in the publication of the *General Paper on Foreign and Security Policy*. In it, the existing 'internationalist' approach was abolished, together with any endeavour to maintain a 'middle power' status. The military apparatus was to be reorganized and Canada's obligations to NATO reduced (troops were to be withdrawn from Europe in due time, while no missiles would be stationed in Canada). To a large extent, this review of Canadian defence policy and its consequences in terms of level of expenditure, derived from the fact that apparently no political consensus could be reached on devoting a large part of the country's economic resources to the military (see Thordarson, 1972: Ch. 6).

In Japan, the final example here, other circumstances play a part. For, notwithstanding the country's vast economic resources and its rapid industrial development, the share of military expenditure is only about 1 percent of GDP. Of course, this is due largely to its imposed military stance: demilitarization directly after the Second World War and the constitutional abolition of (aggressive) war in 1947. However, it should also be noted that, since then, strong public feeling against remilitarization (or 'saigumbi') has arisen and is also apparent in the political stance of the majority in parliament (see Emmerson and Humphreys, 1973). This public and political consensus was even strong enough to resist American pressure, although the USA tried as early as the 1950s to change this attitude. In 1953, for example, Vice President Nixon declared: 'our earlier advocacy of total disarmament of Japan has been a mistake' (Borton et al., 1976: 245). The only form of remilitarization in Japan has been limited to the so called 'Self Defence Forces', which should be capable of coping with an attack, but are incapable of attacking (see Japan Defense Agency, 1970, pp. 38-40). This not only demonstrates how Japan differs from the overall pattern, and from Austria and Finland regarding its economic strength, but also it shows the — albeit indirect — impact of domestic politics.

What these examples have in common is that domestic politics may, to some extent, affect military policy formation, and that such a shaded impact may have consequences for the actual defence outlay in due time. In other words, although domestic political agents are incapable of changing the fundamental ends of external security, they are capable of retarding or even arresting certain developments (such as the 'modernization' of nuclear armament in Europe recently, or resisting the requested increase of military expenditure by the USA).

The assertions above are also compatible with our contention that the 'guns or butter' equation is most unlikely to be tenable in its simplest formulation (see also Table 4) and is probably also, to a large extent, subject to forces similar to those that limit the impact of domestic politics, namely the impact of economic opportunities and of geopolitical factors. To this we now turn.

### The impact of geopolitical factors

As predicted, the results reported in Table 4 indicate the considerable explanatory significance of geopolitical factors in determining the variation in military expenditure levels within our universe of discourse. Since these geopolitical factors do not themselves change in the period under survey, and since the level of association reported is consistently high, we may surmise that here we have an important clue to the nature of the constant structure of military expenditure patterns. It is our view that the relationships here made apparent reflect the way in which much of the postwar history of international relations is structured around the realities of the Cold War (see Halle, 1967; Horowitz, 1971; Kolko and Kolko, 1972).

The impact of the Cold War is twofold: it legitimates the commonly defined 'adequate' level of military effort almost without saying, and it has caused a partial shift in political decision-making from the national to the transnational level in most allied countries (see Albrecht, Joxe and Kaldor, 1980). These elements constitute both a political climate and obligations (although not in an absolute sense), from which it appears obvious that the countries vary differently as to the level of military expenditure, although this may foster a pattern of similarity in the long run.

Earlier in this chapter (see pp. 188-89), we distinguished several types of behaviour with regard to a country's reaction to the 'threat of the Cold War' and suggested that participation in an alliance merely constituted a non-neutral stance, whereas participation in NATO also implied active involvement in the Cold War. The indicators of both NATO and alliance membership indeed explain differences between countries regarding the level of military expenditure and thus also the dependence on transnational decision-making. For in any military alliance the participating nation-state commits itself to share the burden of collective security, which implies mutual agreement on the effort made by each member. The history of NATO shows that this process of mutual agreement does indeed take place and is supposed decisively to influence political decision-making on a national level (see Keman, 1978). Developments like this may be operative as underlying factors for a growing pattern of similarity. Moreover, some authors suggest (Russett, 1970; Kennedy, 1975; Kaldor, 1979) that there seems to be an implicit mechanism at work within alliances, implying that 'the pact leader seems an important determinant for military expenditure' (Pryor, 1968: 126). Although this appears to be an acceptable statement, we nevertheless would like to reformulate it by suggesting that 'pact leaders' (like the USA) merely urge the other participants to follow the established level of military expenditure rather than determining the levels of others. For in the formative years of NATO, it was indeed a foregone conclusion that the larger countries, which were also the 'victors' of the Second World War, bore a large share of the collective burden (i.e. the USA, the United Kingdom and Canada). However, since 1951 other countries have rapidly increased their respective level of expenditure (partly as a consequence of the Korean War) while agreeing to maintain a high level in the next years (at the 'Lisbon' conference of NATO; see Halperin, 1971: 41). Similar events also occurred later on in SEATO (during the Vietnam War) and this development points to two important features regarding the explanation of the constant structure of levels of military expenditure: first, that alliance membership apparently implies a higher level of expenditure than in other countries; and, second, that there is an inherent tendency to maintain a relatively high level over time, but not for the countries that were the largest spenders originally.

The results reported in Table 4 do indeed support the above mentioned conclusions, and thus also our ideas concerning the role of alliances with regard to the determination of the defence outlay and the similarity thereof in time. At the same time, however, the alliance indicators cannot explain the constant structure of military expenditure for all countries of our population.

An answer to this question can be found, as we already stated above, in assessing both status and degree of activity of the different nations in the international arena and especially in their involvement in the Cold War. It is our contention that a nation-state's room to manoeuvre with regard to its military policy formation is determined predominantly by its military stance, which thus explains the overall pattern of similarity to a large extent. To test this thesis we regressed the level of military expenditure against military stance (Table 5). Even a cursory glance at the table reveals that our thesis appears to be largely substantiated: all the countries fit the equation within the bounds of $\pm 2 \times$ s.d. (standard deviation) and remain largely constant — that is, from 1965 onwards. As far as countries deviate from the expectation, they do so consistently, except for the year 1955. Apparently the predominant postwar pattern of military expenditure was still in the process of crystallization, a process that seems to have come to an end during the 1960s. Belgium, Germany, Italy, Japan, Norway and to some extent Denmark provide examples of countries falling gradually into the expected pattern, whereas Canada is, as could be expected, the only country to drop out (see p. 195 above). This deviant behaviour during the 1950s has an obvious explanation: almost all of these countries had suffered badly from the Second World War and were in those days in a stage of economic recovery, which prevented them from an immediate restoration of their military apparatus. Certainly, they were in no position to afford an expansion of their defence outlay according to their military stance.[11]

The losers of the Second World War were in particular subject to these constraints, and moreover they were relatively 'late-starters' regarding the restoration of a military apparatus; for both Italy and Germany were allowed only moderate remilitarization (see, for Italy, Zarisky, 1972; 326-7); and Germany not even until 1955 (see Kolko and Kolko, 1972: 653-62). However, this does not explain the Japanese case. No military establishment was rebuilt after the war, a condition incorporated in the constitution of 1947 (the famous 9th article) and imposed by the allied nations (especially the USA). And yet, it appears that in the 1950s this country was — considering its military status — overspending on defence. This however was caused by the events of the Korean War, when the

## TABLE 5
### Residuals of the regression between level of
### military expenditure and military stance, 1955-1975*

| Country | 1955 | 1965 | 1975 |
|---|---|---|---|
| Australia | 0.49 | 0.67 | 0.53 |
| Austria | −0.59 | 0.15 | 0.17 |
| Belgium | −1.63 | −1.02 | −0.41 |
| Canada | 1.17 | −1.23 | −1.61 |
| Denmark | −2.22 | −1.43 | −0.91 |
| Finland | 0.81 | 0.65 | 0.47 |
| France | 0.97 | 0.97 | 0.39 |
| Germany | −1.33 | 0.07 | 0.09 |
| Ireland | −1.51 | −1.24 | −0.57 |
| Italy | −1.73 | −0.93 | −0.71 |
| Japan | 1.01 | −0.15 | −0.13 |
| Netherlands | 0.27 | −0.33 | −0.01 |
| New Zealand | −0.61 | −0.54 | −0.57 |
| Norway | −1.53 | −0.53 | −0.31 |
| Sweden | 1.69 | 1.36 | 1.12 |
| Switzerland | −0.31 | 0.06 | −0.27 |
| UK | 2.77 | 1.67 | 1.49 |
| USA | 2.25 | 1.69 | 1.25 |
| Standard deviation | ±1.54 | ±1.04 | ±0.82 |

*The linear equation is for:

1955: $Y = 0.79 + 2.3(X)$   $R^2 = 67\%$
1965: $Y = 1.05 + 1.6(X)$   $R^2 = 58\%$
1975: $Y = 1.03 + 1.2(X)$   $R^2 = 62\%$

where $X$ = military stance and $Y$ = levels of military expenditure.

All results are significant; that is, the standard error of the regression coefficient was less than twice the outcome (see Hill, 1978: 59 and Blalock, 1979: 418-23).

commander of the occupation forces, General MacArthur, demanded that the Japanese government recruit auxiliary troops to act as replacements in Japan for the allied occupation troops (see Emmerson and Humphreys, 1973: 7).

It is clear from these explanations that during the 1950s specific conditions played a considerable part in the shaping of the constant structure during this period. With the exception of Ireland in 1965, four countries remain to some extent outliers over the whole period

under survey (if we take the standard deviation as a demarcation
line of being an, albeit moderate, outlier): Denmark, Sweden, the
United Kingdom and the USA. Denmark and the United Kingdom
have already been discussed earlier in the text and seem to have
been hampered by domestic economic problems. However, this was
not the case with regard to Sweden and the USA. A more likely explanation here seems to be each country's respective view of its
place in the world and in the changed 'international theatre' during
and directly after the Second World War (see Kolko and Kolko,
1972; Krippendorf, 1975). The USA clearly altered its geopolitical
attitude from an 'isolationist' position to a 'globalist' perspective,
defending the interests of the 'Free World'. This change has
resulted in a role as a 'pact leader' and as the world's 'policeman'
and subsequently in the maintenance of a high level of military expenditure since the 1950s (see Halperin, 1971; Horowitz, 1971).
The development of Sweden, the other outlyer, can to some extent
be compared with that of the USA, although on a rather smaller
scale. After the Second World War the Swedish government, supported by all major political parties, chose to continue its policy of
non-alignment. However, unlike the prewar period, it was considered necessary to base this policy on a strong defence, capable of
deterring any intruder, who would lose more than he would gain
by an attack. Evidently, such an external security policy must absorb a large share of the national resources (see Andrén, 1967).

Notwithstanding these somewhat 'deviant' cases, it can be concluded that the explanation of the constant structure by a country's
military stance makes both theoretical and empirical sense. In a
way this conclusion is enhanced by the discussion of the separate
countries. For all these 'deviant' cases can be reasonably explained
in terms of geopolitical factors. In sum, in this section we have
showed that the differences between countries are to a large extent
determined by their status in the international arena (see Vogel,
1979). Moreover, the overall similarity of the pattern of military expenditure is dependent on the nature and degree of any nation-
state's involvement in the Cold War. The question that remains to
be answered is: to what extent do socioeconomic factors also play a
part in this process?

*The impact of socioeconomic factors*

There seems to be little disagreement among students of military policy that the effort on external security constitutes a considerable 'burden on a nation's economy' (see Pryor, 1968; Knorr, 1970; Russett, 1970; Kennedy, 1975; Hill, 1978). In general, it is argued that the degree to which a nation-state can afford such a 'burden' is largely dependent on its economic strength and, in addition, on the availability of a 'disposable surplus' (see Knorr, 1970: 49ff).

As we already stated above (see pp. 186-88), economic strength can be considered as a certain threshold with respect to the possible level and expansion of military expenditure. This threshold stems mainly from a constraint in economic resources, which limits any nation in its military build-up and maintenance, especially in terms of manpower and finance. The extent of such a threshold is, of course, dependent also on other factors, such as the impact of the international arena, which influences the perceived need to establish an 'adequate' level of military preparedness. However, we may also consider economic strength as a 'background' condition for military expenditure rather than as a straightforward determinant. This argument rests partially on the notion of 'disposable surplus', which denotes the level of total GDP in combination with the level of economic development (or: GDP per capita). This combination is thought to indicate the potential to increase the 'burden of defence' (see Pryor, 1968: 89), especially if non-economic developments (like war or actual threat) make an enlargement of the military beyond the existing level necessary.

In the light of these views, we will examine in the remainder of this section the impact of both economic strength and prosperity on the levels of military expenditure. We shall discuss first of all the general outcome of the socioeconomic variables, and then the impact of economic strength and economic prosperity.

Judging from the results reported in Table 4, it would appear that both total GDP and GDP per capita are highly related to the level and to some extent to the change in military expenditure. At the same time, it should be appreciated that the degree of association tends to decrease over time. To some extent, this tendency results from the economic growth and the slackening of the growth in military expenditure which has characterized almost all countries of our universe in the period under review. Therefore the outcome should be treated with some care, for this development may very well be an example of Wildavsky's 'counter-Wagner law'.[12] Furthermore, it should also be kept in mind that this very period is characterized by a decrease in tension between East and West (the 'détente'), which may have negatively influenced the political will to mobilize economic resources beyond the existing level for military expenditure. This line of reasoning is compatible with the results of Table 4 regarding the relationship of change with the levels of military expenditure: change in total GDP is negatively related to military expenditure, whereas the relationship of change in GDP per capita declines, but remains positive. In our opinion this outcome not only signifies the decreasing and temporary impact of economic prosperity, but also means that economic strength, as it changes over time, becomes less crucial to the level of military expenditure and apparently develops into a 'background' condition. In sum, it appears that, although both economic strength and prosperity are associated with the levels of military expenditure, these relationships are not sufficiently conclusive during the whole period in an explanatory sense. Therefore in the following subsections we shall examine more closely the differential impact of total GDP and per capita GDP on military expenditure.

*Sharing the 'burden of defence'*
*and economic strength*
The assumption that the size of a nation, or its resources, expressed in total GDP is at least a 'background' condition for explaining its military effort also implies that this relationship is to some extent dependent on other factors. One of these factors, often mentioned in the literature, could very well be the so-called 'alliance behaviour' of nation-states, which developed after the Second World War. The extent to which economic resources are devoted to effort on external security seems largely dependent on the manner of participation (or non-participation) in transnational arrangements of collective security, and several studies have emphasized this point (see Kennedy, 1975: 71-3; Russett, 1970: 91-100). The basic idea behind this approach is that the 'burden of defence' will be shared equally (i.e. proportionally), and that the overall military strength of an alliance will increase by its united effort. According to these studies, however, the larger nations within the alliance tend to carry most of the burden. In this respect, the distinction between large and small(er) nations lies in the relationship between economic strength and level of military expenditure respectively, especially in connection with the degree of 'alliance behaviour'.

Some of these studies analysed the relationship in absolute figures, which however meant that the results were biased because of implicit trends (e.g., the impact of inflation) and difficulties in comparing currencies (e.g., disparities in purchasing power). These biased results not only led to erroneous statistical conclusions, but also reinforced the impression that the USA took most of the burden of any alliance in which she participated.

Other studies, not biased in this respect, attempted a more elaborated explanation of the allocation of military effort (expressed as a percentage of GDP) by taking into account the implication in the basic assumption of the theory of 'public (or collective) goods', that countries within alliances, as well as outside the 'club', may benefit from a system of collective security (see Ypersele de Strihou, 1968; van der Doel, 1980). This approach is sometimes called the 'theory of parasitic behaviour', the expectation being that countries with a comparatively small total GDP tend to spend less than the larger nations. This hypothesis applies to both members and non-members of an alliance.

We have already shown the difference between allied and other countries, especially that between NATO members and other nations. In terms of actual level, only Sweden proved to be an exception to both the 'rules' that a small and non-allied nation spends considerably less on external security than others. Thus, at first sight the above-mentioned approaches seem tenable. If so, it may help us to understand even more thoroughly why the levels of military expenditure differ among countries, and it may also aid our understanding of the constant structure embodied in these differences. In order to test the 'theory', we regressed total GDP with the level of military expenditure. Table 6 shows the results of the equation, also expressed in terms of the residuals as well as the rank orders of GDP at the different point of time employed in the analysis.[13] Considering the information contained in the table, it would seem too harsh to reproach some countries with displaying a kind of 'parasitic behaviour'. Both Ypersele de Strihou and Kennedy claimed that small nations, especially those outside an alliance, tend to have lower levels of military expenditure than one would expect from their economic strength. Kennedy even points specifically to Sweden, Finland, Ireland and Austria (Kennedy, 1975: 71). However, as demonstrated above, with the exception of Austria, this simply does not hold true. Austria, and Japan too, are indeed negative outliers, but — as we know by now — not entirely by their own choice. They are a class by themselves together with Finland, because of their military stance (see p. 189). All other (relative) outlyers — Germany and Italy in 1955 and Canada in 1975 — can be explained in terms of their own specific development

## TABLE 6

**Regression and residuals of the relationship between the level of military expenditure and total GDP and rank orders of GDP, 1955 – 1975**

| Country | 1955 | | 1965 | | 1975 | |
|---------|------|------|------|------|------|------|
| | R.O. | Resid. | R.O. | Resid. | R.O. | Resid. |
| Australia | 8 | – 0.51 | 9 | 0.19 | 8 | 0.04 |
| Austria | 15 | – 2.23 | 14 | – 1.27 | 13 | – 1.08 |
| Belgium | 11 | 0.17 | 11 | 0.22 | 11 | 0.51 |
| Canada | 5 | 1.34 | 7 | – 0.97 | 6 | – 1.37 |
| Denmark | 13 | 0.43 | 13 | 0.23 | 14 | 0.32 |
| Finland | 17 | – 0.17 | 16 | – 0.50 | 16 | – 0.60 |
| France | 4 | 0.40 | 5 | 0.81 | 4 | 0.36 |
| Germany | 3 | – 1.96 | 2 | – 0.38 | 3 | 0.05 |
| Ireland | 18 | 0.65 | 18 | 0.03 | 18 | 0.18 |
| Italy | 6 | – 1.53 | 6 | – 0.71 | 7 | 0.45 |
| Japan | 7 | – 3.37 | 3 | – 3.55 | 2 | – 2.87 |
| Netherlands | 9 | 1.88 | 10 | 0.78 | 10 | 0.80 |
| New Zealand | 16 | 0.25 | 17 | 0.24 | 17 | – 0.12 |
| Norway | 14 | 1.33 | 15 | 1.42 | 15 | 1.05 |
| Sweden | 10 | 1.02 | 8 | 0.78 | 9 | 0.70 |
| Switzerland | 12 | – 0.44 | 12 | – 0.15 | 12 | – 0.41 |
| UK | 2 | 1.99 | 4 | 1.50 | 5 | 1.59 |
| USA | 1 | 0.85 | 1 | 1.36 | 1 | 1.43 |
| Standard deviation | ±1.52 | | ±1.23 | | ±1.10 | |

*The linear equation is for:

1955: $Y = – 19.51 + 3.50(X)$   $R^2 = 65\%$
1965: $Y = – 11.33 + 1.96(X)$   $R^2 = 50\%$
1975: $Y = – 6.96 + 1.28(X)$   $R^2 = 35\%$
where $X$ = total GDP (logged) and $Y$ = level of military expenditure.

Resid. = residual; R.O. = rank order of total GDP; all results are significant following the rule explained in Table 5.

(see pp. 195 and 198) and therefore do not negate the overall outcome of the model. In our opinion, the results of Table 6 show that the 'alliance behaviour' approach is by and large compatible with the development of military expenditure at the various points of time. But we cannot escape the conclusion that the theory of 'parasitic behaviour' is exaggerated and not tenable for our universe of discourse. For the latter approach implies not only that large(r) nations spend considerably more than small(er) ones, but also that the differences between them (relative to their economic strength) will increase. However, the evidence in Tables 1 and 4 also shows that this is not so. We might even suggest that the opposite is the case. The original 'big spenders' showed the most remarkable decrease in military expenditure, whereas the other countries experienced a less drastic decrease or none at all. And this suggestion applies especially to the smaller and non-allied nations such as Austria, Finland, Ireland and Japan (after 1965).

Therefore, it seems more plausible to argue that, to some extent, the thesis of 'alliance behaviour' explains the differences between nations in military expenditure in conjunction with their economic strength. For most countries have experienced a level of military expenditure that is compatible with their overall economic resources. Only Japan is an exception in this respect, because it also differs from the other non-aligned countries like Austria and Finland in terms of its economic strength. As far as there is a tendency towards unequal sharing of the 'burden of defence', it may even point to the efficacy of the arrangement of collective security. For as Russett has stated, 'The failure of burden-sharing would thus indicate the success of deterrence' (Russett, 1970: 99). To some extent, this paradox of 'alliance behaviour' explains the relatively high(er) levels of military expenditure of the pact leader and 'would-be' (or original) pact leaders like France and the United Kingdom. In our opinion, however, this seeming contradiction is overstressed in the theory of 'parasitic behaviour', for the outcome of Table 6 is not compatible with the idea that small(er) nations always enjoy a 'free ride' at the expense of others. On the contrary, as we have already asserted, the larger countries, and especially the pact leader, appear to have established a pattern of defence outlay during the 1950s that has been followed by most other countries in the course of time as far as their economic resources could tolerate such a burden.

Therefore, the conclusion of this subsection must be that countries develop a level of military expenditure according to their respective economic strength, which is to some extent influenced by the existence of and participation in arrangements of 'collective security'. This also means that the level of total GDP can indeed be considered as a determinant of external security effort, whereas 'alliance behaviour' is merely an additional factor, contributing to our understanding of why and how nations have a different level of military expenditure under relatively similar economic conditions.

And as this additional factor is unique for the postwar era, it may also account for the growing pattern of similarity over the period under review together with the impact of economic strength per se.

## Military expenditure and economic prosperity

It is often postulated that the relative prosperity, or stage of economic development, of a country is an important factor in explaining both the level and change of military expenditure. Most of these ideas refer in one way or another to the notion of 'disposable surplus'. As both economic strength and economic prosperity are, to some extent, linked in this concept (see Knorr, 1970: 54; Kennedy, 1975: 71), it is necessary to disentangle the diverse influences of both factors. To this end we will examine more closely in this subsection the ideas of Hoffmann (1969) and of Smith (1977). For both authors have rather specific ideas on the impact of economic prosperity (or per capita GDP) on military expenditure, which may help us to discover the role played by this socioeconomic factor and hence the tenability of the concept of 'disposable surplus'.

Hoffmann has developed a rather straightforward thesis of the impact of economic prosperity on the level of military expenditure, stating that 'of course a rich country can better afford to arm itself than a poor country' (Hoffmann, 1969: 297) and, secondly, that 'there is a tendency for the share of defence expenditure in GNP to increase with per capita income' (1969: 300). To some extent, this assertion regarding the relationship between the level of per capita income and military expenditure is compatible with the results reported in Table 4. However, taking into account the specific selection of countries in this analysis, it should be noted that we are dealing here with most of the developed and industrialized nations of the world. If one takes (almost) all countries of the world as a point of departure — as Hill did in his analysis of military expenditure — then the bivariate relationship would seem to be insignificant: $r = 0.23$ for 1965 (see Hill, 1978: 46). Thus, Hoffman's thesis seems tenable only for a specific population and for specific periods, when the level of military expenditure is relatively high. However, it seems not tenable in general and in times of decreased tension (as for instance in 1975, when the bivariate relationship is 0.48, which is less than in 1965: $r = 0.63$; see Table 4).

Regarding Hoffmann's second thesis, it should be noted that the change in per capita GDP is negatively related to the change in military expenditure (between 1955 and 1975 $r = -0.42$), and positively related to the level of military expenditure (see Table 7). These results imply that per capita income is related to change in defence outlay either inversely or only to a minor degree. In short: differences and changes in per capita GDP seem to have no direct and simple bearing on a nation's effort on external security.

Although Hoffmann's thesis can be dismissed as too simplistic and too general, we still can assert that a substantial 'disposable surplus' (that is, beyond the level of what can be considered necessary for private and public non-military consumption and investment; see Knorr, 1970: 48-9) may affect both level and change of military expenditure. This will especially be the case in countries with a capitalist economy. Smith and other (neo-)Marxists argue that it is necessary to 'absorb' this surplus in a non-reproductive way; for any other method of surplus absorption would inevitably contribute (directly or indirectly) to an enlargement of the 'disposable surplus', a development that 'leads, or would lead if unchecked, to economic crisis and breakdown. This breakdown arises either because of a problem of realization or because of the inevitable tendency of the rate of profit to fall' (Smith, 1977: 65). Military expenditure is the solution to this problem, for it maintains effective demand and absorbs the surplus simultaneously without enlarging the 'disposable surplus' (see Baran and Sweezy, 1966; Kidron, 1970; Mandel, 1975; Smith, 1977; Reich, 1973). This approach is known nowadays as the 'under-consumption thesis'.

The 'surplus absorption' approach can be tested in two ways: first, by following the orthodox under-consumption thesis, which leads us to expect a positive relationship between total GDP and per capita GDP on the one hand, and the level of military expenditure on the other. Economic strength is introduced here in order to control for the differences across the countries involved (see Smith, 1977: 66). The second way involves the expectation that relatively prosperous countries spend more than other countries with a lower per capita GDP, irrespective of the fact that these latter countries may be larger (see p. 188 above). Table 4 shows the level of both total GDP and per capita GDP positively related to the level of military expenditure. It therefore makes sense to expect that the change in these factors will also be positively related. For it is our supposition here that any enlargement of total GDP and per capita GDP necessitates the absorption of an increased 'disposable surplus' by non-reproductive consumption and investment. And

**TABLE 7**
Bivariate relationships between military expenditure
and economic strength and economic prosperity
(level and change)*

|  | Level of military expenditure, 1975 |  | Change in military expenditure, 1955-75 |
|---|---|---|---|
| Level of: |  |  |  |
| Total GDP in 1975 | 0.60 | in 1955 | −0.72 |
| per capita GDP in 1975 | 0.48 | in 1955 | −0.63 |
| Change in: |  |  |  |
| Total GDP, 1955-75 | −0.47 |  | 0.16 |
| per capita GDP, 1955-75 | 0.32 |  | −0.42 |

*See explanations under Tables 3 and 4; no of cases = 18.

this goal can be reached by means of increasing (or at least not decreasing) military expenditure only. In this respect, we differ from Smith's formulation of a research design to test the implied hypotheses (though he admits this implication to be true; see Smith, 1977: 67). From this point of view, the (neo-)Marxists approach may be expected to be tenable, if:

1. a high level of both total GDP and per capita GDP subsequently leads to an increase (or less substantial decrease) in military expenditure; and if

2. an increase of both total GDP and per capita GDP leads to an increase (or less substantial decrease) of military expenditure and consequently to a relatively high level of expenditure in 1975.

Table 7 shows the relevant bivariate relationships for the period between 1955 and 1975. In fact, these results reflect the opposite of what was expected. Both economic strength and economic prosperity appear not to lead to an increase in either change or level of military expenditure. On the contrary, both level and change in total GDP and GDP per capita are negatively or hardly related to change in military expenditure. Only change in per capita GDP is weakly related to the level of defence outlay in 1975, which is a doubtful outcome, as we have already explained (see p. 201). It must therefore be concluded that the (neo-)Marxist approach is not tenable for our universe of discourse and may be applicable only in

separate case studies, using time-series analysis. It seems more likely that both this approach of 'surplus absorption' and the notion of
'disposable surplus' may indicate the degree of tolerance regarding
a nation's potential military effort rather than denoting a necessary
prerequisite for increasing the level of military expenditure. The
only obvious result of Table 7 is that apparently both economic factors contribute to the already observed pattern of similarity over
the period under survey; for the levels of GDP per capita and total
GDP in 1955 are highly related to the subsequent change in military
expenditure, which may indicate that the economically stronger
and more prosperous nations tend to decrease their military effort
and thus help to develop a convergent trajectory in the long run.

Our general conclusion with regard to the impact of
socioeconomic factors is that economic strength appears to be more
important than any other economic variable throughout the period
under review. Furthermore, the 'alliance behaviour' approach is a
valuable contribution in addition to economic strength for our
understanding of the pattern of similarity. However, the impact of
factors such as economic prosperity and 'disposable surplus' are
negligible, as appeared from the discussion of the ideas of Hoffmann and Smith.

Given the outcome of this section, one may reasonably expect
that the level of military expenditure and its supposed constant
structure can best be understood from the combined perspective of
economic strength on the one hand and the geopolitical position of
a nation-state on the other.

### Towards a multivariate model of military expenditure patterns

In the previous sections we have analysed the various factors and
their impact on external security effort separately. It appeared that
two variables in particular had a major impact on both the differences between the nations and the apparent constant structure
underlying it: on the one hand, the military stance of a nation
regarding its position in the international arena (see pp. 197-200),
and on the other the relative economic strength of a country (see
pp. 202-06). Although other factors also contributed substantially
to an explanation of the shaping and maintaining of the constant
structure of military expenditure, both military stance and
economic strength seem to have the most important impact on a

nation-state's effort on external security.

The next logical step therefore seems to be an investigation of the extent to which the pattern of similarity in military expenditure is caused by these two factors. To this end we formulated the level of military expenditure ($=ME$) as a function of military stance ($=MS$) and economic strength ($=ES$), which is:

$$ME = A + B(MS) + B(ES)$$

of which the regression outcome in 1955 is:[14]

$$ME = -12.87 + 1.45(MS) + 2.11(ES)$$
$$\qquad\quad (0.59) \qquad (0.41) \qquad\qquad R^2 = 0.81$$
beta-weight:   0.50        0.51

and the regression outcome in 1965 is:

$$ME = -6.72 + 1.18(MS) + 1.12(ES)$$
$$\qquad\quad (0.29) \qquad (0.40) \qquad\qquad R^2 = 0.77$$
beta-weight:   0.60        0.40

Finally, the regression outcome in 1975 is:

$$ME = -3.36 + 1.15(MS) + 0.60(ES)$$
$$\qquad\quad (0.20) \qquad (0.28) \qquad\qquad R^2 = 0.79$$
beta-weight:   0.74        0.28

These results support our model very well,[15] and therefore it can be concluded that, to a large extent, the constant structure of military expenditure is a consequence of a nation's military stance and its economic strength, at least in the case of a capitalist democracy. At the same time, some changes within the model can be surmised. In the first place, it is obvious, and not quite unexpected, that military stance not only is more stable over time, but also gains more weight. This is due partly to the fact that the impact of total GDP as such on military expenditure lessens in the course of time, and partly to Japan's deviant position in this respect (see note 15). To some extent, this observed shift is indicated by the change in the beta-weights at the subsequent points of time. The precise value of this development cannot be fully inferred from this model, for other factors, such as actual threat and international tension, are not comprehensively included in the operationalization of military stance. Finally, it should be noted that, although this model is rather static, it is the most successful in terms of robustness and explained variance as well as being parsimonious. All other combinations of relevant factors that employ two independent variables yielded less fruitful results and did not make more theoretical sense than the model demonstrated on p. 210.

In order to show the efficacy of this model, we will now examine the residuals for the different countries. For an essential question in this chapter remains: to what extent can the pattern of military expenditure be said to be more or less similar for all nations of our universe of discourse? Until now, we have discovered that nations differ either from an economic point of view or in terms of their geopolitical position. As both aspects play a part in the multivariate model, there will be supposedly fewer outlyers than in the preceding analysis, a nation-state's position now being considered from a dual point of view.

The overall impression of Table 8 is, compared with the outcome of Tables 5 and 6, that indeed the number of outlyers is less and seems to be restricted to rather obvious odd cases. To be more precise, there are no significant outlyers in statistical terms (i.e. being at a distance of more than twice of the predicted curve). In relative terms, there are however four countries that remain constantly at a greater distance than the other countries from the expected outcome: Italy, Japan, Sweden and the United Kingdom. Other former outlyers, such as the USA, Denmark and Austria, now fit the model.

Although both Sweden and the United Kingdom constantly spend more than may be expected from their respective military stance and economic strength, this can be understood from the factors underlying the model from which both countries deviated for specific and historical reasons (see, for the United Kingdom, p. 194 and, for Sweden, p. 200). Moreover, both nations appear to fall gradually into the pattern of similarity, judging from their change in the residuals (see Table 8) and their considerable decrease in military expenditure over the last 20 years (see Table 1).

Italy and Japan apparently belong to those countries in which effort on external security is less than can be expected from the factors underlying our model. Notwithstanding Italy's low contribution compared with other NATO members, it still spends considerably more than other countries that have experienced the same level of economic development (e.g. Austria, Finland and Ireland). Although this factor cannot be considered as a prime determinant,

## TABLE 8
### Residuals of the multiple regression of the level of military expenditure with military stance and economic strength, 1955-1975*

| Country | 1955 | 1965 | 1975 |
|---------|------|------|------|
| Australia | 0.12 | 0.66 | 0.45 |
| Austria | −0.84 | 0.06 | 0.23 |
| Belgium | −0.82 | −0.60 | −0.32 |
| Canada | 0.95 | −1.36 | −0.69 |
| Denmark | −0.88 | −0.76 | −0.67 |
| Finland | 1.04 | 0.72 | 0.61 |
| France | 0.28 | 0.60 | 0.04 |
| Germany | −2.05 | −0.46 | −0.31 |
| Ireland | 0.12 | −0.30 | −0.68 |
| Italy | −1.93 | −1.08 | −0.93 |
| Japan | −0.90 | −1.36 | −0.78 |
| Netherlands | 0.96 | 0.03 | 0.04 |
| New Zealand | 0.20 | 0.13 | −0.21 |
| Norway | −0.05 | 0.31 | −0.01 |
| Sweden | 1.53 | 1.25 | 1.08 |
| Switzerland | 0.13 | 0.16 | −0.18 |
| UK | 1.95 | 1.30 | 1.20 |
| USA | 0.45 | 0.72 | 0.51 |
| Standard deviation | ±1.16 | ±0.87 | ±0.64 |

*The linear equations belonging to these results can be found on p. 210.

it does not mean that it is entirely devoid of importance. Especially in the less developed countries, a certain level of economic prosperity may be an additional component for achieving an 'adequate' effort on external security, in the sense that it indicates possible means of employing economic resources to this end (see Kennedy, 1975: 80; and Knorr, 1970: 56-7).

In terms of the model, Japan clearly is the oddest case of all: it contradicts most of what is implied in the factors underlying it. The country has vast economic resources (which have increased considerably during the period under review) and, apart from its imposed demilitarized and accepted neutral status, is in a rather delicate geopolitical position in South-East Asia. Hence, the explanation cannot follow these lines, and Japan can be understood only in terms of a development peculiar unto itself (see pp. 195 and 198-99). In this Japan differs not only from an economic point of view, but also geopolitically, from countries like Finland and Austria, which fall into the same category of military stance. Japan has maintained a neutral stance (which in practice can hardly be said to be imposed) and pursues this policy of non-alignment, which, at best, can be characterized as contrary to the Swedish (expensive) way.

All other outliers are only temporarily in an odd position with regard to the expected curve, and they all fall gradually into the basic pattern. It is our contention, therefore, that the constant structure of military expenditure patterns is largely dependent on the military stance and economic strength of a nation-state belonging to our universe of discourse. Furthermore, it can be observed from the outcome of Table 8 that there indeed seems to be a convergent trajectory in the development of military expenditure. For almost all countries show a tendency to move towards the regression-line (and this is also expressed in the decrease of standard deviation over time), and have indeed experienced a decrease in the level of military expenditure between 1955 and 1975. Therefore, in the concluding section of this chapter we will elaborate briefly on the factors that may account for this development and on whether this leads to consequences in terms of a trade-off between welfare and warfare.

## Convergence, trade-off and politics

The growing pattern of similarity and the observed downward trend in military expenditure are thus predominantly the result of the factors that feature in the multivariate model developed in the previous section. This outcome signifies that the countries in this study have apparently become more alike over time and that this process is reflected in the historical development of the Cold War on the one hand, and of the increasing prosperity of the capitalist economy during this period on the other. Especially during the latter half of the period under survey, the pressures within the 'international theatre' diminished considerably (the 'détente'), which may explain the overall decrease in military expenditure as well as the fact that the differences between the nations have declined.

At the same time, the capitalist economy was 'booming' and resulted in relatively high growth rates almost everywhere, making the 'burden of defence' easier to carry.

In sum: the observed convergent trajectory can indeed be described as the historical outcome of a combination of decreased international political tension and the greater availability of economic resources. This very outcome is also supported by statistical evidence: both economic strength and military stance are negatively related to change in military expenditure between 1955 and 1975 (total GDP in 1955: $r = -0.72$ and military stance: $r = -0.56$), which means that the trend in both is apparently moving in opposite directions.

Apart from these factors underlying the constant structure of military expenditure, it seems plausible to suggest that the original level of effort on external security (that is: 1955) also plays a part in this uniform tendency (see Nutter, 1978; Schmidt, 1980: 123); for, as we already could infer from Table 2, the original level of defence outlay appears to be highly related to subsequent levels of spending. Moreover, the higher the previous level, the higher the change afterwards. Again, this is supported by statistical evidence: the bivariate relationship between the level of military expenditure in 1955 and the subsequent change between 1955 and 1965 is $r = -0.82$, and between 1955 and 1975 is $r = -0.90$. In our opinion, this finding — in combination with the prime determinants of the constant structure — explains the convergent trajectory of the pattern of military expenditure between 1955 and 1975 to a large extent.

The above conclusion regarding the pattern of convergence may also have consequences for a possible trade-off between welfare and warfare. Obviously, any such process is feasible only in countries that have decreased their military expenditure considerably since 1955. As we have already asserted, a straightforward process of trade-off is hardly a tenable proposition.[16] We also put forward the view that a trade-off, if it occurs, is to be expected mainly in countries that can be characterized as either left-wing or right-wing-dominated (see pp. 185-86). According to this view, one may thus expect that the domestic political agents will be related to the change in military expenditure, for the trade-off process implies a change in the priorities of public expenditure (see Table 9). Except for social democratic seats in the first decade, only the outcome over the whole period seems to indicate a relationship for GAPS and the Left. Moreover, it can be noted that in countries where social democrats are strongly represented and are in government for a longer period of time, the change in military expenditure is

## TABLE 9
### Bivariate relationships between domestic politics and change in military expenditure between 1955 and 1975*

|  | 1955-65 | 1965-75 | 1955-75 |
|---|---|---|---|
| Social democratic seats in parliament | 0.47 | 0.32 | 0.45 |
| Right-wing seats in parliament | -0.08 | -0.29 | -0.11 |
| Complexion of government and parliament (GAPS)(x) | 0.09 | 0.33 | 0.49 |

*See explanations under Tables 3 and 4; no. of cases = 18.

less than in other nations (except for Sweden and, to some extent, the United Kingdom). This result is compatible with the 'modified' trade-off thesis, for it strengthens our argument not only that right-wing-dominated countries more easily decrease their level of military expenditure, but also that in these countries a trade-off may occur in order to create room for other public policies, without enlarging the public economy as a whole. This argument is also supported by the results reported in Table 3; for strong right-wing representation appears to be negatively related to change in non-military expenditure ($r = -0.61$). Such a finding seems to confirm our ideas that, in right-wing-dominated countries, a trade-off will occur only within the given level of public expenditure, whereas in left-wing-dominated countries the public economy may be expanded to achieve more welfare provisions without disturbing the existing level of effort on external security.

Given this relationship between domestic politics and establishing public policy priorities, it is obvious that the 'modified' trade-off thesis apparently depends more on the factors that determine the constant structure of military expenditure and the observed convergent trajectory between 1955 and 1975 (see also Pluta, 1978). In other words: as far as 'modified' trade-offs have occurred, these must be considered as more or less a 'by-product' of the waning of the Cold War and of a favourable economic climate, and to a much lesser extent as a result of the impact of domestic politics. However, whether this conclusion will hold for the period of 1975 and after, in which the above-mentioned conditions appear to have changed, is very doubtful. For since the mid-1970s the international tension and the economic climate seem to have reversed somewhat: conflicts between, as well as within, the different 'blocs' have developed and have led to a renewal of the Cold War. Furthermore, the economic situation has deteriorated during the latter half of the 1970s, and capitalism is no longer 'booming', while at the same time the democratic nations are confronted with an already developed welfare state, which takes up a considerable part of the economic resources.

In sum, the present situation is apparently altered to a large degree, which may imply that effort on external security could very well be increased again — however, unlike the 1950s, not in a climate of reconstruction and subsequent economic prosperity, but in a situation of severe crisis. And such a situation, together with a political climate of alarmism' (see Albrecht, Joxe and Kaldor, 1980) may easily lead to pressure from transnational agencies like NATO to increase military expenditure and to 'modernize' nuclear equipment (a process already in motion) on the one hand, and from national political parties of the Right to uphold (or even expand) military effort as well as to restore private economic development at the expense of welfare-oriented public policies on the other. Such a development, of which the omens are ample and increasing (e.g. Reagan's present policy priorities; the fiscal policy of Thatcher; the ambiguous assertions of Schmidt concerning welfare and warfare) will undoubtedly restrict the political and ideological mobility of the Left. Given the outcome of our analysis, such a development may signify that warfare priorities will be likely to receive more emphasis than welfare priorities, irrespective of the domestic political complexion (see also Wilensky, 1975: 79-80).

From this rather gloomy perspective it may well be that the present international and economic situation has serious political consequences for the intra-national development of public policy formation in the near future; for if we allow ourselves some speculation based on the main findings of this chapter, it must be conceded that the 'guns before butter' argument probably does bear more weight than might have been thought. As has been demonstrated in the foregoing analysis, the constant structure of military expenditure is still extremely important, whereas the convergent trajectory appears to be more or less a result of the postwar history of democratic capitalist nations until the mid-1970s. If, however, the recent developments persist, it may very well signify that a renewed military effort must be financed from declining economic resources at the cost of man's future. The question, which remains unanswered here, is: to what extent can both political and popular support be aroused for such an emphasis on military preparedness? This may have been possible during the 'coldest' stage of the Cold War, but that does not necessarily imply that it will be still the case. Especially in Western Europe, the very centre of Cold War activities, there are ample signs within both political parties and NATO indicating less popular consensus and support for stressing warfare priorities than for fighting unemployment and preserving welfare programmes. And that might be a serious test for the constant structure of military expenditure in the near future, as it appears to have developed since the mid-1950s.

# NOTES

1. To some extent the following studies have dealt with the subject from a cross-national point of view: Pryor (1968); Hoffmann (1969); Russett (1970); Szymanski (1973); Smith (1977); and Hill (1978). However, most of these studies merely concentrate on the effect of military expenditure rather than on the determinants of this particular field of public policy.

2. It should be noted, however, that, although the trend is apparently downward as measured in relative figures, the level of military expenditure is substantially higher than in the period before the Second World War (apart from the Axis powers: Germany, Italy and Japan). See Albrecht (1973: 52); Knorr (1970: 47-8); and Russett (1970: 130-2).

3. It should be noted that in the preceding years this pattern was still to come into existence. Particularly, the formation of NATO in 1949 and the outbreak of the Korean War in 1950 led to a considerable increase in military expenditure in various countries (e.g. Belgium, Denmark, Norway and the USA, which doubled their level compared with that in 1950; see Wilensky, 1975: 76-7). However, in terms of rank order the difference is less dramatic, and merely points to the ongoing process of growing similarity.

4. The adjective 'optimum' is used here neutrally. That is to say, a country is expected, given its economic and human resources, to attempt a maximum military effort on the one hand, and is also dependent on factors like fiscal constraints, political compliance and the international situation on the other.

5. Most studies on war and defence stress the phenomenon of perceived and actual threat and relate it to geopolitics and human and economic resources. See also Dankbaar and Keman (1979); Schelling (1966); Gray (1977); and Knorr (1970).

6. Until now, the trade-off argument has received relatively little attention, and if so mostly from an economic perspective. See for instance OECD (1978: 23-4); Russett (1970: 137-56); Szymanski (1973); Liske, Loehr and McCamant (1975: 21-54). From a more general point of view, some attention has been paid to this phenomenon in the fiscal approach of public expenditure; see for instance Peacock and Wiseman (1961); Musgrave (1969) and Pluta (1978). Finally, Wilensky (1975: Ch. 4) and O'Connor (1973; 150-8) can be mentioned as authors who devote some specific attention to the 'guns and butter' equation.

7. This measure represents all public expenditure except those for military purposes. The data are taken from OECD (1977, 1978). As this indicator is expressed as a ratio of GDP and thus independently from non-military expenditure, there is no implicit danger of bias in the form of a zero-sum relationship. See also Szymanski (1973).

8. We did not include population as an independent variable, because it measures almost in the same way as total GDP does, and moreover the population indicator proved to be less reliable from a statistical point of view. GDP per capita, which is included, is measured at constant prices and the data are taken from OECD (1977).

9. One might suspect that both the economic strength and economic development of Japan could affect the outcome of the bivariate analysis. Although this is, to some extent, the case, it does not however violate the ascertained trend as such. Where necessary, we recalculated all relationships to be used in the subsequent analysis excluding Japan from the sample. If this procedure casts doubt on the original results, it is reported.

10. Until 1967, Det Radikale Venstre was very close to the Social Democrats and could be seen as a progressive/liberal party with a strong pacifist tradition. Although many of its representatives in parliament voted against the decision to join NATO, they nevertheless upheld their support of the existing Social Democratic government (in which they participated) in order to retain as much influence as possible on Danish military policy. See also Raschke (1977: 129-30).

11. Obviously, the Netherlands are an exception here. This is due to the fact that this country had to rebuild its military forces very quickly after the war, irrespective of other priorities, in order to 'defend' its colonies in the East Indies (now Indonesia). And later on this nation responded very eagerly to NATO planning for expanding its forces in order to receive as much 'off-shore procurement' as possible, which meant raw materials and investment goods for further industrialization. See Keman (1978).

12. Wagner's Law referred to an additive linear relationship between economic growth and the expansion of the public economy. Wildavsky, however, claims that the opposite is true: the faster the rate of economic growth, the slower the growth of public expenditure. This argument is based on the assumption that the absolute change in public expenditure more or less disappears in the increased national wealth (see Wildavsky, 1975; Schmidt, 1980). These are the effects to which we are referring in the text, and examples in this respect are Austria and Japan. Although they spend relatively little on defence, both countries nevertheless increased their military expenditure between 1955 and 1975 by, respectively, 7.4 and 6.5 percent annually. This shows that the growth in absolute figures in the countries of this study, which was on average 5.0 percent annually, has been apparently absorbed by the rapid economic development in these countries.

13. Most authors who used this approach (e.g. Ypersele de Strihou; Pryor; van

der Doel; Russett; Kennedy) have utilized a similar research design, in which (1) total GDP is used as the independent variable rather than indicators like population or surface; (2) total GDP is logged to reduce the effect of outlyers and to attain a less skewed distribution; (3) rank orders are sometimes employed to reduce the bias of absolute differences in yet another way; (4) residual plots of the bivariate regression are used to detect 'deviant' cases and to inspect the general pattern of 'behaviour'. See Russett (1970: 100-02; van der Doel, 1980: Ch. 4).

14. The figures in the equation represent the understandardized regression coefficients. The figures in brackets represent the respective standard errors (s.e.); we employed the same criterion for accepting an equation as in Tables 5 and 6. No. of cases = 18; the interrelation of *MS* and *ES* in 1955 is: $r = 0.47$, in 1965: $r = 0.46$, in 1975: $r = 0.42$.

15. We recalculated the model while excluding Japan, the most obvious outlyer in this respect, especially with respect to its economic strength (see also Table 6). The results were by and large identical, although the beta-weights differed to some extent. These showed, without Japan, that the impact of economic strength remained stronger than in the overall model. However, the basic tendency in time remained unchanged: military stance gains weight, while economic strength loses weight. Therefore it is our contention, that, although Japan is a 'deviant' case, it does not violate the tenacity and robustness of the model including Japan.

16. This assertion can also be supported by statistical evidence. Only during the period between 1955 and 1965 was there a more or less significant bivariate relationship between military and non-military expenditure ($r = -0.41$). Between 1965 and 1975, and over the entire period, there were insignificant correlations, respectively: between 1965 and 1975 $r = 0.32$ and between 1955 and 1975, $r = -0.18$.

# REFERENCES

Albrecht, U. (1973). 'Die Struktur der Rüstungsausgaben', *Leviathan*.

Albrecht, U., Joxe, A. and Kaldor, M. (1980). *Against Alarmism*. Berlin and Brighton.

Andrén, N. (1967). *Power-balance and Non-alignment*. Stockholm.

Banks, A.S. (1975). *Political Handbook of the World*. New York, etc.

Baran, P. and Sweezy, P.M. (1966). *Monopoly Capital*. New York.

Barraclough, G. (1979). *Introduction to Contemporary History*. Harmondsworth.

Blalock, H.M. (1979). *Social Statistics*. Tokyo, etc.

Borton, H. et al. (1976). *Japan between East and West*. Westport, Connecticut.

Budge, I. and Farlie, D. (1977). *Voting and Party-competition: A Theoretical Critique and Synthesis Applied to Surveys of 10 Democracies*. London.

Cameron, D.C. (1978). 'The Expansion of the Public Economy: A Comparative Analysis', *APSR*.

Dankbaar, B. and Keman, J.E. (1979). 'Are the Russians Coming?' Conference paper on NATO-WTO Relations. Berlin.

Van der Doel, J. (1980). *Democracy and Welfare Economics*. Cambridge.

Einhorn, S.B. (1975). *National Security and Doemestic Policies in Post-War Denmark*. Odense.

Emmerson, J.K. and Humphreys, L.A. (1973). *Will Japan Rearm? A Study in Attitudes*. Washington, DC.

Gray, C. (1977). *Geopolitics in a Nuclear Age: Heartlands and Rimlands*. New York.

Halle, L. (1967). *The Cold War as History*. New York and Evanston, Illinois.

Halperin, M. (1971). *Defense Strategies for the Seventies*. Boston.

Harrison Wagner, R. (1975). 'National Defense as a Collective Good', in Liske, Loehr and McCamant (1975).

Hill, K.Q. (1978). 'Domestic Politics, International Linkages and Military Expenditures', *Studies in Comparative International Development*.

Hoffmann, W.G. (1969). 'The Share of Defence Expenditures in Gross National Product', *German Economic Review*.

Horowitz, D. (1971). *From Yalta to Vietnam*. Harmondsworth.

Japan Defence Agency (1970). *Report of Director General*. Tokyo.

Kaldor, M. (1979). *The Disintegration of the West*. Harmondsworth.

Keman, J.E. (1978). 'Politics and Economics of the Military Apparatus: the Dutch Experience', *ECPR* (Grenoble).

Kennedy, G. (1975). *The Economics of Defence*. London.

Kidron, M. (1970). *Western Capitalism since the War*. London.

Kirby, S. (1972). 'Britain's Defence Policy and NATO', in M. Leifer (ed.), *Constraints and Adjustments in British Foreign Policy*. London.

Knorr, K. (1970). *Military Power and Potential*. Lexington, Mass.

Kolko, J. and Kolko, G. (1972). *The Limits of Power. The World and the United States Foreign Policy (1945-1954)*. New York.

Krippendorf, E. (1975). *Internationales System als Geschichte. Einführung in die Internationale Beziehungen*, 1. Frankfurt aM.

Liske, C., Loehr, W. and McCamant, J. (1975). *Comparative Public Policies. Theories, Issues and Methods*. New York, etc.

Mandel, E. (1975). *Late Capitalism*. London.

McLin, J.B. (1967). *Canada's changing Defense Policy (1957-1963)*. Baltimore.

Miliband, R. (1969). *The State in Capitalist Society*. London.

Musgrave, A. (1969). *Fiscal Systems*. New Haven, Connecticut.

Nutter, G. W. (1978). *Growth of Government in the West*. Washington DC.

O'Connor, J. (1973). *The Fiscal Crisis of the State*. New York.

OECD (1977). *National Accounts 1950-1975*. Paris.

OECD (1978). *Public Expenditure Trends*. Paris.

Peacock, A.T. and Wiseman, J. (1961). *The Growth of Public Expenditure in the United Kingdom*. Princeton.

Pluta, J.E. (1978). 'National Defence and Social Welfare; Budget Trends in Ten Nations of Postwar Western Europe', *International Journal of Social Economics*.

Pryor, F.L. (1968). *Public Expenditures in Communist and Capitalist Nations*. Homewood, Illinois.

Raschke, J. (1977). *Die politischen Parteien in Westeuropa*. Hamburg.

Reich, M. (1973). 'Military Spending and the U.S. Economy', in S. Rosen (ed.), *Testing Theories of the Military Industrial Complex*. Lexington, Mass.

Ricardo, D. (1951). *The Principles of Political Economy and Taxation* (ed. P. Sraffa). London.

Richardson, L.F. (1960). *Arms and Insecurity*. Pittsburgh.

Russett, B.M. (1970). *What Price Vigilance? The Burdens of National Defense*. New Haven, Connecticut.

Schelling, Th. (1966). *Arms and Influence*. Cambridge, Mass.

Schmidt, M.G. (1979). *Determinanten der Staatlichen Politik in industriell-kapitalistischen Demokratien*. Konstanz.

Schmidt, M.G. (1980). *Wohlfahrstaatlichen Politik unter bürgerlichen und sozialdemokratischen Regierungen*. Konstanz.

Sipri (1975, 1978). *Yearbook*. Stockholm.

Singer, J.D. and Small, M. (1972). *The Wages of War, 1816-1965*. New York.

Smith, Adam (1874). *An Inquiry into the Nature and Wealth of Nations*. London and New York.

Smith, R.P. (1977). 'Military Expenditure and Capitalism', *Cambridge Journal of Economics*.

Smoker, P. (1964). 'Fear in the Arms Race: A Mathematical Study', *Journal of Peace Research*.

Szymanski, A. (1973). 'Military Spending and Economic Stagnation', *AJS*.

Thordarson, B. (1972). *Trudeau and Foreign Policy*. Toronto.

Tufte, E.R. (1974). *Data Analysis for Politics and Policy*. Englewood Cliffs, New Jersey.

Vogel, H. (1979). *Der Kleinstaat in der Weltpolitik*. Zürich.

Wallace, M.D. (1971). 'Power, Status and International War', *Journal of Conflict Resolution*.

Weber, M. (1968). *Economics and Society*. London.

Wildavsky, A. (1975). *Budgeting. A Comprehensive Theory of Budgeting*. Boston.

Wilensky, H.L. (1975). *The Welfare State and Equality*. Berkeley, California.

Wilensky, H.L. (1976). 'The "New Corporatism", Centralization and the Welfare State', *Sage Professional Papers*, 06/020.

Ypersele de Strihou, J. van (1968). 'Sharing the Defence Burden among Western Allies', *Yale Economic Essays*.

Zarisky, R. (1972). *Italy, The Politics of Uneven Development*. Hinsdale.

# II

# The Determination of Incomes

# 5

# Determining the Level of Wages: The Role of Parties and Trade Unions

Klaus Armingeon
University of Konstanz

## Introduction: the social democratic paradox

**In its 1959 party programme** — the Bad Godesberg programme — the German Social Democratic Party (SPD) declared that the distribution of incomes was unfair and that the SPD would work for a more egalitarian distribution of incomes. Seven years later, at the end of 1966, the SPD came to power for the first time since the Weimar Republic. Yet no redistribution of incomes in favour of wage and salary earners occurred! On the contrary, the share of wages and salaries as a percentage of national income actually decreased in the ensuing period, and, as a corollary, the residual (usually called the 'profit share') increased.

A variety of explanations might be advanced for this seemingly paradoxical development: the continued influence of the CDU coalition partners, the impact of the 1966/67 recession and, quite definitely a contributory factor, the increased moderation of union wage claims. However, there is some evidence that union moderation was itself closely connected to the new political configuration in Germany. The trade union movement has close, if informal, links with the Social Democratic Party. It is the party that unionists, leadership and rank and file alike, have traditionally seen as being both willing and able to further policies favourable to the union membership. Thus, the unions were interested in Social Democratic participation in government. On the other hand, one of

the reasons that a coalition deal was clinched was because the conservatives perceived that the SPD might be able to use its co-
operative relations with the unions to effect a co-ordination of
wage policies with the economic policies of the state in such a way
as to ameliorate the impending economic crisis. Further, the Keynesian methods of steering the economy advocated by the SPD as the
background for promised social reforms required a substructure of
economic stability that might best be procured by a degree of union
support in moderating wage claims (see Schmiede, 1979).

Thus, the paradox would appear to be that the SPD claims to be
the party that advocates policies in favour of the working class and
rests its claim for union support on the prospect of such policies being enacted, and yet is dependent on the willingness of the union
movement to underpin these reform policies by a more or less
voluntary wage restraint. The aim of this chapter is to explore this
paradox further; to examine whether there is a systematic relationship between wage policy outcomes and the nature of the socialist
party-trade union nexus not only in West Germany, but also in other
European capitalist democracies. In other words, our concern is to
ask the question: Do trade unions behave differently under social
democratic and bourgeois governments?

It will be noted that this research question is more sharply focused than those that arise in the context of the other essays in this
volume. Whereas their concern was to map whole fields of public
policy, such as public expenditure or macroeconomic policy, ours is
to examine a specific relationship between parties and interest
groups and to determine the nature of its implications for wage
policies. Despite its more delimited focus, this essay is nevertheless
quite obviously complementary to the others. Like them, it attempts to understand the policy outcomes in democratic capitalist
states in terms of the complex interaction of socioeconomic and
political factors; and, like them, it proceeds from an initial
presumption that neither set of factors is likely to be alone sufficient to explain the phenomenon under investigation. Moreover,
the issue that is our central concern here, i.e what trade unionists
get in return for allegiance to particular political parties, is merely
an aspect of a wider question about the trade-off between policy
outcomes and socialist voting, which has been raised, implicitly or
explicitly, throughout this volume. Looked at from a socialist point
of view, the question is whether the working class gets greater
welfare, equality, full employment and price stability if the Left is
strong, either in terms of controlling the reins of government or of

having the capacity to bring extra-parliamentary pressure to bear on the government. Wage policy is clearly a crucial element in this trade-off. Does the working class get higher wages where socialist parties have great influence, or, as has often been suggested, is wage restraint the price that must be paid for the achievement of other policy goals?

Seeing the basic issue of wage policies in terms of a potential trade-off is suggested by the very fact that the majority of West European trade unions have formal or informal ties with political parties, mostly of social democratic complexion.[1] The prevalence of such ties must, presumably, be premised on mutual benefits to both partners in the arrangement. If, as a number of writers have argued, trade unions tend to accept wage restraint or impose self-restraint in wage policies when a party is in office that has strong links to the unions,[2] the reasons must be sought in the probable resulting balance of benefits. One such reason may lie in the union movement's hopes that a social democratic government will be both willing and able to realize policies in favour of working-class interests. The realism of such hopes may be regarded as partially dependent on the extent to which the government can act free of the constraints of wage disputes, inflation and low growth rates.[3] In other words, there is an implicit trade-off beween union self-restraint directed towards economic stabilization and legislative benefits for the working class. Such a trade-off idea becomes wholly explicit if there is a formal agreement between government and unions: by wage restraint the trade unions facilitate the government's macroeconomic policy in exchange for clearly defined reform policies. In intention, if not in realization, the Social Contract of the British Labour government in the latter part of the 1970s was of this nature. The government was to repeal Conservative industrial relations legislation and to increase the 'social wage' by taxation and public expenditure policies; and, in exchange, the trade unions would refrain from using their full industrial muscle in wage negotiations, in the hope of thereby reducing the rate of inflation.[4]

A further reason for wage restraint may be found in the trade unions' desire not to endanger the electoral success of the party with which they have ties. All the West European social democratic parties rely to some extent on middle-class supporters with no tradition of union organization. Since such voters are likely to be alienated in circumstances where the party is unable to demonstrate that it can command the loyalty of the unions, there may be a strong incentive for the unions to exercise self-restraint, in so far as they consider the policies of a future social democratic government would be more advantageous to their interests than would be the policies of a bourgeois government.[5]

The issue of wage policies in capitalist democracies is of particular interest because it is closely linked to some of the central debates in the public policy field. Clearly, it relates to the question of whether, and in what ways, politics really matters. A number of authors have concluded that under certain conditions the participation of social democratic parties in government has led to policies that are markedly more favourable to working-class interests than those pursued by bourgeois parties.[6] This suggests the importance of party political activity for the working class, but if the social reforms thus secured are at the cost of lower wage levels, it may be that politics alters the form, rather than the substance, of the class struggle. An argument along these lines is a common feature of Marxist criticism of the social democratic political strategy. In this view, social democratic governments are little more than instruments for the pacification of the working class; their function is to integrate the labour movement with the goal of steering the economy by keeping wage levels down.[7]

Finally, wage policy questions are of critical importance in the current debate on the nature of liberal corporatism, and, in particular, on the tendency for corporatist arrangements to result in the adoption of incomes policies. It can be strongly argued that social democratic government is an extremely favourable condition for the emergence of neo-corporatist institutions. That this should be so is inherent in the logic of the trade-off between parties and unions, with the linkages becoming the institutionalized basis for decision-making on a variety of aspects of economic policy.[8] Indeed, as Lehmbruch has recently noted, the ties between social democratic party and unions may make the formal institutionalization of tripartite arrangements between government, employers and unions more or less superfluous (see Lehmbruch, 1979a, 1979b). From a viewpoint of corporatist analysis, the central question is whether the links between parties in government and trade unions are the fundamental element in incomes policy, and thus whether the macroeconomic steering capacity of a socialist government depends heavily on the homogeneity and loyalty of the trade union movement.

This essay examines only a single aspect of the complex trade-off between political action and working-class interests. Because a full evaluation of the relationships involved would necessitate a complete survey of the public policy field (especially of the distribution of personal incomes, taxation policy, the distributive and redistributive impact of public expenditure and the outcomes of macroeconomic policy in general), we are unable to suggest any final conclusions concerning the situation of the working class in capitalist democracies. What we shall attempt to do, by focusing on the structural conflict between labour and capital concerning the distribution of gross wages and gross profits, is to provide a fragment of the evidence, albeit an important one, that would be required in such a total evaluation. Moreover, it should be emphasized that wage determination is by no means the only activity of trade union organizations, and that other aspects of their role in modern society (e.g. their overall role in economic decision-making) cannot be considered here.[9] Just as the discussion of the wage share tells us only a part of what happens to the working class under capitalism, so an understanding of the trade unions' role in the determination of the wage share describes only a part of the impact of trade union activity in the democratic capitalist nations.

The attempt to use quantitative empirical methods to test for the presumed relationship between the political complexion of governments and wage policies involves a major methodological problem, the consequences of which must be recognized at the outset. Our difficulty is that we cannot directly measure wages policy, but only the outcomes of such policies, i.e. wage levels or, as in this chapter, wage shares. This means that we cannot, on the basis of the evidence presented here, reach determinate conclusions as to the mechanisms by which partisan control of government is translated into diverse wages outcomes — assuming, of course, that our results show this to be the case. However, this need not present insuperable problems of analysis. On the one hand, in terms of the consequences of partisan control, our results should be sufficient to establish whether the party in office and the nature of its linkages to the trade union movement does make a difference to wages. From the point of view of investigating the extent of a political trade-off for the working class in capitalist democracies, this is in itself an important objective. On the other hand, it is not unreasonable, in the absence of counter-indications, to make rather firm presumptions concerning the nature of the causal mechanisms involved. Even if there is direct state intervention by legislative or executive branch to determine levels of wages and profits, it is by no means clear that such action will be successful. If unions and employers at the various levels of the collective bargaining process do not agree with the policy, the probability of failure will be very considerable. For instance, national wage agreements in Ireland in the period 1974-75 were undermined by local unions and employers setting wage levels below the prescribed norm (OECD, *Economic Survey: Ireland*, 1975). This argument points strongly to the presumption that in capitalist democracies wages are ultimately settled by an interaction between trades unions and employers (or their organizations), and that the ratio between profits and wages is an outcome of the perceptions these actors hold concerning the relative benefits accruing from the courses of action adopted. The social democratic paradox we have essayed suggests merely that, where a social democratic government is in office, associated trade unions will be likely to experience contradictory pressures as to the balance of benefits they are likely to receive from pursuing diverse wages strategies.

Our investigation proceeds from what may be described as an agnostic position concerning the many theories that have been advanced to explain the relative shares of wages and profits in the capitalist economy. We do not deny that economic factors, such as productivity and the rate of unemployment, are crucial in determining union perceptions in the bargaining process. But for all the reasons suggested above, we are willing to entertain the possibility that political factors may also be influential. Obviously, this contradicts the purely economistic hypotheses, which state that it is only economic factors, such as economic growth, unemployment or productivity, that determine the extent of increases or decreases in wage levels with probable effects on the functional distribution of incomes. Proceeding from the belief that there are good reasons to suppose that the wage policies of trade unions may well be influenced by perceptions induced by the partisan composition of government, we shall devote considerable attention to the channels and limits of party influence on union policies. The few authors who have dealt with the party-union relationship have tended to focus on the union influence on party politics and policies (cf. Windmuller, 1974: 3). Because this pressure group approach is clearly asymmetrical, neglecting the reverse impact of party on unions, we shall first attempt to set out some hypotheses about the nature of the probable interaction of trade unions and parties.

Having delineated some of the general factors affecting the ties between unions and social democratic parties and examined the ways in which these may be conditioned within particular national

**TABLE 1**

**Major trade unions and left-wing parties under consideration, 1970**

| Country | Trade union | Left-wing party to which union is linked |
|---|---|---|
| Austria | Österreichischer Gewerkschaftsbund (ÖGB) | Sozialistische Partei Österreichs (SPÖ) |
| Belgium* | Fédération Générale du Travail de Belgique (FGTB) | Belgische Socialistische Partij/Parti Socialiste Belge (BSP/PSB) |
| Denmark | Landesorganisationen (LO) | Socialdemokratiet (SD) |
| Finland | Suomen Ammattiliittojen Keskusjärjesto (SAK) | Suomen Sosialdemokraattinen Puolue r.p. (SDP) |
| France* | Confédération Générale du Travail (CGT) | Parti Communiste Français (PCF) |
| West Germany | Deutscher Gewerkschaftsbund (DGB) | Sozialdemokratische Partei Deutschlands (SPD) |
| Ireland | Irish Congress of Trade Unions (ICTU) | Labour Party (LP) |
| Italy* | Confederazione Generale Italiana del Lavoro (CGIL) | Partito Comunista Italiano (PCI) |
| Netherlands* | Nederlands Verbond van Vakverenigingen (NVV) | Partij van de Arbeid (PvdA) |
| Norway | Landsorganisasjonen (LO) | Det Norske Arbeiderparti (DNA) |
| Sweden | Landsorganisationen (LO) | Socialdemokratiska Arbetarepartiet (SAP) |
| United Kingdom | Trades Union Congress (TUC) | Labour Party (LP) |

*There exist powerful trade unions not linked to parties or linked to bourgeois parties. In Belgium the second most important trade union is the catholic Confédération des Syndicats Chretiens (CSC). In France the Confédération Française Democratique du Travail (CFDT) is not linked to a party, while the Italian Confederazione Italiana Sindicati Lavoratori (CISL) has links to the Democrazia Cristiana (DC). In the Netherlands the Nederlandse Katholiek Vakverbond (NKV) is linked to the Catholic Peoples Party and Christelijk Nationaal Vakverbond (CNV) has connections to the Anti-Revolutionary Party and the Christian-Historical Union. Apart from the above mentioned trade unions, there are several other, but less important, unions in these countries, as well as in other countries.

contexts, we offer an empirical test of our argument. This test is in two parts. First, we employ a longitudinal design to analyse the relationship between partisan control and wage policy for the period 1960-74. As in the other chapters in this volume, we see this period as one of economic optimism and economic growth, and contrast it with the economic crisis of the mid-1970s. Thus, a second part of our test is concerned with what happened to union wage policies in the subsequent period of recession. The study is based on data from 12 West European countries, with non-European capitalist democracies being excluded on the ground that labour movement development outside Europe was too diverse to allow sufficient comparability. In Table 1, we list the major trade unions under consideration together with the left-wing parties with which they are respectively linked. Owing to lack of data, Denmark could not be included in the analysis of the period of economic crisis.

## Hypotheses

The potential for a political party to exercise influence over union wage policies can be viewed as the outcome of an interaction between a number of actors in a particular context. The most important of these actors are:

1. the party (i.e. the influencer);
2. that part of the union membership which conducts collective bargaining (i.e. the bargainers);
3. the mass membership of the union (i.e. the rank and file);
4. other unions (i.e. rivals).

An initially abstract analysis of the range of possible relationships between these actors makes it possible to generate hypotheses concerning the determination of wage policies.

A party can have an impact on union wage policies only if the union bargainers are influenced by the party. However, no union can, in the long term, pursue a policy of wage restraint in favour of a particular party in government unless the rank and file of the membership acquiesces to such a policy. The power base of union leaders is their membership. For this reason, unions cannot simply be used at will to meet the functional requirements of the capitalist economy; they must represent the interests of their members as well. Union bargainers, who are influenced to follow the path of co-operation in the name of the overall interest of the working class or the national good, must always mediate between those interests and the perceived interests of the rank and file (see Bergmann et al. 1976). Unless the union leaders represent the views of the mass membership, they will, sooner or later, be confronted by rank-and-file protest.

Such protest can take a variety of forms, including wildcat strikes, decreases in union density, refusal to pay higher union dues and a generally increasing apathy about union affairs.[10] Most of these indicators of rank-and-file alienation from the policies pursued by the leadership tend to be gradual in effect; and, even in the case of the most dramatic, the wildcat strike, it would be unrealistic to assume that such protest will automatically result from each wage settlement to which the membership is opposed. Because strikes carry high risks for individual workers, it is more reasonable to assume that this form of protest will be a consequence of accumulated discontent over a period of time. Thus, it may be that the adverse reaction of the rank and file takes a considerable time to manifest itself. During such a period, it is possible that a trade union may pursue a wage policy that is disapproved by much of its membership.

This raises the obvious question of why union bargainers should adopt policies against the wishes of the rank and file. There would appear to be two possible answers. The first, which is commonly argued in intra-union polemics, is that the leadership consists of 'class enemies' or 'dupes of the ruling class'. The second, which is far less dramatic, but which fits the evidence far better, is that union bargainers are frequently unaware of the wishes of the membership. There is considerable support for the view that the greater the degree of centralization in the collective bargaining process, the greater will be the gap between union leadership and the rank and file. In Sweden, for instance, the centralized union confederation (LO) actually uses survey techniques to acquire information about membership views in order to attempt to close this gap (Otter, 1975: 204-5). The absence of adequate information about rank-and-file wishes may have serious repercussions, not only in misjudging the membership's reaction to co-operation with government wage policy, but also in the context of industrial disputes, where the leadership may be unaware of the extent of, or absence of, worker militancy. In contrast, where collective bargaining is primarily conducted at plant level, the likelihood decreases that union bargainers (e.g. the shop stewards in Britain) will be badly informed about the views of their members.

These relationships between a government attempting to influence union wage policy, union bargainers and rank-and-file members suggest a number of alternative scenarios for the success or failure of a wage restraint policy. First, where the influencer is able to convince only the union bargainers, but not the rank and file, we might expect a policy of political wage restraint to be moderately effective in the short run, but to founder on the rocks of rank-and-file protest thereafter. Second, where the mass membership and the union bargainers can both be convinced by the party in office that wage restraint is desirable, we might expect a successful and relatively long-term wages policy to result. Third, if the members are not influenced by the party, and if the system of collective bargaining is highly decentralized (as, for example, in Italy since the late 1960s), political wage restraint of any kind will be impossible, even if the union as a whole is committed to that party.

A final general point which needs to be emphasized is that unions obtain their legitimation by demonstrating the success of their bargaining. On the one hand, this means that, in situations where several unions are rivals in organizing a particular group of workers, it is rather unlikely that a given union will be able or willing to accept a policy of political wage restraint, since the inevitable consequence will be a loss of membership to another union willing to act more militantly in defence of members' interests.[11] On the other hand, it also means that unions in general are likely to accept wage restraint only if they really expect to reap certain advantages from the participation of their party in government. If they have prior experience of their party-breaking promises in respect to social and industrial legislation, they will be that much less likely to make concessions in the wage-bargaining arena.

To sum up, the probability of political wage restraint can be determined by the answers to the following questions:

1. Are there strong ties between union bargainers and a particular political party in office?

2. Are there strong links between the rank-and-file union member and that party?

3. Is the system of collective bargaining centralized or decentralized?

4. How does the union handle protest by its members and how effective are the channels of communication and information from membership to leadership?

5. Is there competition and rivalry between several unions, or does a single union organize an entire group of employees?

6. What can the unions realistically expect to gain if their party obtains or retains governmental office as compared with other types of government?

Generalizing from all these elements, we would advance the core hypothesis that there will be political wage restraint if union bargainers are influenced by the social democratic party and if the rank and file fail to protest against, or even agree with, this policy. The null hypothesis is that union wage policy is not dependent on political factors, but is rather determined by a variety of economic factors.

## Channels and limits of party influence on union wage policies

This section examines the nature of the links between social democratic parties and trade unions in the West European nations. Party influence may be exerted through a variety of channels, including institutional ties between party and union, overlapping membership of party and unions and ideological affinities between party and union goals.[12] The strength of the influence is a function of whether all, or only some, of these links exist. It is also a function of the national context in which a particular labour movement has developed. As we shall see, a variety of national factors serves to limit or reinforce the way in which party influence impinges on union policy-making.

### Channels of influence

The linkages most frequently referred to in the literature are the institutional links between trade unions and parties. There are three major types of institutional linkage: (1) collective affiliation, whereby union members automatically become party members; (2) ex officio representation of the union leadership on the party executive (or vice versa); and (3) liaison committees. There is a fourth form of institutional linkage peculiar to Austria, where, although the ÖGB is not affiliated to the Socialist Party, the socialist faction within the ÖGB gets some 35 seats at the party conference (Klenner, 1966: 437ff.).

Collective affiliation exists in the United Kingdom, Ireland, Sweden and Norway, although in Norway affiliation is restricted to the union branch level. Only 15 percent of Norwegian LO members were collectively affiliated to the Labour Party in 1965. In Sweden, some 42 percent of LO members were affiliated to the Social Democratic Party, constituting approximately 75 percent of party membership in 1967. Britain has the highest level of collective affiliation, with around 50 percent of TUC members paying Labour Party dues, and making up almost nine-tenths of the party membership in 1977. Figures for Ireland are not dissimilar, with 45 percent affiliation in 1968 and a virtual monopoly of the party membership.[13] While it is apparent that collective affiliation is a strong weapon in the hands of a union wishing to influence the party with which it is linked (see Raschke, 1977: 278), it is less obvious that the linkage is one that can be readily used to party advantage. The behaviour of the British unions in attacking the industrial relations legislation proposed by the second Wilson administration, and the 'winter of discontent' in 1978-79 in response to the Callaghan administration's call for a 5 percent pay limit, are both examples of the failure of collective affiliation to act as a force of moderation between the two wings of the labour movement.[14] Moreover, it is by no means clear whether the failure of union members to contract out of political affiliation is a measure of the strength of party identification or merely a response to social pressures from fellow unionists (see Elvander, 1974a: 63). Finally, many of those collectively affiliated are simply not aware of the fact, and their formal status as party members has no implications for party influence. Thus, for instance, a survey of British trade unionists has revealed that 27 percent of those collectively affiliated to the Labour Party did not know it (Goldthorpe, 1970: 35).

Ex officio membership in party executive committees exists in Denmark, and in Ireland at the lower party levels.[15] Liaison committees between party and unions can be found in Belgium between the FGTB and the Socialist Party, in Norway and in Great Britain. In this last case there are, in fact, two separate liaison committees: one that brings together representatives of the TUC, the Labour Party national organization and the Co-operative Union, and another linking the TUC, the Parliamentary Labour Party and the National Executive Committee. While it might seem that this plethora of institutionalized access points for the British trade unions was a measure of the unions' capacity to influence Labour thinking, there is some reason to believe successive linkages have been elaborated precisely because the unions felt that the Parliamentary Labour party, and in particular Labour governments, were unresponsive to their views.[16] Generally speaking, ex officio membership of union representatives in party directorates and liaison committees serves as a basis for exchange of information and for policy co-ordination. This co-ordination — in our case, of wage policies — can work only if union representation in these bodies is in tune with the views of the mass membership or, as in the more centralized systems of collective bargaining, if it speaks for a leadership that has the authority to impose such policies.

The existence of formal links of the kind just discussed are not the only means by which union and party leaders can exchange views and co-ordinate policies. Indeed, informal linkages, such as ad hoc working groups, informal liaison committees or the customary selection of one or more prominent unionists to serve on the party directorate, are a common feature in most of the countries under study. Indeed, it may well be that, for communication and co-ordination purposes, informal ties would be sufficient.[17] The point is that the formal symbolism of institutionalized links serves a further function in signifying the unity of the labour movement as a whole. What is particularly interesting in terms of an analysis of wage policy is that such a public identification of the common identity and goals of party and union may have important repercussions on the stance taken by the latter in wage bargaining. Because voters may well hold the party responsible if the unions press their claims too strongly, there are likely to be very strong party pressures to moderate claims and very strong internal pressures to avoid destroying the electoral chances of the party representing the labour movement.[18] Although the British Labour government fell in May 1979 partly in consequence of its failure to persuade the unions to adopt a moderate stance in the previous six months, what is more remarkable is the strength of the resolve of union leaders from 1976 to 1978 that they must rally around to help a weak administration survive to fight another day. Those years of incomes policy might be taken as some sort of measure of the degree to which ties, formal and informal, between party and union leaders, in combination with the threat of electoral defeat, can push the unions towards wage restraint. The defeat of 1979 is witness to the fact that rank-and-file frustration cannot be contained indefinitely.

Collective affiliation is a kind of overlapping membership, but one that does not necessarily betoken strong commitment of union members to the linked social democratic party or left-wing party. The situation is quite otherwise where there is a strong tendency for union members to join the party as individuals. The greater the coincidence of voluntary membership of both wings of the labour movement, the more likely it is that the rank-and-file unionist will identify with the party and its goals. High overlapping membership is found in Austria, Belgium, the Netherlands, and West Germany, and to a lesser extent in Finland, France (CGT and Communist Party), Italy (CGIL and Communist Party) and Denmark. At the level where collective bargaining is conducted, overlapping membership is high in Belgium, the Netherlands, Austria, West Germany, Denmark, Finland and Norway. Although in Finland there has been a history of division within the labour movement, social democrats have, for the most part, held the leading trade union posts, and so have played a predominant role in the centralized system of collective bargaining.[19]

A further channel of party influence exists where the wings of the labour movement manifest a high degree of ideological homogeneity. Measuring the strength of ideolgical commitment is, however, notoriously difficult. Certainly, the most commonly used measure, i.e. the propensity of unionists to vote for a given party, is difficult to interpret in a positive sense. As Reynaud has argued in the French case, the demonstration of party loyalty on polling day and the demonstration of party loyalty in the interim are very different matters (Reynaud, 1975: 219). Nevertheless, we may well be entitled to make the negative interpretation that low electoral support by trade unionists for the party to which their union is, formally or informally, committed is indicative of a low degree of ideological homogeneity. This would seem to be the case in Ireland, where in 1969 only 34 percent of the union membership favoured the Labour Party (compared with 38 percent for Fianna Fáil and 16 percent for Fine Gael).[20] The same holds true of France (see Reynaud, 1975). In general, one might expect there to be a low ideological homogeneity in countries like France, Italy and Finland, where working-class political representation is in the hands of a number of parties and the trade unions have a tendency to be fissiparous. Obviously, if union and party divisions matched closely, homogeneity, if not unity, could be achieved; but if, as in Finland and Italy in recent years, there is markedly less division on the union that on the party side, homogeneity is most unlikely.[21] Finally, the declining voter loyalty of trade unionists to the Labour Party in Britain, together with overt opposition by the unions to the Party's position on industrial relations in the late 1960s and the covert destruction of the Party's wage restraint policy in 1978-79, suggests that Britain must also be classified as manifesting low labour movement ideological homogeneity.[22]

Establishing which countries do manifest high degrees of homogeneity involves an overall assessment of the available literature on party-union relationships. Writers on the Scandinavian countries, all of which have high union density together with a high working-class electoral turnout for the social democrats and strong traditions of regarding the two wings of the labour movement as parts of a single whole, would probably list Sweden, Norway and Denmark, in descending order of homogeneity.[23] All would, however, be homogeneous in comparison with the countries previously discussed, although Denmark from the early 1970s showed a marked decline in working-class support for the social democrats.[24] As we shall point out below, there is also clear evidence of ideological commitment by union members to linked social democratic parties in the consociational countries of Belgium, the Netherlands (particularly during the early 1960s) and Austria. These are countries in which party and union divisions do tend to match, and in which union and allied party are seen as aspects of a single political community. Recent discussion of the ideological loyalties of German trade unionists suggests that the Federal Republic is also characterized by a strongish ideological homogeneity of the labour movement (see Bergmann and Müller-Jentsch, 1977).

In summary, we would argue that wage restraint policies will be more likely to be adopted in countries in which there are personal and ideological links between trade unions and the party in office. But a number of national factors serve to limit or reinforce the capacity of a given party to influence union wage policies. It is to the nature of these factors that we now turn.

## The limits to influence

As a consequence of diverse historical and cultural factors, the development of the labour movement in our 12-country sample has been anything but uniform. This is, of course, already apparent in the varying strength of the linkages between social democratic parties and unions, and is also manifested in a whole host of organizational and ideological differences, which are frequently pertinent to the possibility of a party successfully pressing for union wage restraint. Nevertheless, it is possible and useful to group labour

**TABLE 2**
**Types of union-party nexus**

|                    | *Division of labour*                                                          | *Autonomous*                      |
| ------------------ | ----------------------------------------------------------------------------- | --------------------------------- |
| Consociational     | Austria<br>Belgium<br>Netherlands                                             |                                   |
| Non-consociational | Denmark<br>Finland<br>France (CGT)<br>Germany<br>Ireland<br>Norway<br>Sweden<br>UK | France (CFDT)<br>Italy (CISL)     |

movements in terms of criteria, which to some extent delimit the nature of the union-party nexus:

1. whether there is a clear division of labour within the working-class movement between a party carrying out political functions and a union organization carrying out economic/industrial functions:[25] such a division of labour is normal in most countries, but where, in contrast, unions conceive of their role as an autonomous one, they will clearly be less open to influence and pressure from political parties;

2. whether there has occurred a pillarization of the labour movement as a consequence of its development in the context of a consociational political culture. The salient features of consociational development are that the major social groupings ('pillars' — including Catholic, Protestants, the labour movement, etc.) emphasize their distinctiveness and separateness, avoid contact except at elite level, and conduct politics by compromises and coalitions among group leaders.[26] In such a political culture, the ideological homogeneity of union and party is not merely a question of working-class solidarity, but part of a principle of social organization. While that facilitates labour movement unity, the reverse side of the coin is that social democratic-affiliated unions will not have a monopoly in collective bargaining, but will have to co-operate with unions from other pillars, with linkages to their own parties.

Thus, in general terms, pillarized labour movements make for stronger links between party and union, but offer a lesser scope for influencing the entire organized labour force.

Since the concept of a union organization autonomous from political control is unthinkable in the consociational context, these two criteria yield a threefold typology of the union-party nexus. This is illustrated in Table 2, together with each country's location within the classification. This broad typology describes the overall parameters in which party influence is exercised, but within each type there remains a substantial range of variation.

## *The influence of socialist parties on union wage policies in Great Britain, Germany, Ireland and the Nordic countries*

In Great Britain, agreements between the government and the TUC are of limited effectiveness because a dual union structure corresponds with a dual system of collective bargaining. National agreements negotiated by the national leadership are regarded as minimum marks, and are systematically renegotiated at plant level by shop stewards, whose bargaining authority is a direct function of their success in improving local wage rates and conditions (see Donovan Report, 1968). The obvious difficulties facing national union leaders in delivering policies of the kind desired by the Labour administrations of the mid- to late 1960s were not the only reason for a growing distance between Labour and the unions in this period. For their part, the unions were concerned that Labour was moving towards industrial relations legislation of a kind felt to be antithetical to union interests, while simultaneously trying to woo the middle-class voter by abandoning egalitarian rhetoric in favour of a technocratic image. This perceived shift to the right by the Labour government was matched by a leftward movement in the unions, clearly indicated in the views of the new generation of union leaders elected in the late 1960s.

Compared with the British shop stewards, the German works councillors (Bertriebsräte) have only a limited opportunity, and no legal right, to participate in collective bargaining.[27] Moreover, as a group they appear to be strongly committed to the social democrats, with as many as a third being individually affiliated to the SPD (Bergmann and Müller-Jentsch, 1977: 278). Most bargaining is conducted at the regional level or in selected large enterprises by official union officers, and here too the evidence points to a strong tendency to SPD membership.[28] When in 1966, after 36 years in the political wilderness, the social democrats joined the government, the union movement had considerable hopes that the resulting 'Grand Coalition' would lead to major domestic reform (see Schmidt, 1978), and, in anticipation, implemented a wage restraint policy. By 1969 a series of wildcat strikes indicated growing rank-and-file discontent with the rapid increase in profits, although it does not appear to have spilled over into anti-union or anti-SPD feeling (Schumann et al., 1971). This led to a reorientation towards a more expansive wages policy (Jacobi, 1972: 132), and to a somewhat greater distancing of the social democrats and the DGB. In 1973 the SPD established a work group (Arbeitsgemeinschaft für Arbeitnehmerfragen) to close the gap between the unions and the SPD and to reduce the influence of the leftist Young Socialists.[29]

When the Irish Labour Party entered into coalition with Fine Gael after the 1973 election, it was to confront a wholly transformed collective bargaining arena. Until 1970 trade union bargaining had been decentralized, and the potential for political wage restraint therefore minimized. However, in response to worsening economic conditions and an implicit threat from the government that the unions must put their house in order, the trade unions adopted a centralized bargaining structure. The conjunction of a Social Democratic Party in power and a more authoritative union leadership provides a potential, in terms of our basic hypothesis, for the party to exercise influence in favour of wage restraint. It should be noted, however, that Irish political traditions and the social base of Irish politics lead to divisions in working-class political loyalties, and that the peculiar conformation of the Irish party system means that Labour must enter into coalition with the party regarded by most commentators as being most conservative.[30]

In Norway, Sweden, Finland and Denmark, the unions have strong central organizations and highly centralized systems of collective bargaining. In Denmark the ability of the Social Democratic-oriented union leadership to deliver wage restraint is sometimes threatened by conflict between craft unions and general workers unions, the latter organizing the vast mass of semi-skilled and unskilled workers. In 1974 some unions went as far as to decide to support not only the Social Democratic party, but also the other left-wing parties (including the Communists and Socialist People's Party).[31] In Finland the labour movement is clearly weakened by the political rivalry of the Social Democrats and Communists, but on the whole the former dominate among the union leadership.

Over the years the relationship between the Swedish Social Democrats and LO has been virtually symbiotic, particularly at leadership level, but in the early 1970s there were some signs that the Centre Party was attracting some unionist support. Moreover, a series of wildcat strikes, the most serious in the Norrboten iron ore industry, suggested that the loyalty of the rank and file could not simply be assumed. Norway has also experienced a degree of disruption to the traditional good relationships between Labour Party and unions, but that was less a consequence of debate on wage policy issues than of the fierce controversy concerning the EEC referendum in 1973. In addition, the Norwegian wage bargaining scene contains one element that is unusual in centralized systems, in that rank-and-file members have the right to vote on proposed wage agreements.[32] It might be argued that this unusual stuctural feature of union bargaining in Norway had the potential to counter the predicted impact of union centralization, since it means that union members have already access to channels of communication with union leaders.

Despite the evidence of diversity and minor fluctuation in the relationship between social democratic parties and unions in Finland, Sweden, Denmark, Ireland and West Germany, the general conclusion must be that the potential for successful party influence in favour of union wage restraint exists in these countries. In contrast, the absence of effective centralization in Britain, and the chequered history of party-union relations in the last two decades, suggests that successful influence would be either slight or non-existent. The ambiguous case is Norway. The ties between DNA and LO could hardly be stronger or more amicable, but LO has mechanisms that allow the rank and file to pronounce on the agreements reached at the top of the labour movement hierarchy. In terms of our hypothesis, the interesting question is whether strong ideological and personal ties or rank-and-file demands for higher rewards is the major determinant of the success or failure of wage restraint policy.

## The influence of socialist parties on union policies in Austria, Belgium and the Netherlands

Belgium and the Netherlands are countries where the labour movement has been — and in Belgium still is — divided into three union confederations, each of which is linked to a particular political party. In Austria there is only one confederation (the ÖGB), but this too is internally divided into three factions, of which the socialist faction is the largest and most influential. In general, this pillarized organization of labour movement is only marginally favourable to wage restraint policies, since the advantage of high ideological homogeneity within pillars is offset by the fact that governmental parties seeking wage restraint can at best only influence the trade unions within the pillars to which they belong. This situation is somewhat indeterminate in regard to the possibility of political wage restraint, and the major differentiating factor would appear to be the extent to which the 'cartel of elites' inherent in consociational arrangements is created at the cost of dissolving distinct party identities at the policy-making level.

In the period of Grand Coalition in Austria, after the war until 1966, such dissolution of identity was apparent both at cabinet and union leadership levels. Moreover, a coalition mentality was just as obvious in the context of collective bargaining. The ÖGB has been characterized in terms of its willingness to act as a 'social partner' ('Sozialpartnerschaft'), and such an attitude is reflected in the fact that the tripartite Paritätische Kommission für Preis — und Lohnfragen de facto settles wages issues (see Lang, 1978). The major change in Austrian politics from 1966 onwards, when coalition government was replaced by single-party majority government, clearly involves a greater distinctiveness in party stances on policy issues, and from 1970, when the social democrats took office, suggests a greater potential for political wage restraint influence being directed from the party to the socialist faction within the ÖGB.

Despite emergent regional differences, the Belgian trade unions, in many ways, conform to what might be regarded as the ideal type of industrial bargaining in a pillarized society. The Belgian Socialist Party is closely connected with the FGTB at all levels, demonstrating a high degree of ideological homogeneity and overlapping membership. The action commune is a liaison committee of the Party, the socialist union, the friendly societies and the co-operatives. The organizations of the socialist pillar are integrated by a series of interlocking directorates and there are close personal ties among the leaderships of the various bodies (Lorwin, 1975: 246). The three 'most representative' union confederations have a history of elite co-operation in collective bargaining through bi- and tripartite commissions.[33] However, there has been greater tension between the various union leaderships than among the factions of the Austrian union movement, and there has been a tendency for inter-union co-operation to cease when the parties to which the confederations are affiliated cease to collaborate in parliament.[34] At the rank-and-file level there is no co-operation, and 'members of one confederation feel no obligation to support industrial action taken by members of the other organisation, and in general the crossing of a picket line carries no stigma in Belgium' (Carew, 1976: 36). In recent years, growing rank-and-file militancy and discontent with the wage settlements reached in the 'programmation sociale', the major bipartite collective bargaining body, have become evident.[35] Although there is co-operation at the elite level within the unions, there is less blurring of identity than in Austria. Moreover, at the political level there is marked conflict and competition among the parliamentary parties.[36] Overall, these factors would suggest a modest political wage restraint effect when the PSB is in office, based on high homogeneity rather than total control of the union movement. This is the more probable, since the PSB is usually in coalition with the Social Christians, who are themselves affiliated with the major union rival to the FGTB.

As in Austria, the 1960s was a period of transformation for the labour movement in the Netherlands. In respect of the possibility of effecting political wage restraint, the developments were contradictory in their impact. On the one hand, the depillarization of Dutch society, which rapidly gained pace from the mid-1960s onwards, meant that the parties became more distinctive in their policy stance and more competitive in the parliamentary and electoral arenas. On the other hand, the decline in religious cleavages permitted greater co-operation between the union confederations, which led to a series of mergers by the mid-1970s. This closer co-operation at both elite and rank-and-file levels necessarily led to a concomitant weakening of the linkages between union confederations and particular political parties. Moreover, during the same period, the centralized system of collective bargaining, with the Social and Economic Council at its apex, was weakened in its power to determine wage levels both because of the impact of multinational companies in the domestic market and because of increasing rank-and-file militancy.[37] Thus, while depillarization of the party system might have been conducive to greater political influence on union wage policies, the developments within the unions themselves counteracted such a tendency.

## The influence of socialist parties on union wage policies in France and Italy

In both France and Italy the situation is not propitious for political wage restraint. In general, there is a tendency for the unions to take a more autonomous stance than elsewhere in Europe, and the closest linkages have been between the communist parties and their respective affiliated union confederations (the CGT in France and CGIL, until 1969, in Italy). Moreover, each country has three major confederations, which, in contrast to the practice in pillarized societies, compete for membership. Apart from these features of the linkage between parties and unions in France and Italy, there are two overall impediments to political wage restraint. The most obvious is that, with the exception of minor socialist participation in centre-left-wing coalitions in Italy, no party of the Left has held office in the period 1960-74. Even if the focus is on non-socialist parties with union affiliations (the Christian Democratic link with CISL until the late 1960s), no single party in office has had strong links with a majority of the relevant union movement. Second, it should be noted that union density is extremely low in both countries, and that, certainly until the late 1960s, the impact of the unions on overall national wage levels was negligible. As we shall see in discussing developments in the 1970s in a subsequent section, there has been some change in the Italian situation. There has been a trend towards greater inter-union collaboration in plant level bargaining, which has simultaneously led to a weakening of party linkages and a somewhat greater effectiveness in collective bargaining (see Farneti, 1978).

## Partisan control and wages policy: a longitudinal analysis

In this section we shall employ a longitudinal research design to establish whether our hypothesis concerning the impact of social democratic government on union wage policies holds for each of 12 West European countries in the period 1960-74. The alternative, or null, hypothesis would suggest that wage policies will be dependent on economic factors, and not on politcal factors. It should be clear that, in employing this type of research design, we are not looking for some summary indicator of the general strength of the relationship between party control and wage policies valid across all countries, but rather are seeking to compare the experience of each individual country with predictions based on our analysis of the strength of party-union ties and the national context in which their impact is limited or reinforced. Thus, in some countries we would expect only a very weak social democratic influence (i.e. Great Britain), and in others (i.e. Sweden or Denmark), with stronger trade union-party links, we would expect such influence to be far more pronounced.

## The variables

### The dependent variable[38]

In the absence of any valid cross-national indicator of union wage policies, we utilize a measure of policy outcomes, the wage share, as our dependent variable. This measure indicates the share of wages and salaries relative to the total of domestic factor incomes (i.e., income from employment plus the sum of operating surpluses of all resident industries). This seems to be an appropriate measure in the context of our study, since the objective of social democratic and other left-wing trade unions is, at a minimum, to hold the wage share constant, and preferably to increase it vis-à-vis profits. This measure does not allow for any differentiation between state and private industry; nor does it permit analysis of possible intra-class redistribution of income. This loss of differentiation is not of serious consequence for this study, since (1) our interest is in the conditions under which unions succeed or fail in their presumed aim of protecting or enhancing labour's factor income vis-à-vis profits, and (2) the traditional emphasis of the working-class movement has always been on inter- rather than intra-class distribution.

It might be argued that certain problems arise in using the wage share as a measure of the success or failure of union wage policies, since unions will have a differential impact on wage levels and wage shares from country to country, depending on degrees of union density, the percentage covered by collective agreements and other aspects of organizational strength. This problem is, however, to a large extent minimized because, in the context of a longitudinal design, utilizing annual readings of the wage share, national differences are not involved, and changes in union strength are unlikely to be dramatic in any given year. Another problem lies in the fact that, during the period under review, the percentage of wage-earners in the total labour force was increasing in virtually all 12 countries, as a consequence of the decline in the importance of the self-employed sector. In order to cope with this, it is necessary to make two adjustments, one to control for the impact of this change and the other to ensure that the sum of the wage and profit share is 1.0 or, as measured here, 100 percent.[39]

It might be argued that real money wages or labour costs could have advantages to the wage share as measures of union wage policies. But the problems are, if anything, greater. Real wages do not reflect changes in quasi-income, like greater leisure time, changes in working conditions, etc.[40] Moreover, to use real wages, it would be necessary to control for the effects of economic growth on the development of wage levels. There is also no question that the international comparability of data relating to the wage share is much greater than for real wages.

### The independent variables

Our basic hypothesis suggests that wage restraint will result from the presence of a social democratic party in government and our null hypothesis affirms the importance of labour market factors. Accordingly, we utilize a number of political and economic measures as follows.

1. *Socialist party participation.* If the party to which the union is committed (see Table 1 above) has been in government for more than six months in a given year, no matter whether the prime minister is a member of this party or not, the score for this variable is 1.0: in all other cases it is 0.0.

2. *Socialist party prime minister.* If the above mentioned party has been in office for more than six months in a year and at the same time if the prime minister is a member of this party, the score for this variable is 1.0: otherwise it is 0.0.

3. *Unemployment.* In the traditional Marxist theory, unemployment weakens the power of labour thus allowing for increases in the rate of surplus value by means of lower wages. This variable is operationalized as the percentage of the unemployed in that part of the labour force on which the unemployment data are based.

4. *Change rate of unemployment.* Since it might be argued that the wage policies of unions are a consequence not merely of the level of unemployment, but also of changing labour market conditions, we also provide a measure sensitive to such change. This is operationalized as the difference between unemployment rates in successive years.

5. *The situation of the economy as a whole.* Because the rate of economic growth is closely related to certain types of unemployment, and because expansion or contraction of the economy sets the basic parameters within which the relative shares of wages and profits are determined, we have used the percentage change in real GDP as a measure of the overall situation of the economy. Economists point out that the wage share and indicators of economic growth move countercyclically due to decreasing productivity and thus profits, whereas initially wage levels remain constant and accommodate later to the new economic situation (cf. King and Regan, 1976). On the basis of this hypothesis, we would expect a negative correlation between economic growth and the wage share. Since it is expected that in periods of low economic growth unemployment will be high, there will be a positive correlation between unemployment and the wage share.

6. Considering that inflation may be perceived as a threat to working-class standards of living, it could be that unions will be reluctant to claim higher wages if inflation is high. If this were the case, we would expect the wage share either to remain constant or to decrease in periods of high inflation. On the other hand, arguing from currently fashionable cost-push theories, it may make more sense to consider the wage share as the independent variable and inflation as the dependent one. If this is so, it would be expected that, in so far as the wage share is increasing, employers will attempt to restore their profit margins by increasing prices. Thus, high wage shares and/or increases in the wage share would tend to be accompanied by high rates of inflation.

For each country, we have undertaken a bivariate correlation analysis of the wage share on the various independent variables. Given a number of statistical problems inherent in the small number of observations, and the difficulties stemming from both autocorrelation and assumptions of linearity in the context of time-series analysis, we have adopted the simplest mode of analysis possible under the circumstances.[41] The strategy employed was to check the results both by comparable modes of analysis and by reference to the raw data. The latter method allows us to procure information that is lost in the employment of models assuming linear relationships. In this section, hypotheses will be regarded as confirmed where the correlation coefficients are either less than $-0.30$ or greater than $0.30$; i.e., if the variation in the independent variable accounts for about 10 or more percent of the variation in the dependent variable.

*The determinants of the wage share in*
*an era of prosperity: 1960-74*

Our analysis demonstrates that, although there was a systematic
relationship between economic conditions and the wage share,
social democratic incumbency combined with close links to the
workers' movement was a potent factor making for wage restraint.

*The economic context of working-class*
*distributional advantage*
The overall result of the analysis reported in Table 3 is that there is
a strong relationship between economic growth and the level of the
wage share.[42] In accordance with the 'economic' hypothesis, this
relationship is negative; i.e., the wage share is high precisely where
economic growth is low. Moreover, this observation is further confirmed when looking at the change in the wage share: the wage
share goes up when economic growth rates are low. Simultaneously, we find a high degree of association between levels of and
changes in unemployment and economic growth. Unemployment is
higher, and tends to increase, when economic growth is low.
However, although the wage share is negatively correlated to
economic growth, and growth is negatively correlated to rates of
unemployment, it is difficult to discern a systematic relationship
between unemployment and development of the wage share. There
would appear to be little evidence of any systematic relationship
between the wage share and the level of inflation. Neither the notion of the redistributive effects of inflation in favour of non-wage
incomes nor the cost-push hypothesis is confirmed across our sample of European nations.

*The political context of wage restraint*
In reporting our findings on the linkage between the political composition of government and the outcomes of union wage policies, it
should be re-emphasized that our hypothesis is predicated not on the
wage-restraining impact of social democratic partisan influence
alone, but rather on the influence of socialist partisanship when
combined with close institutional and personal linkages with the
trade union movement. Thus, in Austria, Belgium, Denmark,
Finland, Germany, Ireland, Norway and Sweden we would predict
that trade unions will be more reluctant to claim higher wages in

**TABLE 3**

**Correlation analysis: economic variables, 1960-1974**

| Country | Wage share with unemployment | Wage share with economic growth | Economic growth with unemployment | Wage share (change) with economic growth | Unemployment (change) with economic growth | Wage share (change) with unemployment (change) | Wage share with inflation | Wage share (change) with inflation |
|---|---|---|---|---|---|---|---|---|
| Austria | 0.84 | −0.27 | 0.13 | −0.60* | −0.61 | 0.06* | −0.72 | 0.08* |
| Belgium | 0.20 | −0.46 | 0.05 | −0.64* | −0.46 | 0.40* | −0.55 | 0.30* |
| Denmark | 0.15 | −0.50 | −0.37* | −0.52* | −0.73* | 0.46* | 0.41 | 0.41* |
| Finland | −0.22 | −0.17 | −0.18 | −0.50 | −0.78* | 0.31* | −0.69 | −0.50* |
| France | −0.86 | 0.28 | −0.47 | −0.56 | −0.73* | 0.35 | −0.48 | 0.69* |
| Germany | 0.21 | −0.50 | −0.53 | −0.45* | −0.90* | 0.38* | 0.07 | 0.53* |
| Ireland | 0.12 | −0.46 | 0.14 | −0.52* | −0.20* | 0.12* | 0.43 | 0.27* |
| Italy | −0.15 | −0.41 | 0.28 | −0.39* | −0.59* | −0.22* | 0.52 | 0.49* |
| Netherlands | 0.62 | −0.48 | −0.19 | −0.59* | −0.38* | −0.16* | 0.68 | −0.07* |
| Norway | 0.17 | 0.09 | 0.12 | 0.50* | −0.03* | 0.02* | −0.31 | −0.13* |
| Sweden | 0.21 | −0.23 | −0.68 | −0.44* | −0.71 | 0.66* | −0.39* | −0.06* |
| UK | 0.63 | −0.30 | −0.03 | −0.48* | −0.50* | 0.23* | 0.84* | 0.38* |

* Durbin-Watson statistics between 1.36 and 2.64, i.e. no autocorrelations.

## TABLE 4
### Correlation analysis: the wage share and the political variables, 1960-1974

| Country | Wage share with socialist party prime minister | Wage share with socialist party participation | Wage share (change) with socialist party prime minister | Wage share (change) with socialist party participation |
|---|---|---|---|---|
| Austria | -0.94 | -0.21 | -0.20* | 0.00* |
| Belgium | -0.42 | -0.48 | -0.14* | -0.39* |
| Denmark | -0.72 | -0.55 | -0.19* | -0.44* |
| Finland | -0.47 | (n.a.) | -0.60* | (n.a.) |
| France | (n.a.) | (n.a.) | (n.a.) | (n.a.) |
| Germany | -0.17 | -0.53 | 0.44* | -0.03* |
| Ireland | (n.a.) | 0.09 | (n.a.) | 0.29* |
| Italy | (n.a.) | (n.a.) | (n.a.) | (n.a.) |
| Netherlands | 0.34 | 0.35 | 0.02* | 0.25* |
| Norway | 0.05 | | -0.24 | |
| Sweden | (n.a.) | (n.a.) | (n.a.) | (n.a.) |
| UK | -0.05 | | 0.20* | |

* Durbin-Watson statistics between 1.36 and 2.64, i.e. no autocorrelation. In Denmark, Norway and in the UK the social democratic parties when in government have always been the leading party. Thus there are no differences between the values for socialist party prime minister and socialist party participation.

periods when social democratic parties are in office. In general, we would not expect the trade unions to exercise political wage restraint in Britain, France, Italy or the Netherlands.

In overall terms, the findings presented in Table 4 strongly support the hypothesis that political wage restraint is a consequence of a close social democratic-trade union nexus. A table showing the year-by-year development of the wage share in each of the 12 countries is presented in the Appendix. The degree of fit between the hypothesized relationship and actual wage policy outcome in each country may be summarized as follows.

1. *Austria*. The expected relationship was moderation in wage policy after 1970 as a consequence of the advent of single-party SPÖ government, but, certainly, no political effect prior to 1966. Austria fits the hypothesis very well. Although the wage share shows a secular decline since at least 1954 (see Lang, 1978: 89), the wage share under social democratic government was stabilized at the low point to which it had descended by 1970.

2. *Belgium*. Here the expected result was wage restraint under social democratic rule, although mitigated by the presence of nonsocialist unions. This is confirmed to the degree that moderate wage restraint has characterized each period of PSB participation in government. (The statistical association between a social democratic prime minister in office and wage restraint does not justify interpretation, since the finding is an artefact of only a single year's governmental leadership.)

3. *Denmark*. While the expected relationship was wage moderation in all periods of social democratic rule, the findings seem to demonstrate an interaction between incomes policy, partisan composition of government and the prevailing economic situation. The incomes policy of the mid-1960s was partially viable because the unions were willing to accept the social democratic assertion of the need for restraint in a period of unstable economic development. When the economic situation improved in the years after 1965/66, the unions and rank and file did not feel under pressure strongly enough to continue such moderation (see Ulman and Flanagan, 1971: 140-5), and thus the wage-earners gained ground in the distribution struggle. It is also notable that the combination of established incomes policy and improving economic environment led to a loss in votes to the Social Democrats in the election of 1966, with the major gainers being, significantly, the Socialist People's Party, to the left of SD.

4. *Finland*. The expected result of wage restraint after 1968 is

also confirmed. A similar moderation-recovery process as in Denmark is also apparent in Finland. The Finnish experience is particularly instructive because successful wage restraint emerges at precisely that conjuncture where major union divisions were more or less healed and the Social Democrats re-established themselves in government (see Helander, 1978). Nevertheless, there have been some disturbances in the system. In 1971, after three years of wage moderation, the metal workers and building workers refused to accept a proposal by the President, which was generally seen as a compromise between the divergent claims of unions and employers. The metal workers went on strike, and the deadlock was only resolved by wage concessions which exceeded the guidelines stipulated in the presidential compromise (see OECD, *Economic Surveys: Finland*, 1971: 15-16). In subsequent years, despite some difficulties, centralized agreements between government, unions and employers were usually possible (except in 1973 and 1977).

5. *France*. In the absence of any period of socialist government in the period under survey, no predictions are appropriate within the scope of our model. However, the more or less continuous decline in the French wage share could reasonably be interpreted as a reflection of the weakness and disunity of the French working-class movement.

6. *Germany*. In Germany, our survey of the changing relationship of Social Democrats and unions would suggest wage restraint in the period of the Grand Coalition followed by a more pragmatic attitude consequent on the disappointments engendered by the first period of social democratic rule. Again, as in Denmark and Finland, we encounter the moderation-recovery and frustrated expectations on the part of unionists. The development of the wage share, as reported in the Appendix, clearly shows the impact of the incorporation of the unions into a system of incomes policy. When the economic situation improved, and it became progressively more obvious that the distributional share accruing to the working class was rapidly being attenuated, the unions were forced by rank-and-file demands to pursue a more aggressive wages stance. It is true that, if we examine only the period in which the SPD has been the leading party in government, no systematic relationship can be discerned, but this would not appear to be a consequence of the absence of political effect. Rather, as in the Danish and Finnish caes, it represents the 'recovery' phase of the incomes policy cycle. In reality, the moderation-recovery cycle is testimony to the joint

impact of economic and political factors in the determination of the wage share.

7. *Ireland*. The expected relationship of wage restraint under social democratic rule is not confirmed. While in 1973 there is some evidence for the assumed relationship, the sharp up-swing in 1974 clearly contradicts our hypothesis. Two points should, however, be noted. First, the 1974 change in the wage share may well be associated with the initial impact of the economic crisis and the greater flexibility of the profit margin of firms (see previous section and the next section on the economic crisis). Second, the statistical basis for generalization is, in the Irish case, far from secure, owing to the extremely limited period of social democratic participation in government.

8. *Italy*. Although we have regarded socialist participation in government in Italy as too marginal to include in our analysis, it may be regarded as significant that the downturn in the wage share occurred at the height of the experiments into an 'opening to the Left' in the mid-to late 1960s. The subsequent advance in the wage share could be seen partially as a manifestation of the moderation-recovery cycle, but is probably chiefly attributable to the increasing unity of the Italian trade union movement in this latter period.

9. *Netherlands*. In this case, as predicted, there is no apparent political wage restraint effect. Unions do not curb their wage claims under PvDA government and, indeed, there seems to be a significant tendency for wage policy outcomes to be more favourable to the working class when the social democrats participate in government.

10. *Norway.* There was a question mark over our predictions concerning the development of the wage share in Norway. On the one hand, the social democrats and union leadership have a virtually symbiotic relationship; on the other, the union rank and file have mechanisms at their disposal to check leadership concessions to the party. Owing to certain problems in the National Accounts data for Norway (i.e. a change in the basis for compiling time-series), there must be some doubts as to reliability. Our interpretation, based on the data available, must still leave something of a question mark. The correlation of level of wage share and social democratic incumbency demonstrates no obvious impact of political wage restraint, suggesting, perhaps, the control that the rank and file is able to exert through referenda on wage settlements. On the other hand, it is noticeable that the major wage share decline — from 1962 to 1965 — occurred under Social Democratic rule, and in the

run-up period to an election in which the party had strong reasons to seek union moderation to protect an increasingly weak electoral position.

11. *Sweden.* As in the French case, the absence of any alternation in government makes prediction impossible. However, it is worth noting that the 1968-70 and 1971-73 declines in the wage share (see Appendix) coincided with the run-up periods to obviously dangerous elections for the Social Democrats. The possibility of such an electoral effect is strongly suggested by the fact that, overall, the wage share declined in a period characterized by intense rhetoric about the need to increase the degree of equality in Swedish society. In the next section, which also includes a period of 'bourgeois' rule, it will be shown that wage policy outcomes have been more favourable to the wage- and salary-earning groups under the new dispensation.

12. *United Kingdom.* As expected, the evidence concerning the development of the wage share in Britain points to the failure of the wholly explicit attempts of the Labour administration of 1964-70 to get the unions to adopt a more moderate wages stance than under Tory government.

Overall, the evidence from the era of prosperity from 1960 to 1974 suggests strongly that political factors do have an impact on the development of the wage share. We now turn to the question of whether a similar phenomenon is also characteristic of periods of economic crisis.

## Wage policy outcomes in a period of economic crisis

The economic prosperity and stability of the 1960s was succeeded in the middle 1970s by a much more unsettled period. In a previous chapter, it has already been noted that this change in the economic climate had major repercussions in respect of the relationship between macroeconomic policy outcomes and a range of economic and political variables. There is every reason to suppose that the economic crisis would also herald changes — or an intensification of existing trends — in the determination of labour market outcomes. On the one hand, increasing and mass unemployment — compared with the modest rates of unemployment in the 1960s and early 1970s — should provide the acid test for the thesis relating unemployment and the power of the working class in the distributional struggle. On the other, economic recession combined with hyperinflation provided an incentive, as never before, for exercising political wage restraint. Our fundamental question is, therefore, whether social democratic governments, and particularly those with close links to the trade unions, were more successful in effecting a moderation of union wage policies in the period of economic crisis.

## Economic and political hypotheses

The general consensus of economic theories concerning wage determination in periods of crisis would suggest the intensification of postulated links between productivity, unemployment and wages policy.[43] For instance, the traditional Marxist view — which in this respect departs little from the neoclassical approach — is that high unemployment and low economic growth combine in such a way as to lead to stagnation or a decrease in real wages.[44] Nevertheless, as we have noted previously, this need not, in the short run, result in a decrease in the wage share. On the contrary, as a consequence of the greater responsiveness and flexibility of profits, we would expect the advent of a severe recession to be associated with an increase in the distributional share accruing to wage and salaried employees. Only after a period in which prior collective agreements had time to work through would we expect to find a gradual reversal of this trend. In other words, the most promising hypothesis linking wage policy outcomes to labour market conditions would appear to be one that postulates a time-lag between the beginning of the crisis and the decrease in the wage share.[45] Given that the crisis of the 1970s was associated with hitherto unexperienced rates of inflation, it is necessary to control for this factor's possible impact on the development of the wage share, even though our prior longitudinal analysis of the period of economic crisis did not point up any significant inflationary effects.

In the widest sense, the argument that politics can affect wage determination is presumed by all governmental attempts, whether overt or covert, to introduce an incomes policy. The mid-1970s was, par excellence, the era of incomes policy aimed directly at containing the inflationary consequences of the economic crisis. Such a policy was adopted irrespective of party labels, and our interest is in whether the close ties with the trade unions enjoyed by some — but not all — social democratic parties were particularly propitious in determining the success of wage restraint through incomes policy.

As previously, it is important to note that the likely impact of a social democratic government on union wages policy will be dependent on both the formal and informal linkages between the wings of the labour movement and on the particular national context in which they occur. Obviously, both of these factors are subject to change. In particular, national contexts were subject to change in the 1970s as a consequence of assessment of the degree to which the economic crisis impinged on national prosperity and the previously accepted goals of public policy. For this reason, we cannot simply be content to argue that a party-union nexus that led to wage restraint in the earlier period of prosperity would have a similar effect subsequently, but must undertake a brief review of ensuing changes and ways in which they effect our predictions.

1. *Countries with close party-union links which conformed to the prediction of political wage restraint in the period 1960-74.* These countries include Austria, Belgium, Denmark, Finland and Germany.

As we have noted previously, an absence of comparable data makes it impossible to include Denmark in our analysis of wages policy in the period of the economic crisis. In the other instances, the evidence is such as to suggest that political wage restraint would persist under circumstances of social democratic rule. In both Austria and Finland, the previously established frameworks of incomes policy remained in existence. In Germany there was a breakdown in the concerted action ('Konzertierte Aktion') between trade unions, employers and the state in 1977. Nevertheless, the unions seem to have persisted in a moderate stance owing to a number of factors, including loyalties to the SPD-led coalition, a belief that wage restraint would rapidly ease the crisis,[46] and a strongly felt national priority on avoiding inflation. The continuing pillarization of Belgian politics, despite the recent complications of regional fragmentation, suggests the continuity of a moderate wage restraint effect.

2. *Countries with close party-union links which failed to conform with the prediction of political wage restraint in the period 1960-74.* Ireland is the only case that unequivocally falls into this category, although with the caveat that the period of Labour rule under review was of insufficient duration to base firm conclusions. However, the period of economic crisis was one in which centralized and corporatist modes of regulating the labour market were fur-

ther developed (see OECD, *Economic Surveys: Ireland*, 1976). Since we would expect such changes to be conducive to a political wage restraint effect, we reaffirm our original prediction for Ireland in the period of ecomomic crisis.

3. *Countries in which there must remain some question about the impact of the party-union nexus in the period, 1960-74.* The reasons for such a question mark vary, and the cases include Norway, France, Italy and Sweden.

Assuming the Norwegian data to be reliable, there was little statistical evidence in the early period for a wage restraint effect, although it seemed possible that the social democrats may have mobilized union support to moderate wage demands in the run up to the 1965 election. In the 1970s there were clear signs that the national context may have changed in such a way as to further constrain union members to support joint leadership and social democratic initiatives for wage restraint. Norway's close integration into the world economy makes her extremely vulnerable to inflationary pressures that threaten the competitiveness of the export sector. In the 1970s, overt incomes policy has been adopted by the DNA, with the agreement of the union leadership, in a well publicized attempt to limit the degree of such vulnerability. Although channels of protest remain open between rank-and-file unionists and the leadership, we would assume that strong links between the two arms of the labour movement would, in a period presented as an international crisis, lead to solidarity in support of the attempted incomes policy.

The French, Italian and Swedish cases did not lead to confirmed predictions in the earlier longitudinal analysis, since in none of these countries was there any alternation of partisan control in the period under review. As explained in the next sub-section, the methodology employed in the analysis of the economic crisis period is cross-sectional in kind. This, despite other disadvantages, means that these countries can now be included, although, of course, Sweden at last experienced a change in partisan composition in the mid-1970s. Our basic hypothesis suggests a very strong political wage restraint in Sweden as a consequence of the almost symbiotic relationship between the Social Democrats and LO established over four decades of socialist government. In the period up until the 1976 Social Democratic defeat, it was possible to reconcile the increasingly conflicting claims of LO and the employers' organization (see Fulcher, 1976). In the latter years of Social Democratic rule (1974-76) the mechanism for such agreements were the so-called Haga conferences, in which the main trade unions, the employers' confederation, the parties and central bank participated. There the central issues of economic and tax policy were settled. The third conference (1976) failed because of competitive stances predicated on the coming election (see Nedelmann and Meier, 1979), and, thereafter, attempts to resolve industrial conflict by corporatist means have failed. The major strike-cum-lock-out of spring 1980 is an indication of the markedly more aggressive stance of the unions in the absence of a moderating Social Democratic government.

In the French and Italian cases question marks must remain even for our predictions concerning the development of the wage share in the period of economic crisis. On the one hand, the continuation of non-socialist government in France until 1981 seemed to indicate an aggressive stance by the trade unions. On the other, the weakness and disunity of the union movement, and its paralysing disappointment after the failure of the Federation of the Left, would seem to suggest the continuation of the double disadvantage under which the French working class has suffered, i.e. the simultaneous emasculation of the political and industrial wings of the labour movement (see Sellier, 1979). In Italy the situation is different, although no less complex. Although moves towards greater union political unity had ceased by 1974, there were visible signs of achievement in the 'scale mobile', which automatically adjusts wages in light of inflation (see Farneti, 1978). On the other hand, the PCI has supported the programme of austerity of the Christian Democrats between 1976 and 1979. This leaves it an open question as whether PCI pacification of the trade union movement or the 'scale mobile' has had the major impact on the development of the wage share.

4. *Countries with relatively weak party-union links which conformed to the prediction of an absence of political wage restraint in the period, 1960-74.* There are two cases in this category, the United Kingdom and the Netherlands. In the British case, we have seen that Labour attempts to introduce an incomes policy in the 1960s foundered on a trade union structure insufficiently centralized to damp down initiatives stemming from shopfloor militancy. There is some debate about the success of the next exercise in incomes policy, the Social Contract between government and unions, first essayed in 1974. Some authors have argued that it contributed to an overall decline in the distributional share of the working class, while others have maintained that the Social Contract was, at best,

only minimally effective in holding down wages.[47] This latter view is premised, once again, on the weakness of the leadership's structural position vis-à-vis the rank and file. Moreover, it has been argued that rank-and-file discontent was fuelled not merely by an absence of obvious advantages in the trade-off between reform policy and wages promised by the Contract, but also by the nature of flat-rate wages increases, which led to discontent based on the erosion of differentials.[48] In general, the literature would appear to support the view that in the 1970s the British situation was no more propitious for Labour-initiated wage restraint than it had been earlier.

The absence of political wage restraint in the Netherlands in the earlier period was largely a consequence of the disruptive impact of depillarization on trade union solidarity. There were, however, important changes in the 1970s, amounting to a re-orientation of the trade union movement in the Netherlands.[49] While previously the movement had been religiously fragmented, there was now a marked tendency for class politics to provide the major dividing lines in industrial conflict. Thus, the normal trade union stance in the 1970s has become more closely linked to the policy platforms of the left-wing parties and, in particular, PvDA. Precisely because in the 1970s relations between state, employers and unions have become more conflict-laden, we would now expect the Netherlands to conform more closely to our guiding hypothesis, which states that a political wage restraint effect will be observable when social democratic parties are in office.

*Research design*

Between 1960 and 1974 economic conditions remained relatively stable (except for 1974) in all the countries under consideration. Obviously, the economic crisis of the 1970s demanded a re-orientation of union attitudes to wages policy in light of the changed economic conditions. Union members and leaders experienced, or at least perceived, the crisis in terms of a heightened risk of unemployment and escalating prices. Even if a particular country had not yet been touched by the full force of the recession, it made sense to take these factors into account when developing a wage bargaining position. This was the more so in countries with open or exposed economies — like the Netherlands, Norway and Sweden — where the wages-inflation-export competitiveness equation was well understood.

Because the economic crisis had a similar impact throughout the capitalist democracies in pressurizing unions to adopt a more moderate bargaining stance, it would be extremely difficult to continue our analysis by means of the longitudinal approach utilized in the earlier sections. At a minimum, it would be necessary to control for the economic variables by use of a multiple regression analysis, which included a dummy variable for the impact of the recession on the attitudes taken by union wage negotiators. Furthermore, it would also be necessary to control for the differential impact of unemployment, inflation and economic growth. Clearly, within the scope of an analysis with such a limited number of cases, a multiple regression with so many potential sources of variance would be statistically meaningless.

Under these circumstances, we employ a cross-national, cross-sectional design, which, by focusing on the development of wage policy outcomes in several countries under similar conditions of economic crisis, helps to resolve the dummy variable problem. Clearly, the cost of such a design is that only the most important variables can be embodied in the analysis. Thus, only modest correlations for the political aspects of wage policy development can be expected, since we are unable to take account of the predicted variation within our guiding hypothesis, i.e. that we would predict a strong political effect in Sweden and none in Britain. This means that the substance of our analysis must take care not to over-interpret the correlation findings, but must devote considerable attention to an examination of the fit between wage share development and predictions for each individual country.

Although the impact of the recession was general, its manifestation, timing and degree were different in each country. To control for this, it was necessary to calculate change rates for all the major variables.[50] Moreover, dealing with the crisis implies defining crisis compared with a period of previous economic stability. To avoid results that are merely an artefact of when different nations perceived the onset of recession, we have constructed a series of change measures. The first relates the period 1970/73-1974/77; the second relates the period 1972/74-1975/77; and the third relates the period 1971/73-1975/77.[51] Obviously, the use of change rates throughout our analysis modifies the formulation of our basic hypothesis, which now states that: trade unions will tend to restrict their wage demands to a greater degree when the political complexion of government shifts to the Left in the period of economic crisis than in the previous period of economic stability. Finally, it should be noted that, in addition to calculating the change rate in office holding by social democratic parties, we have used a further measure consisting of the percentage of time a social democratic government has been in office during the period of economic crisis. For both measures of party strength, the operationalization is in terms of the number of months in office for each relevant party.

## The economic context of wage policy outcomes in a period of economic crisis

Looking at the development of the wage share and its relationship to economic growth, a clear pattern is discernible. In 10 out of 11 countries — only Finland is an exception — the average wage share in the period of economic crisis is higher than the average wage share in periods of economic stability. Moreover, although somewhat weaker, there is a further pattern in so far as 7 out of 11 countries manifest an increase in the first half of the crisis followed by a subsequent decline in the wage share. Thus, with the exceptions of Belgium, Italy, Norway and Sweden, there is some support for the hypothesized lag between the beginning of the crisis and the decline in the wage share. On the other hand, the extent of the economic crisis explains little or nothing of the variation in the wage share. There is no empirical evidence that decreases in economic growth are directly related to the development of the wage share. In none of the three periods delineated above — hereinafter designated I, II and III — can one discern a significant relationship ($r_I = 0.16$; $r_{II} = -0.14$; $r_{III} = 0.15$). A similar conclusion applies to changes in unemployment ($r_I = 0.18$; $r_{II} = -0.06$; $r_{III} = 0.24$) and in rates of inflation ($r_I = 0.18$; $r_{II} = 0.35$; $r_{III} = 0.02$).

It is important to emphasize the conclusions that can be legitimately drawn from this set of findings. On the one hand, it is quite clear that a serious economic crisis of the kind experienced in the 1970s does have an impact on the development of the wages share. Moreover, there is some evidence that the mechanism by which this comes about is the greater flexibility of profit margins over trade union wage policies. On the other hand, it is apparent that the extent of wage change and the associated bargaining behaviour of the trade unions cannot simply be explained by the economic dimensions of the crisis.

## TABLE 5
### Correlation matrix between wage share change and
### social democratic office-holding

|  | Change rate, wage share I | Change rate, wage share II | Change rate, wage share III |
|---|---|---|---|
| Socialist prime minister I (change rate) | −0.20 |  |  |
| Socialist party participation I (change rate) | −0.13 |  |  |
| Socialist prime minister II (change rate) |  | −0.30 |  |
| Socialist party participation II (change rate) |  | −0.54 |  |
| Socialist prime minister III (change rate) |  |  | −0.14 |
| Socialist party participation III (change rate) |  |  | −0.11 |
| Socialist prime minister percentage, 1975-77 |  | −0.35 | −0.33 |
| Socialist party participation percentage, 1975-77 |  | −0.58 | −0.54 |
| Socialist prime minister percentage, 1974-77 | −0.28 |  |  |
| Socialist party participation percentage, 1974-77 | −0.44 |  |  |

*Wage policy outcomes, economic crisis
and the political complexion of government*

There is substantially greater empirical support for the political
hypothesis than for the economic ones. Our findings provide support for the hypothesis that, with the provisos made on p. 258ff.
above,
1. the longer a social democratic party has been in office in the
   period of economic crisis *compared with the previous period of
   economic stability*, the greater the moderation in wage policy
   outcomes; and

## TABLE 6
### Actual and estimated results of regressions between wage share change and social democratic office-holding

| Country | Residual of the regression estimates: wage share II = − 0.0529 (socialist party participation II) + 2.4698 (Pearson's r = − 0.54) | Rank order (1 = most deviant case; 11 = less deviant case) | Residual of the regression estimates: wage share III = − 0.0088 (socialist party participation III) + 2.2265 (Pearson's r = − 0.11) | Rank order |
|---|---|---|---|---|
| Austria | − 1.0 | 6 | − 1.4 | 7 |
| Belgium | − 0.6 | 7 | + 2.4 | 6 |
| Finland | − 5.2 | 1 | − 7.5 | 1 |
| France | − 0.5 | 8.5 | − 0.1 | 11 |
| Germany | − 2.4 | 5 | − 1.2 | 8 |
| Ireland | − 0.2 | 10 | − 0.6 | 10 |
| Italy | + 3.4 | 2 | + 3.9 | 3 |
| Netherl. | + 0.5 | 8.5 | − 0.8 | 9 |
| Norway | − 0.1 | 11 | − 2.5 | 5 |
| Sweden | + 3.2 | 3 | + 4.3 | 2 |
| UK | + 2.6 | 4 | + 3.6 | 4 |

2. the longer a social democratic party has been in office in the period of economic crisis, the greater the moderation in wage policy outcomes.

The evidence for such conclusions may be derived from the correlation matrix presented in Table 5 and from an analysis of the degree of fit between our predictions and wage share development in each individual country. The question of the degree of fit may be seen as an issue of which countries conform to our guiding hypothesis and which, in various ways, depart from it. In Table 6 we report the differences between actual changes in the wage share and those that are predicted by the successful regression equations. In order to make a safe identification of the countries that do not conform with the basic hypothesis, we present both the residuals for the regression estimates with the strongest (measurement II, SP-participation (change rate)) and the weakest (measurement III, SP-participation (change rate)) correlations between the changes of the wage share and change rates of the political variables. In fact, both regressions produce remarkably similar patterns, with the countries having least difference between actual and estimate figures being much the same in each (Spearman's $r = 0.75$).

The countries where there are only small differences between estimated and actual figures are Austria, Belgium, France, Germany, Ireland, the Netherlands and Norway. The deviating cases are Finland, Italy, Sweden and the United Kingdom. The fact that in Britain a social democratic government was unable to control the impact of union wage demands is exactly as predicted on the basis of the weak linkage between party and union membership. The aggressive attack on the profit shown by the Swedish unions under 'bourgeois' rule does not contradict our basic hypothesis, but, clearly, it assumed unusually great dimensions, which may well be explained by the fact that this was LO's first opportunity for decades to show that it was a militant champion of working-class aspirations. The Italian question mark raised on p. 260 above seems resolved in favour of the view that the trade union success in procuring the scala mobile was of more potent influence than implicit PCI support for the government's income policy efforts. The apparent overwhelming success of the Finnish Social Democratic coalition in securing wage restraint must be put down to the long-term institutionalization of a sophisticated incomes policy mechanism.

A substantially similar pattern emerges when we cross-tabulate the degree of Social Democratic office-holding in the period of the economic crisis with the change rate in the wage share. This is shown in Table 7. We present both the results for the analysis with the strongest and weakest correlations between the change rate of the wage share and the political variables. Obviously, there is a certain information loss in using the cross-tabulation procedure, since the dichotomization into high and low categories makes it impossible to observe the degree to which some countries manifested even more wage restraint (Finland) or markedly less (Italy) than would have been expected on the basis of a linear interpretation of our basic hypothesis. Nevertheless, the procedure does show very clearly the countries that conform and those that deviate from the hypothesis. Both the United Kingdom and France are deviant cases in each of the two cross-tabulations. That this should be so is wholly in line with the predictions on pp. 260-61 above: in the British case because of the structural impediments to Labour Party control over the union movement, and in the French case because of the extreme weakness of the trade union movement itself. Both the Irish and

## TABLE 7
### The relationship between social democratic office-holding and the change rate of the wage share

| | *(a) Socialist party participation, 1975-77 (percentage)* | | |
| | *Less than mean* | *Mean = 67.4%* | *More than mean* |
| --- | --- | --- | --- |
| Change rate of wage share below mean; i.e. more moderation | France | | Austria Netherlands Norway Finland Germany Ireland |
| Mean = 2.38% | | | UK |
| Change rate of wage share above mean; i.e. less moderation | Belgium Italy Sweden | | |

| | *(b) Socialist party prime minister, 1974-77 (percentage)* | | |
| | *Less than mean* | *Mean = 57.2%* | *More than mean* |
| --- | --- | --- | --- |
| Change rate of wage share below mean; i.e. more moderation | France Ireland | | Austria Netherlands Finland Norway Germany |
| Mean = 1.69% | | | Sweden |
| Change rate of wage share above mean; i.e. less moderation | Belgium Italy | | UK |

Swedish cases are exceptions in respect of the impact of socialist party governmental leadership. The finding for Sweden is, in a sense, an artefact of the timing of both economic and political events. The SAP government, which remained in office until September 1976, managed simultaneously to contain the effects of the recession and to hold the wage share down, and it was only with the advent of the bourgeois government that LO mounted a massive offensive against the profit share. The Irish case illustrates a point that might also have been made concerning Germany in the longitudinal analysis of the period 1960-74 (see Table 4). There too it was apparent that the presence of the political wage restraint effect was more a consequence of socialist party participation in government than of governmental leadership. In other words, the mechanism making for wage restraint is the closeness of the link between party and unions rather than the degree of dominance exercised by the party within a governing coalition.

The overall finding of our cross-sectional analysis is that union wage policy, or at least its outcomes, are not merely a consequence of economic factors, but are also crucially effected by the political complexion of governments. The incomes policies of social democratic governments, or governments in which social democratic parties participate, have the intended results provided that the negotiations are conducted centrally and all sections of the trade union movement regard themselves as bound by the agreement. If the system of collective bargaining is decentralized and/or the rank and file do not feel themselves committed to agreements made between government and union leadership, incomes policy will necessarily fail, as in the United Kingdom.

But it would appear that it is not merely the existence of institutionalized mechanisms for regulating the conduct of industrial relations that produces the wage restraint effect. In Germany that mechanism broke down in 1977, but without thereby leading to greater union wage militancy. It is our view, therefore, that it is the relationship between party and union that is the prior condition for effective wage restraint, rather than the institutional and legislative mechanisms of income policy.

### The role of Social Democracy in
### a capitalist society

The aim of this chapter has not been to provide a definitive account of the factors determining the development of the relative shares of wages and profits in the economies of the advanced capitalist nations. More modestly, we have attempted to demonstrate that, apart from the undoubted importance of economic factors, political variables must be taken into account in understanding union wage policies and their outcomes. The evidence derived from both our longitudinal study of wage policy outcomes in the period of economic stability and our cross-sectional analysis of developments in the economic crisis points clearly to the importance of the partisan composition of government in this context. Which party is in office is significant because it has an effect on the wage policies pursued by trade unions, in so far as trade unions that are closely linked to a ruling social democratic party tend to curb their wage demands. However, our analysis also points to the fact that a necessary condition of such political wage restraint is a strong degree of commitment by union wage negotiators to the goals of the party. Where, as in Britain, the negotiating machinery is decentralized and the degree of commitment, as demonstrated by individual membership of the party, is low, incomes policy is unlikely to be successful. More ambiguously, where the rank-and-file union member has an effective veto on the agreements entered into by the leadership, a social democratic party may also encounter problems in limiting wage demands. The Norwegian case is virtually unique in combining strong centralized bargaining with such a veto mechanism, and the evidence is ambiguous because there is a strong degree of party loyalty among the union rank and file. This commitment would appear to have facilitated wage moderation in face of the perceived threat of the economic crisis, but to have been less effective in the period of economic prosperity.

The overall finding that social democratic governments seem to be more successful than their bourgeois counterparts in controlling the problems of the capitalist economy can be interpreted in two rather different ways. Since the size of the wage share may be taken as a crude measure of inter-class distribution, it may be argued that social democratic control of government serves to integrate the trade union movement into the functional requirements of the capitalist economy. Far from the traditional Leninist picture of the party of the working class pressurizing the unions away from their inherent 'economism', the domesticated social democratic parties of contemporary capitalism contain union wage demands aimed to tip the balance of inter-class distribution in favour of working-class interests. In such an interpretation, social democratic parties can hardly be seen as the agency of a transition from capitalism to socialism (see Stephens, 1979), but must be characterized as contributing to the smoother operation and development of the capitalist economy.

On the other hand, a rather different interpretation may emerge in terms of the patterns of trade-off between wages policy and other aspects of public policy. As emphasized in the introduction to this chapter, the size of the wage share is only one element in the complex equation of what the working class may expect to gain or lose from a social democratic presence in government. It could be argued that, if the economic stability procured by wage moderation is used by such a government to effect welfare reforms, reduce unemployment and inflation or effect redistribution by means of a progressive taxation policy, the immediate loss in terms of inter-class distribution may be more than offset in other areas. Clearly, the possibility of such trade-offs is suggested by many of the find-ings in this volume concerning the political factors affecting public expenditure, macroeconomic policy and income distribu-tion. However, the assessment of exact nature of the balance of ad-vantage and disadvantage in each particular country remains an ex-traordinarily complicated issue, and certainly not one that is readily amenable to analysis in terms of the strictly quantitative modes of analysis utilized here. Perhaps, all that we would wish to claim for our own discussion of the development of the wage share under social democratic government is that it suggests that the working class in contemporary capitalism have something to lose as well as to gain by seeking power within the framework of existing society.

# NOTES

1. Throughout, the term 'trade union' is used synonymously with 'confederation of trade unions'. 'Social democratic party' is used synonymously with 'socialist' or 'labour parties' as designated in Table 1.

2. See Headey (1970) and Bergmann (1979).

3. Certain important aspects of the differences in economic policy-making of social democratic and bourgeois governments are discussed in the chapters in this volume dealing with macroeconomic policy and income distribution in capitalist democracies.

4. There is an extensive literature on the nature of the Social Contract and its ef-fectiveness. See, for example, Crouch (1975, 1977, 1978); Goodman (1975); Minkin and Seyd (1977); Tarling and Wilkinson (1977).

5. It is quite apparent that such considerations enter into the calculations of members of the British Parliamentary Labour Party. For documentation, see Minkin (1974: 36; 1978).

6. See the chapter on public expenditure in this volume and the literature quoted there.

7. This view has been advanced extensively in the recent literature. See, for instance, Parkin (1972: 105); Deppe et al. (1976: 388); Hirsch (1974: 59); and Huffschmid (1972).

8. See Lehmbruch (1977); Panitch (1979); and Lehmbruch (1979a, 1979b).

9. Cf. Neumann (1978), Mayer (1973); and Crusius and Wilke (1971).

10. These manifestations have been discussed by Bergmann (1979). Also see Lipset (1954) and Clegg (1976: 40-54).

11. In this brief presentation it is impossible to discuss the intricacies of the relationship and competition between white-collar and blue-collar trade unions. See Beyme (1977: 44-60). Our presentation focuses almost exclusively on the linkages between blue-collar trade unions and social democratic parties.

12. Although in a slightly different context, this is the same three fold distinction applied by Raschke (1977: 278).

13. The sources for the discussion of collective affiliation are as follows: Norway — Martin (1974: 77); Fivelsdal and Higley (1970); Carew (1976: 51); Valen and Katz (1964); Ferraton (1960: 153); Sweden — Elvander (1974); UK — May (1975: 49); Minkin (1974, 1978); Hartmann (1978a); Ireland — Chubb (1970); Murphy (1978).

14. Such a summary conclusion is necessarily a major simplification of an extensive body of literature. See Panitch (1976); Goodman (1975); Degen (1976, 1979); Crouch (1978); Hughes (1979); Cox (1979).

15. On Denmark, see Lund (1976). On Ireland, see Murphy (1978).

16. See Minkin (1974); May (1975); Panitch (1976).

17. Cf. Elvander (1974a: 61). Kuhn (1978: 309) argues that cooperation between the Swedish trade union confederation and the social democrats has actually become more effective since the old formal links were abandoned and replaced by more informal co-operation.

18. See Minkin (1974). Also see Martin (1974) for an analysis of the Norwegian case.

19. The literature cited in note 13 is also relevant here. In addition, see Raschke (1977: 278) and Bergmann and Müller-Jentsch (1977) (for West Germany); Hänsch (1978) (for France); Helenius (1977: 281-2); Nousiainen (1971: 116); Pesonen and Rantala (1978b: 146-7) (for Finland).

20. Cf. Whyte (1974: 633). The figures cited are from a Gallup Poll conducted in Dublin in April 1968. It is possible that the socialist party preferences of trade unionists in other — more rural — areas could be higher.

21. See Weitz (1975) and Bechtle and Heiner (1979).

22. In addition to the literature cited in notes 4 and 14, see Goldthorpe (1970: 32-4) and Wendt (1975).

23. On Denmark, see Lund (1976). On Norway, Valen and Katz (1964); Fivelsdal and Higley (1970); Martin (1974); and Heidar (1977). On Sweden, Board (1970: 63) and Hancock (1972: 57).

24. See Galenson (1969) and, for developments in the 1970s, Lund (1976).

25. For the concept of the division of labour in this context, see Deppe et al. (1978).

26. For various discussions of the pillarization phenomenon, see Lijphart (1968, 1974); Lorwin (1974) and Lehmbruch (1967).

27. A 'Betriebsrat' need not be, but usually is, a member of one of the DGB

unions. He has no right to settle collective agreements ('Tarifvertraege') with the employer, which is a function reserved for union representatives outside the factory. Although he can bargain — without much power — about conditions of work, social affairs and forms of payment, he is not supposed to intervene on matters concerning the amount of payment (see Betriebsverfassungsgesetz 87, Tarifvertragsgesetz 2). In reality, he often is unwilling to accept such a restriction on his sphere of activity.

28. This view is based on a survey conducted in three unions. See Bergmann and Müller-Jentsch (1977: 278).

29. See Schmollinger (1973); Bachsleitner (1976); Deppe et al. (1976: 408).

30. Detailed information concerning the Irish labour movement is to be found in Chubb (1970); Boyd (1972) and Orridge (1977).

31. See Elvander (1974b) and Lund (1976).

32. There is also a system of membership voting in Denmark, but it is not as extensive as that in Norway. See Ferraton (1960: 121); Bull (1960: 123); Elvander (1974b: 371); Carew (1976: 188).

33. See Blanpain (1975); Carpreau (1967) and Janne and Spitaels (1975).

34. See Claeys (1973: 163ff); Mabille and Lorwin (1977); Kendall (1977: 220).

35. See Blanpain (1975), and Kendall (1977).

36. See Weil (1970: 67); Mabille and Lorwin (1977: 395-6) and Hartmann (1978b: 58).

37. See Albeda (1973, 1974); Teulings (1973); Peper (1975) and Wolinetz (1977).

38. The data sources for the dependent and independent variables are as follows:
Wage share and unemployment data: Lang (1978); OECD (1963, 1975, 1976, 1979a); Oesterreichisches Statistisches Zentralamt (1979); Sachverständigenrat (various years); Statistisches Bundesamt (1968); Statistisches Bundesamt (various years); UN (various years).
Partisan composition of government: Paxton (various years); Pesonen and Rantala (1978a); Spuler et al.(1977).
Domestic product: OECD (1975, 1979a); UN (various years).
Inflation: OECD (1973, 1977, 1979b); UN (various years).

39. The wage share is calculated according to the formula:

$$l_{adj} = \frac{w_t A_0}{w_t A_0 + k_t S_0}$$

$l_{adj}$    adjusted wage share.

$A_0$    number of employees in 1960

$S_0$    number of employers including active family members in 1960

$w_t$    mean income of the employees in year $t$; calculated according to the formula: $w_t = C_t : A_t$.

$k_t$    mean income of the employers in year $t$; calculated according to the formula: $k_t = P_t : S_t$.

$C_t$    all wages and salaries, in cash and kind, paid to employees, the contributions made by employers to social security schemes in respect of their employees and the contributions, paid or imputed made by employers to private pension arrangements, family allowances, health insurance, layoff and severance pay and other casualty insurance, life insurance and similar schemes in respect of their employees in year $t$.

$A_t$    number of employees in year $t$.

$P_t$     the excess of the value added of resident industries over the sum of their cost of employee compensation, consumption of fixed capital, and indirect taxes reduced by subsidies in year $t$.

$S_t$     number of employers including active family members in year $t$.

For a more detailed analysis of this procedure, see Köstl (1979).

40. Obviously, using the wage share as our indicator of union wage policy means that this concept is operationalized very broadly. Thus, union wage policy is taken to consist of all policies that have an impact on the distribution of wages and profits. If, for example, a union succeeds in reducing normal working time by some stipulated percentage without a commensurate decline in wage payments, this might be regarded as equivalent to a wage increase.

41. The problem stemming from linear assumptions results from the fact that our predictions concerning the development of the wage share in each individual country were more detailed than the broad expectations derived from our guiding hypothesis. Thus, while the basic hypothesis states that the wage share will be higher under bourgeois than social democratic rule, in some countries (e.g. Germany and Denmark) it was argued that initial moderation when a social democratic government enters office will be followed by an upsurge of union militance to restore the previous relationship between wages and profits. Obviously, in such cases the use of models assuming linearity is inappropriate.

Irrespective of the occurrence of this problem, we also necessarily confront difficulties stemming from autocorrelation. The usual response to such difficulties is to calculate change rates, but in cases where linearity cannot be assumed this must be particularly problematic. This can be illustrated as follows. If at the beginning of a period of social democratic rule the wage share goes down by, say 10 points, and stays that way only to jump by 10 points just prior to the advent of a fresh period of bourgeois rule, the consequence will be that there is no correlation between changes in the wage share and party composition, despite the fact that the level of the wage share has been markedly lower throughout much of the social democratic incumbency.

Our response to these problems is to focus our primary attention on the correlation between the level of the wage share and partisan composition. Since this means that autocorrelation remains an inherent feature of the research design, it would be misleading to use our estimates as a basis for predicting the future development of the wage share. However, the procedure seems far less objectionable as a basis for deriving a quantiative description of past trends. It is for this purpose that we have used a measure of the level of the wage share. Under these circumstances, the problem of autocorrelation amounts to saying that important factors have not been specified in our model, the most significant of which is generally the fact that the wage share at time $t$ is partially dependent on the level at $t-1$. In addition to our primary focus on the level of the wage share, we also computed the correlations between changes in the wage share and partisan composition. While the resulting indicators meet the requirement of non-autocorrelation, they cannot, as indicated above, provide us with a meaningful assessment of situations where nonlinear relationships prevail.

In all cases, our basic response to the statistical problems outlined was to check all statistical results by reference to the raw data on the wage share, and thus to attempt to incorporate statistical analysis and findings 'by eye' into a meaningful structure of argumentation.

42. The analysis of the relationship between the wage share and economic

variables involves problems of autocorrelation of the same kind as those adduced in note 41. It is, therefore, necessary to exercise extreme caution in interpreting these findings.

43. The relationship between unemployment and wage rates is the theme of the discussion of the Phillips Curve. For an analysis of the interconnection between wages, economic growth and productivity, cf. Himmelmann (1971).

44. Marx (1974), and Zoll (1976).

45. See Risch (1978) and Möller (n.d.).

46. See Arbeitsgruppe Soziale Infrastruktur (1976); Bierbaum et al. (1977); and Schumann (1979).

47. See OECD, *Economic Surveys: UK* (1975, 1976, 1977); Cambridge Political Economy Group (1975).

48. See Hughes (1979) and Cox (1979).

49. We have to admit that such a reading of the evidence is necessarily somewhat speculative. Cf. Peper (1975); Wassenberg (1978);Akkermans and Grootings (1978).

50. The change rates were calculated as first-order differences; i.e., the mean of the respective variable in the crisis period minus the mean of the same variable in the preceding period of economic stability. The advantage of this type of calculation is that an increase from, say, 0.1% unemployment to 0.2% (i.e. 100% increase) does not appear as the same as an increase in the unemployment rate of 2.5 to 5.0% (i.e. 100%).

*Example:* If the period of economic crisis is defined as 1975-77 and the period of economic stability as 1972-74, the change rate in the wage share and the political variables were calculated as follows:

1. Wage share: the mean of the wage share in Ireland in 1972-74 was 62.5. The mean of the wage share in 1975-77 was 63.6. Thus, the change rate of the wage share was $63.6 - 62.5 = 1.1$.

2. SP participation: The Irish Labour Party participated in government for 61.1% of the period 1972-74 and 83.3% of the period 1975-77. Thus, the change rate of SP participation was $83.3 - 61.1 = 22.2$.

51. The reasons for this choice were as follows:

1. 1970-73 to 1974-77: the periodization coincides with the generally held view that the world-wide recession started with the onset of the Oil Crisis in late 1973.

2. 1972-74 to 1975-77: this periodization takes account of the fact that the crisis took effect in different countries at different times. The implication here is that by 1975 it was universal.

3. 1971-73 to 1975-77: an alternative way of coping with the transition from stability to crisis is to omit 1974 altogether. Calculations of the change rates of gross domestic product, unemployment and inflation — the normal indicators of economic recession — suggest that no particular periodization is unequivocally better than the others.

| | Change rate of: | | |
| | GDP | Unemployment | Inflation |
| --- | --- | --- | --- |
| Measure I: | | | |
| 1970-73 to 1974-77 | − 2.4 | 1.9 | 5.2 |
| Measure II: | | | |
| 1972-74 to 1975-77 | − 2.4 | 2.3 | 2.0 |
| Measure III: | | | |
| 1971-73 to 1975-77 | − 2.5 | 2.3 | 4.3 |

Thus, computations were undertaken for all measures.


# REFERENCES

Akkermans, T. and Grootings, P. (1978). 'From Corporatism to Polarisation: Elements of the Development of Dutch Industrial Relations' in C. Crouch and A. Pizzorno (eds), *The Resurgence of Class Conflict in Western Europe Since 1968*, vol. I. London: Macmillan.

Albeda, W. (1973). 'Zur Situation der niederländischen Gewerkschaften', *Gewerkschaftliche Monatshefte* 4/1973.

Albeda, W. (1974). 'Recent Trends in Collective Bargaining in the Netherlands', in *Collective Bargaining in Industrialised Market Economies*. Geneva: ILO.

'An Underlying Question in the British General Election' (1978). *Government and Opposition*, 4/1978.

Arbeitsgruppe Soziale Infrastruktur (1976). 'Wirtschaftliche Rezession, Konflikpotential und Reformbestrebungen der Arbeitnehmerschaft-Bericht über eine empirische Untersuchung'. *Gewerkschaftliche Monatshefte* 6/1976.

Bachsleitner, K. (1976). 'Zur Entstehung und Funktion der AfA als "Arbeitnehmerflügel" der SPD', *Blätter für deutsche und internationale Politik*, 7/1976.

Bechtle, G. and Heiner, S. (1979). 'Die Schwierigkeiten einer Klassenpolitik. Der Fall der italienischen Gewerkschaften 1968-1978' in J. Bergmann (ed.), *Beiträge zur Soziologie der Gewerkschaften*. Frankfurt: Edition Suhrkamp.

Bergmann, J. (1979). 'Von den Septemberstreiks zur Wirtschaftskrise. Veränderte Bedingungen der gewerkschaftlichen Politik', in J. Bergmann (ed.), *Beiträge zur Soziologie der Gewerkschaften*. Frankfurt: Edition Suhrkamp.

Bergmann, J. and Müller-Jentsch, W. (1977). *Gewerkschaften in der Bundesrepublik, Bd. II*, Frankfurt: Aspekte.

Bergmann, J. et al. (1976). *Gewerkschaften in der Bundesrepublik*, vol. I. Frankfurt: Aspekte.

Beyme, K.v. (1977). *Gewerkschaften und Arbeitsbeziehungen in kapitalistischen Ländern.* Munich/Zürich: Piper.

Bierbaum, Ch. et al. (1977). *Ende der Illusionen? Bewusstseinsveränderungen in der Wirtschaftskrise.* Cologne/Frankfurt: EVA.

Blanpain, R. (1975). 'Die Gewerkschaften und die Entwicklung der Beziehungen zwischen Gewerkschaften und Unternehmer in Belgien', *Gewerkschaftliche Monatshefte,* 8/1975.

Board, J.B. (1970). *The Government and Politics of Sweden.* Boston: Houghton Mifflin.

Boyd, A. (1972). *The Rise of the Irish Trade Unions 1729-1970.* Tralee: Anvil Books.

Bull, E. (1960). *Die norwegische Gewerkschaftsbewegung.* Cologne: Bund Verlag.

Cambridge Political Economy Group (1975). 'Englands Krise — Ursachen und Abhilfen', *Leviathan,* 3/1975.

Carew, A. (1976). *Democracy and Government in European Trade Unions.* London: Allen & Unwin.

Carpreau, R. (1967). *Ziele und Instrumente der belgischen Wirtschaftspolitik.* Tübingen: Mohr.

Chubb, B. (1970). *The Government and Politics of Ireland.* Stanford: University Press.

Claeys, P.H. (1973). *Groupes de pression en Belgique.* Brussels: ULB and Crisp.

Clegg, H.A. (1976). *Trade Unions and Collective Bargaining.* Oxford: Basil Blackwell.

Cox, A. (1979). 'The Social Contract and the Problems of Incorporation', University of Hull, mimeo.

Crouch, C. (1975). 'The Drive for Equality', in L. Lindberg et al. (eds), *Stress and Contradiction in Modern Capitalism: Public Policy and the Theory of the State.* Lexington, Mass.: D.C. Heath.

Crouch, C. (1977). *Class Conflict and the Industrial Relations Crisis.* London: Heinemann.

Crouch, C. (1978). 'The Intensification of Industrial Conflict in the United Kingdom', in C. Crouch and A. Pizzorno (eds), *The Resurgence of Class Conflict in Western Europe since 1968,* vol. I. London: Macmillan.

Crusius, R. and Wilke, M. (1971). *Elemente einer Theorie der Gewerkschaften im Spätkapitalismus.* Berlin: Die Arbeitswelt.

Degen, G.R. (1976). *Shop Stewards-Ihre zentrale Bedeutung für die Gewerkschaftsbewegung in Grossbritannien.* Frankfurt/Cologne: EVA.

Degen, G.R. (1979). 'Das Dilemma der britischen Gewerkschaften. Gewerkschaftliche Kampfkraft zwischen betrieblicher Stärke und gesellschaftlicher Ohnmacht', in J. Bergmann (ed.), *Beiträge zur Soziologie der Gewerkschaften.* Frankfurt: Edition Suhrkamp.

Deppe, R., Herding, B. and Hoss, D. (1976). 'Gewerkschaftliche Organisation und politische Orientierung der Arbeiterschaft', in R. Ebbinghausen (ed.), *Bürgerlicher Staat und politische Legitimation.* Frankfurt: Edition Suhrkamp.

Deppe, R. Herding, B. and Hoss, D. (1978). 'The Relationship between Trade Union Action and Political Parties', in C. Crouch and A. Pizzorno (eds), *The Resurgence of Class Conflict in Western Europe Since 1968,* vol. II. London: Macmillan.

Donovan Report (1968). *Report of the Royal Commission on Trade Unions and Employers' Associations, 1965-1968,* Cmnd 3623. London: HMSO.

Elvander, N. (1974a). 'In Search of New Relationships: Parties, Unions and Salaried Employee's Associations in Sweden', *ILRR*, 28(I).

Elvander, N. (1974b). 'The Role of the State in the Settlement of Labor Disputes in the Nordic Countries: A Comparative Analysis', *EJPR*, 2/1974.

Farneti, P. (1978). 'The Troubled Partnership: Trade Unions and Working Class Parties in Italy 1948-78', *Government and Opposition*, 4/1978.

Ferraton, H. (1960). *Syndicalism ouvrier et Social-démocratie en Norvêge.* Paris: Armand Collin.

Fivelsdal, E. and Higley, J. (1970). 'The Labor Union Elite in Norway', *SPS*, 5/1970.

Fulcher, J. (1976). 'Class Conflict: Joint Regulation and Its Decline', in R. Scase (ed.), *Readings in the Swedish Class Structure.* Oxford: Pergamon Press.

Galenson, W. (1969). *The Danish System of Industrial Relations. A Study in Industrial Peace.* New York: Russel & Russel.

Goldthorpe, J. (1970). *Der 'wohlhabende' Arbeiter in England*, vol. II. Munich: Goldmann.

Goodman, J. (1975). 'Great Britain: Toward the Social Contract', in S. Barkin (ed.), *Worker Militancy and Its Consequences 1965-75. New Directions in Western Industrial Relations.* New York: Praeger.

Hancock, M.D. (1972). *Sweden: The Politics of Post-Industrial Change.* London: Holt, Rinehart & Winston.

Hänsch, K. (1978). 'Frankreich', in J. Raschke (ed.), *Die politisichen Parteien in Westeuropa.* Reinbek bei Hamburg: Rowohlt.

Hartmann, J. (1978a). 'Grossbritiannien', in J. Raschke (ed.), *Die politischen Parteien in Westeuropa.* Reinbek bei Hamburg: Rowohlt.

Hartmann, J. (1978b). 'Belgien', in J. Raschke (ed.), *Die politischen Parteien in Westeuropa.* Reinbek bei Hamburg: Rowohlt.

Headey, B. (1970). 'Trade Unions and National Wage Policies', *JoP*, 2/1970.

Heidar, K. (1977). 'The Norwegian Labour Party: Social Democracy in a Periphery of Europe', in W.E. Paterson and A.H. Thomas (eds), *Social Democratic Parties in Western Europe.* London: Croom Helm.

Helander, V. (1978). 'A Liberal Corporatist Subsystem in Action: The Incomes Policy System in Finland'. Turku/Grenoble (ECPR), mimeo.

Helenius, R. (1977). 'The Finnish Social Democratic Party', in W.E. Paterson and A.H. Thomas (eds), *Social Democratic Parties in Western Europe.* London: Croom Helm.

Himmelmann, G. (1971). *Lohnbildung durch Kollektivverhandlungen.* Duncker & Humblot.

Hirsch, J. (1974). *Staatsapparat und Reproduktion des Kapitals.* Frankfurt: Edition Suhrkamp.

Huffschmid, J. (1972). *Die Politik des Kapitals.* Frankfurt: Edition Suhrkamp.

Hughes, J. (1979). 'Die Entwicklung der britischen Gewerkschaften in den Krisen der 7oer Jahre', *WSI-Mitteilungen*, 4/1979.

Jacobi, O. (1972). 'Einkommenspolitik contra Lohnpolitik', in O. Jacobi, W. Müller-Jentsch and E. Schmidt (eds), *Gewerkschaften und Klassenkampf. Kritisches Jahrbuch 1972.* Frankfurt: Fischer.

Janne, M.-H. and Spitaels, G. (1975). 'Belgium: Collective Bargaining and Concertation Mold a New System', in S. Barkin (ed.), *Worker Militancy and Its Consequences 1965-75. New Directions in Western Industrial Relations.* New York: Praeger.

Kendall, W. (1977). *Gewerkschaften in Europa.* Hamburg: Hoffmann & Campe.

King, John and Regan, Philip (1976). *Relative Income Shares.* London: Macmillan.

Klenner, F. (1966). 'Der Österreichische Gewerkschaftsbund', in Pütz (ed.), *Verbände und Wirtschaftspolitik in Österreich.* Berlin: Duncker & Humblot.

Köstl, F. (1979). 'Eine Bemerkung zur Bereinigung der Lohnquote', *WSI Mitteilungen,* 1/1979.

Kuhn, K. (1978). *Partizipation in schwedischen Parteien. Eine Untersuchung über Massenloyalität im Wohlfahrtsstaat.* Stuttgart: Kuhn & Maier.

Lang, W. (1978). *Kooperative Gewerkschaften und Einkommenspolitik. Das Beispiel Österreichs.* Frankfurt: P. Lang.

Lehmbruch, G. (1967). *Proporzdemokratie. Politisches System und politische Kultur in der Schweiz und Österreich.* Tübingen: Mohr.

Lehmbruch, G. (1977). 'Liberal Corporatism and Party Government', *CPS,* 1/1977.

Lehmbruch, G. (1979a). 'Wandlungen der Interessenpolitik im liberalen Korporatismus', in U. von Alemann and R.G. Heinze (eds), *Verbände und Staat. Vom Pluralismus zum Korporatismus.* Opladen: Westdt. Verlag.

Lehmbruch, G. (1979b). 'Concluding Remarks: Problems for Future Research on Corporatist Intermediation and Policy-Making', in G. Lehmbruch and P.C. Schmitter (eds), *Trends Toward Corporatist Intermediation.* Beverly Hills/London: Sage.

Lijphart, A. (1968). *The Politics of Accommodation: Pluralism and Democracy in the Netherlands.* Berkley and Los Angeles: University of California Press.

Lijphart, A. (1974). 'Consociational Democracy', in C.D. McRae (ed.), *Consociational Democracy. Political Accommodation in Segmented Societies.* Toronto: McClelland & Steward.

Lipset, S.M. (1954). 'The Political Process in Trade Unions: A Theoretical Statement', in M. Berger, T. Abel and C.H. Page (eds), *Freedom and Social Control in Modern Society.* New York: Van Nostrand.

Lorwin, V.R. (1974). 'Segmented Pluralism: Ideological Cleavages and Political Cohesion in Smaller European Democracies', in C.D. McRae (ed.), *Consociational Democracy. Political Accommodation in Segmented Societies.* Toronto: McClelland & Steward.

Lorwin, V.R. (1975). 'Labor Unions and Political Parties in Belgium', *ILLR,* 28(2).

Lund, R. (1976). 'Die dänische Gewerkschaftsbewegung von 1945 bis 1975', *Gewerkschaftliche Monatshefte,* 9/1976.

Mabille X. and Lorwin V.R. (1977). 'The Belgian Socialist Party', in W.E. Paterson and A.H. Thomas (eds), *Social Democratic Parties in Western Europe.* London: Croom Helm.

Martin, P.G. (1974). 'Strategic Opportunities and Limitations. The Norwegian Labour Party and the Trade Unions', *ILLR,* 28(1).

Marx, K. (1974). *Das Kapital,* vol. I (MEW 23). Berlin (Ost): Dietz.

May, T. (1975). *Trade Unions and Pressure Group Politics.* Farnborough, Hants: Saxon House/Lexington Books.

Mayer, E. (1973). *Theorien zum Funktionswandel der Gewerkschaften.* Frankfurt: EVA.

Minkin, L. (1974). 'The British Labour Party and the Trade Unions: Crisis and Compact', *ILLR,* 28(1).

Minkin, L. (1978). 'The Party Connection: Divergence and Convergence in the British Labour Movement', *Government and Opposition,* 4/1978.

Minkin, L. and Seyd, P. (1977). 'The British Labour Party', in W.E. Paterson and A.H. Thomas (eds), *Social Democratic Parties in Western Europe*. London: Croom Helm.

Möller, H.-H. (n.d.). *Die Entwicklung von Lohn-und Gewinneinkommen im Konjunkturverlauf aus theoretischer und empirischer*. Sicht, Blaeschke Verlag.

Murphy, D. (1978). 'Ireland', in J. Raschke (ed.), *Die politischen Parteien in Westeuropa*. Reinbek bei Hamburg: Rowohlt.

Nedelmann, B. and Meier, K. (1979). 'Theories of Contemporary Corporatism: Static or Dynamic?' in G. Lehmbruch and P.C. Schmitter (eds), *Trends Toward Corporatist Intermediation*. Beverly Hills/London: Sage.

Neumann, F.L. (1978). 'Die Gewerkschaften in der Demokratie und in der Diktatur', in F.L. Neumann, *Wirtschaft, Staat, Demokratie. Aufsätze 1930-1954*. Frankfurt: Edition Suhrkamp.

Nousiainen, J. (1971). *The Finnish Political System*. Cambridge, Mass.: Harvard University Press.

OECD (1963). *Statistical Bulletins. Manpower Statistics, 1950-1962*. Paris: OECD.

OECD (1973). *Main Economic Indicators. Historical Statistics 1955-1971*. Paris: OECD.

OECD (1975). *National Accounts Statistics*, vol. 1. Paris: OECD.

OECD (1976). *Basic Statistics. B Labour Force Statistics, 1963-1974*. Paris: OECD.

OECD (1977). *Economic Outlook 23*. Paris: OECD.

OECD (1979a). *National Accounts Statistics*, vol. I. Paris. OECD.

OECD (1979b). *Economic Outlook 26*. Paris: OECD.

OECD (various years). *Economic Surveys*. Paris: OECD.

Oesterreichisches Statistisches Zentralamt (1979). *Statistisches Handbuch fuer die Republik Oesterreich*, Vienna: Oesterreichisches Statistisches Zentralamt.

Orridge, A. (1977). 'The Irish Labour Party', in W.E. Paterson and A.H. Thomas (eds), *Social Democratic Parties in Western Europe*. London: Croom Helm.

Otter, C. van (1975). 'Sweden: Labor Reformism Reshapes the System', in S. Barkin (ed.), *Worker Militancy and Its Consequences, 1965-75. New Directions in Western Industrial Relations*. New York: Praeger.

Panitch, L. (1976). *Social Democracy and Industrial Militancy. The Labour Party, the TUC and Incomes Policy 1945-1974*. Cambridge: University Press.

Panitch, L. (1979). 'The Development of Corporatism in Liberal Democracies', in G. Lehmbruch and P.C. Schmitter (eds), *Trends Toward Corporatist Intermediation*. Beverly Hills/London: Sage.

Parkin, F. (1972). *Class Inequality and Political Order*. St Albans, Herts: Paladin.

Paxton, J. (various years). *The Stateman's Yearbook*. London: Macmillan.

Peper, B. (1975). 'The Netherlands: From an Ordered Harmonic to a Bargaining Relationship', in S. Barkin (ed.), *Worker Militancy and Its Consequences 1965-75. New Directions in Western Industrial Relations*. New York: Praeger.

Pesonen, P. and Rantala, O. (1978a). 'Change and Stability in the Finnish Party System', mimeo.

Pesonen, P. and Rantala, O. (1978b). 'Finnland', in J. Raschke (ed.), *Die politische Parteien in Westeuropa*. Reinbek bei Hamburg: Rowohlt.

Raschke, J. (1977). *Organisierter Konflikt in westeuropäischen Parteien. Eine vergleichende Analyse parteiinterner Oppositionsgruppen*. Opladen: Westdt. Verlag.

Reynaud, J.-D. (1975). 'Trade Unions and Political Parties in France: Some Recent Trends', *ILLR*, 28(2).

Risch, B. (1978). *Der Zusammenhang zwischen Arbeitslosenrate, Lohnquote und Inflation*, Kieler Arbeitspapiere no. 76, Kiel.

Sachverständigenrat (various years). *Jahresgutachten*. Bonn: Bundestagsdrucksache.

Schmidt, M.G. (1978). 'The Politics of Domestic Reform in the Federal Republic of Germany', *Politics and Society*, 8, pp. 165-200.

Schmiede, R. (1979). 'Das Ende des westdeutschen Wirtschaftswunders 1966-1977', in *Die Linke im Rechtsstaat*, vol. II. Berlin: Rotbuch.

Schmollinger, H. (1973). 'Gewerkschafter in der SPD-Eine Fallstude', in J. Dittberner and R. Ebbinghausen (eds), *Parteiensystem in der Legitimationskrise*. Opladen: Westdt. Verlag.

Schumann, M. (1979). 'Entwicklungen des Arbeiterbewusstseins', *Gewerkschaftliche Monatshefte*, 3/1979.

Schumann, M. et al. (1971). *Am Beispiel der Septemberstreiks—Anfang der Rekonstruktionsperiode der Arbeiterklasse*? Frankfurt: EVA.

Sellier, F. (1979). 'Die französischen Gewerkschaften angesichts der Krise—Krisenentwicklung und Krisenerscheinungen: Arbeitslosigkeit, Inflation und Wirtschaftsstrukturen', *WSI-Mitteilungen*, 4/1979.

Spuler, B. et al. (1977). *Rulers and Governments of the World*, vol. 3: *1930-1975*. London/New York: Bowker.

Statistisches Bundesamt (1968). *Allgemeine Statistik des Auslandes. Länderkurzberichte, Finnland*. Stuttgart, etc.: Kohlhammer.

Statistisches Bundesamt (various years). *Statistisches Jahrbuch für die Bundesrepublik Duetschland*. Stuttgart etc.: Kohlhammer.

Stephens, J.D. (1979). *The Transition from Capitalism to Socialism*. London: Macmillan.

Tarling, R. and Wilkinson, F. (1977). 'The Social Contract: Post-war Incomes Policies and Their Inflationary Impact', *Cambridge Journal of Economics*, 1, pp. 395-414.

Teschner, E. (1977). *Lohnpolitik im Betrieb*. Frankfurt/New York: Campus.

Teulings, A. (1973). 'Arbeitskonflikte und Gewerkschaften in den Niederlanden', in O. Jacobi, W. Müller-Jentsch and E. Schmidt (eds), *Gewerkschaften und Klassenkampf. Kritisches Jahrbuch 1973*. Frankfurt: Fischer.

Ulman, L. and Flanagan, R. (1971). *Wage Restraint: A Study of Incomes Policies in Western Europe*. Berkeley: University of California Press.

UN (various years). *Statistical Yearbook*. New York: UN.

Valen, H. and Katz, D. (1964). *Political Parties in Norway*. Oslo: University Press.

Wassenberg, A. (1978). 'Creeping Corporatism: A Cuckoo's Policy'. Delft/Grenoble (ECPR), mimeo.

Weil, G.L. (1970). *The Benelux Nations. The Politics of Small-Country Democracies*. New York: Holt, Rinehart & Winston.

Weitz, P. (1975). 'Labor and Politics in a Divided Movement: The Italian Case', *ILLR*, 28(2).

Wendt, B.-J. (1975). 'Industrial Democracy. Zur Struktur der englischen Sozialbeziehungen', in *Aus Politik und Zeitgeschichte*, 46/1975.

Whyte, J.H. (1974). 'Ireland: Politics without a Social Base', in R. Rose (ed.), *Electoral Behaviour: A Comparative Handbook*. New York: Free Press.

Windmuller, J. (1974). 'European Labor and Politics. A Symposium', *ILLR*, 28(1).

Wolinetz, S.B. (1977). 'The Dutch Labour Party: A Social Democratic Party in Transition', in W.E. Paterson and A.H. Thomas (eds), *The Social Democratic Parties in Western Europe*. London: Croom Helm.

Zoll, R. (1976). *Der Doppelcharakter der Gewerkschaften*. Frankfurt: Edition Suhrkamp.

# APPENDIX
## Adjusted wage share data, 1960-1974*

| Countries | 1960 | 1961 | 1962 | 1963 | 1964 | 1965 | 1966 | 1967 | 1968 | 1969 | 1970 | 1971 | 1972 | 1973 | 1974 |
|---|---|---|---|---|---|---|---|---|---|---|---|---|---|---|---|
| Austria | 59.0 | 59.3 | 59.8 | 59.4 | 58.3 | 58.1 | 58.0 | 58.7 | 57.8 | 56.4 | 53.7 | 54.9 | 53.2 | 53.2 | 52.9 |
| Belgium | 57.0 | 55.7 | 56.3 | 56.7 | 55.6 | 55.5 | 56.9 | 57.0 | 56.3 | 55.3 | 52.2 | 53.5 | 53.6 | 52.8 | 54.2 |
| Denmark | 58.4 | 59.6 | 59.9 | 60.6 | 59.4 | 61.6 | 64.3 | 65.8 | 65.1 | 64.6 | 64.4 | 66.2 | 61.2 | 60.3 | 65.0 |
| Finland | 56.7 | 56.2 | 57.4 | 57.3 | 56.3 | 56.6 | 57.4 | 56.4 | 54.6 | 52.3 | 50.3 | 52.8 | 50.1 | 46.8 | 43.7 |
| France | 58.3 | 58.8 | 58.3 | 58.4 | 58.1 | 57.2 | 56.1 | 55.1 | 55.4 | 54.7 | 54.2 | 54.0 | 52.3 | 52.1 | 54.2 |
| Germany | 59.9 | 61.9 | 61.3 | 61.3 | 59.8 | 59.7 | 60.4 | 60.4 | 58.0 | 57.8 | 58.2 | 59.0 | 59.1 | 59.9 | 61.7 |
| Ireland | 57.5 | 59.2 | 63.1 | 63.3 | 64.0 | 62.2 | 64.8 | 63.5 | 62.4 | 62.6 | 64.1 | 64.2 | 61.5 | 60.1 | 66.0 |
| Italy | 52.4 | 50.8 | 50.1 | 51.2 | 52.4 | 51.6 | 50.2 | 50.2 | 49.3 | 47.7 | 50.4 | 52.0 | 50.8 | 51.4 | 52.7 |
| Netherlands | 58.1 | 59.9 | 60.2 | 61.3 | 60.9 | 61.0 | 63.2 | 62.6 | 61.7 | 61.4 | 62.4 | 63.7 | 62.8 | 62.2 | 63.7 |
| Norway | 64.6 | 63.8 | 65.8 | 60.6 | 59.0 | 57.3 | 58.2 | 63.7 | 63.0 | 62.5 | 60.7 | 63.3 | 63.0 | 61.3 | 59.0 |
| Sweden | 66.3 | 65.8 | 70.9 | 70.9 | 68.9 | 68.5 | 69.0 | 68.9 | 70.8 | 69.3 | 66.1 | 70.2 | 69.2 | 65.8 | 65.7 |
| UK | 73.4 | 74.9 | 75.0 | 77.9 | 73.6 | 73.3 | 74.5 | 75.6 | 75.0 | 76.0 | 78.3 | 78.2 | 78.1 | 78.5 | 82.8 |

* For method of calculation see end note 39.

# 6

# Do Parties Affect the Distribution of Incomes? The Case of Advanced Capitalist Democracies

J. Corina M. van Arnhem
and Geurt J. Schotsman
University of Amsterdam

## Introduction

*The purpose of the study*

**In this study** we shall analyse the distribution of incomes in capitalist democracies. A generally accepted theory of income distribution does not yet exist. The theories that have been developed — some rival, others complementary — alternatively stress factors such as ability, choice, luck, education, economic structure or inheritance.[1] Recently, attention has also been given to the effects of politics on the distribution of incomes. In particular, the analysis has focused on the impact of movements with egalitarian ideologies, such as parties of the Left and labour unions. The empirical results of these studies, to be discussed below, suggest that these movements have had a significant positive effect on income equality.

In the present study we intend to assess the impact of structural phenomena on the distribution of incomes in capitalist democracies, thus leaving aside factors like ability, choice or inheritance. These structural phenomena may be divided into two groups: on the one hand, phenomena belonging to the socioeconomic structure, and on the other hand, those belonging to the political structure. However, as we shall subsequently note, there are important interrelationships between these groups of factors.

An examination of the literature arguing for the impact of socioeconomic variables on the distribution of incomes suggests the following variables for analysis: level of economic development, economic growth, rate of inflation, unemployment, proportion of the population over 65, education expansion, and openness of the economy. The political structure will be represented by variables measuring the parliamentary and governmental strength of parties of both the Left and the Right and also the extra-parliamentary strength of organized labour. The potential importance of these political agencies is indicated in a study of Kirschen and associates (1964: 227). They found, in a survey of party stands on economic objectives, that parties of the Left and of the Right differed most in their ranking of economic priorities on the issue of 'improvement in income distribution': for parties of the Left this was recorded as a 'dominant objective', while it was a 'negligible objective' for parties of the Right.

As to the distribution of income, several kinds of income will be considered: primary income, income after transfers, and income after both transfers and taxes. The first income concept refers to the incomes as generated by the economic process. However, these primary incomes are not equivalent to the final distribution of disposable incomes among individuals or households. Both transfers and taxes change the distribution of incomes. Thus, we will also consider the distribution of income after transfers and after both transfers and taxes, and the changes in inequality brought about by transfers and taxes.

Specifying the distribution of incomes in such detail is appropriate, since the socioeconomic and political variables to be considered differ with regard to the aspects of income distribution they affect. Further, this specification is a prerequisite for obtaining a better understanding of the nature of the relationship between politics and income distribution than can be found in the studies dealing with this subject referred to above. In our opinion, a shortcoming of these analyses is that they examine only isolated aspects of this relationship. For instance, most studies take into account only one income concept, e.g. income after transfers (generally without bothering about whether this is the appropriate concept), and many studies deal with the impact of parties of the Left but do not consider that of parties of the Right, although, arguably, this

## TABLE 1
**Developed capitalist democracies included in the analysis**

| | |
|---|---|
| 1. Australia (AUS) | 8. Italy (IT) |
| 2. Canada (CND) | 9. Japan (JA) |
| 3. Federal Republic of Germany (FRG) | 10. Netherlands (NL) |
| 4. Finland (FIN) | 11. Norway (NOR) |
| 5. France (FR) | 12. Sweden (SWE) |
| 6. Ireland (IRE) | 13. United Kingdom (UK) |
| 7. Israel (ISR) | 14. United States (US) |

may be just as important in explaining income inequality.

Since the impact of the socioeconomic and political structure may be very different in developed and underdeveloped countries, this analysis has been limited to those countries that can be considered 'highly industrialized'. The number of countries that fitted this criterion has been further reduced by the exclusion of countries where state ownership of the means of production prevails and where the political system is not distinguished by democratic procedures. Also excluded are countries for which the data on the distribution of personal income were judged to be not sufficiently robust to warrant an international comparison (Austria, Belgium, Denmark, Luxembourg, New Zealand and Switzerland). The remaining developed capitalist democracies are listed in Table 1.

### The plan of the study

In the following section we first discuss our dependent variable: the distribution of income in developed capitalist democracies. Apart from presenting the data available on personal income distribution, this section also contains a comparison of inequality of incomes before and after transfers and taxes in the countries included in our study. The third and fourth sections deal with the impact of socioeconomic and political factors on the distribution of incomes. In these sections we discuss the relevant literature, evaluate hypotheses and present empirical results.

As to the methodology followed, it should be noted that analysis of cross-national data for a small number of countries is associated with several difficulties. First, as is noted in the Introduction to this volume, the restricted number of countries may bias the results.[2] Further, with a small number of cases, it is, for statistical reasons, inappropriate to use multiple regression techniques or path analysis. A possible alternative would be to use factor analysis. This statistical technique consists of constructing variables, called factors, which altogether represent the total 'common' variance that is present in each variable.[3] The meaning of these factors has to be interpreted by reference to the variable with which they are most strongly associated. Thereafter, the association between these constructed factors and the dependent variable may be examined. This technique is suited to study the sensitivity of the dependent variable for various clusters of independent variables. It is, however, less suited to study the pattern of interaction between specific independent variables and the phenomena that are to be explained.

Therefore, we have decided to use bivariate correlation as our basic mode of analysis. A deficiency of this kind of analysis is that it does not adequately control for the influence of other factors. For this reason, we have avoided basing our conclusions on the reading of isolated correlation coefficients, but rather have attempted to build up a persistent pattern of findings, in which the reported relationships concerning both levels and changes in the distribution of incomes are mutually reinforcing. Further, with respect to the correlations to be reported in this study, it should be noted that in cross-sectional studies relatively low degrees of association may occur even if the model is a satisfactory one, because of the large variation that is inherently present in the data.

To solve some of the limitations inherent to a study based upon bivariate correlation analysis, we have complemented the information provided by the statistical analysis with a descriptive comparative analysis of political systems, industrial relations and policies in separate countries. This is the subject matter of the fifth section. The final section concludes with a summary and overview of the major results of the study.

## Income inequality
## in developed capitalist countries

### Data on inequality

The data on income inequality used in this study are in the form of decile shares, that is, the share of total income accruing to successive tenths of income receiving units ranked by size of income. Thus, in contrast to the previous chapter, where the focus was on the broad inter-class distribution of wage and profit shares, the main subject matter of our analysis concerns the distribution of individual incomes. Most of these size distributions of income are derived from the meticulous study of Sawyer (1976), which brings together comparable data on the distribution of income for a relatively large number of OECD countries. Some other size distributions have been derived from Jain (1975) and Schnitzer (1974), or have been calculated according to the definitions suggested by Sawyer[4] from data reported by the national statistical offices of Finland, Ireland, Israel and the Netherlands.[5] Compared to the data that used to be available before the appearance of Sawyer's research, the size distributions included in our study are to be judged of good quality. This is not to say that these size distributions are without deficiencies. As Sawyer notes: 'Even when an international project on income distribution was mounted, the results from the participating countries were not strictly comparable' (1976: 3). Some of these deficiencies are purely statistical, while others result from economic factors or are linked to noneconomic considerations. For a discussion of these problems we refer to Sawyer (1976: 12-14).

The available data allowed us to construct three sets of size distributions: an 11-country set with respect to primary income, a 13-country set with respect to income after transfers, and a 14-country set with respect to income after both transfers and taxes. All size distributions refer to years around 1970. Primary income is defined as the sum of wages, salaries, entrepreneurial and property income. Income after transfers covers the same items as primary income, but includes public money transfers. These transfers are benefits with respect to old age, invalidity, sickness, death, physical deficiencies, unemployment and family circumstances. Income after both transfers and taxes equals income after transfers less direct personal taxes (income tax and social security contributions). Generally, the data conform to these definitions. However, it should be noted that the data on primary income distribution are somewhat less comparable than the other series owing to divergent statistical definitions (Sawyer, 1976: 34).

As indicated above, the three sets of countries that constitute the various size distributions are not identical. This was unavoidable to the degree that we wished to maximize our coverage of the relevant universe of discourse to the greatest degree possible, and yet were confronted by serious divergences in the availability of data in respect to the varying aspects of income distribution. The absence of an identical set of cases presents a methodological disadvantage, implying as it does the possibility of incorrectly relating differences in findings for the respective sets to differences in income concepts underlying these sets, while in fact such differences may stem from the inclusion of different countries. However, it is our contention that the broad thrust of our conclusions is unaffected by this problem, and that the disadvantages it involves are less serious than the loss in breadth of analysis that would have resulted from a more restricted universe of discourse. Throughout this study, we have taken pains to isolate where the inclusion or exclusion of particular countries affects the findings, and have commented in the text on the possible distortions so caused. Furthermore, the descriptive analysis of the fifth section, covering all the countries in the study, provides a further safeguard against spurious explanation stemming from a changing data-base.

## Measures of inequality

To measure the degree of income inequality, we have used the following indicators: the Gini coefficient, the Theil coefficient, the share of total income received by the top decile, and the share received by this decile divided by the sum of shares received by deciles three, four and five.[6] The Gini coefficient is based on a so-called Lorenz curve, which relates the cumulative share of income to the cumulative proportion of income units. The divergence of this curve from a straight-line diagonal gives an image of the degree of inequality. A simple way to express this numerically is to calculate the Gini coefficient, which shows the area between the diagonal and the Lorenz curve, as a proportion of the total area under the diagonal. The Gini coefficient, therefore, can have values between zero for complete equality and one for extreme inequality. Figure 1 shows the Lorenz curve for a hypothetical income distribution. It should be noted that the Gini coefficient is a relatively insensitive measure of inequality.

The Theil coefficient is based on the difference between a weighted[7] sum of the actual shares accruing to income-receiving units and of shares that would result if total income were equally divided. Unlike the Gini coefficient, the value of the Theil coefficient has of itself no specific meaning: it is useful only in compari-

**FIGURE 1**

**Lorenz curve for a hypothetical income distribution.
The horizontal axis measures proportion of income-earners,
the vertical axis, proportion of income earned**

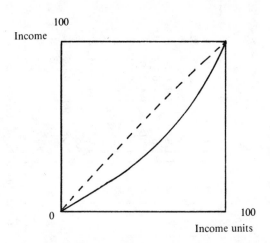

sons. The two decile measures are provided because of their emphasis on income inequality at its extremes. An advantage of such measures is that they are easily understood; a disadvantage is that only part of the information available is used, and that in a relatively arbitrary way. This does not hold for the two overall measures discussed above: they condense the many facets of an income distribution into a single number. As to these two overall measures, it may further be noted that the Theil coefficient is particularly sensitive to transfers of income between high-income groups while the Gini coefficient is particularly sensitive to income transfers between middle-income groups. Table 2 presents these four measures of inequality for the three sets of countries used in the analysis.

*General characteristics of inequality*

We now turn to consider the general characteristics of the size distributions of personal income. In Table 3 information is presented on the central tendency and dispersion indicated by the mean and the coefficient of variation[8] of each of the measures of inequality. Because we intend to compare the changes in dispersion brought about by transfers and taxes, which requires the coeffi-

## TABLE 2

### Measures of inequality of the distribution of personal income, years around 1970
(countries ranked according to respective Gini* coefficient of inequality)

| | Pre-tax, pre-transfer | | | | Pre-tax, post-transfer | | | | Post-tax, post-transfer | | | |
|---|---|---|---|---|---|---|---|---|---|---|---|---|
| | G | T | 10 | 10/(3+4+5) | | G | T | 10 | 10/(3+4+5) | | G | T | 10 | 10/(3+4+5) |

| | | G | T | 10 | 10/(3+4+5) | | G | T | 10 | 10/(3+4+5) | | G | T | 10 | 10/(3+4+5) |
|---|---|---|---|---|---|---|---|---|---|---|---|---|---|---|---|---|
| 1. SWE | | 0.471 | 0.402 | 28.8 | 1.88 | FR | 0.416 | 0.290 | 31.0 | 1.82 | FR | 0.414 | 0.287 | 30.4 | 1.77 |
| 2. FR | | 0.462 | 0.363 | 33.7 | 2.22 | US | 0.406 | 0.273 | 28.4 | 1.62 | IT | 0.398 | 0.270 | 30.9 | 1.77 |
| 3. US | | 0.446 | 0.347 | 31.6 | 1.85 | FRG | 0.396 | 0.266 | 31.1 | 1.84 | FRG | 0.384 | 0.249 | 30.3 | 1.77 |
| 4. FIN | | 0.438 | 0.333 | 28.4 | 1.64 | CND | 0.383 | 0.244 | 27.1 | 1.44 | US | 0.380 | 0.237 | 26.6 | 1.44 |
| 5. NL | | 0.437 | 0.329 | 34.0 | 2.14 | IRE | 0.380 | 0.237 | 26.8 | 1.42 | IRE | 0.363 | 0.216 | 26.0 | 1.33 |
| 6. IRE | | 0.437 | 0.325 | 29.1 | 1.68 | ISR | 0.357 | 0.208 | 25.4 | 1.30 | CND | 0.354 | 0.207 | 25.1 | 1.26 |
| 7. CND | | 0.430 | 0.325 | 28.0 | 1.56 | NOR | 0.355 | 0.206 | 24.5 | 1.24 | ISR | 0.327 | 0.175 | 22.6 | 1.07 |
| 8. UK | | 0.418 | 0.314 | 26.9 | 1.41 | NL | 0.355 | 0.218 | 29.5 | 1.52 | FIN | 0.321 | 0.166 | 23.5 | 1.15 |
| 9. NOR | | 0.415 | 0.294 | 26.3 | 1.46 | SWE | 0.344 | 0.191 | 24.4 | 1.26 | UK | 0.319 | 0.165 | 23.5 | 1.11 |
| 10. FRG | | 0.404 | 0.277 | 27.3 | 1.48 | UK | 0.343 | 0.193 | 24.7 | 1.22 | JA | 0.316 | 0.174 | 27.2 | 1.30 |
| 11. ISR | | 0.403 | 0.270 | 26.7 | 1.47 | FIN | 0.334 | 0.179 | 25.1 | 1.32 | AUS | 0.312 | 0.162 | 23.7 | 1.09 |
| 12. | | | | | | JA | 0.333 | 0.195 | 28.6 | 1.41 | NOR | 0.309 | 0.155 | 22.2 | 1.03 |
| 13. | | | | | | AUS | 0.313 | 0.163 | 23.8 | 1.09 | SWE | 0.302 | 0.148 | 21.3 | 0.99 |
| 14. | | | | | | | | | | | NL | 0.292 | 0.140 | 23.3 | 1.08 |

*abbreviations of measures of inequality: G = Gini coefficient; T = Theil coefficient; 10 = decile 10; 10/(3 + 4 + 5) = decile 10 divided by the sum of deciles 3, 4 and 5; for abbreviations of countries see Table 1.

Source: calculated from size distributions (see text).

## TABLE 3

**Central tendency and variation of measures of inequality of the distribution of personal income in developed capitalist democracies around 1970**

| Measures | Pre-tax, pre-transfer | | Pre-tax, post-transfer | | Post-tax, post-transfer | | Ratio of change through transfers to change through taxes |
|---|---|---|---|---|---|---|---|
| | Mean | Coefficient of variation | Mean | Coefficient of variation | Mean | Coefficient of variation | |
| G | 0.433 | 5.1 | 0.370 | 7.6 | 0.342 | 11.4 | 2.3 |
| T | 0.325 | 11.7 | 0.228 | 16.2 | 0.195 | 24.6 | 2.9 |
| 10 | 29.2 | 9.4 | 27.1 | 9.4 | 25.0 | 12.4 | 1.0 |
| 10/(3 + 4 + 5) | 1.71 | 16.4 | 1.45 | 15.4 | 1.27 | 22.0 | 1.4 |
| Mean of coefficients of variation | | 10.7 | | 12.2 | | 17.6 | |

*Source:* Table 2.

cients of variation not to be at the same time subject to changes owing to inclusion of more countries, the figures in Table 3 are based on the set of countries occurring in every column in Table 2.[9] From Table 3 it can be seen that the mean of each of the measures of inequality decreases significantly through both transfers and taxes. In the case of transfers, the decrease in inequality varies from 7 percent (decile ten measure) to 30 percent (Theil coefficient); in the case of taxes from 7 percent (decile ten measure) to 14 percent (Theil coefficient). The last column in Table 3 compares the equalizing impact of transfers to that of taxes. For all measures of inequality the equalizing impact of transfers is greater than that of taxes, except for the decile ten measure, which shows an equalizing impact of taxes as large as that of transfers. Further, in general, both transfers and taxes increase the dispersion between countries. Only in the case of transfers, and measuring inequality by the decile ratio $10/(3+4+5)$ (stressing the extremes of inequality), dispersion decreases slightly. Thus, we may conclude that there is a tendency for redistributive policies to increase inter-country differences in inequality of personal income distribution.

These findings are illustrated in Figure 2 with the example of the Gini coefficient of inequality. In this figure, the range consisting of the mean of the Gini coefficient plus and minus the standard deviation is given for income distributions before and after transfers and taxes.

The picture that emerges from these comparisons reinforces the conclusion of the UN (1967: 41) study that transfers are most important in equalizing the distribution of income. With regard to the impact of the tax system, however, our results give more credit to the equalizing effect of taxes than is done in the UN study, in which the tax system as a whole — direct taxes and indirect taxes — is characterized as tending to be regressive. We do not deem it plausible that inclusion of indirect taxes in our data would have neutralized the equalizing impact of direct taxes. This may have been the case in the 1950s and early 1960s, when indirect taxes of OECD countries on average amounted to some 45 percent of total taxes, but it seems unlikely for the period after 1965, in which indirect taxes fell on average to some 33 per cent of total taxes.[10]

**FIGURE 2**
**Mean of Gini coefficient of inequality. The length of the shaded area indicates the range of average Gini values plus and minus the corresponding standard deviation**

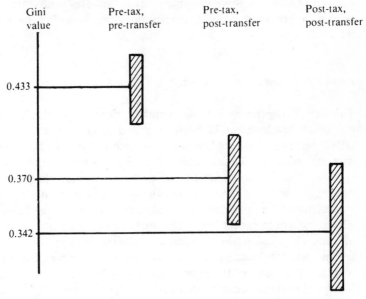

**Socioeconomic structure**

*Introduction*

The distribution of personal income is initially created in the economy. Thus, a priori, it seems plausible that variables pertaining to the socioeconomic structure may have an impact on the distribution of primary income. If these variables are also to affect the distribution after transfers and after both transfers and taxes, this has to be through influencing the extent of transfers and taxes. We will argue that, for some of the socioeconomic variables considered in this study, an impact on the distribution of income both before and after transfers and taxes may be expected, while for others this only holds for the distribution of primary income. To the first category of variables belong the level of economic development and the openness of the economy. The postulated impact of these variables on the redistributive system will be argued to be a consequence of a relationship between these variables and the political structure. Level of unemployment and the proportion of old-aged pensioners in the population also belong to the first category. In these cases an impact on the redistributive system may be expected through the volume of transfers. Inflation, economic growth and education belong to the second category of variables. In our opinion, for these variables only hypotheses postulating an impact on primary income distribution can plausibly be constructed.

*Level of economic development*

The view that primary income inequality depends on the level of economic development is fairly accepted since Kuznets's study (1955) on income inequality and economic growth. In this study Kuznets noted that the development in the direction of more equality observable for countries for which data are available (roughly since 1900 for the United Kingdom, Germany and the United States) is something of a puzzle. He referred to two factors on the basis of which one would expect income inequality to increase after a lapse of time.The first is the concentration of savings in the upper-income brackets, leading to a concentration of income-generating wealth in the hands of the upper-income groups. The second factor follows from the sectoral structure of the income distribution. Economic growth involves a shift away from agriculture, a process usually referred to as 'industrialization and urbanization'. Since the income distribution in the agricultural sector is more equal than in the industrial sector, the shift away from agriculture implies an increase of inequality in the total income distribution.

Kuznets went on to investigate which factors could negate the effects of the concentration of savings and sectoral shifting. He suggested the following categories of factors:
— a reduction in inequality within the non-agricultural sector through economic changes as well as through increased political power of low-income groups;
— political legislation and intervention to limit the yield of accumulated wealth;
— differential rates of increase between the rich and the poor (family control having first spread to the former), implying an influx of newcomers with little or no accumulated wealth into the highest-income classes;
— rampant technological change, causing a reduction in returns on existing wealth in old branches of industry;

— less incentive and possibility of having high incomes increase as much as low incomes; for low income groups, more possibilities to increase incomes by switching from low-income to high-income industries.

This enumeration shows that, according to Kuznets, economic as well as political factors cause economic growth to be accompanied by a narrowing of income inequality. Kuznets added to this the fact that these factors presumably make their influence felt only in the later phases of industrialization and urbanization. This would suggest that the early phases of economic growth are characterized by a widening of income inequality. In this way there would be a kind of long swing in the degree of income inequality: widening in the early phases of economic growth, becoming stabilized for a while, and then narrowing in the later phases. Kuznets did not have adequate empirical evidence to test this hypothesis. However, he would place the phase of increasing income inequality from about 1780 to 1850 in the United Kingdom and from about 1840 to 1890 in Germany and the United States.

If there really is such a long swing in the development of primary income inequality, then it is reasonable to suppose that a like movement occurs, to an ever greater degree, in the development of the income distribution after tranfers and after both transfers and taxes. Taxes and transfers have been of great quantitative importance only in the more recent period of economic growth, and they must have accentuated the downward trend in the long term movement of income inequality.

After his analysis of the development in income distribution through time in the United Kingdom, Germany and the United States, Kuznets considered a cross section of developed and underdeveloped countries around 1950, in which the distribution of income in India, Ceylon and Puerto Rico is compared with that in the United Kingdom and the United States. This comparison showed that the income distribution in the developed countries was somewhat more equal than in the underdeveloped countries. Kuznets noted further that it is tempting to consider the historical trends in the now developed countries as the present and future trends of the underdeveloped countries. Although such an interpretation may include an important element of truth, he pointed to the dangers of such a view, since the circumstances in which the underdeveloped countries find themselves now differ in many respects from those in which the developed countries found themselves at the early phase of their economic growth.

**FIGURE 3**
**Stylized representation of the relationship between income inequality (Gini coefficient) and GNP per capita expressed in 1971 US dollars**

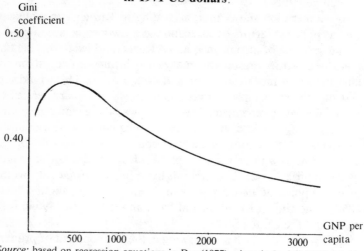

*Source:* based on regression equations in Das (1977), given in Lydall (1979, table 8.1).

**FIGURE 4**
**Income inequality and successive stages of economic development**

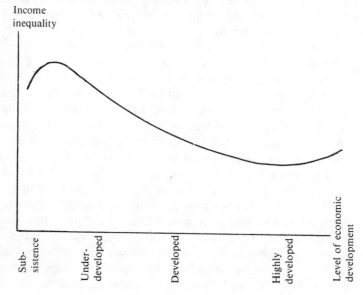

Later studies by Kuznets and others[11] have produced results in agreement with those in Kuznets' (1955) study. They have pointed to a relationship between inequality of personal income and level of economic development as shown in Figure 3. However, some studies restricted to highly developed countries have suggested that, at high levels of economic development, there exists a tendency towards increased inequality of primary incomes.[12] This tendency may be explained as a consequence of the fact that at high levels of development there are some factors that work cumulatively towards a concentration of higher and lower incomes in certain social categories. Thus, increases in level of education, activities in the well-paid service sector, female employment, families with more than one income from labour and the presence of property income often coincide, resulting in an increased concentration of income in the upper end of the income distribution. The opposite mechanism is effective at the bottom of the income distribution. If these arguments are correct, they would imply a partial modification of Kuznets's argument. The amended theory would postulate a relationship between level of economic development and income inequality as represented schematically in Figure 4.

The initial rise and consequent fall of inequality suggested in Kuznets's argument are expected to hold for inequality of income both before and after transfers and taxes, while the arguments for increased inequality at high development pertain to primary income. Of course, if the latter effects are too strong to be wiped out by transfers and taxes, this inequality may also be reflected in the distribution of income after transfers and taxes.

Table 4 presents correlations reflecting the degree of association between gross national product per capita (GNP p/c)[13] and measures of inequality. For all three income concepts, inequality tends to be higher as GNP p/c is higher. For the distribution of income after both transfers and taxes the associations are very weak, but for primary income and income after transfers they cannot be neglected. The changes brought about by transfers and taxes tend to be larger as GNP p/c is higher. For the separate changes the associations are weak; in the case of the total change the relation appears to be somewhat more robust. These results support the hypothesis that in highly developed economies primary income distribution tends to become more unequal. This is further confirmed by evidence on changes in inequality during approximately the 1960s. In the four countries scoring highest on GNP p/c

## TABLE 4
## Correlations between GNP p/c and inequality of income distribution

|  | Primary income | Income after transfers | Income after transfers and taxes | GNP p/c | Change through transfers | Change through taxes | Change through transfers and taxes |
|---|---|---|---|---|---|---|---|
| G | 0.42 | 0.49* | 0.18 | $\Delta G$ | 0.11 | 0.17 | 0.30 |
| T | 0.48 | 0.49* | 0.16 | $\Delta T$ | 0.15 | 0.14 | 0.36 |
| 10 | 0.32 | 0.35 | 0.06 | $\Delta 10$ | −0.03 | 0.10 | 0.18 |
| 10/(3+4+5) | 0.36 | 0.48* | 0.16 | $\Delta 10/(3+4+5)$ | 0.06 | 0.17 | 0.26 |

* significant at 5% level.

(United States, Federal Republic of Germany, Sweden and Canada) there has been either a trend towards inequality or a stabilization of inequality.[14] A similar conclusion is reached by Deleeck (1977: 38-40) after surveying evidence on postwar changes in inequality of pre-tax income in Western societies. The positive association between GNP p/c and change (i.e. decrease) through transfers and taxes suggests that part of Kuznets's argument still holds for highly developed economies, namely the proposition that the equalizing impact of transfers and taxes increases with GNP p/c. However, these effects are not strong enough for GNP p/c to be associated with less inequality of distribution of income after transfers and after both transfers and taxes.

## Openness of the economy

One reason why the openness of the economy may have an impact on income inequality is to be found in the market situation characteristic of an open economy. The more open an economy is, the more foreign competition is experienced. Home-made products face competition of foreign products both in the foreign and in the national markets. Thus, in an open economy firms have less scope to pass rising costs into prices than in a closed economy. Phelps-Brown (1957) has argued that, in a situation with few possibilities to pass rising costs into prices — a hard market environment — bargaining power of labour unions will cause a shift from capital income to labour income. In a market environment with ample opportunities to pass rising costs into prices — a soft market environment — rising money wages will result mainly in a rising general level of prices and costs. Examples given by Phelps-Brown include New Zealand after the return of a Labour government in 1936 and France in 'L'experience Blum'. In these cases the combined action of government and labour unions to raise money wages resulted mainly in a raising of the general level of prices and costs. Firms seem to have experienced a soft market environment in which they generally felt able to pass rises in costs. In the case of New Zealand, an increase of 50 per cent in wages was accompanied by only a 4 to 5 percent increase in share of wages in national product. On the other hand, according to Phelps-Brown, in the United Kingdom in 1870-73 and 1890-91 profit margins were squeezed between strong union pressure and a hard market environment.

A shift from capital income to labour income implies a fall in overall inequality of income distribution, since entrepreneurial and investment income is less equally distributed than labour income (cf. Sawyer, 1976: 12). Thus, if the argument stated above is correct, we might expect variations in openness of the economy to be related to variations in the inequality of primary income distribution. However, this argument is not the only one that may be forwarded for more equality of income distribution in an open economy. Cameron (1978) has argued that openness of the economy is accompanied by destabilizing effects on production, employment and consumption. He notes that governments may try to dampen these effects by expanding the role of the state. This will imply an increase in the number and intensity of the policy instruments utilized. These policy instruments may include not only public employment, transfer payments and other public consumption expenditure, but also progressive taxation, incomes policies and labour market policies. Independently of the ideology of the government, the use of such instruments to counteract the instability of the market economy may lead to decreases in the inequality of income distribution.

More important, however, is Cameron's proposition that open economies are characterized by a high degree of industrial concentration, which means that an unusually large share of production and employment is realized in a few large firms. This is a consequence of the sharp competition in the export field, which has tended to force out the smaller and less efficient companies. According to Cameron, industrial concentration tends to be accompanied by high unionization, a wide scope of collective bargaining, strong labour confederations and, related to these phenomena, frequent leftist-dominated governments. Both leftist governments and labour unions have egalitarian ideologies. Thus, in this argument openness of the economy will result in the formation of egalitarian forces. These forces may be of importance for the distribution of income both before and after transfers and taxes. A similar argument can be found in Stephens (1979: 43ff).

Table 5 represents correlations between openness of the economy, measured by exports as a percentage of gross national product,[15] and measures of income inequality. For all three income concepts used, openness of the economy tends to be accompanied by less inequality of income distribution. This tendency is most pronounced for the distribution of income after both transfers and taxes. This may be due to the cumulative effects of the postulated equalizing impact of the openness of the economy on primary in-

## TABLE 5
## Correlations between openness of the economy and inequality of income distribution

|  | Primary income | Income after transfers | Income after transfers and taxes |  | Change through transfers | Change through taxes | Change through transfers and taxes |
|---|---|---|---|---|---|---|---|
|  |  |  |  | Openness of the economy |  |  |  |
| G | −0.30 | −0.13 | −0.39 | ΔG | 0.15 | 0.59* | 0.36 |
| T | −0.34 | −0.19 | −0.40 | ΔT | 0.07 | 0.56* | 0.22 |
| 10 | −0.24 | −0.23 | −0.38 | Δ10 | 0.18 | 0.45 | 0.40 |
| 10/(3+4+5) | −0.16 | −0.24 | −0.36 | Δ10/(3+4+5) | 0.23 | 0.40 | 0.35 |

* significant at 5% level.

come distribution and on the distribution of income after transfers
and taxes. Further, as expected, changes in income inequality — in
particular those through taxes — are larger, the more open the
economy. These findings support the arguments both of Phelps-
Brown and of Cameron and Stephens, albeit they are somewhat
more favourable to those of Cameron and Stephens.


*Other socioeconomic variables*

Earlier we noted that, for some socioeconomic variables,
hypotheses may be constructed according to which these variables
influence the distribution of income both before and after transfers
and taxes, while for others only an impact on primary income
distribution can plausibly be hypothesized. Two of the variables
belonging to the first category (i.e., the level of economic development and the openness of the economy) have already been discussed. To this category also belong the level of unemployment and the
proportion of the population over the age of 65. The more
unemployed and old-age pensioners there are, the higher is the proportion of the population earning little or no primary income.
Other things being equal, this will result in greater inequality of
primary income.[16] Since those concerned receive transfers and have
to pay little tax, this inequality may be mitigated in the distribution
of income after transfers and taxes.

Table 6 presents the coefficients of correlation between levels of
unemployment and proportions of old-age pensioners on the one
hand and measures of income inequality on the other;[17] we did not
include the correlations with changes in inequality through
transfers and taxes because these tended to be effectively zero.
Looking first at the correlations with level of unemployment, we
may conclude that associations are either absent or weak. Only in
the case of the distribution of income after transfers and after both
transfers and taxes, and measuring inequality by Gini or Theil coefficients, does unemployment tend to be associated with less
egalitarian distributions of income. Surprisingly, this does not hold
for the distribution of primary income. This may be explained partly by the circumstance that the set of countries with respect to income after transfers and after both transfers and taxes includes
respectively 13 and 14 countries, while that with respect to primary
income only includes 11 countries. Indeed, recalculating the cor-

## TABLE 6
### Correlations between level of unemployment and proportion of the population over 65 on the one hand and inequality of income distribution on the other

| | Level of unemployment | | | Proportion of the population over 65 | | |
|---|---|---|---|---|---|---|
| | Primary income | Income after transfers | Income after transfers and taxes | Primary income | Income after transfers | Income after transfers and taxes |
| G | −0.01 | 0.33 | 0.29 | 0.31 | 0.31 | 0.21 |
| T | −0.03 | 0.27 | 0.23 | 0.35 | 0.28 | 0.21 |
| 10 | 0.02 | −0.07 | −0.01 | 0.11 | 0.13 | 0.14 |
| 10/(3 + 4 + 5) | −0.13 | −0.01 | 0.01 | 0.23 | 0.28 | 0.24 |

* significant at 5% level.

relations with the Gini and Theil coefficients for this set of 11 countries yields lower correlations.[18]

The correlations with the proportion of old-age pensioners are somewhat more pronounced than those with unemployment, although none of them is statistically significant. In line with the hypothesis, in all cases the higher the proportion of old-age pensioners, the higher the inequality of income distribution. However, the correlations are weak and should therefore be interpreted with caution.

We will now discuss the remaining socioeconomic variables to be considered in this study. For these, only hypotheses with regard to primary income distribution will be developed. These variables are inflation, economic growth and education expansion. It has been argued, among others by Olson (1963), that rapid economic growth is positively associated with income inequality. Olson points out that economic growth proceeds mainly through innovation and technical change. These processes involve vast changes in the methods of production, in the importance of different industries and in the types of labour demanded. In the long run these processes will benefit the income of all classes. In the short run, however, the main result will be a relatively high proportion of gainers and losers. This rise of groups of 'nouveaux riches' and 'nouveaux pauvres' may lead to greater income inequality by its impact on the upper and the lower ends of the income distribution. This tendency may be reinforced by the fact that, according to Olson, there exists 'a tendency for wages to become more sticky than prices. Thus, as demand increases with economic growth, businessmen may raise prices *pari-passu* with the increases in demand, but wages may rise more slowly' (Olson, 1963: 536). Thus, in this argument we may expect a high rate of economic growth and, more specifically, of inflation to be positively associated with income inequality, especially with the measures stressing inequality at its extremes.

However, from Table 7 it can be seen that none of the correlations with inflation[19] is as expected. The income of the top 10 decile most sensitive to the amount of profits realized tends to be lower as inflation is higher. According to Olson's argument, this should be the other way around. The results with respect to economic growth[20] are more in accordance with the hypothesis. The decile 10 measure and the decile ratio $10/(3+4+5)$, which both stress inequality at its extremes, show a tendency, albeit not statistically significant, to be positively associated with economic growth.

## TABLE 7
## Correlations between inflation, economic growth and education expansion and inequality of primary income distribution

|  | Inflation | Economic growth Primary income | Education expansion |
|---|---|---|---|
| G | − 0.03 | − 0.03 | 0.56 |
| T | − 0.04 | − 0.02 | 0.43 |
| 10 | − 0.17 | 0.28 | 0.63* |
| 10/(3 + 4 + 5) | − 0.06 | 0.34 | 0.65* |

* significant at 5% level.

However, it should be noted that the direction of the explanation may also be reversed by arguing that a high income share of the top 10 decile furthers investment and thus economic growth.

Expansion of education may be interpreted as a factor leading to income equality. In this regard the theory of Tinbergen (1975) is well known. Tinbergen argues that the distribution of income is determined mainly by the interplay of supply and demand of labour of various qualifications. If education expands and the number of the highly qualified increases while that of the ill qualified decreases, there will be a tendency for highly qualified labour to experience a relative decline of income compared with the movement of income of unskilled labour. In recent years this evolution seems to have become increasingly pronounced. In some sectors the supply of the academically trained is so large that they perform jobs that used to be performed by the less educated. This has been accompanied by a relative, or in some cases even an absolute, decline in income. On the other hand, in some other sectors unskilled labour is very hard to get. These jobs have tended to become better paid. In Tinbergen's view, then, expansion of education is a strategic instrument for decreasing the inequality of income distribution.

Tinbergen's theory may however be criticized. First, expansion of education is effective in decreasing inequality only if it concerns expansion of the kind of education that is needed in the economy. This type of education does not necessarily coincide with the type of education that is in effect chosen. Further, Jencks (1972) has provided evidence that a decrease in inequality of amount of schooling experienced does not result in decreased income inequality. According to Jencks this is due to the fact that social inequality and the difficulties associated with social mobility are not diminished by education expansion. Desayere, Tavernier and Van Loon (1973) have argued that education expansion will be concentrated in higher social strata and will thus cause inequality of income distribution to increase. (This argument is related to the proposition that a highly developed economy is characterized by a trend towards income inequality; the correlation coefficient between GNP p/c and education expansion for the group of countries in our study is 0.43.)

To test these conflicting arguments we carried out correlations between average years of formal education on the university level of the total population aged 24-64[21] and measures of income inequality. The results, presented in Table 7, are not in accordance with the argument of Tinbergen. Better than average education expansion on the university level tends to be associated with greater than average inequality of primary income distribution. This does not necessarily imply that Tinbergen's theory is wholly wrong: it may be that education has not yet expanded enough. More education implies that more people earn the higher incomes associated with higher education. These higher incomes, on the other hand, will show a relative decline when the supply of educated labour increases. It depends on the relative strength of the first effect versus the second one whether income inequality increases or decreases. It may be that the first effect has dominated the second effect, and that this has resulted in the recorded positive association between education and inequality. On the other hand, it is also possible that Desayere, Tavernier and Van Loon are right in postulating that education expansion leads to increased income inequality.

*Summary*

The analysis presented in this section did not reveal any very pronounced associations between the distribution of incomes and elements of the socioeconomic structure. However, some provisional conclusions do seem to be justified. First, the examination of the effects of economic development suggested that inequality tends to be higher as levels of economic development are higher. This tendency may be caused by a concentration of higher and lower incomes in certain social categories that arise at high levels of economic development. This result contradicts the general impression that the wealthier a country is, the more egalitarian is its distribution of income. Thus, the optimism present in the analyses of Kuznets and others has to be tempered.

Second, the openness of the economy was found to exert a modest equalizing impact on income inequality. Several hypotheses were mentioned to explain this. First, it may be possible that in open economies employers have less scope for passing wage increases into prices; second, it may be that the government interference called for by the instability of open economies has an equalizing impact. Finally, we mentioned the possibility that the industrial structure of open economies creates a favourable milieu for labour unions and socialist parties, both committed to an egalitarian ideology.

Third, education expansion on the university level appeared to be related with greater income inequality. This may be interpreted to support the argument according to which a highly developed economy is characterized by a trend towards inequality. As to the remaining socioeconomic variables examined, the results are not very straightforward. As expected, unemployment and the proportion of the old-age pensioners in the population tended to be associated with greater inequality. However, the associations are not very pronounced. Inflation and economic growth did not show a clear relationship with measures of income inequality.

It is, however, important to interpret the conclusion that the socioeconomic structure is of limited importance in explaining cross-national variations in income inequality in its proper perspective. This conclusion does not imply that socioeconomic variables do not matter; neither does it challenge the proposition of Kuznets and others that differences between developed and underdeveloped countries are crucially related to the level of economic development. However, it does challenge the proposition that cross-national differences in income inequality between advanced capitalist democracies depend largely on differences in socioeconomic structure.

## Political structure

*Overview of the literature*

The question of whether politics influences the distribution of personal incomes has often been discussed.[22] However, systematic empirical research started to be carried out only in the 1970s. Adelman and Taft Morris (1973) found that for underdeveloped countries the impact of social-political variables on inequality of income distribution was as important as that of economic variables.[23] Interpreting evidence in a somewhat impressionistic way for some Western societies, Parkin (1972: 120-1) argues that socialist governments have no marked impact on the shape of the distribution of income. The more rigorous study of Jackman (1975) seemed to support Parkin's conclusions. For a group of 60 developed and underdeveloped countries, Jackman found no discernible association between strength of socialist parties[24] and income inequality. However, the results of Jackman's analysis were contradicted by those of a group of studies confined to developed capitalist countries (Cameron, 1976; Hewitt, 1977; Dryzek, 1978; Tufte, 1978; Stephens, 1979; and Borg and Castles, 1981). Generally the authors of these studies have defended the restriction of the analysis to developed countries by arguing that the effects of political factors may be very different in developed and underdeveloped countries. To check this argument we recalculated Jackman's test for a subset of 18 developed capitalist democracies out of the 60 countries included in his study. In this case strength of socialist parties turned out to be of importance in explaining the variance in income inequality.[25] This finding supports the case for focusing cross-national research on the relationship between politics and income inequality on sets of countries that are comparable as to level of economic development. As pointed out in the Introduction to this volume, there is no implication here that socioeconomic factors are unimportant in the determination of levels of income inequality in general, but rather that the strategies appropriate for analysing the differences between developed and underdeveloped countries (where socioeconomic factors are of undoubted significance) and those that may be useful in discerning the causes of variance within the group of advanced capitalist democracies are necessarily rather different.

On the basis of cross-sectional data on 13 developed countries, Cameron (1976) found that the experience of socialist parties[26] is significantly related to variations in inequality of income after transfers and before taxes. His findings are based upon a measurement of income inequality by the income share of the top 20 percent of the population. A similar conclusion was reached by Hewitt (1977) after examining the relationship between, on the one hand, the income share of the top 10 and the top 5 percent of the population and, on the other hand, strength of socialist parties[27] for a group of 25 'modern industrial' countries. However, neither author is particularly clear as to how the strength of socialist parties leads to decreased income inequality. Hewitt only notes that 'only if the lower classes use their votes to elect socialist governments will democracy result in more equality, since nonsocialist governments will not be concerned with redistribution and social equality (Parkin, 1971: 105)' (Hewitt, 1977: 451). Looking in the study of Parkin at the place referred to by Hewitt we find the following passage:

> Social Democrats claim that leftwing governments have consistently introduced legislation designed to improve the lot of the less privileged. By initiating reforms in taxation and education, by the expansion of health and welfare programmes, full employment policies and the like, the position of the working class and the poor has been significantly improved under Labour regimes. Even when the means of production are largely in private hands, and where the economy is still organized along market principles, a government with a democratic socialist ideology, it is suggested, is still able to some extent to shift the balance of advantages in an egalitarian direction. [Parkin, 1971: 105]

According to Cameron (1976: 22), the degree to which governments are able to pursue the kind of policies mentioned by Parkin is related to the size of the public sector. However, in testing this hypothesis it was found that it is the expansion rather than the size of the public sector that is associated with inequality of the distribution of income before taxes. This awkward finding is not well explained by Cameron. A simiiar finding was reported by Cameron in a later article. In a study of the public sector (Cameron, 1978) he found inequality of the distribution of income after both transfers and taxes to be smaller in countries that had experienced large increases in the public sector.[28]

The results of the analyses of both Cameron and Hewitt may be judged to be vulnerable to criticism because they are based on somewhat dubious measures of income inequality. For instance, Deleeck (1977: 39) has shown that in postwar Europe during both the 1950s and the 1960s the share of the top ten decile decreased, while more general measures of inequality show a decrease of inequality during the 1950s but a tendency to increased inequality during the 1960s. The study of Dryzek (1978), however, based on measuring inequality by the Gini coefficient and the ratio of the top ten and bottom decile, yielded results consistent with those of Cameron and Hewitt. In discussing the variations in income inequality in capitalist democracies Dryzek distinguishes between the impact of two different groups of independent factors referred to by him as characterizing an underlying dimension of, respectively, 'development' and 'class politics'. He argues that 'development' pertains not only to economic but also to political development as expressed in the degree of democracy.[29] As to 'class politics', Dryzek notes that in societies where class is important politically — as expressed in high strength of socialist parties[30] — other social cleavages, such as ethnolinguistic, religious and regional differences, tend to be weak; in these cases the public sector will tend to be large because of the relatively frequent presence of socialist governments which are more prone to state expansion than nonsocialist governments. Using factor analysis, Dryzek constructed two factors corresponding, respectively, to the 'development' dimension and the 'class politics' dimension.[31] These two factors were then used as independent variables in multiple regressions with inequality as the dependent variable. Dryzek performed regressions for two sets of countries, one consisting of 11 cases and the other of 20. According to Dryzek, the data on income distribution for the 11-country set are strictly comparable, while those for the 20-country set are 'somewhat less comparable'. However, this is a rather misleading statement. Actually, Sawyer (1976: 20), from whom Dryzek derives his data, characterizes the data pertaining to the 11-country set as being 'as comparable as possible', not as 'strictly comparable'. Worse, however, is the position with regard to the 20-country set. In this set Dryzek indiscriminately uses pretax and post-tax data. Therefore, these data are 'incomparable' instead of 'somewhat less comparable'.

For the 11-country set the 'class politics' factor turned out to be significantly associated with inequality, suggesting that countries where socialist parties are strong and non-class cleavages weak tend to have the most equal distributions of income. The 'development' factor showed no association with variations in inequality. For the 20-country set, however, no significant results were obtained, although the relationship between 'class politics' and inequality is again in the anticipated direction. Normally, the poor results for the larger sample should cast serious doubt on the general character of the findings resulting from the smaller sample.[32] In this case, however, we judge it better not to cling too much to the outcome of the 20-country set because of the incomparability of the data.

The results of Dryzek's analysis point both to the strength and the weakness of the factor analysis technique used by him. The strength is that it enables one to analyse the impact of broad categories of factors. This may be useful in early stages of research to find out in which direction research should proceed. The technique is, however, less suited to study the pattern of interaction between specific independent variables and the phenomena to be explained.

Stephens (1979) and Borg and Castles (1981) offer a more viable account of the relationship between politics and income distribution. According to Stephens, strength of labour organization is the main causal factor in the equalization of incomes. This is not to say that the party composition of the government makes no difference for policy outcomes. In fact, Stephens argues that socialist rule is a condition of increasing the equality of incomes. However, in his view governmental activity of socialists needs to be supported by labour union activity. Stephens is not clear as to the question of whether unions and socialist parties have an impact on the distribution of income by interference with the economic process, thus influencing the distribution of primary income, or by the redistributive system. The fact that he often stresses 'welfare statism' as the goal of socialist policy during the 1950s and 1960s shows his preoccupation with redistribution through transfers and taxes. To check his argument concerning the importance of labour unions, Stephens calculated coefficients of correlation with measures of income inequality (Gini coefficient and income share of the highest quintile). On this basis, he concludes that labour union strength is more closely related to equality of income than socialist rule.[33] However, the difference is only slight in the case of the distribution of income after transfers and taxes, and still smaller in that of the estimated distribution of income after transfers, taxes and public spending; the difference is most pronounced with the distribution of pre-tax, post-transfer income. This suggests that unions are effective in equalizing the income by interference with the income-generating processes, while socialist rule is more effective in equalizing through taxes and public spending.

In Borg and Castles (1981) and Tufte (1978: 94-7) the change in inequality brought about by taxes is related to strength of political parties. Tufte shows that income equalization (measured by the change in income share of the highest quintile) resulting from taxes is greatest in countries where parties of the Left have governed longest.[34] The research reported by Borg and Castles confirms the results of Tufte. Borg and Castles also draw attention to a hitherto unstudied phenomenon: the impact of parties of the Right.[35] They show that strength of parties of the Right is accompanied with less equalization through taxes. Surprisingly, moreover, the impact of these parties turned out to be much more significantly related to changes in inequality than was the impact of the parties of the Left. From this finding the authors argue that in a number of important areas of public policy it is the strength of the Right that may be the determining factor instead of, as is usually assumed, the strength of the Left.

It will be recalled that the results of studies measuring inequality by the income share of the top 10 or top 20 percent of the population may be criticized because these measures are not necessarily representative for overall inequality. However, we also pointed out that subsequent studies based on overall measures of inequality like the Gini coefficient yielded similar results, thus supporting the findings of the earlier analyses. Neglecting these studies, Jackman (1980) argues that the results of Hewitt (1977) and Tufte (1978) are not reliable, since attention is focused on the wealthiest population groups only. Rightly, Jackman argues that the shape of the whole distribution should be considered. However, he does not mention the studies of Dryzek and Stephens which are based on the whole distribution of income and yet yield associations consistent with those of Hewitt and Tufte.

On the other hand, it may be argued that it is not enough to use measures of inequality based on the whole distribution of income, but that the separate elements of the shape of the distribution should also be considered. This is done in the study of Jackman. He analyses the relationship between the income share of successive quintiles and the strength of socialist parties[36] for two sets of industrialized Western countries. The first set consists of 14 countries and refers to pre-tax income; the second set consists of 10 countries and refers to post-tax income. For both sets Jackman reports similar results: the share of the top quintile is negatively associated with strength of socialist parties, while that of the other quintiles is positively associated with strength of socialist parties. This finding is not inconsistent with the proposition that strength of socialist parties results in less income inequality. However, only in the case of the three highest quintiles are the relationships statistically significant. From this Jackman concludes that the redistribution that may be attributed to socialist parties has benefited the two quintiles below the top quintile, but not the two bottom quintiles. This conclusion would be correct were it not for the fact that the data referring to the lower end of the income distribution are much less reliable and less fit for cross-national comparison than those for the upper end of the income distribution. Low incomes are highly sensitive to errors or changes in statistical procedures. For instance, an increase of women or students working part-time may decrease the income share of the bottom quintiles because this makes these quintiles contain more part-time and fewer full-time working income recipients. Not only may countries differ in these respects, but also statistical procedures may differ between countries as to which part-timers are to be included and which not.

However, the fact that data on lower quintiles are less comparable, does not mean that they are not at all comparable. It is very difficult, if not impossible, to determine how much distortion exists in consequence of statistical deficiencies. Thus, on these grounds we cannot exclude the possibility that Jackman is correct in stating that the redistribution associated with socialist party strength has mainly benefited the middle classes. Some support for this hypothesis may be derived from the fact that the middle classes in Western democracies generally have enjoyed a pivotal role in electoral contests between the political representatives of the rich and the poor, and may well have been able to exploit this advantage to their own benefit (Stigler, 1970; Van den Doel and Grondsma, 1979; 473-4).[37]

Summarizing the results of the studies discussed, we may suggest that it is clear that politics cannot be neglected in accounting for cross-national variations in income inequality. This is not to say that no questions are left. Inequality of the distribution of income after transfers and after both transfers and taxes were found to be smaller when socialist parties are stronger (Cameron, 1976; Dryzek, 1978; Stephens, 1979). However, Stephens has argued that strength of labour organization is the main causal factor in the equalization of incomes. On the other hand, he does not indicate whether the latter is realized through interference with the primary income-generating process or through the redistributive system. The findings of Borg and Castles (1981) are of importance in this respect. They suggest that parties of the Left are much less effective in accentuating the equalizing impact of taxes than parties of the Right are in curbing these effects. This creates some doubt as to whether parties of the Left and labour unions have their main impact on the distribution of income through the redistributive system. The findings of Borg and Castles also create interest in a further exploration of the relationships that may exist between parties of the Right and the distribution of income. In the following sections we will deal with these questions and try to clarify the underlying pattern yielding the associations reported in the studies discussed.

*Definitions of party and union strength*

Between the countries examined in this study major differences exist in the strength of political parties and labour unions, which may have important consequences for the policies that can be pursued and the distributional outcomes that result. In this section we discuss the definitions of party and union strength and offer some comments on these definitions.

Labour unions are organizations that seek to maximize their membership. The larger the membership of a union, the stronger is its bargaining position vis-à-vis employers and government. Therefore, the measure of labour union strength to be used here expresses labour union membership as a percentage of non-agricultural labour force.[38]

The appropriate measure of party strength is less easy to decide on. In the literature several measures of party strength are used: percentage of the total vote, percentage of seats in the legislature, number of years in office, and percentage of cabinet seats. Percentage of the total vote measures political sympathies within the population; since our study deals with the policy impact of political parties, we decided not to use this measure as it indicates political sympathies rather than power. Percentage of seats in the legislature, which is employed in our study, measures the extent to which political sympathies within the population are 'translated' into legislative power. This measure also takes into account the impact that parties may have even when in opposition, to the degree that the governing parties may try to forestall the electoral appeal of the opposition by adopting some of its policies.

Number of years in office is related to the direct impact of political parties on policy. This measure does not differentiate between presence in government and control of government. The distinction may be of crucial importance in countries in which governments are formed by coalitions. Cameron (1976) illustrates this with the Swedish and Swiss cases. In both countries parties of the Left have been in office throughout the period considered by Cameron (1956-73). Therefore both countries scored identically on the variable measuring years in office. However, during this period the party of the Left in Switzerland held only two seats in the government, while that in Sweden possessed a majority. To be in government as a minority member in the coalition or as a majority member makes a lot of difference. We therefore decided to use percentage of cabinet seats as a variable tapping the direct impact of political parties on policy. Finally, we included a composite measure derived from the political complexion of governments and political systems.[39] More specifically, this measure is based on cabinet seats, length of time in office and party size. This measure compresses these elements into a rank-order scale of strength of the party of the Left compared with that of the party of the Right. (This scale is identical to that used in the earlier chapter on public expenditure outcomes.)

To sum up, the following measures are used in the present analysis:

1. the average percentage of seats in the legislature held by the selected party of the Left over a period of 10 years (LL);[40]
2. ditto for the selected party of the Right (LR);
3. the average percentage of cabinet seats held by the selected party of the Left over a period of 10 years (CL);
4. ditto for the selected party of the Right (CR);
5. a rank-order scale derived from the political complexion of governments and political systems (GAPS); this scale is based on a 10-year period, and indicates strength of the Left versus that of the Right.
6. labour union membership as a percentage of the non-agricultural labour force (UN).

As a criterion for selection of parties of the Left, membership of the Socialist International was used. The operational definition of the Right covers both conservative and Christian democratic parties. The latter are included when they do not have a conservative rival polling at least 10 percent of the vote. The selected parties are listed in Table 8. An impression of the political structure in

## TABLE 8
### Parties of the Left and of the Right in 14 countries

| Country | Left | Right |
|---|---|---|
| Australia | Labour | Liberal/Country |
| Canada | New Democratic | Conservative |
| Germany | Social Democratic | Christian Democratic |
| Finland | Social Democratic | National Coalition |
| France | Socialist | Gaullist |
| Ireland | Labour | Fine Gael |
| Israel | Labour | Likud |
| Italy | Socialist | Christian Democratic |
| Japan | Socialist | Liberal Democratic |
| Netherlands | Labour | Liberal |
| Norway | Labour | Conservative |
| Sweden | Social Democratic | Moderate Unity |
| UK | Labour | Conservative |
| USA | (none) | Republican |

*Source:* based on Mackie and Rose (1974).

## TABLE 9
### Variables measuring party and union strength, years around 1970*

| Country | LR | LL | CR | CL | GAPS | UN |
|---|---|---|---|---|---|---|
| | % | % | % | % | | % |
| Australia | 59 | 41 | 100 | 0 | 2 | 50 |
| Canada | 46 | 6 | 34 | 0 | 2 | 26 |
| Germany | 50 | 39 | 70 | 15 | 2 | 35 |
| Finland | 15 | 24 | 7 | 22 | 4 | 39 |
| France | 55 | 14 | 49 | 0 | 2 | 25 |
| Ireland | 34 | 14 | 5 | 4 | 2 | 36 |
| Israel | 25 | 51 | 0 | 100 | 5 | 80 |
| Italy | 43 | 14 | 72 | 6 | 2 | 23 |
| Japan | 61 | 31 | 100 | 0 | 1 | 27 |
| Netherlands | 11 | 27 | 18 | 8 | 4 | 30 |
| Norway | 20 | 48 | 20 | 47 | 4 | 46 |
| Sweden | 14 | 49 | 0 | 100 | 5 | 71 |
| UK | 47 | 51 | 35 | 65 | 3 | 44 |
| USA | 35 | 0 | 39 | 0 | 2 | 27 |

* For explanation of variables see text.
*Source:* Mackie and Rose (1974); Korpi and Shalev (1980: cf. note 38).

the 14 countries included in our study may be obtained from the data on party and union strength contained in Table 9.

Obviously, if we had adopted the procedure of labelling all political parties within a given country as either Left or Right, we would by definition have obtained perfect negative correlation between the percentage of both legislative and cabinet seats for the two political tendencies. However, such a procedure would hardly be true for the realities of any but two-party systems, and, in the case of many Western European party systems, would give rise to a frequent attribution of power-sharing by left- and right-wing parties within the context of joint coalition cabinets. For this reason, the political variables used in this study are not based on such an unnatural dichotomy, but involve a selection out of the range of political parties of one party of the Left and one of the Right. In this procedure countries with a greater than average share of legislative seats for the Left do not necessarily have a less than average share for the Right and vice versa, as would be the case in the Left-Right dichotomy. Indeed, from Table 10 it appears that there exists hardly a relationship between percentage of seats in the legislature of the party of the Left and of the Right ($r = -0.17$). With respect to the relationship between cabinet-sharing of parties of the Left and of the Right a negative correlation is more to be expected, at least, if one accepts the supposition that polarization between these parties does not easily yield joint cabinet participation. This expectation is indeed borne out, as Table 10 demonstrates ($r = -0.56$).

Thus, we may conclude that the procedure of selecting only one party of the Left and one of the Right does not in general justify the assumption that a high value of percentage of seats in the legislature for the one party implies a low value for the other. If, however, one measures the strength of parties by degree of cabinet-sharing, the assumption of a negative relationship between strength of party of the Left and of the Right is justified to some extent.

Concerning the relationship between the strength of parties of the Left and of the Right, it is also interesting to examine the extent to which these parties 'translate' their legislative seats into cabinet seats. From Table 10 it can be seen that, for parties of both the Left and the Right, there exists a significant and positive relationship between percentage of legislative seats and cabinet seats. Calculation of the elasticities of cabinet seats with respect to legislative seats yields about the same results for Left and Right, implying that Left and Right tend to be about equally efficient in translating

## TABLE 10
### Coefficients of correlation between variables measuring party and union strength in 14 countries

|      | LR     | LL    | CR     | CL      | UN     |
|------|--------|-------|--------|---------|--------|
| LR   |        | −0.17 | 0.81*  | −0.49   | −0.42  |
| LL   |        |       | −0.14  | 0.75*   | 0.75*  |
| CR   |        |       |        | −0.56*  | −0.44  |
| CL   |        |       |        |         | 0.87*  |

\* significant at 5% level.

*Source:* Table 9.

legislative seats in to cabinet seats.[41] Finally, from Table 10 it may also be concluded that labour union strength is significantly and positively associated with left-wing party strength and negatively, but less significantly, with right-wing party strength. This is not surprising: sympathies among the population favourable to labour unions generally tend to be favourable to leftist parties too.

### The impact of political parties and labour unions

A common view among authors in the domain of income inequality is that the impact of political parties via government or legislature is of importance mainly for the distribution of income after transfers and taxes. This view is not surprising, as in a free market economy the role of government in changing the distribution of income through transfers and taxes is much more commonly recognized than is government interference with the distribution of primary income. Indeed, the concept of the welfare state is for a large part based on the redistributive tax and transfer system.

Although we agree with the argument that the role of political parties is to be expected to be of greater importance for the distribution of income after transfers and after both transfers and taxes than for that of primary income, we do not exclude the possibility that political parties may have an impact on the distribution of primary income. This holds especially for parties of the Left and labour unions, because these, owing to their interventionist ideology, are more prone to interference with the economy than are parties of the Right. In a comparative analysis of a priori preferences regarding the use of instruments of economic policy, Kirschen and associates (1964: 241-3) recorded socialists and labour unions to have a positive attitude towards 10 out of 16 selected instruments, while conservatives only favoured 2; the interests among socialists and labour unions turned out to be almost identical. Further, a 'law of preference' was observed

> for instruments in inverse ratio to the degree of intervention that they involve... [This law] is particularly valid for the political families and groups of interests defending acquired positions and, more generally, defending private property, free enterprise and the market... Its field of validity is much more restricted with the Socialists and the Trade Unions who are more concerned with altering certain social structures and with extending the role of economic policy rather than preserving freedom of choice which seems to them more mythical than real. [Kirschen, 1964: 243-4]

Thus, parties of the Left may have a direct equalizing impact on the distribution of primary income through wage policies, labour market policies (including job retraining and prohibition of artificial scarceness of labour in certain professions, e.g. doctors) and through control on profits and prices. It is less easy to argue for a direct impact of parties of the Right, since these parties are hostile to interference with the economic process.

Apart from direct influences, there also may be some indirect influences, mainly owing to redistributive policies and education policies. Redistributive policies may increase the inequality of primary income distribution because in the bargaining processes determining primary incomes allowances are made for the workings of the redistributive system. To the extent that this kind of shifting occurs, the effectiveness of the redistributive system is reduced. From a study of the OECD (1978a) it appears that these kinds of shifting processes do occur in some OECD countries, notably in Sweden. To see to what extent a progressive tax system is associated with inequality of primary income distribution, we performed a correlation between a measure of progressivity of taxes as calculated by the OECD (1978a:57) and measures of primary income inequality. Of these, the Gini and Theil coefficients turned out to be significantly, and positively, associated with progressivity of taxes.[42]

We further performed a correlation between progressivity of

**TABLE 11**
Correlations between political variables on the one hand
and progressivity of taxes and education expansion on the other

|      | Progressivity of taxes | Education expansion |
|------|------------------------|---------------------|
| LR   | −0.31                  | −0.12               |
| LL   | 0.02                   | −0.56*              |
| CR   | −0.38                  | −0.06               |
| CL   | 0.33                   | −0.36               |
| GAPS | 0.18                   | −0.21               |
| UN   | 0.53*                  | −0.19               |

* significant at 5% level.

taxes and the political variables discussed above. The figures shown
in Table 11 demonstrate that progressivity of taxes is positively,
although with the exception of labour union strength not
significantly, correlated with variables measuring strength of parties of the Left and labour unions,[43] while it is negatively related,
although again not significantly, with variables measuring strength
of parties of the Right. We may therefore tentatively hypothesize
that strength of labour unions and parties of the Left is accompanied by an indirect effect of the discussed nature on the distribution of primary income. The data in Table 11 also suggest that for
parties of the Left it is cabinet seats rather than legislative seats that
matter in this respect.

As to education, the analysis of Parkin (1975) indicates that in
countries where the Left is strong there is greater equality of educational chances than in countries where the Right is strong.
However, this conclusion is challenged by Hewitt (1977), who
draws opposite conclusions from his analysis. Hewitt explains his
results by observing that parties of the Right place greater emphasis
on equality of opportunities than parties of the Left, which are
more concerned with the actual level of material equality. To see
which of the two arguments holds for the countries used in this
study, we considered the relationship between education expansion
at the university level and strength of political parties. From Table
11 it would seem that parties of the Left are associated with less
education expansion at the university level, while for parties of the

## TABLE 12
### Correlations between political variables and primary income distribution

|  | LR | LL | CR | CL | GAPS | UN |
|---|---|---|---|---|---|---|
| G | 0.07 | −0.38 | −0.05 | −0.11 | −0.20 | −0.11 |
| T | 0.07 | −0.28 | −0.04 | −0.01 | −0.22 | −0.01 |
| 10 | 0.35 | −0.66* | 0.36 | −0.56* | −0.45 | −0.52* |
| 10/(3 + 4 + 5) | 0.12 | −0.48 | 0.15 | −0.35 | −0.14 | −0.31 |

* significant at 5% level.

Right the association is negligible. In the preceding section, education expansion was found to be accompanied with greater income inequality. Thus we may interpret the data in Table 11 to suggest that parties of the Left have an indirect equalizing impact on the distribution of income via less than average education expansion.

Labour unions may have a direct equalizing impact on the distribution of primary income through bargaining with employers and by exercising pressure on the government and an indirect equalizing impact by their commitment to an egalitarian redistributive system. Summarizing for both parties and unions, we judge it legitimate to state that the discussed direct impacts are probable, while the indirect ones are only possible. Thus we expect the strength of parties of the Left and labour unions to be negatively associated with inequality of primary income distribution, and the strength of parties of the Right, positively associated. The latter relationship is expected to be less pronounced than the former, since interference with the economy is less likely with parties of the Right. The correlations in Table 12 tend to confirm these expectations. With two negligible exceptions, all correlations are in the expected direction. The figures in this table also indicate that the impact of parties and labour unions is most pronounced with respect to the measures of inequality stressing the extremes of inequality, decile 10 and decile ratio 10/(3 + 4 + 5).

One of the correlations in Table 12 is presented graphically in Figure 5. From this figure it can be seen that the position of Sweden (characterized by both high strength of party of the Left and high inequality of primary income distribution) disturbs the pattern.

**FIGURE 5**
**Relationship between distribution of primary income**
**and legislative strength of parties**
**of the Left; including Sweden,**
**r = − 0.38; excluding Sweden, r = − 0.78**

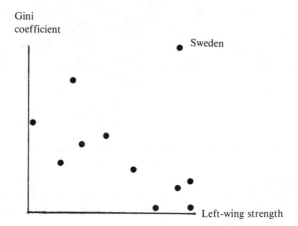

Several explanations for the inequality of primary income distribution in Sweden may be put forward. According to Sawyer (1976: 13, 18), part of the recorded inequality results from statistical peculiarities. Further, the inequality of primary income distribution in Sweden may result from unique political circumstances. In Sweden the party of the Left (the Social Democratic Party) has been the dominant party; it was in office from 1932 to 1976. Between this party and the Confederation of Trade Unions (LO), which is the largest employee organization, there exist strong ties. Therefore, the LO has had ample opportunities to represent the workers' interests in the formal political structure. In all probability, this hegemonic position of the Swedish Social Democrats and labour movement has caused the highly egalitarian character of the Swedish redistributive system. This egalitarian character is reflected in Table 2 (above), where Sweden switches from being most unequal as to primary income distribution to second most equal as regards the distribution of income after transfers and taxes. The skewedness of transfer payments in favour of households in the lower-income groups and the highly progressive nature of direct taxes is also recognized in studies on the Swedish income distribution (Schnitzer, 1974: 91; UN, 1967: Ch. 4, pp. 10,

11). However, these studies also point to the failure of policies directed at the structure of primary incomes. It will be recalled that, in discussing the impact of political parties and labour unions on the distribution of income, we suggested that redistributive policies may increase primary income inequality, because in the bargaining processes determining primary incomes allowances are made for the workings of the redistributive system. Since progressivity of taxes in Sweden is highest of all OECD countries, it is not surprising that studies on these shifting processes suggest that they tend to occur in Sweden (OECD, 1978a: 51ff). In the descriptive analysis contained in the next section we shall discuss the situation in Sweden in more detail, and in relation to patterns found in other countries.

Excluding Sweden, the coefficients of correlation as presented in Table 13 would result. In this table all coefficients are considerably higher than in Table 12. Both legislative and cabinet seats of parties of the Left and strength of labour unions are significantly associated with inequality of primary income distribution. As in Table 12, the degree of association with legislative seats of the Left is higher than for cabinet seats. We will pay attention to this finding later. Further, strength of labour unions appears to be somewhat less related to inequality than is strength of parties of the Left. However, the differences are small and do not justify the conclusion that parties of the Left have a more important impact on the distribution of primary income than do labour unions. Comparing the strength of association for parties of the Left and unions with that for the Right, we find, as expected, that the former is considerably more significant than the latter. The use of the composite measure indicating the balance of Left and Right in the political system (GAPS) does not yield closer associations than those for the variables exclusively measuring strength of the Left. These results confirm our hypothesis that the Right is less active than the Left in attempting to influence the distribution of primary incomes.

Transfers and taxes may alter the distribution of primary income. In principle, not only transfers in cash should be included in the analysis, but also those in kind. However with respect to the latter kind of transfers, no statistical data are available. We therefore leave these kinds of transfers out of consideration. Further, we also leave indirect taxes out of consideration.

Since taxes and transfers are instruments in the hands of governments, it seems a priori plausible that political parties are of importance with respect to the scope and possible redistributive ef-

## TABLE 13
### Correlations between political variables and primary income distribution, excluding Sweden

|              | LR   | LL      | CR   | CL      | GAPS    | UN      |
|--------------|------|---------|------|---------|---------|---------|
| G            | 0.40 | − 0.78* | 0.25 | − 0.68* | − 0.56* | − 0.63* |
| T            | 0.47 | − 0.75* | 0.30 | − 0.64* | − 0.58* | − 0.65* |
| 10           | 0.37 | − 0.70* | 0.38 | − 0.67* | − 0.56* | − 0.61* |
| 10/(3 + 4 + 5) | 0.24 | − 0.63* | 0.28 | − 0.63* | − 0.40  | − 0.56* |

* significant at 5% level.

## TABLE 14
### Correlations between political variables and inequality of income after transfers and after both transfers and taxes

| Measures of inequality of income | LR    | LL      | CR      | CL      | GAPS    | UN      |
|----------------------------------|-------|---------|---------|---------|---------|---------|
| **After transfers**              |       |         |         |         |         |         |
| G                                | 0.15  | − 0.57* | − 0.22  | − 0.21  | − 0.17  | − 0.43  |
| T                                | 0.24  | − 0.59* | − 0.10  | − 0.29  | − 0.35  | − 0.49* |
| 10                               | 0.41  | − 0.48* | 0.21    | − 0.41  | − 0.55* | − 0.63* |
| 10/(3 + 4 + 5)                   | 0.28  | − 0.49* | 0.01    | − 0.29  | − 0.52* | − 0.54* |
| **After transfers and taxes**    |       |         |         |         |         |         |
| G                                | 0.46  | − 0.60* | 0.17    | − 0.38  | − 0.51* | − 0.51* |
| T                                | 0.49* | − 0.59* | 0.23    | − 0.40  | − 0.59* | − 0.54* |
| 10                               | 0.61* | − 0.51* | 0.47*   | − 0.51* | − 0.86* | − 0.68* |
| 10/(3 + 4 + 5)                   | 0.52* | − 0.50* | 0.33    | − 0.42  | − 0.77* | − 0.62* |

* significant at 5% level.

fects of these instruments. Above, we concluded that political parties of the Left and labour unions contribute to equality of primary income distribution, while the opposite holds for parties of the

Right, although the latter association is less pronounced. It is to be expected that traces of the impact of parties and unions on primary income distribution are left in the distribution of income after transfers and after both transfers and taxes. These traces are now combined with the impact of parties and unions through the medium of transfers and taxes. We expect parties of the Left to place greater emphasis on progressive taxation and social welfare payments than would parties of the Right. Unions also may have an impact on the redistribution of income by way of reconciliation of wage bargaining with wider social and economic aims such as equalization through transfers and taxes. If these expectations are correct, strength of parties of the Left and labour unions will tend to be accompanied by less, and strength of parties of the Right by greater, inequality of incomes after transfers and after both transfers and taxes. This expectation is indeed confirmed by the data presented in Table 14.

For political parties, legislative seats tend to show higher associations than cabinet seats. Note that a similar finding was reported with primary income distribution; we will comment on this later. Further, the correlations with parties of the Left and labour unions are more pronounced than those with parties of the Right. However, examination of the scatterplots underlying these correlations suggests that the associations with parties of the Right would be considerably higher if Australia and Japan — both characterized by strength of the Right and also, equality — were excluded.[44] Owing to lack of data, these two countries could not be included in our analysis of primary income distribution. In Australia the party of the Right (the Liberal/Country Party) enjoyed ministerial authority from 1949 to 1972. However, the labour movement and the political left are strong in Australia compared with other countries having a strong Right (Japan, France and Italy). This may explain the relative equality in Australia. An explanation of why Japan has an equal distribution of income in the absence of leftist governments and strong labour unions may be found in the patriarchal and beneficient relationships between employers and employees that characterize the Japanese industrial structure. In the next section we shall discuss these matters in greater detail.

Considering the associations for the composite measure indicating strength of the Left versus that of the Right (GAPS), we observe close associations in the case of post-transfer, post-tax income distribution. This is not surprising, since both the Left and the Right tend to be closely associated with the final distribution of income.

Table 14 also offers evidence that the associations are stronger in the case of the distribution of income after both transfers and taxes than after only transfers. Apart from the fact that in the former case the impact of transfers and taxes is included, this may also be due to the fact that, although through transfers considerable equalization is achieved (cf. Table 3), the primary purpose of transfers is not equalization, but the provision of welfare and security. Thus, it is comprehensible that inequality of the distribution of income after transfers is less closely associated with political factors than the inequality of the distribution of income after transfers and taxes.

*Changes in income inequality through
transfers and taxes*

Table 15 presents the coefficients of correlation between variables measuring the strength of political parties and labour unions and changes in measures of income inequality through transfers and taxes. The pattern of associations emerging from this table is as expected. Parties of the Left and labour unions are associated with a greater equalizing impact of transfers and taxes, and parties of the Right with a less equalizing impact. With a slight exception in the case of union strength, the correlations with respect to the change through taxes, and through transfers and taxes, are more significant than the correlations with respect to the change through transfers alone. This is in line with our earlier argument that the equalizing impact of transfers, while considerable, is related less to political choices than is the equalizing impact of taxes. In the case of labour unions, there is no clear difference between the associations with changes through transfers and those with changes through taxes.

Table 15 demonstrates an impressive degree of association between certain aspects of domestic policies and change in inequality. The single most outstanding result is the 0.9 correlation between GAPS and change in the decile 10 measure, but, overall, the significant point that emerges from an examination of the table is just how much more strongly parties of the Right are associated with changes in inequality through transfers, taxes or both than are parties of the Left and labour unions. As far as taxes are concerned,

## TABLE 15
## Correlations between political variables and changes in inequality

|  | LR | LL | CR | CL | GAPS | UN |
|---|---|---|---|---|---|---|
| **Change through transfers** | | | | | | |
| G | −0.56* | 0.14 | −0.63* | 0.37 | 0.43 | 0.34 |
| T | −0.45 | 0.10 | −0.57* | 0.35 | 0.30 | 0.32 |
| 10 | −0.37 | −0.11 | −0.54* | 0.13 | 0.31 | 0.15 |
| 10/(3 + 4 + 5) | −0.44 | −0.07 | −0.55* | 0.16 | 0.30 | 0.18 |
| **Change through taxes** | | | | | | |
| G | −0.88* | 0.14 | −0.63* | 0.32 | 0.75* | 0.20 |
| T | −0.85* | 0.04 | −0.61* | 0.25 | 0.66* | 0.11 |
| 10 | −0.86* | 0.11 | −0.60* | 0.37 | 0.75* | 0.29 |
| 10/(3 + 4 + 5) | −0.87* | 0.04 | −0.66* | 0.38 | 0.75* | 0.29 |
| **Change through transfers and taxes** | | | | | | |
| G | −0.80* | 0.31 | −0.71* | 0.44 | 0.80* | 0.41 |
| T | −0.69* | 0.27 | −0.66* | 0.45 | 0.60* | 0.39 |
| 10 | −0.76* | 0.11 | −0.72* | 0.30 | 0.90* | 0.32 |
| 10/(3 + 4 + 5) | −0.71* | 0.05 | −0.67* | 0.26 | 0.62* | 0.29 |

* significant at 5% level.

this is in accordance with the study of Borg and Castles (1981), in which the strength of parties of the Right was found to be more closely associated with changes in inequality through taxes than was the strength of parties of the Left. According to the data in Table 15, this also holds for the changes brought about by transfers. These findings are in clear contrast to those that emerged from the analysis of levels of personal income inequality, where the explanatory power of the strength of the parties of the Left outweighed those of the Right.

These findings suggest that the Right is more successful in curbing the equalizing character of the redistributive system than the Left is in accentuating it. The fact that, none the less, levels of inequality tend to be significantly associated with strength of parties of the Left and labour unions can thus not be explained by the redistributive impact of the Left. It can, however, be explained by assuming that strength of the Left and labour unions leads to less inequality in the level of primary income distribution, and that it is this effect that largely accounts for the association between strength of the Left and labour unions with measures of income inequality after transfers and taxes. This assumption is in accordance with the findings on primary income inequality. These findings indicated that strength of parties of the Left and labour unions tended to be highly significantly associated with inequality of primary income when Sweden was excluded, while strength of parties of the Right appeared to be only weakly related to primary income distribution.

Now, Sweden may also be fitted into this argument by observing that the Swedish Social Democrats and labour movement rely much more heavily on the equalizing effect of the redistributive system than do parties of the Left and labour unions in general. That is, the Swedish Left has reached its goal — a relatively equal distribution of disposable (i.e. post-tax, post-transfer) income — in a manner differing from the one that tends to have been used by parties of the Left and labour unions in general. This may be due to the fact that the Swedish Left has had a hegemonic position in the political system for more than four decades.

Another interesting result of Table 15 is that, in the case of parties of the Right, both legislative and cabinet seats show a pronounced association with changes in inequality, while for parties of the Left it is mainly cabinet seats that seem to be of importance. This is probably due to the fact that for parties of the Left the main effort is directed towards changing the existing inequality of income distribution, while for parties of the Right the important thing is to maintain the existing structure of incomes. Voting power in the legislature may be an effective instrument to realize the latter since it enables a party to obstruct policy proposals aimed at changing the distribution of incomes. However, it seems unlikely that legislative strength by itself enables a party to increase the equalizing impact of transfers and taxes. To create and implement such a policy in practice requires a position in the government. This may explain why, with parties of the Left, it is mainly cabinet seats that are related to changes brought about by transfers and taxes.

## Discussion

In analysing the relationship between levels of income inequality and parties of the Left we found that legislative seats tended to be more closely related to income inequality than cabinet seats. In respect of changes in inequality brought about by transfers and taxes, however, we observed the opposite phenomenon. We explained the latter finding by pointing out that to increase the equalizing impact of transfers and taxes requires governmental power. We have not as yet paid explicit attention to the linkage between legislative strength and levels of income inequality. For an understanding of this linkage, we have to consider the relationships between parties of the Left and both levels of inequality and changes through transfers and taxes. To this end, we may first note that, in the case of changes in inequality, the equalizing impact of transfers and taxes may be changed by governments in the short run. Therefore, the degree to which parties of the Left or of the Right have been in government during the 10-year period considered is of immediate relevance in this respect. Political strength in the form of legislative seats only is no guarantee of a large equalizing impact through transfers and taxes.

The situation is different, however, in respect to the level of income inequality. This level is in the first instance determined by the inequality resulting from the market system. The market system is contained in an institutional setting which influences the distributive structure of the economy. Not only can this institutional setting and the distributive structure related to it be not readily changed in the short run, but also, political parties are not alone in determining these. In the case of the Left, the leftist tradition and milieu in general, and strength of labour unions in particular, may be as important or even more important than the specific political power of parties of the Left at a particular moment. Obviously, there is a strong possibility that, in a leftist institutional setting, a substantial part of the electorate will vote for parties of the Left, which will be expressed in a high score on the variable measuring legislative strength. Thus, a high score on legislative seats for the Left may be interpreted as an indicator of a strong leftist milieu. While the translation of left-wing legislative strength into cabinet incumbency may be crucial for effecting short-term changes in redistributive policies, it is, arguably, less significant in terms of shaping the basic parameters of levels of inequality, which stem from an institutional setting of which left-wing political strength is only one aspect.

This interpretation raises the question of the relative importance with respect to income inequality of political parties versus the leftist milieu in general. More specifically, the question is whether it is parties of the Left, labour unions or both that matter. It will be recalled that strength of parties of the Left is closely related with strength of labour unions. Therefore it is statistically almost impossible to determine whether it is party, union or both that have an impact on the shape of the distribution of income. In the following section we will try to answer this question by studying patterns of political and industrial relations in the countries included in our study. However, some preliminary thoughts on this subject may be formulated now.

First, it is of importance that we could explain the pattern of findings by assuming that strength of the Left and labour unions leads to less inequality in the distribution of primary income. Labour unions explicitly direct their efforts at the distributive structure in the market system, while after the Second World War social democratic parties have shifted their attention from control of the market economy towards the creation of the welfare state. The welfare state is characterized by state provision of welfare in the framework of a capitalist economy and a parliamentary democracy. The logic of the welfare state is related to Keynesian economic theory. Keynes's theory undermined the socialist case for central planning and public ownership, which had rested on the inefficiency and injustice of the allocative mechanism under capitalism. According to Keynes, the government's job was to secure an aggregate volume of output corresponding to full employment. Broadly, this 'demand management' could be achieved through indirect and general measures, mainly fiscal and monetary policy. The market could continue to allocate resources and rewards as hitherto. In this conception of the welfare state, attempts to equalize the distribution of income have to be realized through transfers, progressive taxation and public expenditure directed at welfare. Thus, it is implied that the state can achieve equality without the traditional means of public ownership and control of production, distribution and exchange.[45] However, our findings regarding the changes through transfers and taxes suggest that parties of the Left have not been very successful in accentuating the equalizing potential of the welfare state. In this respect, it should be noted that the general resistance against further increases in taxes makes it hardly possible to achieve further income equalization through redistributive policies alone.

On the other hand, the abandonment of traditional socialist means of controlling the economy should not be equated with a total absence of interference with the market economy. Further, the countries included in this study differ in the degree to which they have endorsed the ideology of the welfare state. Thus it would be premature to conclude that, owing to their inclination towards the ideology of the welfare state, parties of the Left have no impact on the distribution of primary income. We may, however, conclude that in the case of parties of the Left the intention to change the distribution of primary income is less unambiguous than with labour unions.

The question of the relative importance of parties of the Left versus labour unions is considered from a different point of view by Marxists. Marx's work is often interpreted as economic-deterministic. Obviously, economic determinism leaves little scope for political influence as an autonomous factor. This interpretation is however challenged by others (e.g. Poulantzas, 1973: 14). Be that as it may, the traditional vision of Marxists concerning the role of governments within the democratic political systems of the advanced capitalist countries corresponds with the analysis of Marx and Engels, who labelled governments in capitalism 'bourgeois-democratic', i.e., instruments in the hands of the dominant classes and used by these classes to exercise their power. A most unambiguous expression of this view is found in Miliband's (1973) analysis of the nature and the role of the state in the advanced capitalist societies. According to Miliband, governments in capitalist societies accept the capitalist context in which they operate and shape their policies and actions in accordance with the priorities of the dominant classes. In Miliband's view, this also holds for governments of the Left. These governments, Miliband (1973: 92) writes,

> have found in the difficult conditions they inevitably faced a ready and convenient excuse for the conciliation of the very economic and social forces they were pledged to oppose, and for the reduction of their own ambitions to the point where these ceased to hold any kind of threat to conservative forces. And the longer they have been in office, the more marked have become these tendencies.

Recently, however, some Marxist authors have questioned this instrumental view of the state.[46] They argue, instead, that the state in capitalist societies is 'relatively autonomous' from the direct manipulation of the dominant classes. However, until now these Marxist authors have not given a satisfactory analysis of the way in which the state in capitalist society is supposed to produce policies that are in the interest of the dominant classes, while at the same time the state maintains a certain degree of autonomy from the manipulation by these classes.

Although Marxist scholars argue that governments in advanced capitalism are not able to shift the balance of material rewards in an egalitarian direction, they tend to attach more importance to labour unions to improve the lot of the less privileged. This stems from the view that labour unions represent people in the centre of the capitalist mode of production, that is, in their role as individuals who sell their labour power to the owners of the means of production. Labour unions are thus, in the Marxist view, rooted in the economic class struggle and are more prone to express their resentments against the prevailing distribution of material rewards. However, Marxists differ in their evaluation of the extent to which unions have realized material gains. Some argue that the economic demands asserted by labour unions have indeed changed the distribution of material rewards, although these results have in general been accompanied by a de facto acceptance of the capitalist mode of production by the unions. This view is clearly expressed by Gramsci (1920), who argued that the stable and progressive development of capitalism has been made possible only by the involvement of the unions. The price unions had to pay for the resulting material gains was a commitment to capitalist legitimacy. Other Marxists, however, are more negative in their evaluation of unions. Miliband (1973: 144) has argued that the growing importance of the relations of organized labour with employers and governments has not improved the bargaining position of labour. In his view the process of collaboration has turned union leaders into

> junior partners of capitalist enterprise... In fact, their incorporation into the official life of their countries has mainly served to saddle them with responsibilities which have further weakened their bargaining position, and which has helped to reduce their effectiveness. [Miliband, 1973: 144]

The involvement of labour unions into 'the official life' is, however, valued more positively by other (non-Marxist) authors. For instance, Wilensky (1976: 21-3) argues that the involvement of labour unions in a national bargaining pattern with the government and employers yields an effective social contract. On the one hand, labour, interested in wages and social security, takes account of inflation, productivity and the need for investment; on the other hand, employers take account of the demands of the labour union movement. These 'corporatist' processs, as Wilensky calls them, are also valued as effective channels of labour union influence by Van der Vall (1970: 12). In his view, corporatist union activity is more effective than economic unionism, which stresses mainly wages, hours and working conditions. The argument of Stephens (1979) is related to that of Wilensky and Van der Vall, although Stephens mainly pays attention to corporatist processes in the framework of social democratic governments and labour unions.

However, one may wonder whether the gains that result for labour from the integration in the politics of the welfare state are not accompanied by losses (cf. the discussion in Chapter 5 of this volume). Labour's participation in corporatist processes may restrict its scope for economic unionism. For instance, labour may mitigate wage demands in exchange for tax measures (cf. Lindbeck, 1974: 145). In the argument of Wilensky, this trade-off character is implicitly present. It is, however, more explicitly discussed by Leynse (1977: 159-63). According to him, the most important advantage of centralized bargaining versus decentralized bargaining is that it offers more scope to realize welfare and security. In this regard, Leynse points out that the highly developed system of social security in the Netherlands has been brought about by the centralized labour union movement. Leynse also notes that the situation in the United Kingdom and the United States, where the labour union movement is much less centralized, contrasts with that in the Netherlands. In these countries the system of social security is much less developed. Centralized bargaining not only offers scope for developing the system of social security, but it also enables labour to achieve immaterial demands (like workers's comanagement, arrangements with respect to retirement and dismissal, etc.) that are difficult to negotiate in the context of decentralized bargaining.

On the other hand, centralized bargaining also has certain disadvantages. According to Leynse, centralized bargaining weakens the grip of unions on what really happens to wages in the firms. Such a grip can be realized only by decentralized wage bargaining, in which workers of the industry itself participate. Only these workers have the knowledge and the power to change the structure of payments in the firm. In view of these offsetting tendencies, Leynse concludes that neither too much centralism nor too much decentralism is desirable: an effective union strategy requires elements of both centralism and decentralism.

Stephens (1979) also recognizes the possibility that the 'Social Contract', while favourable for an expansion of social services and progressive taxation, results in an enrichment of capitalists through wage restraint. However, he is less positive in his judgement on the merits of decentralized bargaining. According to Stephens, decentralized bargaining may lead to high levels of inflation, to a deterioration of the country's competitive position in foreign markets, to capital flight and to a decrease in investment. To prevent such things, an incomes policy and wage restraint are necessary. In this argument Stephens neglects the fact that corporatist processes are characterized by the principle of quid pro quo (he states so himself; see Stephens, 1979: 122): the increase of social security and government spending resulting from centralized bargaining may just as well be a source of inflation, deterioration of competitive position, etc., as of unrestrained wage demands resulting from decentralized bargaining. Thus, this is no legitimate argument against decentralized bargaining compared with centralized bargaining.

Finally, with respect to the question of the effectiveness of labour unions versus parties of the Left, it also matters whether labour-linked parties are in office frequently. If so, this may weaken the union's bargaining power. In a study of British wage politics, Dorfman (1973: 152) writes that British union leaders found the relationship during the early 1960s with the Conservative government more satisfying than that with subsequent Labour governments. When the Labour Party governed, an enormous pressure was exerted on unions to agree to wage policies that were contrary to union purposes, while when the Conservatives were in office the unions could pursue their objectives a great deal more easily. Dorfman (1973: 152) illustrates this by quoting a study according to which 'Throughout the dark days of the Labour Government a surprising number of union worthies used to sigh secretly for those 13 years of Tory misrule...'

## Summary

In the last two sections we have evaluated a series of hypotheses concerning the impact of various economic, social and political factors on the distribution of income in the advanced capitalist democracies. The statistical findings all point to the importance of political factors. Although these findings should be interpreted with caution, the persistence of significant relationships between the political variables on the one hand and income inequality on the other seems to warrant the conclusion that political factors do explain income inequality to a considerable extent.

Both strength of parties of the Left and labour unions were found to be accompanied with less income inequality. A somewhat surprising conclusion following from the statistical analysis was the fact that parties of the Left and labour unions appeared to be only weakly associated with the redistributive processes. On the basis of this finding, it was argued that the relatively strong associations of parties of the Left and labour unions with levels of income inequality should be explained by the impact of these political agencies on the distribution of primary income. Thus, with respect to the equalizing impact of parties of the Left and labour unions it seems to be not the redistributive system, but interference with the processes of primary income formation, that matters.

Strength of parties of the Right was found to be related only weakly to inequality of primary income and income after transfers, but significantly to highly significantly with the distribution of post-tax, post-transfer income and with the changes in inequality effected by the redistributive processes. Thus, parties of the Right seem to pursue a quite different policy strategy from that pursued by parties of the Left. They do not interfere with the processes of primary income formation, but they use their political strength to take care that the redistributive processes do not take too much from the rich and give it to the less well-to-do.

In a discussion of these findings, attention was focused on the question of whether it is parties of the Left or labour unions that matter with respect to income equality. It was argued that the emphasis on the mechanisms of the welfare state weakens the case for an impact of parties of the Left on the distribution of primary income. It was further remarked that the ardour with which labour unions pursue wage interests is weakened by union integration into the politics of the welfare state. Such integration is the more likely when labour-linked parties are in office frequently.

**TABLE 16**

**Classification of countries according to their scores on party and union strength**

| Country | Party % seats in legislature Right | Left | Union | Degree of income inequality Pre-tax, pre-transfer income | Post-tax, post-transfer income | Degree of equalization through transfers and taxes |
|---|---|---|---|---|---|---|
| 1. France | Strong | Weak | Weak | High | High | Low |
| Italy | Strong | Weak | Weak | (High)* | High | (Low)* |
| United States | Medium | Weak | Weak | High | High | Medium |
| Canada | Strong | Weak | Weak | Medium | Medium | Medium |
| Japan | Strong | Medium | Weak | (Low)* | Low | (Low)* |
| 2. Ireland | Medium | Weak | Medium | Medium | Medium | Medium |
| Finland | Weak | Medium | Medium | Medium | Low | High |
| Netherlands | Weak | Medium | Weak | Medium | Low | High |
| 3. Australia | Strong | Strong | Medium | (Low)* | Low | (Low)* |
| United Kingdom | Strong | Strong | Medium | Low | Low | Medium |
| Fed. Rep. Germany | Strong | Strong | Medium | Low | High | Low |
| 4. Israel | Weak | Strong | Strong | Low | Low | Medium |
| Norway | Weak | Strong | Medium | Low | Low | Medium |
| Sweden | Weak | Strong | Strong | High | Low | High |

* estimated (see text).

*Source:* Tables 2 and 9.

## Comparative analysis of country patterns

*A classification of countries*

In this section we will analyse the pattern of relationships between political parties, labour unions and income inequality. The 14 countries included in our study may be classified in four groups. This classification is based on a grouping of the countries according to their scores on party and union strength. Table 16 presents the results.

Before discussing the patterns in separate countries, we will first characterize the four groups in general terms. Group 1 contains five countries. These tend to have a strong party of the Right, a weak party of the Left and a weak labour union movement. With one exception, they have a high to medium income inequality. (The exception is Japan, which has comparatively low income inequality.) Group 4 contrasts most strongly with Group 1. The pattern in this group is the reverse of that in Group 1. The countries in Group 4 tend to have a weak party of the Right, a strong party of the Left and a strong labour union movement. These countries are characterized by low income inequality. In the case of primary income, however, an exception has to be made for Sweden, which has a high primary income inequality.

Groups 2 and 3 are intermediate to Groups 1 and 4. In Group 2 neither the party of the Right nor that of the Left is strong. The labour union movement is either weak or of medium strength. However, the party of the Left tends to be somewhat stronger than that of the Right. The countries in this group have a moderate to low income inequality. Group 3 is characterized by a strong Right, a strong Left and moderately strong labour unions. The countries in this group tend to have a low income inequality. The exception to this pattern is the Federal Republic of Germany, characterized by an equal distribution of primary income and an inequality of post-tax, post-transfer income distribution.

The overall pattern arising from Table 16 is clear. Going from top to bottom, the relative strength of the Right compared with that of the Left decreases. This is accompanied by a decrease of income inequality. In the two groups that are at opposite poles to each other, i.e. Groups 1 and 4, the relation between the pattern of politics and that of income inequality is unambiguous. Neglecting for the moment the exceptional cases of Japan and Sweden, we may state that strength of the Right and weakness of the Left are accompanied by inequality, while equality results when the Right is weak and the Left strong. In situations where both Left and Right are of weak to medium strength (Group 2) or where both Left and Right are strong (Group 3), inequality tends to be low or moderate. Thus, when strength of the Left is about equal to that of the Right, the results tend to be in the direction of low income inequality. Before trying to explain this overall pattern, we will first consider the patterns in separate countries for the postwar period up to 1970.[47] In several countries, the patterns established in the two or so decades after 1945 changed quite dramatically in the 1970s, and sometimes early signs of such change can be distinguished in the late 1960s. Since our basic focus is on the determinants of personal income distribution circa 1970, our focus in the following pages is on the broad patterns characteristic of the postwar period.

### Country patterns

#### Group 1
In *France* levels of unionization are low. At the same time, the labour union movement is divided in political outlook: the largest confederation, the CGT (Confédération du Travail), has close ties with the Communist Party. The CFDT (Confédération Française Démocratique du Travail) is of progressive Christian origin. In 1964 the CFDT committed itself to an anti-capitalist position and advocated democratic planning and workers' control. The Force Ouvrière is a social democratic splinter from the CGT. The limited degree of unionization and internal divisions have so far prevented the elaboration of a common incomes policy. The difficulties of elaborating such a policy are intensified by the decentralization of wage bargaining. In general, collective agreements are concluded for a particular industry.

The divisions and decentralization of the French labour union movement may also contribute to an explanation of why labour has failed to make an impact on the distribution of income after transfers and taxes. A prerequisite for this is that labour unions be strongly organized and centralized and meet regularly with politicians and employers to bargain out national economic and social policy. In France such corporatist processes have not been developed.

Turning to the redistributive processes, it can be noted that the

Right, which had had a solid governmental position in France from the advent of the Fifth Republic until 1981, did not effect much redistribution through transfers and taxes when compared with other countries. This is due mainly to the structure of the tax system. In France indirect taxes and social security contributions, both of which tend to be regressive, are the most important source of revenue. Direct taxes, which tend to be progressive, account for only a relatively small percentage of total tax receipts. Thus, on balance the French tax system does not lead to redistribution.

*Italy* is characterized by low levels of labour union organization. The industry is the main bargaining unit in Italy, although since the 1960s bargaining also takes place at plant level. The attention of labour unions to plant-level questions had been stimulated in the 1960s by the dissatisfaction of labour with the Centre-Left government. In the early 1960s the Christian Democrats brought the Socialists into their coalition. Although leading Christian Democrat progressives and Socialists were given important positions in the government, the key positions, in particular that of the Treasury, were reserved by Christian Democrat conservatives.The failure of the Centre-Left alliance to realize its reform programme, and the subsequent decrease in labour's attention to national economic and social questions, were not conducive to the creation of a corporatist model of policy-making.

Since data are not available on the distribution of primary income and of income after transfers in Italy, it is difficult to assess the impact of government redistributive policies. However, an indication of the role of transfers may be found in an OECD (1978a: 25) study in which transfers as a percentage of gross domestic product are specified for a number of OECD countries. The percentage for Italy is 10.4 in the mid-1970s, which is more than the average expenditure on transfers for all OECD countries (9.5 percent). This finding suggests that some redistribution may have taken place. Redistribution through taxes is probably not an important factor, since until 1970 Italian governments relied heavily on indirect taxes of a regressive kind (OECD, 1978a: 25).

The *United States* is characterized by low levels of labour union organization and a high degree of decentralization of wage bargaining. Consequently, American labour unions have not succeeded in developing a unified and national incomes policy. The narrow base of union membership and the decentralization of wage bargaining authority have effectively prevented unions from exercising an influence on national economic and social policy.

Turning to the redistributive process, it can be noted that the policy of the American governments has effected a medium degree of equalization through transfers and taxes. In this regard, several authors have noted that the tax system could be more favourable to redistribution if tax loopholes were not so extensive. Thus, Schnitzer (1974: 57) remarks:

> The effective rate of [tax] progression has been reduced through a series of loopholes that have been written into tax laws over time. In general these loopholes have worked to the advantage of upper-income families. Capital gains realized from the sale of assets are subject to a lower tax rate than ordinary income, and interest income from state and local bonds is completely exempt from federal income taxation. These and other loopholes were designed to encourage certain activities that have been deemed beneficial to the national economy. The end result, however, has been to deprive the U.S. Treasury of additional revenue.... .

Criticism has also been directed to government transfer policy. Relative poverty in the United States is widespread (OECD, 1976: 72), and this phenomenon seems to be largely attributable to insufficient provision of social assistance to those outside the labour market.

As noted before, *Japan* is an exception to the pattern in Group 1, since it is characterized by a strong Right, a weak Left *and* low income inequality. In Japan, in the postwar period, conservative governments have allowed private business the first claim on resources in a context in which private demand was so high that government 'Keynesian' policies were not necessary. Consequently, governments held down public expenditure to a level that is considerably below that in Western Europe and the United States. Welfare and social insurance programmes were consequently neglected by the conservative governments.

Since there are no reliable data available on the distribution of primary income in Japan, no definite statements can be made on the equalizing impact of the transfer policy of the Japanese governments. However, on the basis of the OECD (1978a: 25) study mentioned above, in which it is remarked that in the 1960s transfers in Japan account for only 2 to 3 percent of gross domestic product, it must be surmised that the relative equality of the post-transfer income distribution is not a consequence of the transfer process; therefore, it must be a consequence of the equal distribution of primary income. Turning to taxation policy, the empirical evidence available (cf. Table 2) indicates that government action in this area did not have an equalizing impact on the distribution of income.

According to Sawyer (1976: 19), equality in Japan is partly a statistical artefact: compared with other countries, Japan has few one-person households. This biases the results towards equality. The equality of the Japanese income distribution in the absence of leftist governments and strong labour unions may further be explained by the patriarchal and beneficent relations between employers and employees. In Japan the enterprise is considered to be a social unit which provides the employee with benefits such as free medical care, retirement allowances, family allowances and many other benefits. The enterprise is thus regarded

> as an industrial family. The employee, rather than being hired, is adopted as a member of the family, and his participation in it is based on grounds larger than his actual contribution in terms of skill. The wage system is not simply compensation for work but is rather a kind of 'life income' determined by the employee's age and family changes. [Schnitzer, 1974: 203]

Summarizing the pattern for the countries in Group 1, the following picture arises: levels of unionization are low, bargaining authority is decentralized, and no corporatist processes have been developed. In these countries, where conservative governments have prevailed a low to medium degree of income equalization is realized through the redistributive processes. Taxes would appear to be particularly ineffective in decreasing income inequality. With the exception of Japan, the inequality of income distribution tends to be high in these countries.

## Group 2

In the *Netherlands*, levels of unionization are low and wage bargaining is often conducted at a central level. During the 1950s the Netherlands was the only European country where pay settlements could be applied only with government approval, and where such settlements determined maximum as well as minimum pay. The institutional framework for the negotiations between labour, employers and government was established immediately after the Second World War. In their joint forum, the Foundation of Labour, the three confederations of labour unions, the corresponding confederations of employers and government agencies periodically sought to reach agreements on wages and related issues such as employment and price stability.

In the first 10 years after the war, central agreements took the form of modest increases which were justified only by increases in the cost of living. As a result, by 1954 the Netherlands was about the only country in Western Europe in which there had been no increases in real hourly wage earnings since 1948 (UN, 1967: Ch. 4, p. 3). In 1959, however, a new pay system was developed on the central level in which pay increases were related to increases in productivity. This system became exposed to severe stresses which made it virtually inoperative by the mid-1960s. Owing to the pressure of the economic development and dissatisfaction in the rank and file with the central agreements, which gave them less than they hoped for, the central bargaining structure broke down. Since then, industry-wide bargaining has become the principal element in the bargaining structure, though the parties occasionally settle issues at the national level.

The Netherlands, further, has a party of the Left of medium strength and a weak party of the Right. The pattern of policy-making in this country can be characterized as corporatist: the political elites generally accept that basic interests of the major groups in society should not be challenged.[48] These elites, therefore, carefully work together in order not to exclude major groups from decision-making processes. As a consequence of this model of policy-making in the Netherlands, government redistributive policies are structured with at least one eye to the interests of the working class even when non-labour-linked parties are in office. This may explain the highly egalitarian character of the Dutch redistributive system.

In *Finland* labour unions are moderately strong. Since the Second World War, central negotiations have been the rule, but on various occasions these negotiations have come close to breakdown. Compared with the other Scandinavian countries, industrial relations in Finland are more troubled. In 1956, and again in 1965, central negotiations were broken off and government intervention was needed to restore working relations between the two sides of industry.

The party of the Left in Finland is of medium strength and that of the Right is weak. The Social Democrats took part in a coalition until 1957 and they rejoined the government in 1966. The pattern of policy-making in Finland is to a certain extent similar to the Dutch pattern. Again, redistribution through transfers and taxes is considerable, but it is not as large as in the Netherlands.

The degree of unionization in *Ireland* is moderate. During the 1950s the Irish union movement tended to devote itself 'more to the grass-roots business of getting more money for its members than to any long-term social and economic planning' (Coogan, 1966: 164). In the 1960s efforts have been made to create a national system of collective bargaining. Initially, these were not very successful, and in 1965 attempts to replace independent industry bargaining by a central agreement failed. But from 1970 onwards wage bargaining has assumed a much more highly centralized character, with frequent intervention into the process of wage formation. However, in terms of a focus that is restricted to pre-1970 developments, Ireland clearly lacks many of the characteristics typical of corporatist industrial structures, such as the Netherlands and Finland.

The relation between the strength of political parties of the Right and the Left in Ireland is the reverse of that in Finland and the Netherlands. In the latter countries the Right is weak and the Left is of medium strength, but in Ireland it is the other way around. As to government redistributive policies, it should be noted that the equalizing impact is less than that of Finland and the Netherlands.

Summarizing the pattern for the countries in Group 2, the following picture arises: labour unions and parties of the Right and the Left tend to be weak or of medium strength. In the Netherlands and Finland corporatist processes have been developed. It seems likely that these corporatist processes have played an important role in the creation of an egalitarian redistributive system. In Ireland, where the Right is stronger than in the Netherlands and Finland, corporatist processes have hitherto been of much less importance, and redistribution has had a less egalitarian character. In these countries, inequality of disposable income is low (in the Netherlands and Finland) to medium (in Ireland).

### Group 3

In *Australia*, the party of the Right (the Liberal/Country Party) enjoyed continuous authority at the federal level from 1949 to 1972. The party pursued an economic and social policy that can be described as 'Keynesian' in character, but with a commitment to low levels of taxation. The Left in Australia has considerable strength in the legislature, but throughout the 1950s and 1960s found the preferential voting system to be a massive obstacle to its governmental aspirations.

Since the only reliable data pertain to the distribution of income after transfers and after both transfers and taxes, no direct conclusion can be reached concerning the equalizing impact of the transfer policy of the conservative governments. However, an indication of the role of transfers in this respect may be found in the OECD study (1978a: 25) mentioned above, in which it is noted that in the 1960s transfers in Australia accounted for only 4 to 5 percent of gross domestic product. Thus, as in the Japanese case, it may be inferred that government transfer policy does not lead to significant redistribution of income. The empirical evidence available (cf. Table 2) further indicates that the taxation policy of the rightist governments did not lead to redistribution, either. It therefore seems likely that the relative equality of the distribution of income after transfers and taxes in Australia derives from the equality of the primary income distribution.

According to Sawyer (1976: 19), the relative equality of the distribution of income in Australia is partly a consequence of the data-base utilized. In the source of data on income distribution, one-person households are under-represented, and this implies a bias of the results towards equality. A further explanation of the relative equality of the income distribution may be found in the strength of the labour union movement. Levels of unionization in Australia are high. The labour union movement is further characterized by decentralized wage bargaining. In the postwar period the unions, negotiating against a background of continued full employment, have achieved many concessions from the employers. Probably, the specific structure of industrial relations existing in Australia, and especially minimum wage setting in the context of a complex industrial arbitration system, has favoured union efforts to make substantial material gains.[49]

In the *Federal Republic of Germany* levels of unionization are medium. As to wage bargaining, during much of the postwar period the situation has not been unlike that in the United Kingdom and Australia, with the initiative resting largely with the individual unions, and the industry or plant being the prime focus for bargaining. According to a United Nations study (1967: Ch. 4, p. 26), German unions have tended to resent government interference over wage bargaining, since past experience has taught them that they tend to be more successful in circumstances where government participation is minimized. Thus, in the period that matters for our analysis, it seems fair to conclude that few corporatist developments of any major significance had occurred.[50]

In Germany both the party of the Right and that of the Left are strong. However, in the postwar period the CDU was in office until the mid-1960s. From late 1966 until 1969 a 'Grand Coalition' of the

CDU and socialists held office. The general election of 1969 brought an important political change, in so far as it marked the end of 20 years of political supremacy by the CDU. The long period during which the conservatives held the reigns of government may explain the failure of the redistributive system to exert an equalizing impact of any significance. Thus, the situation is not unlike that in Australia; in both countries the distribution of primary income is relatively equal and redistribution is of little importance. The fact that in the ranking of inequality of post-tax, post-transfer income Germany is among the unequal countries, while Australia is among the equal countries, may be explained in terms of the difference in primary income inequality in Australia and Germany. Both belong to the countries with the most equal distribution of primary income; but, none the less, the data suggest that inequality of primary income distribution in Australia is considerably lower than that in Germany. However, this may be due partly to the already mentioned bias in the Australian data-base.

In the *United Kingdom* the labour union movement is characterized by a medium level of unionization. The Trade Union Congress (TUC) often negotiates for the affiliated unions with the government and the employers on a central level. However, these negotiations do not have binding consequences, since the affiliated unions are not obliged to behave in accordance with the central agreements and in practice often go their own way. Related to this, most wage bargaining in the United Kingdom takes place at the industry, or plant, level. Another characteristic of the British labour union movement is the existence of many craft unions. This fragmentation does not facilitate the formation of a national incomes policy. According to Scase (1976: 37):

> one of the main features of wage bargaining in Britain has been the efforts of the specific unions to preserve, if not to increase, differentials as they exist between themselves and others. Different craft and trade unions have tended to compete with each other, thus emphasising the sectionalism and the divisions that exist within the British working-class movement.

Governments in the United Kingdom have made several attempts to get some kind of control on the wage agreements and, consequently, to develop a consistent national incomes policy. Most attempts in that direction failed in the 1950s and the 1960s. Roberts and Rothwell (1974: 353) thus state: 'until the passing of the Industrial Relations Act in 1971 it could be claimed that the British system of industrial relations was less regulated by law than that of any other industrialised country.'

As in Australia and Germany, the parties of the Right and of the Left are both strong in Britain. After the Second World War the Labour Party has held office for three periods — 1945-51, 1964-70 and 1974-79. Reforms introduced by these governments were often minimized by subsequent Conservative governments. For instance, in the 1950s Conservative governments introduced fees for a number of services that were previously free, cut down welfare expenditure and made taxes more regressive. Turning to government redistributive policies, it should be noted that a medium degree of equalization is realized in Britain. In particular, transfers mitigate primary income inequality. Taxation also has an equalizing impact, although this effect is considerably less than that of transfers. It has been argued in a UN study (1967: Ch. 6, p. 29) that this is a consequence of the degree of progression of income tax scales, which becomes really steep only for the top decile of personal income.

Summarizing the pattern for the countries in Group 3, the following picture arises: levels of unionization are comparatively high and wage bargaining authority is decentralized. In these countries no corporatist processes have been developed. Parties of both the Left and Right are strong. Only in the United Kingdom, where the Labour Party has been in office for about half the postwar period, has substantial equalization been effected through the redistributive processes. In the countries belonging to this group inequality of primary income is low, while that of disposable income is low (Australia and the United Kingdom) to high (Federal Republic of Germany).

*Group 4*

In *Norway* labour unions are of medium strength. The principle of central wage bargaining was accepted by the Norwegian unions in 1949. However, not all of the bargaining in the 1950s and 1960s has been conducted at a central level. While the employers and the government have been in favour of central agreements, the unions have been more divided and have several times opted for decentralized bargaining at the industry level. This union opinion was related to the feeling that occasional decentralized bargaining is important for unions that feel that their interests have been neglected at the central level.

In Norway, the party of the Right is weak and that of the Left is strong. During the postwar period, the party of the Left was in office till the mid-1960s. During the latter half of the 1960s the Conservatives were in government, although in coalition with other non-socialist parties. In this coalition the Conservatives were the biggest coalition partner. The equalizing impact of the redistributive system in Norway is of medium strength. (The redistributive system in Norway is the most equalizing of the countries classified as having a medium egalitarian redistributive system.)

In *Israel* the labour union movement (the Histadrut) and the Ma'arach (a combination of two parties of the Left — the Labour Party (Mapai) and Mapam — dating from 1969) both have a strong position. The Labour Party was the largest party in the Israeli legislature until 1977, when it was surpassed by the Likud (a combination of right-wing parties). The Labour Party also has been in office for many years (1948-77). The ties between the Labour Party and the Histadrut are different from those characterizing union-party links in other countries. Whereas in most Western European countries, labour unions tend to be relatively independent from political parties and to have developed their own policy-making bodies, in Israel labour union leaders are nominated by the political parties and elected in accordance with the amount of support that the party receives in the elections. Thus, the parties control the Histadrut; and, to be more exact, until 1965 the Labour Party controlled the Histadrut because of its strong electoral position. There are some further differences between the Israeli labour union movement and that in other countries. Whereas elsewhere the labour unions participate in industrial and economic activities on only a small scale, the Histadrut in Israel is a vast industrial, commercial and financial empire. This empire is known as the 'labour economy', and it includes companies in building, industry, public works, banking, insurance, marketing and supply together with pension and loan funds. The Histadrut furthermore has its own kindergartens, hospitals and clinics.

As a result, the Histadrut has enormous prestige and great authority, which is reflected in the effectiveness of the wage policy and social policy conducted by it. Taken together with the fact that private employers in Israel are relatively weak in their bargaining position (there is no strong employer's organization), it is not surprising that the Histadrut is practically able to impose any wage policy that it desires upon the employers and the rest of the country. However, during the period concerned the Histadrut has abstained from making absurd wage demands, and instead has been concerned with the realities and the problems of the general economic situation and with the effects of their demands upon society at large. Wage negotiations between labour, employers and government have not been very problematic because of the weakness of the employers, the sympathy of the government to the needs and demands of the workers and the general concern of the Histadrut with the economic situation (Medding, 1972: 184, 205-6).

Although the Israeli Left is strong in terms of both union organization and political power, the impact of the redistributive system is only moderate. This may be related to the highly egalitarian distribution of primary income.

In *Sweden*, the party of the Left (the Social Democratic Party) is the dominant party; between 1932 and 1976 it maintained a continuous presence in government, partly as a consequence of an exceptionally high level of working-class electoral solidarity, and partly owing to the disunity that prevailed among the 'bourgeois' opposition (see Castles, 1978: 105-18). Between the Social Democrats and the Confederation of Trade Unions (LO), which is the largest employee organization, there has been a virtually symbiotic relationship.

After the Second World War the LO adopted an incomes policy attempting to reduce the range of inequalities in the pay structure. This policy is known as the 'wage policy of solidarity' and rests on the principle of 'equal pay for equal work', implying that wage levels should be determined by the nature of the work and not by the efficiency and profitability of the individual companies. This policy has had several consequences. First, it has stimulated the use of job evaluation to provide objective pay criteria, and second, it has led to the acceptance of the idea that low-wage companies that are unable to pay the 'standard' wages should go out of business. The workers thereby released were provided with new jobs through an active labour market policy consisting of job retraining, the provision of information on jobs available, unemployment benefits, etc. According to several authors in this field,[51] the wage policy of solidarity has been rendered almost abortive by the operation of 'wage drift'. This wage drift, largely affecting better paid workers, has tended to restore original income differentials, despite attempts in the bargaining process to equalize wage differentials. This is one of the reasons why the distribution of primary income in Sweden has changed very little in the 1950s and 1960s.[52] However, it should be noted that the 'wage policy of solidarity', even if successful, can create only limited equalization. This is because it attempts to eliminate differences in pay for equal work, and is not directed against existing differences between unequal kinds of work.

It has repeatedly been argued by labour unions that wage policies should be accompanied by regulation of other income, especially of profits. Apart from taxation, control of profits can be effected by control of prices. However, in Sweden direct price control did not exist in the 1950s and 1960s. Instead, the Swedish labour unions favoured indirect price control by publicity, consumer information and the promotion of competition between companies.

Another characteristic of the Swedish labour union movement is that it participates in corporatist processes in order to influence the redistributive processes. Sweden is probably the clearest example of a corporatist organization of the economy, because it has a small number of strongly organized and highly centralized organizations, both on the employee and the employer sides, which meet regularly with politicians on the national level to negotiate national economic and social policy.

Turning to the political parties, it can be noted that one of the main objectives of the Swedish Social Democratic Party has been to move Sweden towards equality in the distribution of income. To achieve this objective, the Social Democratic governments have utilized broadly based economic and social policies, such as full employment, redistribution, education and labour market policies. The empirical evidence available indicates that the transfer policy of the government has indeed contributed in a major way to a more egalitarian distribution of income. The taxation policy, which relies heavily on progressive taxation, has further equalized the distribution of income. It is important to note, however, that Swedish taxes, given the fact that they are very progressive, may increase the inequality of primary income distribution, because in the bargaining processes determining primary incomes allowances are made for the workings of the redistributive system. To the extent that this kind of shifting occurs, the effectiveness of the redistributive system is reduced. Already we have referred to a study of the OECD (1978a), according to which these kind of shifting processes do in fact occur in Sweden. More evidence for this can be found in Lindbeck (1974) and Martin (1979). In these studies it is demonstrated how the creation of the welfare state in Sweden has had a strong feedback on behaviour in the market economy. In this context Lindbeck (1974: 147) remarks that there seems to be an inconsistency in the behaviour of the unions as political pressure groups on the one hand and as partners in wage bargaining on the other. Pressure for highly egalitarian redistributive policies appears to be incompatible with equality of primary incomes in a capitalist market economy.

Finally, it should be noted that, according to Sawyer (1976: 13-19), the large number of one-person households, old people and women working part-time biases the data on the Swedish income distribution towards inequality. However, the fact that Sweden nevertheless emerges as among the most egalitarian countries in terms of its post-transfer, post-tax distribution of income may, by implication, be taken to suggest that this statistical bias is, by itself, an insufficient explanation of the high degree of primary income inequality.

Summarizing the pattern for the countries in Group 4, the following picture arises: levels of unionization are high; bargaining authority is centralized; and corporatist processes have been developed. These countries are characterized by political dominance of leftist parties. The inequality of both primary and disposable income is low, with the exception of Sweden, where primary income inequality is high. The degree of redistribution is of medium strength in Norway and Israel, while in Sweden a highly egalitarian redistributive system has been developed. The case of Sweden suggests the existence of a trade-off between redistribution and equality of primary income distribution.

*Conclusions*

When we consider the four groups jointly, we may arrive at the following conclusions. First, in none of the countries where the Right is strong have viable corporatist structures been developed, while in all countries where the Right is weak corporatism exists to some extent. Not all of these countries have a strong Left; e.g. in the Netherlands the party of the Left is classified as of medium strength and the labour union movement as weak. Thus, for the creation of a corporatist structure, weakness of the Right seems to be a sufficient condition; the presence of a strong Left is not necessary.

Second, the countries where corporatist processes have been developed are characterized by medium to highly egalitarian redistributive systems. This finding may amplify our interpretation of the negative association between strength of the Right and equalizing impact of transfers and taxes. When we first found this association (pp. 326-28 above), we offered an explanation by suggesting that parties of the Right are more successful in curbing the equalizing character of the redistributive system than parties of the Left and labour unions are in accentuating it. The present analysis of country patterns, however, suggests that the equalizing impact of transfers and taxes depends on the degree to which corporatist processes have been developed. Both explanations may be complementary to each other. However, the latter explanation seems more complete than the former, since it accounts more fully for cases like Finland and the Netherlands where neither Right nor Left are particularly strong, and yet a high degree of equalization through transfers and taxes has been achieved. This finding also complements our earlier proposition that parties of the Left have not been very successful in accentuating the equalizing potential of the welfare state. It now appears that it is corporatism that has effected this.

In summarizing the pattern for Group 4 we noted that the case of Sweden suggested the existence of a trade-off between the amount of equalization through transfers and taxes and equality of primary income distribution. This hypothesis is confirmed by the experience of the Netherlands and Finland. Like Sweden, these countries are characterized by a high degree of equalization through transfers and taxes. But also, like Sweden, these countries have a relatively unequal distribution of primary income. On the other hand, countries with low inequality of primary incomes show only a low to medium degree of equalization through transfers and taxes, even when the Left is strong. This holds even for Israel and Norway, characterized not only by strength of the Left, but also by weakness of the Right. Thus we may formulate a third conclusion; namely that in advanced capitalist societies, the situation with respect to the possibilities for equality of income distribution and the instruments to realize these, resembles that of a 'zero sum game'. The more equality is realized through redistribution, the less equality can be realized through an incomes policy of parties and unions directed at primary incomes.

The relationships between strength of party of the Right, corporatism and redistribution in the framework of the welfare state also increase our insight into the proposition that the equalizing impact of parties of the Left and labour unions is due to interference with primary income formation rather than to the redistributive system. From the country groupings, it appears that when both

Left and Right are strong, redistribution is low to medium, while a combination of a strong Left and a weak Right yields medium to high redistribution. On the other hand, with one exception (Sweden) all countries where the Left is strong have a low inequality of primary income distribution. Thus, our fourth conclusion is that, while the political strength of the Right serves as an impediment to the achievement of a high degree of equalization through the redistributive mechanisms of taxes and transfers even where the left is also strong, it does not impede the achievement of primary income inequality in the same way.

While these conclusions support the argument of Wilensky (1976) that corporatist processes result in an effective social contract, they fit even better with the argument of Leynse (1979), according to which union centralization, characteristic of corporatist processes, is accompanied by both advantages and disadvantages. On the other hand, they refute part of the argument of Van der Vall (1970) referred to above. According to Van der Vall, unions are effective only when they are integrated into the politics of the welfare state; in his opinion economic unionism is not effective. The latter proposition, however, is refuted by the evidence resulting from the country patterns. Van der Vall fails to recognize the trade-off between integration into the politics of the welfare state and the degree of equality that may be realized in the market system directly.

To check the above conclusions we performed some correlations with a measure of 'union centralization' as employed by Stephens (1979: 118-19). For 10 of the countries included in our analysis Stephens specifies this variable. Correctly, he notes that only countries in which economy-wide bargaining is practised can be designed as potentially corporatist. Thus, it is not surprising that all countries where economy-wide bargaining is practised are characterized by high union centralization. We will use this measure as a proxy for corporatist processes. According to the conclusions derived above, we expect this measure to be positively associated with the decrease in inequality through transfers and taxes. Not only do we expect a positive association, but also we expect a stronger positive association than was found with the measure of labour union strength (based on membership) employed in the statistical analysis. Further, the finding from the country studies that it is corporatism rather than strength of parties of the Left that matters with respect to redistribution also leads us to expect variations in changes in inequality through transfers and taxes to be more closely

**FIGURE 6**
**The relationship between union centralization**
**(proxy for corporatist processes) and decrease in**
**inequality through redistribution (measured by Gini coefficient);**
**r = 0.75. Group A respectively B: countries characterized by**
**economy-wide, respectively decentralized, bargaining**

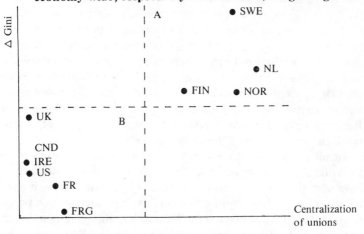

related with union centralization than with strength of parties of the Left.

On the other hand, we expect primary income inequality to be associated less with union centralization than with the measures of strength of parties of the Left and labour unions as employed in the statistical analysis. This expectation is based (1) on the stated trade-off between redistribution and primary income equality; and (2) on the finding from the country studies that inequality of primary incomes tends to be low in countries with a strong Left and labour union movement.

Figure 6 presents graphically the relationship between union centralization and changes in inequality through redistribution. As expected, there appears to be a strong positive relationship between these variables. The relationship is of the same strength (but in the other direction) as the associations reported in the statistical analysis (p. 327 above) between strength of the Right and redistributive changes. This is not surprising, since we have found that corporatism and strength of the Right are inversely related.[53] On the other hand, union centralization turns out to be of negligible importance in explaining cross-national differences in primary income inequality ($r = 0.16$).

We now turn to the question of whether it is strength of labour unions or strength of parties of the Left that matters with respect to income inequality. When we first posed this question, it was with respect to the impact of these political agencies on the distribution of primary income. Now we have enlarged our theory to include also the relationship between corporatism and redistributive equality. Thus, it is appropriate to consider this question also with respect to the development of corporatist processes of policy-making. The latter can be done in terms of the conclusions stated above: the development of corporatist processes requires a centralization of unions (high strength of unions in terms of membership is not enough, or even necessary); such centralization does not require a strong party of the Left, but it does require that the party of the Right be weak. Thus, with respect to corporatism, our arguments stress the importance of the union element.

Turning to the question of whether it is unions or parties of the Left that are most important as to equality of primary incomes, we may note that the analysis of the country patterns again supports the proposition that labour unions are more important than parties of the Left. In Australia and the Federal Republic of Germany, the party of the Left has a strong position in the legislature, but it has either not been in office at all (Australia) or only for a short period (Federal Republic of Germany). This suggests that the equal distribution of primary income in Australia and Germany is due to labour union activities. This hypothesis tends to be supported by the pattern in the United Kingdom, Israel and Norway. In the United Kingdom the party of the Left has been in office frequently. However, we found that the unions did not appreciate this wholeheartedly. When the Labour Party was in office, strong pressure was exerted on the unions to restrict wage demands. It seems that during this period attempts were made by the government to develop a corporatist model of policy-making. This suggests that also in the United Kingdom it has been the labour unions rather than the party of the Left that have been responsible for equality of primary incomes. Furthermore, we have seen that in Israel labour unions dominate the system of industrial relations, and that in Norway the employers and the government have been in favour of central agreements, while the unions have on some occasions pursued decentralized bargaining because they felt that not all union interests were taken properly into account at the central level.

## Overview

In this study we have examined the impact of the socioeconomic and the political structure on the distribution of income in advanced capitalist democracies. Contrary to much current opinion, socioeconomic variables appeared to be of relatively little importance for an explanation of cross-national differences. Furthermore, the optimism of those who hold that increased economic development and education expansion will result in a decrease of income inequality is contradicted by the experiences of the countries included in our analysis.

The variables belonging to the political structure turned out to be more closely related to cross-national differences in income distribution. A correlation analysis yielded some preliminary insights. Both strength of parties of the Left and labour unions were found to be accompanied with less income inequality. However, the statistical results indicated that this could not readily be explained by successful redistributive policies brought about by the Left. Rather, the statistical analysis suggested that the Right is more successful in curbing the equalizing character of transfers and taxes than the Left is in accentuating it. We then argued that the relationship between parties of the Left and labour unions with levels of income inequality should be explained by the impact on the distribution of primary incomes.

To complement the information provided by the statistical analysis, we made a comparative study of country patterns. This study increased our understanding of the relationships derived from the correlation analysis. The strong relationship between variations in strength of the Right and equalizing impact of the redistributive system turned out to be related to the phenomenon of corporatism (i.e. a cast of policy-making characterized by centralized bargaining of employers, unions and government on wages and wider economic and social objectives). It was found that, in countries where the Right is strong, corporatist processes are weak, while the reverse holds for countries where the Right is weak. The country studies indicated that corporatist processes result in considerable redistribution. Corporatism may also explain cases (like the Netherlands) where neither the Right nor the Left is particularly strong, and yet where considerable redistribution is realized.

It was further found that the countries with the most egalitarian redistributive systems (Sweden, the Netherlands and Finland) had an unequal distribution of primary incomes. This suggests that, in advanced capitalist societies, an increase in equalization through transfers and taxes decreases the scope for incomes policies directed at equality of primary incomes.

The findings originating from the country analysis also give more content to the explanation offered for the observed relationships between strength of parties of the Left and labour unions on the one hand and income inequality on the other. The country studies suggest that a strong Right is able to prevent parties of the Left and labour unions from achieving redistribution, but that it does not prevent strong parties of the Left and labour unions from influencing the distribution of primary incomes. Thus, when both Right and Left are strong, strength of the Left tends to yield equality of primary incomes but little redistribution, while strength of the Left combined with weakness of the Right yields varying mixtures of both primary income equality and redistribution. Finally, the information from the country studies supported the proposition that labour unions are more important for equality of incomes than parties of the Left. However, it should be kept in mind, as previously suggested (p. 329), that variables pertaining to labour unions may at the same time be representative of a leftist or egalitarian tradition and milieu.

Our findings stress the importance of political factors in explaining differences in income inequality in advanced capitalism. This is contrary to the functionalist view of society that is dominant in some circles of the social sciences.[54] According to this functionalist view, politics is either of peripheral significance for developments in market economies or harmful to the proper functioning of these economies. For instance, Bronfenbrenner (1977: 407) has argued that an income distribution based on normative criteria, such as the wishes of the electorate or of organized labour, will have as a consequence the fact that efficiency in the market sector is reduced and that insufficient capital is accumulated for investment and innovations.

However, the empirical support for such contentions is scanty or absent. For instance, economic growth, closely related to the level of investment, shows no association with measures of income inequality, but a weak positive relationship with the income share of the top 10 decile (see p. 305). Even if this relationship were much stronger, it would not constitute proof of the proposition that a relatively large share for the higher incomes is necessary to promote investment and economic growth. It may just as well be that economic growth results in a high income share for the top 10 decile.

On the other hand, in evaluating the functionalist approach we should not throw away the baby with the bathwater. Our finding that there exists a trade-off between equalizing impact of redistributive policies and primary income equality indicates that an increasingly intensive use of such redistributive policies becomes ineffective after a certain point. As has been demonstrated so frequently in this volume, the fact that political parties have a major influence on public policy outcomes does not imply that major reform within the structure of the democratic capitalist state is readily attainable.

## NOTES

1. For a survey of theories on personal income distribution, see Sahota (1978).

2. See also Chapter 2 above.

3. Thus, the unique variance that belongs to only a specific variable and shows no association with the other variables is not taken into account.

4. Sawyer (1976: 5, 6, 11).

5. We constructed size distributions of income for these countries from data on the distribution of the population in income groups. The method of logarithmic interpolation used for this purpose is given in Sawyer (1976: 36).

6. For formulae and a more elaborate discussion of the measures of inequality used in this study, see Sawyer (1976: 7, 8).

7. The logarithms of the reciprocals of the income shares are used as weights.

8. Defined as the standard deviation as percentage of the mean.

9. However, basically similar results would have been obtained if, for each kind of income distribution, all countries available had been included (the only difference with Table 3 being decile 10 and decile ratio 10/(3 + 4 + 5) also showing greater dispersions after transfers).

10. OECD (1978a: 77-80).

11. Kuznets (1963), Adelman and Taft Morris (1973), Paukert (1973) and Das (1977).

12. See Deleeck (1977: 33-4, 38-40, 53-8) and Desayere, Tavernier and Van Loon (1973); see also the references given in Deleeck (1977).

13. GNP p/c at constant prices have been derived from OECD (1978b); the data on GNP p/c are for the years to which the size distributions of income refer.

14. For the United Kingdom and Canada, see Sawyer (1976: 26, 29); for the

Federal Republic of Germany, see Schnitzer (1974: 110-12); for Sweden, see UN (1967, Ch. 6: 15).

15. Derived from World Bank (1979: 135).

16. See UN (1967, Ch. 6: 17-21).

17. The data on unemployment, measured by rate of unemployment (10-year average), have been derived from Madsen (1978). The 10-year periods were found by counting 10 years backward from the years to which the data on income distribution refer. The data on old-age pensioners as a proportion of the total population have been derived from ILO statistics. They are calculated for the years to which the data on income distribution refer.

18. However, they are still higher than those recorded in the case of primary income. This may be the consequence of the fact that the data on primary income distribution are somewhat less reliable than those on the distribution of income after transfers and taxes.

19. The data on inflation, measured by rate of inflation (10-year average; cf. n. 17), have been derived from Madsen (1978).

20. The data on economic growth, measured by the relative change in GNP p/c over a 10-year period (cf. n. 17), have been derived from OECD (1978b).

21. Derived from OECD (1974).

22. See e.g. Lenski (1966) or Titmuss (1962).

23. The following social-political variables proved to be most significant: the extent of direct government activity; strength of the labour movement; level of social modernization; importance of the indigenous middle class; extent of political participation; political strength of the traditional elite; percentage of literacy and degree of cultural and ethnic homogeneity. However, the study of Adelman and Taft Morris (1973) is of limited importance for our analysis because it refers to underdeveloped countries only, and because the strength of political parties is not taken into account.

24. Measured by the proportion of seats in the legislature held by parties of the non-communist Left. The variable was created by taking the average of the number of seats in both the last legislature before 1960 as well as the first created after that date.

25. For the 18 advanced capitalist democracies in Jackman's sample, we found that for the Schutz coefficent of inequality ($SCH$), the level of energy consumption ($EN$; used by Jackman as a proxy for economic development) and strength of socialist parties ($SP$; measured on the basis of parliamentary seats) there was the following relationship ($t$-values between brackets):

$$SCH = 80.09 + 0.001828\ EN + 0.230\ SP$$
$$\quad\ (23.19)\quad (3.1)\qquad\quad (3.6)\qquad\qquad\qquad R^2 = 0.45\quad F = 7.99$$

The bivariate correlation between $SP$ and $SCH$ for these 18 democracies yielded $r = 0.46$ ($R^2 + 0.21$), while in the sample of both developed and underdeveloped countries no correlation at all was recorded. Apart from the level of aggregation, one may also criticize Jackman's study for using the degree of intersectoral income inequality between eight economic sectors as a proxy for the degree of inequality in the distribution of personal income. This procedure has been severely criticized (for references, see Hewitt, 1977).

26. Measured by the proportion of the 18 years between 1956 and 1973 in which

social democratic and labour parties (and their leftist allies) possessed a majority of the electoral base of the government.

27. Measured by the annual average proportion of seats held by socialist parties in the legislature, over the period 1945-65.

28. To complement the findings of Cameron, we performed correlations between the increase in the public sector (measured by relative change of total government revenues over a 10-year period (cf. n. 17); data derived from OECD (1978b)) and the changes in income inequality brought about by transfers and taxes for our measures of inequality. As expected, all of these correlations are positive (generally ranging between $r = 0.40$ and $r = 0.60$).

29. Measured in Dryzek's study by competitiveness of the party system, voter turnout, press freedom, electoral irregularity and the number of years of full democracy.

30. Measured by the annual average proportion of seats held by socialist parties in the legislature, over the period 1945-70.

31. See p. 286 above for a summary discussion of the factor analysis technique.

32. It is somewhat embarrassing that Dryzek does not pay attention to this problem.

33. This variable was created by giving a score of one for each year of rule by socialist parties (Social Democratic and/or Communist) from 1945 to 1970.

34. Measured by percentage of years of 'Socialist-Labor' control of government, 1945-69.

35. Borg and Castles have constructed various variables measuring strength of political parties. They have constructed these variables from the average percentage of seats in the legislature won by the major party of the Right respectively the social democratic or labour party, and the number of years and months these parties have been in office. The period considered is 1962-72. The impact of taxes is measured by changes in overall measures of income inequality, including the Gini and Theil coefficients.

36. Measured by the mean percentage of legislative seats held by parties of the non-communist Left, in the years 1945-70.

37. Van den Doel and Grondsma refer to a study by Pommerehne (1978) giving some empirical support to this proposition. On the basis of data for 74 local communities in the Swiss canton Basel-land, Pommerehne concluded that income redistribution realized via the public sector is paid for by the rich, but that it benefits the middle class rather than the poor.

38. Except for Israel, the data on union density employed in our study are derived from Korpi and Shalev (1980). These data refer to the period 1946-76 and are based on union membership standardized by the size of the non-agricultural labour force. Korpi and Shalev do not specify union density for Israel; we estimated this from labour force data in *ILO Yearbooks of Labour Statistics* and union membership data in Sjer (1977: 178-80).

39. The rank ordering is obtained by scoring the two underlying dimensions as follows:

1. Dominant governing party:
   1 = dominance of the Right in
   government (whenever the
   share of cabinet seats
   aggregated over the period
   = 66% and if the party is in
   office for 66% of the period)
   2 = neither Right nor Left
   dominance

   3 = dominance of the Left in
   government

2. Relative size of party:
   1 = when the party of the Right is
   stronger than the party of
   the Left by at least 5% of
   the vote

   2 = when the party of the Right
   and the Left are not separated
   by more than 5% of the vote
   3 = when the Left is stronger than
   the Right (see 1)

The two scores are totalled and one is deducted. The coefficients of correlation with this rank order scale are Spearman's rho's.

40. The 10-year periods were found by counting 10 years backward from the year of observation of the dependent variable in each country; e.g., when the measure of inequality of post-tax, post-transfer income for France refers to 1970 and that for the United Kingdom to 1973, the relevant periods are 1961-70 and 1964-73, respectively.

41. The elasticities are 1.7 and 1.6, implying that a one percent change in seats in the legislature is statistically associated with a 1.7 percent change in cabinet seats for the Left and a 1.6 percent change for the Right. This finding contradicts the argument in Borg and Castles (1981) that right-wing seats translate more easily than left-wing seats. In Chapter 2 above Castles argues that the extent of translation may vary — depending on the specific period under consideration.

42. The coefficients of correlation with the Gini and Theil coefficients are 0.54 and 0.51 respectively; the correlations with the decile measures were not significant.

43. Similarly, Stephens (1979: 107) reports progressivity of taxes to be positively associated with socialist rule and level of labour organization.

44. Exclusion of Japan and Australia also changes the negative association of cabinet seats of the Right with the Gini and Theil coefficients into a positive one.

45. For a discussion of this topic, see Holland (1976: Ch. 1).

46. E.g. Poulantzas (1975), Offe (1975).

47. For the countries discussed the following literature has been used: Barbash (1972), Coogan (1966), Dorfman (1973), Von Freyberg et al. (1977), ILO (1974), Joseph (1979), Lindbeck (1974), Martin (1979), Medding (1972), OECD (1976, 1978a), Patrick and Rosovsky (1976), Roberts and Rothwell (1974), Sawyer (1976), Scase (1976), Sjer (1977), Stephens (1979), UN (1967).

48. The pattern of policy-making in the Netherlands during the period concerned may also be described as consociational. As Lehmbruch (1979: 53-61) has argued, consociational democracies have tended to move strongly towards the corporatist model of policy-making. This is in accord with the experience of the Netherlands: during the period concerned, consociational and corporatist tendencies have closely intertwined.

49. See ILO (1974: 173-204).

50. However, in the late 1960s this changed. In 1967, when for the first time in the postwar period the SPD was in government, the 'Konzertierte Aktion' was set up. Referring to Willey, Harrison (1980: 91) points out that the participation of the unions in the Konzertierte Aktion was a two-edged sword: sharing in national

economic planning also involved 'behaving responsibly in the light of group findings'. This led to the acceptance in 1968 of moderate wage settlements for a longer period than usual. 'The wave of unofficial strikes in 1969 against these contracts were the result. Union officials were abused as traitors to the working class and whistled down at meetings.'

51. See Lindbeck (1974: 197), Martin (1979: 108), UN (1967, Ch. 4; p. 8).

52. Rudolf Meidner, the LO's chief economist, has argued that the 'wage policy of solidarity' has been successful, with 'the spread of wages [declining] by almost a half in fifteen years' (Meidner, 1978: 30). However, it is quite clear from the data Meidner himself presents (p. 31) that the greater part of the decline in the dispersion of average wage levels took place in the late 1960s and early 1970s, i.e. outside the scope of our analysis.

53. The association between legislative strength of the Right (see Table 9) and corporatism (as indicated by union centralization) yields a coefficient of correlation of $-0.86$.

54. Functionalism plays an important role in neoclassical economics and in 'Parsonian' sociology (cf. Gouldner, 1970); for a discussion of functionalism with respect to inequality, see Parkin (1975) and Hewitt (1977).

# REFERENCES

Adelman, I. and Taft Morris, C. (1973). *Economic Growth and Social Equity in Developing Countries*. Stanford: University Press.

Banks, A.S. (1971). *Cross-polity Time Series Data*, Cambridge: MIT Press.

Barbash, J. (1972). *Trade Unions and National Economic Policy*. Baltimore and London: Johns Hopkins Press.

Boggs, C. (1976). *Gramsci's Marxism*. London: Pluto Press.

Borg, S.G. and Castles, F.G. (1981). 'The Influence of the Political Right on Public Income Maintenance Expenditure and Equality', *Political Studies*, vol. XXIX.

Bronfenbrenner, M. (1977). 'Ten Issues in Distribution Theory', in S. Weintraub, *Modern Economic Thought*. Oxford: Basil Blackwell.

Cameron, D.R. (1976). 'Inequality and the State, a Political-Economic Comparison'. Paper prepared for 1976 Annual Meeting of the American Political Science Association, Chicago, 2-5 September 1976.

Cameron, D.R. (1978). 'The Expansion of the Public Economy: A Comparative Analysis', *American Political Science Review*, vol. 72.

Castles, F.G. (1978). *The Social Democratic Image of Society*. London: Routledge & Kegan Paul.

Central Statistical Office of Finland (1976). *Finnish Survey on Relative Income Differences*. Helsinki.

Central Statistical Office of Ireland (1976). *Household Budget Survey 1973*, vol. 2-3. Dublin.

Central Statistical Office of the Netherlands (1978). *Inkomensverdeling 1973 en vermogensverdeling 1974*. The Hague.

Champernowne, D.G. (1973). *The Distribution of Income between Persons*. Cambridge: University Press.

Coogan, T.P. (1966). *Ireland since the Rising*. New York: Praeger.

Cutright, P. (1967). 'Inequality: A Cross-National Analysis', *American Sociological Review* 32: 562-78.

Das, T. (1977). 'Effects of Democratic Change and Choice of Income Unit on the Size Distribution of Income'. PhD thesis, University of East Anglia.

Deleeck, H. (1977). *Ongelijkheden in de welvaartsstaat*. Antwerp; De Nederlandsche Boekhandel.

Desayere, W., Tavernier, K. and Van Loon, E. (1973). 'Meten en verklaren van de personele inkomensverdeling in Belgie', in *De overheid in de gemengde economie*. Universitaire Pers Leuven.

Van den Doel, J. and Grondsma, T. (1979). 'Inkomensverdeling en politieke besluitvormingstheorie', *Acta Politica*, 4: 434-78.

Dorfman, G.A. (1973). *Wage Politics in Britain 1945-1967*. Ames, Iowa: Iowa University Press.

Downs, A. (1956). *An Economic Theory of Democracy*. New York: Harper and Row.

Dryzek, J. (1978). 'Politics, Economics and Inequality: A Cross-National Analysis', *European Journal of Political Research*, 6: 399-410.

Von Freyberg, J. et al. (1977). *Geschichte der deutschen Sozialdemokratie 1863-1975*. Cologne: Pahl-Rugenstein Verlag.

George, V. and Wilding, P. (1976). *Ideology and Social Welfare*. London: New Left Books.

Gouldner, A.W. (1970). *The Coming Crisis of Western Sociology*. London: Heinemann.

Gramsci, A. (1920). 'Sindicati e consigli', *L'Ordine Nuevo*, 12 June 1920.

Ha-Lishkah Hamerkazit Listatistika (1970). *Family Expenditure Survey, 1968/69*, special series no. 330. Jerusalem.

Harrison, R.J. (1980). *Pluralism and Corporatism*. London: Allen & Unwin.

Hewitt, C. (1977). 'The Effect of Political Democracy and Social Democracy on Equality in Industrial Societies: A Cross-National Comparison', *American Sociological Review*, 42: 450-64.

Hibbs, D.A. (1977). 'Political Parties and Macroeconomic Policy', *American Political Science Review*, 71: 1467-87.

Holland, S. (1976). *The Socialist Challenge*. London: Quartet Books.

ILO (1974). *Collective Bargaining in Industrialised Market Economies*. Geneva.

ILO (various years). *Yearbook of Labour Statistics*. Geneva.

Inglehart, R. and Klingemann, H.D. (1976). 'Party Identification, Ideological Preferences and the Left-Right Dimension among Western Mass Publics', in I. Budge, I. Crewe, and D. Farlie, *Party Identification and Beyond*. New York: John Wiley.

Jackman, R.W. (1975). *Politics and Social Equality, A Comparative Analysis*. New York: John Wiley.

Jackman, R.W. (1980). 'Socialist Parties and Income Inequality in Western Industrial Societies', *The Journal of Politics*, 42: 135-49.

Jain, S. (1975). *Size Distributions of Income*. Washington, World Bank.

Jencks, C. (1972). *Inequality: A Reassessment of the Effect of Family and Schooling in America.* New York: Basic Books.

Joseph, M.S. (1979). 'Trade Unions in Western European Politics', in J.E.S. Hayward, and R.N. Berki, *State and Society in Contemporary Europe.* Oxford: Martin Robertson.

Kerr, C., Dunlop, J.T., Harbison, F. and Myers, C.H. (1964). *Industrialism and Industrial Man: The Problems of Labor and Management in Economic Growth.* New York: Oxford University Press.

Kirschen, E.S. et al. (1964). *Economic Policy in Our Time.* Amsterdam: North Holland.

Korpi, W. and Shalev, M. (1980). 'Strikes, Power and Politics in the Western Nations, 1900-1976', in M. Zeitlin, *Political Power and Social Theory*, vol. 1. Boston: Jay Press.

Krupp, H.J. (1977). 'Transfer Policy and Changes in Income Distribution' (see 'Discussion'), in W. Krelle and A.F. Shorrocks, *Personal Income Distribution.* Amsterdam: North Holland.

Kuznets, S. (1955). 'Economic Growth and Income Inequality', *American Economic Review*, 45: 1-28.

Kuznets, S. (1963). 'Quantitative Aspects of the Economic Growth of Nations: VIII. Distribution of Income by Size', *Economic Development and Cultural Change*, vol. XI, no. 2, Part II: 1-80.

Lehmbruch, G. (1979). 'Consociational Democracy, Class Conflict and the New Corporatism', in P.C. Schmitter and G. Lehmbruch, *Trends Toward Corporatist Intermediation.* London: Sage.

Lenski, G. (1966). *Power and Privilege: A Theory of Social Stratification.* New York: McGraw-Hill.

Leynse, F. (1977). 'Centralisatie en decentralisatie van het loonoverleg', in T. Akkermans, *Facetten van vakbondsbeleid.* Alphen a/d Rijn; Samsom.

Lindbeck, A. (1974). *Swedish Economic Policy.* Berkeley/Los Angeles: University of California Press.

Lydall, H. (1979). *A Theory of Income Distribution.* Oxford: Clarendon Press.

Mackie, T.T. and Rose, R. (1974). *The International Almanac of Electoral History.* London: Macmillan.

Madsen, H.J. (1978). *A Political Economic Timeseries Cross-Section System of Data: 1920-75.* Aarhus: Institute of Political Science, University of Aarhus.

Martin, A. (1979). 'The Dynamics of Change in a Keynesian Political Economy: The Swedish Case and Its Implications', in C. Crouch, *State and Economy in Contemporary Capitalism.* London: Croom Helm.

Medding, P.Y. (1972). *Mapai in Israel: Political Organisation and Government in a New Society.* Cambridge: University Press.

Meidner, R. (1978). *Employee Investment Funds.* London: Allen & Unwin.

Metcalf, C.E. (1972). *An Econometric Model of the Income Distribution.* Chicago: Markham.

Miliband, R. (1973). *The State in Capitalist Society.* London: Quartet Books.

OECD (1974). *Educational Statistics Yearbook*, vol. 1. Paris.

OECD (1976). *Public Expenditure on Income Maintenance Programmes.* Paris.

OECD (1978a). *Public Expenditure Trends. Studies in Resource Allocation.* Paris.

OECD (1978b). *National Accounts of OECD Countries*, vol. II. Paris.

Offe, C. (1975). 'The Theory of the Capitalist State and the Problem of Policy Formation', in L. Lindberg, et al., *Class and Contradiction in Modern*

*Capitalism*. Lexington, Mass.: Lexington Books.

Olson, M. (1963). 'Rapid Growth as a Destabilizing Force', *Journal of Economic History*, 23: 529-52.

Parkin, F. (1972). *Class Inequality and Political Order*. St Albans: Paladin.

Patrick, H. and Rosovsky, H. (1976). *Asia's New Giant*. Washington, Brookings Institution.

Paukert, F. (1973). 'Income Distribution at Different Levels of Development: A Survey of Evidence', *International Labour Review*, no. 2-3: 97-125.

Pen, J. (1977). 'The Role of Power in the Distribution of Personal Income: Some Illustrative Numbers', in W. Krelle, and A.F. Shorrocks, *Personal Income Distribution*. Amsterdam: North-Holland.

Phelps-Brown, E.H. (1957). 'The Long-term Movement of Real Wages', in J.T. Dunlop, *The Theory of Wage Determination*. London: Macmillan.

Pommerehne, W.W. (1978). 'Public Choice Approaches to Explaining Fiscal Redistribution', Paper Conference IIPF, Hamburg.

Poulantzas, N. (1973). *Political Power and Social Classes*. London: New Left Books.

Poulantzas, N. (1975). *Classes in Contemporary Capitalism*. London: New Left Books.

Roberts, B.C. and Rothwell, S. (1974). 'Recent Trends in Collective Bargaining in the United Kingdom', in ILO, *Collective Bargaining in Industrialised Market Economies*. Geneva.

Sahota, G.S. (1978). 'Theories of Personal Income Distribution: A Survey', *Journal Of Economic Literature*, 16: 1-55.

Sawyer, M. (1976). 'Income Distribution in OECD Countries', *OECD Economic Outlook Occasional Studies*, July 1976: 3-36.

Scase, R. (1976). *Social Democracy in Capitalist Society*. London: Croom Helm.

Schnitzer, M. (1974). *Income Distribution*. New York: Praeger.

Sjer, H. (1977). *Facts about Israel*. Jerusalem: Israeli Information Centre.

Stephens, J.D. (1979). *The Transition from Capitalism to Socialism*. London: Macmillan.

Stigler, G.J. (1970). 'Director's Law of Public Income Redistribution', in *The Journal of Law and Economics*, vol. XIII (1), April 1970.

Taylor, C. and Hudson, M. (1972). *World Handbook of Political and Social Indicators*. New Haven: Yale University Press.

Tinbergen, J. (1975). *Income Distribution*. Amsterdam: North Holland.

Titmuss, R.M. (1962). *Income Distribution and Social Change*. London: Allen & Unwin.

Tobin, J. (1970). 'On Limiting the Domain of Inequality', *Journal of Law and Economics*, 13: 263-77.

Tufte, E. (1978). *Political Control of the Economy*. Princeton: University Press.

United Nations (1967). *Incomes in Postwar Europe: A Study of Politics, Growth and Distribution*. Geneva: UN Economic Commission for Europe.

United Nations (various years). *Statistical Yearbook*. New York/Geneva.

Van der Vall (1970). *Labour Organizations*. Cambridge: University Press.

Wilensky, H. (1976).'The "New Corpôratism", Centralization and the Welfare State', *Contemporary Political Sociology Series*, 2(20).

World Bank (1976). *World Tables 1976*. Baltimore: Johns Hopkins University Press.

World Bank (1979). *World Development Report 1979*. Oxford: University Press.

# Index of Names

# Notes on Contributors

**Klaus Armingeon** is working on the comparative analysis of neo-corporatist policy-making in Western Europe at the University of Konstanz, West Germany. He is also writing a PhD dissertation on new kinds of incomes policies in Western Europe in the 1970s.

**Corina van Arnhem** studied political science at the University of Amsterdam and now works there in the Department of Political Science.

**Francis G. Castles** is Dean of the Faculty of Social Sciences and Reader in Political Science at the Open University. He is the author of *Pressure Groups and Political Culture* (1967), *Politics and Social Insight* (1971), and *The Social Democratic Image of Society* (1978), as well as numerous articles on social democracy, Scandinavian politics, policy, and teaching politics.

**Hans Keman** is Senior Lecturer in Politics and History at the sub-faculty of General Political and Social Sciences at the University of Amsterdam. His publications include articles on military policy, social democratic politics, and the theory of the state.

**Manfred Schmidt** is a lecturer in political science at the University of Konstanz. His publications include books and numerous articles on the analysis of public policy in Western democracies.

**Geurt Schotsman** studied political science and economics at the Faculty of Social Sciences of the University of Amsterdam. In 1977 he finished his university study. After a short-lived career as a teacher in economics at a secondary school, he was employed at the Faculty of Economics (department of macroeconomics) of the University of Amsterdam. He has published in the fields of automation, public policy and income distribution.